I0820499

The Yardbirds

Also by Peter Stanfield

A Band With Built-In Hate: The Who From Pop Art to Punk
Body and Soul: Jazz and Blues in American Film, 1927–63
Dirty Real: Exile on Hollywood and Vine with the Gin Mill Cowboys
The Cool and the Crazy: Pop Fifties Cinema
Hollywood, Westerns and the 1930s: The Lost Trail
Hoodlum Movies: Seriality and the Outlaw Biker Film Cycle, 1966–1972
Horse Opera: The Strange History of the Singing Cowboy
Maximum Movies – Pulp Fiction: Film Culture and the Worlds of Samuel Fuller, Mickey Spillane and Jim Thompson
Pin-Ups 1972: Third Generation Rock 'n' Roll

THE YARDBIRDS

THE MOST BLUESWAILING FUTURISTIC WAY-OUT HEAVY BEAT SOUND

PETER STANFIELD

REAKTION BOOKS

Dedicated to The Commuters –
Hemel Hempstead's finest purveyors of knockout R&B

Published by
Reaktion Books Ltd
Unit 32, Waterside
44–48 Wharf Road
London N1 7UX, UK
www.reaktionbooks.co.uk

First published 2025

Printed and bound in Great Britain
by Bell & Bain, Glasgow

A catalogue record for this book is available from the British Library

ISBN 978 1 83639 077 0

CONTENTS

Prologue: Future Now

When Led Zeppelin cleaned up at the *Melody Maker* poll awards in autumn 1970, dislodging the Beatles from their long-held prime spot, for some it was as if the tectonic plates of contemporary music had shifted and vomited up a crude lumpen mass – the certainties, the absolutes, of pop had been corrupted. The transfer of power triggered a seditious response from rock critics alive to the symbolism of the moment.

Lester Bangs was 23 years old when he wrote 'Psychotic Reactions and Carburetor Dung: A Tale of These Times', published in June 1971 in *Creem* magazine. It was a comic manifesto that was deadly serious in its intent; a vulgar bon mot to his more civilized peers and a rebel's rabble-rousing yell aimed at his adolescent fellow travellers. His piece began with a retreat to 1965, to the verities of recent history, with Bangs acting the role of Uncle Remus, retrieving the past and pushing his tale a few years beyond the present for the edification of his third-generation rock 'n' roll readers: 'Run here, my towhead grandchillen, and let this geezer dandle you upon his knee.'[1] The tale told summoned forth the Yardbirds as his avatar of a future yore:

> They came stampeding in and just blew everybody clean off the tracks. They were so fucking good, in fact, that people were still imitating 'em as much as a decade later, and getting rich doing it I might add, because the original band of geniuses just didn't last that long. Of course, none of their

> stepchildren were half as good, and got increasingly pretentious and overblown as time went on until [in] about 1973 a bunch of emaciated fops called Led Zeppelin played their final concert when the lead guitarist was assassinated by an irate strychnine freak in the audience with a zip gun just fifty-eight minutes into his famous two-and-a-half-hour virtuoso solo on one bass note.[2]

Bangs's story is part wallow in nostalgia and part fantasy of what might yet be. He proceeded with the impact the Yardbirds had on numerous aspirants – 'and then punk bands started cropping up who were writing their own songs but taking the Yardbirds sound and reducing it to this kind of goony fuzztone clatter . . . oh, it was beautiful, it was pure folklore, Old America, and sometimes I think those were the best days ever' – then he pulled up hard with the advent of *Sgt. Pepper* and rock's subsequent embracing of 'Art'.[3] Bangs wasn't opposed to a more sophisticated culture if it exuded noise (and posed in a scuffed leather jacket) but, without such irritants, he was not much interested in refinement.

If Led Zeppelin had run the music he loved down a dead end, he still thought it possible that the Who's and the Yardbirds' legacies might yet be rediscovered. Both bands, Bangs pronounced, had then been 'writing whole new chapters of musical prophecy almost monthly':

> certainly we've never known music more advanced at the time of its inception than the likes of 'I'm a Man', 'Anyway Anyhow Anywhere', 'My Generation' and 'Shapes of Things'. The Yardbirds I especially idolized. Eventually, though, I wised up to the fact that the Yardbirds for all their greatness would finally fizzle out in an eclectic morass of confused experiments and bad judgments.[4]

He thought the Stooges could carry the mantle of a 'primordial rock and roll' underpinned by a willingness to be open to ideas and influences – like the jazz of Archie Shepp and Albert Ayler which held out the prospect of progress to a better future: 'We could all see the possibilities for controlling the distortions of Who/Yardbirds feedback and fuzz for a new free music that would combine the rambling adventurousness of the new free jazz with the steady, compelling heartbeat of rock.'[5] For a while, it seemed as if the Velvet Underground would be the band to shape that fusion, especially with 'Sister Ray', which 'carried the Yardbirds/Who project to its ultimate extension'.[6] The experiments of that band's first two albums 'might at first hearing seem merely primitive, unmusicianly and chaotic' but, out of that pounding beat, in 'Sister Ray' the most basic of funk riffs evolved across the track's seventeen minutes 'into stark structures of incredible complexity'.[7] That capability, the Velvet's daring-do, was presaged and foreshadowed in the Yardbirds' 'metallic clanging cacophony of precisely distorted guitars' before being passed onto the Stooges – 'the first young American group to acknowledge the influence of the Velvet Underground'.[8]

THIS BOOK IS THE STORY of the Yardbirds' magnificent reverberations, those sonic truths that left their mark on Bangs and on the artists he declared an undying fealty towards, like the Velvet Underground, MC5 and the Stooges. The Yardbirds' tale is told through the primary materials they generated, the traces they left in the music, national, regional and local presses, in teenage magazines and fanzines of the day. Contrary to Bangs's version, it is not a history made from reminiscences but a story made from contemporary documents and artefacts. This scrapbook of cuttings is placed within the evolving context of the times, the rapid developments within pop culture as the Yardbirds reached out for their own future-now and helped to spin those revolutions that Bangs came to praise.

Throughout 1963, the nascent London R&B scene was busily inveigling itself within the trad jazz community, a parasite that would hungrily consume its host. The Rolling Stones and their peers moved into jazz's suburban clubs and pubs, occupying its stages and leading astray its young devotees before taking on Soho, the city's centre. With trad vanquished, in 1964 the scene moved out to the provinces and into the record charts, competing with the Beatles and Merseybeat. Always to the fore, the Stones were followed in double-quick time by Georgie Fame, the Kinks, the Pretty Things, Manfred Mann, Long John Baldry, the Animals, Them, the Downliners Sect and the Yardbirds.

The R&B craze of 1964 was not long consolidated, authentic credentials checked against chart placing, before it was all but abandoned and then superseded by the pop rush of the following year; bands everywhere casting off their rehearsed stance of affected sincerity. Forsaking their studies in bluesology, the Yardbirds left Eric Clapton behind and reinvented themselves, in partnership with Jeff Beck, as sonic adventurers. In January of the New Year, Pete Townshend and co. abandoned 'Maximum R&B', their only-just-minted catchphrase, for the more prescient 'The Who – London 1965', before jumping tracks to become Pop-art explorers. Competing head-to-head with the Who as the capital's most daring band, the Yardbirds countered by making themselves absent from the British scene. In the summer, on the back of a brace of hit singles, they took their first trip to the USA – five further tours of the States, each more intense than the last, would follow until the band's demise in June 1968.

The band's touring schedule was relentless, leaving little time to experiment in the studio never mind the space to craft a first studio album. Manager Giorgio Gomelsky set the pace and steered the band from suburban club gigs to supporting the Beatles, hit records, television appearances and then to the USA. He had taken the most blueswailing Yardbirds further out and helped to create the sound of 1975 in 1965, but he lost the band on the way. In spring 1966, he was dropped, and Simon Napier-Bell took over; a new hit single and the long-promised album were recorded. For a brief moment it was as if the Yardbirds were back in contention, but then their bass player/producer, Paul Samwell-Smith, quit. He was burnt out from all the touring, too old, he said, at 23 to play the pop game with any conviction. His place was taken by the band's friend and session man Jimmy Page. Within weeks, Page was touring with the Yardbirds in the States; once there he switched from bass to guitar while Beck, whose fan appeal was only matched by Keith Relf, absconded.

Napier-Bell's influence was felt immediately with the band's fifth hit single in a row, 'Over Under Sideways Down'. It was another audacious experiment in sound, but on this front they were now being challenged, not only by the Who but by their old bandmate Eric Clapton. Armed with a newly enhanced reputation after his time with John Mayall's Bluesbreakers, Clapton formed the Cream (the definitive was part of the band's name until their first single). Still forging their identity (and a set list), the Cream repeatedly dealt with a critical commentary that compared them, often unfavourably, to both the Yardbirds and, more intensely, the Who. In response, the trio mirrored the same moves that the Yardbirds had made a year earlier and sought cover deep inside the pop machine.

While the Cream were establishing themselves on the British gig circuit, the Yardbirds continued to concentrate their activities across the Atlantic. In the United States, the psychedelic scene was fast developing as a response to the waves of British bands that had followed the Beatles and the Stones to those shores. The Yardbirds' relationship with this scene, and its transportation to London in the autumn, had them, for a brief moment, at the head of the new fad. But then their single 'Happenings Ten Years Time Ago' stalled and the emergence of such luminaries as the Jimi Hendrix Experience and the Pink Floyd (the definitive used in front of the band's name was in place until around the release of their debut LP, then, like Syd Barrett, it was gone) threw shadows over their brilliance.

By late 1966, Beck was out of the band and, having managed the guitarist's exit, Napier-Bell had then taken himself out of the picture. Producer Mickie Most and tour manager Peter Grant took over from him; the former understood the hit parade but had no interest in the underground movement, the flourishing American ballroom scene or the growing importance of the university gig circuit and student audiences that Page and Grant would later work to their benefit. With just one single released on the domestic market in 1967, the Yardbirds were all but invisible to Britain's pop fans. Three singles and an album were released in the States, all produced by Most, but these made little headway, even as the band toured and continued to build their reputation as a major live attraction.

With psychedelia exploited to exhaustion, the more downbeat, politically inclined underground scene took centre stage. From subterranean caverns there emerged the latest iteration of British blues and the overarching umbrella term 'progressive rock'. It was a turn away from the glitz and superficiality of psychedelia and pop more generally. Even as they played Covent Garden's underground venue Middle Earth in January 1968, the Yardbirds were heading towards their end – a spring 1968 tour of the States was their final fling. Across the subsequent summer and autumn, Jimmy Page pulled together Led Zeppelin, refitting songs and arrangements from the Yardbirds' playbook to conform to the 'new heavy beat sound' that he was fashioning for his freshly recruited bandmates to better exploit before leaving the underground (and Lester Bangs) behind. Into 1969, Led Zeppelin performed a brand of showmanship, with gestures extravagant and loud, to guide rock 'n' roll's third generation into the new decade.

1

Modybirds and Craw-Daddies, 1963

Wednesdays are good days. I go to my Island. I must tell you all about it, it is an important part of my life. It's in the River Thames. You cross a steep bridge over the river and pay a toll of *4d* to an old lady called Rose. Then walk along a winding road with bungalows on either side. There's lots of trees and it's dark and mysterious. You turn a bend and see a large decrepit hotel and a crumbling facade. You hear loud blues music. Walk through the gates and you are in another world. All material cares disappear and we are the only people who exist.

There's a large converted barn, you go down some steps after conning your way in with *6d* – it's usually 3/*6d* – your wrist is stamped and you go down. It's very dark with just red and green lights. Long John Baldry is singing with his band at one end of the hall. The walls are white flaking and full of cobwebs, with cartoons, murals and names printed over them. People dance there crazily. Next door is the pub, where we and the musicians all congregate, we con drinks and play the jukebox and talk to everyone. I often go there on my own but always end up meeting someone I know to dance with.

Outside there is a long strip of grass down to the river with large stone nuts and bolts lying around and convenient bushes where couples make love and smoke hash. It's the coolest place in England, there's nowhere else like it.

SIXTEEN-YEAR-OLD ANDREA HIORNS
to her American pen pal (*c.* 1963)[1]

In 'Nightbeat', his column for *The Stage*, Peter Hepple in January 1963 looked away from Soho and the West End's more glittery attractions, casting a truant eye over some of the area's 'fringe' activities to 'determine which minority taste will graduate into the big business class':

> At the moment, Central London seems to be full of the music known as rhythm and blues, something which is essentially an urban Negro folk form, was the raw material out of which rock 'n' roll was forged and which has now been taken up in a big way by local musicians, both trad and modern, who feel a call for a return to the roots.[2]

The man responsible for this new trend, wrote Hepple, was the 'fiercely moustachioed Alexis Korner, whose Blues Incorporated group, founded early last year, now pulls in fantastic business to the Marquee Club on Thursdays, to the Flamingo and the Discotheque on other days and who has also invaded the well-paid field of society and student functions'.[3]

The extreme novelty of R&B's attraction was underscored by Hepple's observation that '[in] recent weeks a whole new crop of bands has sprung into being to spread the gospel into the suburbs and provinces, amongst them the Rolling Stones, Dave Hunt, the Blues by Six and Pete Deuchar.'[4] He had already mentioned Georgie Fame in an earlier column, so for this latest tour guide he'd gone to the Roaring Twenties and listened to Cyril Davies, 'almost the "grand old man" of the movement', and his Rhythm and Blues All-Stars:

> You could almost add All-Electric All-Stars, for one of the conventions of R&B is that everything must be amplified except the drums and quite honestly I cannot recommend numbers like 'Chicago Calling' for those gentle souls who

> have been brought up on Max Jaffa. After two minutes they will find themselves praying for a power cut!
>
> Cyril himself plays heavily amplified harmonica, which in his hands becomes an instrument of almost frightening force, and the singer, hollering out earthy blues with savage intensity, is the appropriately named Long John Baldry.[5]

But it wasn't just the aggressive volume generated that caught Hepple's attention, it was the audience, who were as remarkable as the bands themselves: 'For investigators of social phenomena a trip to one of the R&B clubs is also of interest in order to observe the astonishing dance style which has suddenly materialized. Imagine Frankenstein's monster trying to walk like a penguin and you have a rough idea.'[6]

Hepple's piece was published at the end of January; at the start of that month, *Melody Maker* had covered the scene with a piece by Chris Roberts, 'Trend or Tripe'. Unlike Hepple, Roberts began by problematizing the term itself due in good part to its porous boundaries. What was the difference between R&B and 'plain old rock', 'hard bop' or 'soul. Or Any other borderline combinations?', he asked.[7] Were the signs pointing to a boom or a bandwagon existence? If the latter, it spelt 'the story of trad all over again, with purist versus popster battles'.[8] At the moment, the scene was confined to two or three London clubs, its 'king-pins' were Korner and Davies, but they felt praise should go to jazzman Chris Barber, who 'started quite a few things one way or another', said Davies.[9] Last words, however, were left to one of 'the newer faces on the R and B scene, Mick Jagger, singer with the Rolling Stones'.[10] He made the 'thought-provoking suggestion' that the scene had to move out of London: 'Only two or three clubs are making any money at the moment, and it has to spread to live. That's the only way it can become popular, and retain its form at the same time.'[11] If the Rolling Stones were at this point being added to such discussions as a makeweight, they would, within a few short months, be the scene's unchallenged leaders.

Melody Maker didn't catch on to this until much later, its attention focused on what it saw as the contraction in audiences for jazz, both modern and trad – 'rarely has a new year caught the British jazz scene in such a state of flux.'[12] The measure of what was happening in the city's clubs could be seen in the steady emergence of new R&B bands in the gig listings and the sidelining of the old order. At the start of the year, the Piccadilly Jazz Club, on Great Windmill Street, was featuring Dave Hunt's Rhythm and Blues Band and 'Chicago Style R&B' with Cyril Davies. The Ken Colyer Jazz Club at Studio 51, Great Newport Street, was highlighting 'Rhythm & Blues with the Blues By Six' and would soon give over the venue entirely to R&B. Alongside its jazz attractions, the Marquee in Oxford Street, in the first week of January, had Blues By Six, Pete Deuchar's Country Blues and Cyril Davies supported by the Rollin' Stones. In the year's second issue of *Jazz News and Review*, the Rolling Stones advertised gigs every Thursday at the Marquee; Friday, 11 January, at Ricky-Tick, Windsor; every Saturday at Sandover Hall, Richmond; every Monday at the Flamingo and alternate Fridays, beginning 18 January, at the Red Lion, Sutton. The block advert was headed: 'Don't be Mislead [*sic*] ! Hear the Real, Authentic Rhythm and Blues Sound', with a contact number and address: GER 6602 or 102 Edith Grove, London, SW10.[13]

Jazzshows Jazz Club, west of the Marquee at 100 Oxford Street, held out against the young pretenders, but their spirited defence would barely last out the year. New venues were being added to the circuit weekly, it seemed, like the 'Blues Club' at Thames Hotel, Hampton Court, which Pete Deuchar's band opened at the start of February. Hyperbole and ballyhoo were the order of the day: 'R&B IS THE THREAT', shrieked a *Melody Maker* headline. 'Rhythm and-blues', said one jazzman, was just a 'load of rubbish . . . nothing but rock-'n'-roll without the movements!'[14] The following week,

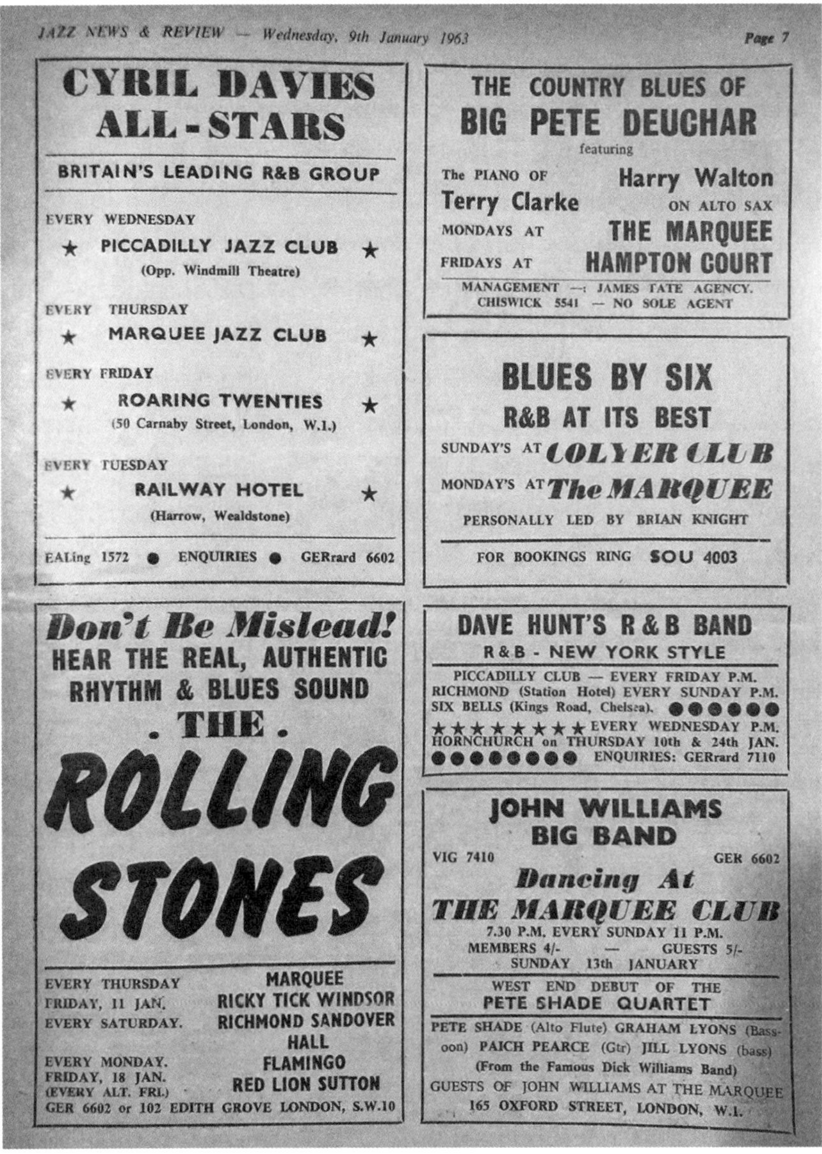

JAZZ NEWS & REVIEW — Wednesday, 9th January 1963 Page 7

CYRIL DAVIES ALL-STARS
BRITAIN'S LEADING R&B GROUP
EVERY WEDNESDAY
★ PICCADILLY JAZZ CLUB ★
(Opp. Windmill Theatre)
EVERY THURSDAY
★ MARQUEE JAZZ CLUB ★
EVERY FRIDAY
★ ROARING TWENTIES ★
(50 Carnaby Street, London, W.1.)
EVERY TUESDAY
★ RAILWAY HOTEL ★
(Harrow, Wealdstone)
EALing 1572 ● ENQUIRIES ● GERrard 6602

THE COUNTRY BLUES OF
BIG PETE DEUCHAR
featuring
The PIANO OF Terry Clarke
Harry Walton ON ALTO SAX
MONDAYS AT THE MARQUEE
FRIDAYS AT HAMPTON COURT
MANAGEMENT —: JAMES TATE AGENCY.
CHISWICK 5541 — NO SOLE AGENT

BLUES BY SIX
R&B AT ITS BEST
SUNDAY'S AT COLYER CLUB
MONDAY'S AT The MARQUEE
PERSONALLY LED BY BRIAN KNIGHT
FOR BOOKINGS RING SOU 4003

Don't Be Mislead!
HEAR THE REAL, AUTHENTIC
RHYTHM & BLUES SOUND
. THE .
ROLLING STONES
EVERY THURSDAY MARQUEE
FRIDAY, 11 JAN. RICKY TICK WINDSOR
EVERY SATURDAY. RICHMOND SANDOVER HALL
EVERY MONDAY. FLAMINGO
FRIDAY, 18 JAN. (EVERY ALT. FRI.) RED LION SUTTON
GER 6602 or 102 EDITH GROVE LONDON, S.W.10

DAVE HUNT'S R & B BAND
R & B - NEW YORK STYLE
PICCADILLY CLUB — EVERY FRIDAY P.M.
RICHMOND (Station Hotel) EVERY SUNDAY P.M.
SIX BELLS (Kings Road, Chelsea). ●●●●●●
★★★★★★★★ EVERY WEDNESDAY P.M.
HORNCHURCH on THURSDAY 10th & 24th JAN.
●●●●●●●● ENQUIRIES: GERrard 7110

JOHN WILLIAMS
BIG BAND
VIG 7410 GER 6602
Dancing At
THE MARQUEE CLUB
7.30 P.M. EVERY SUNDAY 11 P.M.
MEMBERS 4/- — GUESTS 5/-
SUNDAY 13th JANUARY
WEST END DEBUT OF THE
PETE SHADE QUARTET
PETE SHADE (Alto Flute) GRAHAM LYONS (Bassoon) PAICH PEARCE (Gtr) JILL LYONS (bass)
(From the Famous Dick Williams Band)
GUESTS OF JOHN WILLIAMS AT THE MARQUEE
165 OXFORD STREET, LONDON, W.1.

'The Real, Authentic Rhythm & Blues Sound the Rolling Stones',
Jazz News and Review (9 January 1963).

Pete Deuchar – ex-trad banjoist – hit back: 'I changed from trad because I felt I was not having freedom of expression. We seemed to be playing the same old tunes to the same old people – and nobody was getting a kick out of it.'[15]

Kicks aside, this was all to become a sideshow to the three-ring circus that the Beatles were about to command. Two hit singles and now '"the biggest thing to happen to the music scene since Elvis Presley", according to their personal manager Brian Epstein.'[16] Chris Roberts spoke to the band for *Melody Maker*: 'We don't play real rhythm and blues,' John Lennon told him, but played a bit of everything, which included Ray Charles, Arthur Alexander – 'you don't hear much of him over here' – and the Isley Brothers' 'Twist and Shout'. 'That's a knock-out number,' Lennon told Roberts, but 'I don't know whether you'd call it rhythm and blues.'[17] Whatever it was that the Beatles played, 'a hefty shot of their exciting music is just what the meandering pop scene needed,' wrote Roberts.[18] They had cut their first album the Monday following his interview, and weekly reports on their activities continued after they received their first *Melody Maker* cover story on 23 March. Thereafter, they were rarely off the front page.[19]

With regard to its coverage of the pop scene and the trend in R&B, *Melody Maker* lagged behind *Record Mirror*, which put the Beatles on the front cover for their 16 February issue. The paper's most prominent advocate of the new was Norman Jopling, who initiated a series on underexposed artists, mostly American R&B stars, with a feature on the Miracles in the second week of March.[20] Two issues later, he surveyed the British R&B scene, though he focused not on the clubs but on what discs were available and the small number of hits they'd achieved: 'Thirty discs in one year which can be vaguely classed as R&B. Actually, only about five of these are Rhythm and Blues, as opposed to rock, or just blues. So shed a tear for the hordes of U.S. artists who can't get any hits over here because they sing R&B.'[21] That situation would change rapidly over the coming year, and *Record Mirror* would take a lead role in promoting the music, giving serious coverage to a range of American R&B artists, often written by Scene Club DJ Guy Stevens.

In the wake of the Beatles came the Beat explosion with distinct provincial accents: Liverpool, Birmingham and Manchester. London remained R&B central, the capital's bands a counter to the Mojos, the Searchers and the Big Three.[22] The proximity of the London R&B scene to the day's pop and jazz music press no doubt gave it some heft that it otherwise wouldn't have had when weighed against the new regional sounds. *Melody Maker* continued to be obsessed with definitions: 'Well – What Is R&B?' ran one headline: 'Rhythm-and Blues is in the news again this week. The Ronnie Scott Club has joined the Flamingo and Marquee clubs in presenting regular R&B sessions. Only Jazzshows and the Dankworth Club of London's Big Five remain aloof.'[23] Running through the usual gamut of definitions, the National Jazz Federation's Bill Carey provided some tentative answers: 'R&B is what jazzmen call rock-n-roll and the rockers call jazz.'[24] The point was made by him that, at the moment, 'there is really no real R&B scene outside London,' and that in the capital it was best understood as a 'replacement scene really – R&B going into established trad and modern clubs rather than building its own circuit'.[25] Like an oversized cuckoo chick, R&B pushed its smaller rivals out of the nest.

Whether or not R&B was a gluttonous parasite or a contender with genuine artistic ambition, on the BBC and in *Melody Maker* one of the country's biggest booking agents, Harold Davidson, declared the trad boom finished: 'It's a promoter's job to gauge the tastes of the public – well in advance – trad has had a good run and now the public wants something different.'[26] Davidson thought what audiences wanted was the return of big bands, but it was beat and R&B combos that would be filling out his date books. In April, *Melody Maker* listed some of the groups being signed by the majors and noted that 'Pye are jet-propelling a new R&B series on their Pye International label . . . First releases are two LPs, by Chuck Berry and Bo Diddley. Singles feature Sonny Boy Williamson, Howlin' Wolf, another Bo Diddley, and Cyril Davies and His All-Stars –

a British group.'[27] The latter was given some added authenticity (or the planting of another cuckoo's egg) by being marketed alongside these Chicago Chess sides. The real thing, 'Rhythm & Blues – U.S.A. Imported – Chuck Berry, Bo Diddley, Little Walter, Muddy Waters, Dale Hawkins, Sonny Boy Williamson, Howlin' Wolf, Carl Perkins's could be bought from IMHOFS, 112–116 New Oxford St., London WC1 . . . Please send for lists.'[28]

The first four of Pye's singles, including Davies's sides, were advertised on the front page of *Record Mirror* as 'AUTHENTIC R&B'; Norman Jopling provided these releases with some significant coverage. On Davies, he wrote, 'authenticity is his keynote,' which he clearly didn't feel was contradicted by the observation that the harmonica man was 'currently the white hope of Pye's R&B campaign'.[29] Jopling believed the single 'Country Line Special' could break through and make a first hit for what 'has been classed "high class rock 'n' roll"'.[30] Davies himself was not enamoured with that description: 'My kind of R&B just grew out of the blues.'[31] Born in January 1932, he had played through the skiffle and trad eras with Lonnie Johnson and Ken Colyer, partnered Alexis Korner as musician and club entrepreneur (Roundhouse, Wardour Street) then worked with Chris Barber, alongside singer Ottilie Patterson, on the jazzman's R&B sets. That line-up led to Blues Incorporated with Korner and a residency at the Marquee Club on Thursdays. Davies then split with Korner and formed his All-Stars with Long John Baldry; support, as a standalone act and as backing singers, was given by the Velvets, 'three coloured girls comparable only to Ray Charles' Raylets'.[32] The average age of the band member was eighteen: Bernie Watson, guitar; Ricky Fenton, bass; Nicky Hopkins, piano; and Carlo Little, drums. 'Cyril's ambition', Jopling wrote, 'is to go to Chicago – and he intends retiring very young. Which would be a sad thing for the R&B scene which should be thriving like mad before very long.'[33]

By mid-April the Rolling Stones had started a Sunday afternoon residency at the Ken Colyer Jazz Club at Studio 51, and in the evening played at the Station Hotel, Richmond, where they had been performing since the end of February. In the first week of May, the west London show was plugged as the 'Stupendously electrifying R&B sounds of the Unstoppable Rollin' Stones'.[34] The following week's pitch was 'WARNING: R and B Sound Barrier to Be Broken by Rollin' Stones'.[35] In April, the *Richmond and Twickenham Times* gave the band their first write-up with accompanying photographs, the reporter as much intrigued by the audience as by the group:

> The 300 and more in their late teens and early 20s who pack the club on Sunday nights do a dance similar to the craw-daddy. But most improvise on a wildly remote form of the hully gully, similar to the twist . . .
>
> Outside the bar the long hair, suede jackets, goucho trousers and Chelsea boots rub shoulders with the Station Hotel's 'regulars' resulting in whispered mocking, though not unfriendly remarks about the 'funny' clothes.[36]

Not for the last time, but certainly for the first, the Stones were compared to their Mersey peers: 'Hair worn Piltdown style, brushed forward from the crown like "The Beatles" pop group – "we looked like this before they became famous"', said an unidentified Stone.[37]

Jopling wrote up the first music press review of the Stones at the Station Hotel in the 11 May issue of *Record Mirror*. By then, the Beatles had paid a visit to the venue and Jopling recorded this fact along with a list of the Bo Diddley numbers the group played, six in all, and three of Chuck Berry's. He had little doubt in his mind that the Stones were parlaying 'genuine R&B' having 'achieved the American sound better than any other group over here. And the group that in all likelihood will soon be the leading R&B performers in the country.'[38]

In May, both *Record Mirror* and *Melody Maker* began regular columns on the 'Mersey Beat Scene' that also heavily featured the provinces (in June, the latter pit Liverpool against Manchester in the 'Beat wars').[39] In the middle of the month, the Rolling Stones' debut, 'Come On', was released. In a blindfold test, the Isle of Wight's singing milkman, Craig Douglas, reviewed the disc for *Melody Maker*: 'Very, very ordinary. Can't hear a word they are saying and I don't know what all this is about. If there was a Liverpool accent it might get somewhere, but this is definitely no hit. I dislike it, I'm afraid. Take it off!'[40] Despite Douglas's prediction, the record climbed into the Top 30 and stayed there through the summer and into the autumn.

The week of the single's release, the *Daily Mirror*'s avuncular-looking DJ Patrick Doncaster published his report on witnessing the Stones play at the Station Hotel:

> In the half-darkness, the guitars and the drums started to twang and bang. A pulsating rhythm and blues. Shoulder to shoulder on the floor stood 500 youngsters, some in black leather, some in sweaters. You could have boiled an egg in the atmosphere. They began to dance and it was no place for Victor Silvester. They just stood as they were. Their heads shook violently in what can only be described as a paroxysm. 'A sudden attack', says the dictionary of this word.
>
> That's what it looked like in a sweating jazz club that meets at the Station Hotel at Richmond, Surrey. Their feet stamped in tribal style. If they could, the dedicated occasionally put their hands above their heads and clapped in rhythm. Suddenly there would be shaking figures above the rest of the on-the-spot dancers, held aloft by their colleagues, thrashing and yelling 'Yeh, yehs'. No one needed a partner. It was simply shake, rattle and roll on your square foot of the floor. In its fervour it was like a revivalist meeting in America's Deep South.[41]

The *Liverpool Echo* described the Stones' arrival as recording artists as 'The Battle of Denmark Street or Incident at Tin Pan Alley. The troops of groups are lined up. It is Mersey Beat against London Beat, and may the most exciting sound win.'[42] While 'Come On' used 'some of the ingredients involved in the construction of Mersey hits', it lacked 'the essential wildness and the tough rawness of our Northern sounds. The fire glows but never blazes. The vocal talks rather than shouts.'[43]

With the single's release, Norman Jopling had an excuse to once again feature the Stones. Illustrated with a 'moody picture of the great teen R&B group', the disc, he wrote, 'doesn't sound like the Rolling Stones. It's good, catchy, punchy and commercial, but it's not the fanatical R&B sound that the audiences wait hours to hear. Instead it's a bluesy, very commercial group that should make the charts in a smallish sort of way.'[44] As if he recognized and understood this description of his band's record, Brian Jones told Jopling, 'Once we've made an impression then we can try out our real R&B routines.'[45]

Later in the year – around the release of the band's second single, their cover of Lennon and McCartney's gift to them, 'I Wanna Be Your Man' – *Beat Monthly* (precursor of *Beat Instrumental*) introduced the Rolling Stones to its readers as 'Group of the Month'. The band was playing at the Cavern Club, Liverpool, it reported, outside 'fantastic queues of fans – hundreds of whom were later turned away because of the crush'.[46] Their arrival at this point has been slow and steady. Their debut 45, 'Come On', hadn't made it big, but it had been a steady seller, Mick Jagger said. 'I Wanna Be Your Man' had sped things up, but if they hadn't yet charged the charts, like the Beatles, they had at least had time to develop their character: 'It's been said we've deserted the original R and B material we did. Let's be honest – we did for a while. Specially on "Come On". But that was our way of getting accepted. We're back on the good wildies now.'[47] The fire they had helped start was well and truly lit.

Subsequent to the release of 'Come On', Cyril Davies was still calling attention to himself. As Jopling wrote, '[he's] a guy who is as popular with teenagers as he is with the purists.'[48] Interviewed about who he respected in the R&B field, Davies knocked Chuck Berry, Bo Diddley and Jimmy Reed. Of Reed, he said, 'I don't like his singing, which I consider is out of tune, his harmonica playing, and his guitar work. Which means I don't like Jimmy Reed.'[49] Only Muddy Waters came in for fulsome praise; he said he hoped soon to record an album that would include a new ten-minute version of 'Country Line Special'. Asked about those who dismissed his music as 'rock', he told Jopling, 'They don't know the difference anyway... so how can they tell whether I sing R&B or R&R?'[50]

Towards the end of June, *Record Mirror* noted that the Stones had finished their Sunday appearances at the Station Hotel and would now be performing at the Scene Club on Thursday nights: 'this new treat for R&B fans follows the spectacular success of Monday nights at the club, where DJ Guy Stevens holds an R&B disc night.'[51] Alexis Korner continued to find new venues for his Blues Inc., adding the White Lion, Acton, on Monday nights and the Manor House, Finsbury Park, on Tuesdays.[52] The third National Jazz Festival, held on 10 and 11 August at the Athletic Association Grounds, Richmond, was being advertised at the end of July and featured most of the key figures on the R&B scene – the Graham Bond Quartet, Georgie Fame, Cyril Davies, Long John Baldry, the Velvets and the Rolling Stones, alongside jazz favourites Chris Barber, Tubby Hayes, Humphrey Lyttelton, Alex Welsh and Acker Bilk. The scene was evolving at a pace few could have anticipated.

But having predicted the rise of the Stones, Jopling declared that *Record Mirror* had clairvoyant powers. With the band's success came the charge they had gone 'commercial, but in their defence, Jopling wrote:

For the purist in R&B: Cyril Davies in an advertisement for Hohner Harmonicas, *Jazz Beat* magazine (January 1964).

On stage the boys are just about completely uninhibited. They don't bother about what they wear, and they certainly don't have a tightly planned stage act. Their act is wild and loud and carries the new message to the audience of the big R&B sound. And the Stones reckon they have just about managed to cover all fields of R&B now, after practising

> for years. They feel competent to play any number in the R&B vein.[53]

Brian Jones told him that the Liverpool–London controversy was just a 'big thing invented by the newspapers'.[54]

In a sign of the clout their new management, Eric Easton and Andrew Loog Oldham, carried, the Stones were booked in June for an autumn tour supporting the Everly Brothers, with Bo Diddley later added to the bill. Meanwhile, they continued their Sunday afternoon residency at Studio 51 and other club appearances. *Melody Maker*'s first article on the Stones appeared at the end of June – 'The Rolling Stones – London's most talked-about new R and B group – are moving too fast to gather anything except fans.'[55] The band talked about the up-and-coming package tour, stage gear, going 'commercial' by holding off on the Muddy Waters's numbers and featuring Chuck Berry and Bo Diddley covers – 'There'll be plenty of beat there,' said Brian.[56] Haircuts, or their lack thereof, were played up in the profile alongside their mutual admiration for the Beatles; trundling behind them were the bandwagon jumpers: 'They're more familiar with the Coasters, the Shirelles and Chuck Berry, than with Jimmy Reed, or Muddy. But it doesn't worry us. We'll play the stuff we like as long as people come to hear it,' Jagger told Chris Roberts.[57]

At the start of July, the Stones began a Wednesday residency on Eel Pie Island, Twickenham, and Monday evenings at Studio 51, while still playing there every Sunday afternoon. On Fridays, John Mayall's Bluesbreakers were featured at the club, alternating with the Downliners Sect (Mayall had moved from Manchester, where he had led the Blues Syndicate, to London in May).[58] Throughout September, the Stones continued with their Sunday afternoon slot and Monday night residency, but on Friday, 20 September, 'The Yard Birds [*sic*]' made their advertised debut at the club (they had appeared previously on two earlier September dates as the Blue

Sounds). They would be at the Soho club throughout the month and into October; taking over the Sunday slot from the Stones on 29 September, they were now billed as 'The Yard-Birds'.

Across October and into the first week of November, the Everly Brothers and Bo Diddley tour package was documented by each of the Rolling Stones in the pages of *Record Mirror*. Brian Jones went first, writing that he was bowled over by Don, Phil and Bo, the last of whom, he wrote, was 'much more "primitive" (I'm sure he won't mind me saying this) than I expected'.[59] He was equally impressed by the Everlys' professionalism and their 'fantastic equipment'.[60] The following week Mick Jagger carried the news that Little Richard had joined the tour: 'There is no single phrase to describe Richard's hold on the audience. To some it may excite, to others it may terrify.'[61] Jagger was clearly among the excited; he wrote that the band's nerves had settled after the first few nights of the tour.[62] Like his two bandmates who had already written their reports, Bill Wyman got on famously with Bo and his maraca-shaking sideman, Jerome Green.[63] Keith Richards wrote that he had picked up tips from the Everlys' guitarist, Don Peake. He also made time to plug the Stones' soon-to-be-released second single and George Bean's 'Secret Love', on which he revealed he played claves.[64] Charlie Watts signed off the final report in the first week of November; he'd 'enjoyed it all', he wrote.[65]

In mid-October, Giorgio Gomelsky (who had booked the Stones into the Station Hotel) had taken his Crawdaddy Club over the way to the Richmond Athletic Grounds and presented a summons in the music press for people to 'come flying from far and wide to hear R&B's the Yardbirds!!'[66] On the fifth night of their residency, the Yardbirds would be competing for an audience with an 'Encore Appearance' at Croydon's Fairfield Hall of the National Jazz Federation's 'American Negro Blues Festival', featuring Muddy Waters, Lonnie Johnson, Otis Spann, Big Joe Williams, Memphis Slim, Victoria Spivey, Sonny Boy Williamson, Willie Dixon, Bill

Stepney and Matt 'Guitar' Murphy. The Yardbirds had made the trip east to watch the Friday night show of the festival, which Val Wilmer reviewed for *Jazz News*.[67] For her, the first half of the night was stopped by Matt Murphy's 'beautiful long guitar lines' and then capped by Sonny Boy Williamson, who looked

> like a rather uncertain, elderly French army officer, and as he shuffled up to the microphone, the audience must have been totally unprepared for his beautiful performance. The man can really make the harmonica talk, and the highlight of his act was a memorable solo, 'Bye Bye Bird'. On this he placed the harp lengthwise in his mouth and, pushing it backwards and forwards in a 'look ma, no hands!' manner, blew some surprisingly well-conceived choruses.[68]

The second half was all about headliner Muddy Waters, whose photographic portrait, taken by Wilmer, was on the magazine's front cover. Appeasing the blues enthusiasts that questioned his use of electric guitar on his previous visit, Waters had used an acoustic guitar. But amplified or not, the excitement he generated was 'practically unequalled': 'He had the crowd in hysterics and stomping, shouting, screaming for more.'[69]

The two nights of the festival consolidated the idea of R&B as the 'now' sound of the capital; as 1963 started its slide towards the New Year, the Rolling Stones, according to Bob Dawbarn, were now 'priced out of the strictly R&B scene'.[70] Norman Jopling called it the 'quiet revolution': 'Let's get one thing straight. Rhythm and Blues HAS taken over from Trad . . . I wouldn't say R&B "killed" trad. Trad was already dead or dying, long before the public realized they had something with which to replace it.'[71] After this introduction, Jopling gave a potted history of British R&B's main players and the clubs they had come to dominate, going back into the late 1950s with Korner and Davies. The latter was still very much the scene's figurehead, profiled in *Melody Maker* back in June and again in October, but the order of things was about to shift once more.[72] The Stones had already been and gone, but at the Crawdaddy, the Yardbirds 'look set to follow in [their] footsteps', wrote Jopling, who then sounded a concerned note: 'there just aren't enough R and B bands, good bad or indifferent[,] to cater for all the clubs which wish to feature the music.'[73] The arrival of more artists from America will help, he suggested. He completed his précis with some enthusiastic words about the Graham Bond Quartet with Jack Bruce on bass and Ginger Baker on drums.[74]

The 'Craw Daddy R&B Club . . . that launched The Rollin' Stones' and that was 'Now Featuring The Yardbirds' was promoting shows not only in Richmond but at the Star Hotel, Croydon, and Edwina's Club, Finsbury Park. In October, *The Stage* followed an item on the success of 'Authentic Blues in the shape of the American Negro Blues Festival at Croydon's Fairfield Concert Hall' with a note that the Star Hotel in the same district, headquarters of Croydon's jazz club, was to hold a 'preview session of the new Craw Daddy Club, introducing the jazz group, The Yardbirds, this Club having already made a name at Richmond, Surrey'.[75]

Talking to Max Jones, Muddy Waters said:

> I must tell you I have to feel good about what is happening with the blues in Britain, because there's some of my versions in it. I see at the Marquee Club they've got my set-up right on the stage. Of course, I was surprised this time, by Cyril's group, for instance. If you remember, I got a little criticism last time for playing electric guitar . . . Now, when I come back, I find everybody is using electric, and playing as loud as they can get it.[76]

Gomelsky in his club advertisements was promoting his charges with the line 'Presenting the group that got Sonny Boy Williamson "real satisfied" – The Yardbirds'.[77] The following week, the buzz-line had become 'The Most Blueswailing Yardbirds' – a tag that would stay with them right into 1964.[78] In between times, the Yardbirds were playing with Sonny Boy Williamson – 'The King of the Harp, that Menacing Man' – at the Crawdaddy Club and the Ricky-Tick in Windsor.[79] The Yardbirds had not only satisfied Sonny Boy but, as he said of them (according to Gomelsky's Crawdaddy ads), 'These boys play so sweet they wanna make me cry!'[80]

Looking back across the year just passing, *Melody Maker* put all bets for the future on the 'Beat storm' that was then 'gathering all over the country. The thunder will start to roll in the New Year, accompanied by some of the bigger financial flashes of lightning ever seen.'[81] The trend, it wrote, had only just begun, not just the 'famed Liverpool sound' that now dominated everywhere bar London but the R&B that was moving out of the capital.[82] An increasing number of clubs were turning from jazz to beat, but so were universities. These venues, 'once the stronghold of jazz', in the

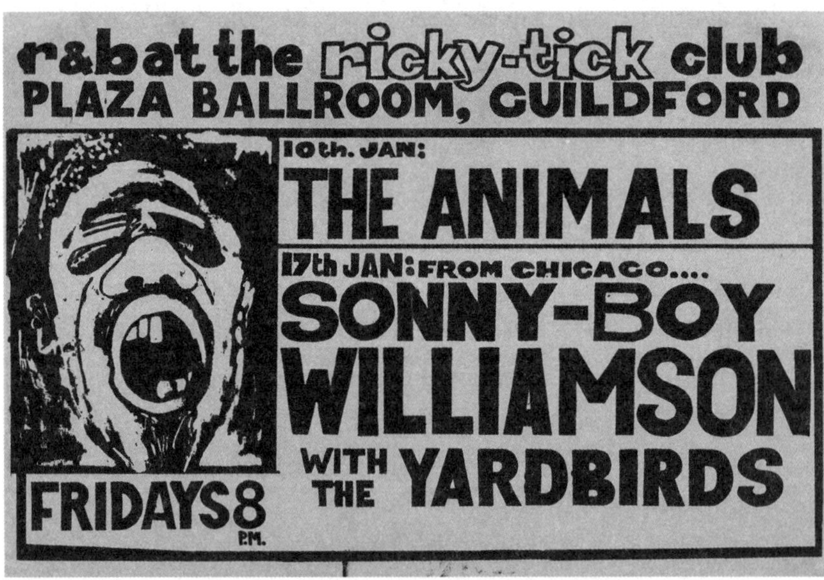

Poster for the Ricky-Tick club in Guildford featuring the Animals and the Yardbirds, 1964.

words of Chris Roberts, were 'now creating a demand for R&B': 'The twin-pronged attack on the scene from commercial and non-commercial aspect might produce an unprecedented situation in the music business, where R&B and good beat groups can build up followings comparable to pop stars – without a hit record or national exposure, except through club and concert tours.'[83] Georgie Fame and the Blue Flames were held up as an example of a band in demand without a hit record.

In its 7 December issue, *Record Mirror* turned its back page over to the Rolling Stones with a colour picture of the band (the Beatles had been granted the paper's first full-colour cover three weeks earlier) alongside news of their single's ascent up the charts and of a forthcoming EP, which was designed to impress upon listeners their authentic R&B bona fides against accusations of commercial selling out. Also boosted was their emerging songwriting talent, with a composition for Gene Pitney, 'That Girl Belongs to Yesterday'. 'And there's another thing that their fans can be thankful for,' wrote Jopling: 'The fact that the Rolling Stones are a group who can sing R&B to a pop audience and be highly appreciated. They really ARE off-beat.'[84]

At the outset of 1964, *Melody Maker* understood that the New Year would be a time of reckoning for trad jazz: 'Rhythm-and-blues continues to infiltrate into former trad strongholds – the latest to be stormed is the Mecca of trad itself, London's Jazzshows Jazz Club.' Cyril Davies was taking up the Thursday residency and Manfred Mann had moved in on Tuesdays. The club had been running seven nights a week for many years; attendance had always been strong on Fridays, Saturdays, Sundays and Mondays, but Monday shows 'had taken a nose-dive and we can't carry four bad days', said club owner George Webb, a man as responsible as anyone for trad's post-war popularity.[85] The professional acts that had won audiences had traded the clubs for concert halls and ballrooms, and the lesser groups weren't able to offer what had been lost: 'They have all the honesty, conviction and sincerity, but they just don't have the jazz thing . . .

After all nobody supports Tottenham Reserves,' said Webb.[86] But if R&B was to be played at his club, he was adamant that it would be the right kind; he would not be booking any bandwagon jumpers.

Whether or not the Rolling Stones were part of the bandwagon-jumping clique who were anathema to Webb wasn't said, though Bob Dawbarn didn't rate them. They were listed in that week's *Melody Maker* as belonging to a group of 'Beat Pursuers' who were lining up to challenge the Beatles. Alongside the Searchers, Bern Elliott and the Fenmen, the Swinging Blue Jeans, the Fourmost, the Merseybeats and the Hollies, the Stones stood out as the only group promoting themselves as advocates of R&B. Mick Jagger said, 'We have always favoured the music of what we consider the R&B greats – Muddy Waters, Jimmy Reed, and so on – and we would like to think that we are helping to give the fans of these artists what they want, as well as doing more commercial numbers.'[87]

By February, Jazzshows was booking the 'new-look' Mike Cotton band. It was his 'regular Dixieland line-up. The faces, several of them Beatle-fringed, are the same but the sound has changed,' *Melody Maker* reported: 'This is the out-and-out R&B group . . . and as wild and loud as can be reasonably expected.'[88] Cotton had been putting R&B numbers into his set for a while, he explained:

> It was last winter really when the jazz thing dwindled, well, definitely since the Beatles started happening. It took a nosedive, and we started planning. So this change is not a sudden thing . . . Playing R&B is a different approach, much more abandon, but the more we do the more we'll feel the whole thing. And we find it very satisfying playing a vital music to a vital audience.[89]

In the final pages of his 1965 autobiography, *Owning-Up*, George Melly paid heed to the recent changes in the jazz scene that had been driven by teenagers and their new beat groups:

> At the Albert Hall around Easter 1963, Diz Disley, Rolf Harris and myself were linkmen for a B.B.C. spectacular of 'Jazz 'n Pop'. The jazz bands got a lot of applause, but the stars of the evening were the Beatles, a group I'd only just heard of. The bell had begun to toll for trad.
>
> Over the last two years trad has died. Clubs closed. Managements turned over to Beat groups . . . At the time of writing rhythm and blues is taking over from Beat. This is nearer allied to trad and several of the [trad] bands have made the jump. What is good about rhythm and blues is that it has meant almost every month one or more Negro blues singers come over on tour.[90]

By the end of 1964, the tide had risen against trad. At the height of the boom in 1961, Dawbarn was reporting that there was an estimated fifty professional trad bands operating in London alone; three years later, there were no more than twelve.[91] Conversely, he had estimated the number of R&B groups in Britain to be more than 2,000 in 1964, though he 'doubted if 20 of these have anything very original to offer'.[92] Whatever the truth in these numbers, as the scene progressed into 1964, clubs would have no problem finding enough R&B bands to put before audiences.

2

An ABC of R&B for the Purists and Bandwagon Jumpers Alike, 1964

First the Beatles. Then the Dave Clark Five. Then the Rolling Stones. As Rhythm and Blues grows more dominant in the beat craze, the appearance of pop groups becomes increasingly bizarre . . .

With the rapidly snowballing success of the Rolling Stones, emphasis in the pop world over the past few months has begun to shift from the Northern 'beat' groups who emulate the Beatles, to groups from the South who play Rhythm and Blues in the manner of the Stones, and who often surpass them in outlandish appearance. Such groups as the Pretty Things, the Yardbirds, the Animals, the Kinks, the Daisies, make the Beatles look almost conventional. Rhythm and Blues attracts a sub-teenage public: the average age for members of the Rolling Stones fan club is 10. Many of these groups originated in art schools; they lead a strange life, poised between the blazing notoriety achieved by the Stones, and the total anonymity in which they began.

SUNDAY TIMES MAGAZINE (12 July 1964)[1]

The New Year got off to a sad start; harmonica man, singer and linchpin of London's blues scene Cyril Davies died in the first week of 1964. A memorial event was held Tuesday, 28 January 1964, at the Jazz Club at 100 Oxford Street, previously known as Jazzshows. Among those listed as performing were Georgie Fame, Manfred Mann, Alexis Korner, Jim Powell, John Mayall, Zoot Money, Long John Baldry, the Animals and the

Yardbirds. By any reckoning it was an impressive line-up, lacking only the Rolling Stones from the generation of young talent that Alexis Korner and Cyril Davies had done so much to help foster.

For *Melody Maker*, Bob Dawbarn provided a career overview and appreciation alongside collected tributes for Davies.[2] The latter was, Dawbarn reported, often difficult to work with, but a man dedicated to the R&B cause that he and Korner had helped promote, which had its inauspicious beginnings in 1955 at London's Roundhouse pub, Soho, 'where they presented rhythm-and-blues long before its most fanatical adherents could ever foresee a real popularity for the music'.[3] Davies had played with Chris Barber on his 'early R&B experiments' and with Korner in Blues Incorporated before leaving to start his own band, the All-Stars, shortly before Christmas 1962. Harold Pendleton, of the National Jazz Federation and Marquee Club, told Dawbarn that Davies 'played hard and worked hard and he was THE harmonica player', and Chris Barber said that 'Cyril was one of the most dedicated men in the whole blues field here. He lived and died a bluesman.'[4] Contrary to myth, Davies did not die on stage at the Crawdaddy but in Harrow General Hospital, on 7 January.[5] He had been suffering from pleurisy and endocarditis. He was just 32 years old, married with two children.

If Davies's death acted as a centrifugal force in bringing together the London blues community, still in its infancy, others such as Bill Carey, on the jazz beat from which the emergent scene had illegitimately been born, were intent on tripping up the rickety orphan child. Having been secretary of the National Jazz Federation and manager of the Marquee Club, both from 1961 to 1963, Carey had made a sizable investment in the London scene's idiosyncratic deployment of Black American music forms. He was also a 'critic, writer, journalist, amateur and semi-professional jazz and R and B publicist'.[6] In the same issue of *Record Mirror* in which the Cyril Davies benefit was advertised, Carey wrote that Rhythm and Blues in clubland was booming, but its integrity was being called into question by 'too many rock groups' jumping on the bandwagon.[7] Carey's pitch to young upstarts was to leave the scene 'to the purists':

> It's infuriating! It really is. For three years, some of us have been sponsoring and encouraging sincere, exciting Rhythm 'n' Blues groups. Now every beat group with money enough to buy a cheap harmonica and hire in a four-chord guitarist is calling itself 'R. and B.' It's a cast-iron certainty that, in 1964, the great heaving mound of Tin Pan Alley-controlled nursery-rhyme beat groups will attach itself to the R. and B. label.[8]

Twelve months later, Carey's prophecy was fulfilled; the bandwagon had rolled on unfettered, his criticism unable to block its wheels. 'In 1962,' he wrote,

> Chris Barber, Alexis Korner, the late Cyril Davies and I were involved in an attempt to create blues-and-jazz-based R and B groups using the material and inspiration of the great American Negro vocalists. We knew it needed the talents of dedicated jazz and blues musicians who knew the idiom, loved it and could create authenticity.[9]

Today, that vision, Carey argued, had fractured into three strands of R&B. The first was country and city blues that was given a full band treatment, including trombone, trumpet and saxophone (for example, Chris Barber's band with vocalist Ottilie Patterson). The second was based on the talent of trained musicians associated with the 'modern' jazz sphere (for example, Alexis Korner, Manfred Mann and Graham Bond). The third was 'the truly authentic R and B, linked with American Negro styles and solo voice/guitar, or harmonica.'[10] The leading exponents of this strand were 'Cyril Davies' All-Stars, now led by Long John Baldry, Johnny Mayall's

Bluesbreakers and the recreated Brian Knight's Blues by Six' (the last of the three had worked with Brian Jones and Charlie Watts before the formation of the Rolling Stones).[11]

The Rolling Stones, Carey wrote, 'are still often authentic, but are now largely concerned with the nursery rhyme market', and 'The Yardbirds are another group of authenticity in danger of becoming kindergarten.'[12] The false R&B prophets were at best aping 'American teenage "twist-rock 'n' roll"' in disguise.[13] 'Let's set the record straight,' he asserted: 'A group is NOT an R and B group unless its total work is based on rhythmic, blues artistry of the American Negro City Blues vocalists/guitarists.'[14] To those riding the trend, he had a message: 'Climb Off the wagon, boys, before you tilt it over and destroy REAL R and B . . . and yourselves with it!'[15]

Southend's Paramounts were a good example of what Carey considered to be the 'nursery rhyme' end of the R&B spectrum. They'd just released their hurried-up version of the Coasters 'Poison Ivy' – 'we had to speed it up because in its original form it was too slow to do any of the modern dances to,' they told *Record Mirror*.[16] The Rolling Stones had also covered the song on their newly released EP; about them, the Paramounts said:

> Well, they're the Kings of the R&B scene. They appeal to everybody. The R&B fanatics and the commercial kids. They busted the scene wide open. If it hadn't been for them there wouldn't have been an R&B scene here in London.
>
> We started gradually switching over to playing more bluesy stuff about a year ago. Why? Well, the main thing is it's more subtle. That's what counts. You get very fed up with rock 'n' roll after a while. The same old sounds. R&B is a challenge. We were lucky – we changed before the boom really came. It was a gradual thing of course. But believe us, on stage our sound is completely different now.[17]

For the Paramounts, there was no simple binary opposition between blues purity and commercialism. They made no claim to being among the advance guard, they paid deference to the Stones, but then staked a position ahead of the trailing pack. Their motive in moving into R&B was a desire for the novel, to avoid getting stale – authenticity, sincerity and truth are not part of their vocabulary. But as Carey suggested, those values were still very much part of the Yardbirds and Stones' glossary. Regardless of Carey's opinion – he would, most likely, have dismissed the Paramounts as pop – the band at least had Mick Jagger and Keith Richards publicly voicing their support, regarding them as among the best in the scene.[18]

Carey saw himself as a custodian of Black American music; like many of his contemporaries who proselytized about jazz, he argued over the merits, authentic and otherwise, of traditional, revivalist, Dixieland, mainstream and modern forms. Purity of intent, if not always delivery, mattered. It mattered a great deal because jazz and R&B were, or should have been, beyond commercial imperatives; exploiting such music for financial gain was a heresy. Commercial interests traded in falsehoods, but authentic Black American music held truths untrammelled by decadent white, Western cultures. As much as this constituted his philosophy, Carey was at that point a very British version of Norman Mailer's 'white Negro', a hipster in self-declared exile, searching for truth in a deceitful world: 'In such places as Greenwich Village, a ménage-à-trois was completed – the bohemian and the juvenile delinquent came face-to-face with the Negro, and the hipster was a fact in American life,' wrote Mailer.[19] There may have been an ocean between them, but, just like Jack Kerouac and his non-conformist Beat cohort, Carey was choosing to live on the margins – an outsider fuelled by a romanticized idea of Black America.

For many, the R&B boom was nothing more than the latest musical fad, and Carey's histrionics were neither here nor there.

Trad jazzman Kenny Ball saw the whole thing as part of an ebb and flow of trends:

> Is there an R and B boom? . . . there most definitely is a boom in a form of music that people like to attach the tag 'Rhythm and Blues' to. Consequently all the beat and rock groups who can get a member to play harmonica after a fashion are calling themselves R and B groups . . . the same thing is happening to it as happened to trad. All the inferior and imitation groups are jumping on the bandwagon.[20]

Hohner Harmonicas had no reservation about pushing the bandwagon a little faster down the hill than Carey (or Ball) would have cared for, using Brian Jones to help sell their product and listing not only the Rolling Stones but Manfred Mann, Sonny Boy Williamson, John Lennon and 'the late Cyril Davies' as playing their Echo Super Vamper.[21]

When questioned on the topic, Acker Bilk had little to say except that he wasn't paying much attention to the emerging scene and hadn't heard Mick Jagger:

> 'I don't know enough about the beat groups to really judge. But the ones I have heard are nowhere near; they don't compare with the musicians in the trad bands . . .' Speaking of beat and the like, how does he think our R&B compares with the American article? 'I don't think it swings as well.'[22]

When asked by *Melody Maker*'s Max Jones which was his favourite beat group, Bilk facetiously offered Count Basie and Louis Prima.[23]

On the other hand, Chris Barber was presented as an elder statesman to the scene; he 'had a good deal to do with the spread of trad', wrote Dawbarn. He 'was also in on the ground floor on the skiffle and R&B trends':

> 'We have played some R&B for a long time now,' says Chris. 'We've been closing our shows with "I've Got My Mojo Working" for all of five years . . . We have always believed in being versatile. We don't like playing one noise all night . . . On our R&B night at the Marquee we just play blues all night – but it varies from a trumpet-alto line-up on "Jeep's Blues" to things with harmonica and guitar . . .
>
> There has been a shift in public favour in jazz to blues, or whatever you care to call it. Some is purely artificial, dictated by the fashion designers, but I feel there is a great deal to be said for the extra guttiness and vigour that has come in with all this.'[24]

Whatever position Britain's jazz musicians held towards the scene, they could do no more than react or comment from the sidelines. Things were moving fast in 1964, even if the year started with a loss.

A number of benefit concerts for Davies were held in small clubs around London, but the most impressive took place on 21 February at the Fairfield Hall in Croydon, with all proceeds going to his family. The bill was a perfect primer of the mixed nature of the nascent R&B scene. Sponsored by the National Jazz Federation, Ottilie Patterson, Chris Barber and Colin Kingwell's Bandits represented the jazz side of things, and the Yardbirds and Alex Harvey's Soul Band covered the rock 'n' roll end. Alexis Korner's Blues Inc. held the middle ground, while American bluesman Sonny Boy Williamson topped the bill.[25] (Ottilie Patterson's swinging Columbia 45 of the blues standard 'Baby Please Don't Go' with harmonica accompaniment from Sonny Boy was released to coincide with the show. In November, Belfast's Them had their own version for sale.[26])

The evening's entertainment was advertised in *Record Mirror* alongside reviews of a glut of recent UK releases of blues discs by Jimmy Reed, John Lee Hooker, Bo Diddley, Lightnin' Hopkins, T-Bone Walker and a number of compilation albums. (Always far behind *Melody Maker* in its coverage of the R&B boom, never mind *Record Mirror*, *Disc* remained steadfastly enthralled with Merseybeat and Cliff Richard; apart from copious coverage of the Stones, the paper didn't recognize the scene until May, when it finally reported on the excess of album, EP and single releases of original American recordings.[27])

With jazzing the blues on the way out, and with plenty of readily available licensed American blues on British labels to provide inspiration and song material, indigenous British bands began to release self-identified R&B discs. The Downliners Sect independently distributed 'New R&B E.P.' *Nite in Great Newport Street* was promoted in a series of adverts in *Record Mirror*. It featured four covers: Jimmy Reed's 'Shame, Shame, Shame', Booker T. and the MG's' 'Green Onions', Chuck Berry's 'Beautiful Delilah' and Bo Diddley's 'Nursery Rhymes'. The Chuck Berry songbook, which featured prominently in the Rolling Stones set lists, provided a bedrock for many of the year's R&B groups. The scene's consistent dipping into his catalogue represented the rock 'n' roll element so many jazzmen disdained.

In its 22 February issue, *Melody Maker*'s listings for London's 'Jazz Clubs' told the tale of just how firmly and quickly the new R&B acts had colonized the city's central and suburban venues. At the Jazz Club, 100 Oxford Street, Jimmy Powell, the Groundhogs, the Art Wood Combo and the Animals played either side of Acker Bilk in the final week of the month. 'Jazz at The Marquee' (still at its Oxford Street location) had the Cheynes (Mick Fleetwood and Pete Bardens's band), Zoot Money, Long John Baldry and the Yardbirds as that week's attractions, alongside Humphrey Lyttelton, Freddy Randall and the Harry South Trio and other jazz disciples. At Ken Colyer Club/Studio 51, Great Newport Street, The Downliners Sect supported by the Impressions (not Curtis Mayfield's combo, I'd wager) were holding an 'All Night R&B Session This Saturday' and Chris Farlow Thunderbirds, as they were named on the advertising material, preceded them earlier in the week. Farlowe was a featured attraction at the All-Nighter Club at the Flamingo, Wardour Street. Georgie Fame and Zoot Money were also part of the bill that evening. The Scene, Great Windmill Street, was all R&B, with record nights led by Guy Stevens and 'Blue Beat Night with Sandra'. The Animals, Alex Harvey's Soul Band and Zoot Money's Big Roll Band made up the club's live acts in the final week of February.

Anticipating the weekly music press's interest in the scene was a small coterie of blues fans who produced specialist magazines – *Blues Unlimited*, *R&B Monthly*, *R&B Scene* and *R&B Gazette* – mimeographed productions. *Jazzbeat* was a much glossier affair. It first circulated in January 1964, incorporating the Marquee Club's listings sheet, *Jazz Today*, and *Jazz News and Reviews*, which ceased in December 1963. That final year of publication had, according to the Editorial,

> been a year of change in the British jazz scene. The trad fad is over and a Rhythm & Blues trend is accelerating. Clubs close and clubs open and a magazine must adjust to the ever changing scene.
>
> With this issue *Jazz News* completes seven years as an independent jazz publication. We have made several changes over the years because we feel a magazine devoted to jazz should be as free from stylistic restrictions as the music itself.
>
> From the next issue we shall resume an official connection with the National Jazz Federation who originally founded *Jazz News* in 1956. We shall merge with their monthly *Jazz Today*. For the new magazine we have chosen a new name, *Jazzbeat*.[28]

The magazine continued to use Val Wilmer's superlative photographs of visiting American blues and jazz artistes and gave regular spots to

Guy Stevens's record reviews and profiles. Early issues also included pieces by Giorgio Gomelsky and photographs by his collaborator Hamish Grimes.

By the beginning of March 1964, 'The Jazz Club' had been rebranded 'The 100 Club' and was promoting a bill of 'Rhythm and Blues' fare to the exclusion of jazz. Graham Bond's R&B Quartet, the Pretty Things, the Animals and John Lee and the Groundhogs were among the featured acts in the week of 12–19 March. Just below the 100 Club advertisement, the R&B Crawdaddy Club was being promoted in *Record Mirror*:

> It started 80 weeks ago with the Rolling Stones in Richmond, the centre of R&B. It is now the most raving R&B Club in Britain, with the most Blueswailing, fan-followed YARDBIRDS who give forth every Sunday – RAA Grounds, Richmond. Every Wednesday and Saturday at the Star Hotel, London Road, Croydon. Come and Feel the Sound!![29]

Outside London, at one or other of the four Ricky-Tick club nights in Windsor, Guildford, Reading and Maidenhead, the Pretty Things, the Animals, the Yardbirds, Manfred Mann and the Embers could be heard. Long John Baldry's Hoochie Coochie Men, featuring Rod 'The Mod' Stewart, had their own 'Baldry's Blues Club' at the Railway Hotel, Wealdstone, on Tuesday nights. That same night of the week, Chingford R&B club at the Royal Forest Hotel 'Klooks (R&B) Kleek' hosted Graham Bond. At the Railway Hotel, West Hampstead, the night's attractions were Georgie Fame and the Blue Flames plus Bill's Bluesers. On Wednesday, South Harrow R&B offered 'The Fantastic Mike Cotton Sound'. The Friday night Blue Opera Club at the Royal Bell on Bromley High Street was headlined by John Mayall's Bluesbreakers. Competing with that venue for an audience was Harringay R&B Bluesville! Club at the Manor House (opposite the tube station). On Saturday, the Annexe, Barnes (on the 'No. 9 bus route'), advertised 'Rhythm & Blues, Name Groups, Bar Adjacent'.

Promotion of Gomelsky's clubs continued into the following weeks, noting 'fantastic attendance on Saturday' and thanking Sonny Boy Williamson 'for all the great raving scenes that the boys had at the Crawdaddy'.[30] Recently relocated to Wardour Street, the Marquee started advertising in *Record Mirror* in the first week of April. The Yardbirds, alongside Long John Baldry, Manfred Mann and John Mayall's Bluesbreakers, were the R&B acts across four nights; a blue-beat session, Stan Getz and Chris Barber made up the acts for the other three evenings' entertainment. If exclusivity was part of the attraction offered by R&B clubs, then in that week's Crawdaddy advertisement, the point was made that the Yardbirds, 'so very most blueswailing', were one of only four acts that they had featured. The other three were the Rolling Stones, Manfred Mann and the Animals.[31]

On Wednesday, 26 February, Liverpool's Cavern Club had hosted the second 'R&B Festival' (the first had been held in Birmingham on 2 February). The day began with a lunchtime double-feature show (noon–2.15) with the Undertakers and the Yardbirds. 'Six truly fantastic Genuine R&B Acts' were featured in the evening show, headlined 'In Person' by the 'Great' American bluesman Sonny Boy Williamson. Filling out the rest of the bill for 'Merseyside's Mightiest R&B Show Ever' were the Yardbirds, the Roadrunners, the Valkyries, the Mersey Bluebeats and St. Louis Checks.[32]

The club-level identification and exploitation of a new musical form practised by ardent young students of Black American blues was quickly picked up by the mainstream press. In April, the *Daily Mail* featured the Pretty Things – a 'down-to-basics rhythm-in-blues group'.[33] Their music was the

> current teenage religion. Meetings are vibrant with the fervour of Holy Rollers. They shake and tremble to power-blasting music with ritualistic delight. As Phil [May] says: 'If the music left you cold it would be useless. It's loud, loud, loud. The very noise gets into you . . . Some of our stuff borders on rock 'n' roll, but we aim to play the blues.'[34]

Chuck Berry played as big a part in the Pretties' scheme of things as he did in the Stones'.

The *Daily Mail* reporter Robert Bickford noted that the Pretty Things were part of the trend, following on from the Beatles and the Rolling Stones, and there are '101' groups in Greater London alone, with a 'club following of more than 100,000'.[35] Manfred Mann, Georgie Fame, the Yardbirds, Long John Baldry's Hoochie Coochie Men, Zoot Money's Big Roll Band, the Bluesbreakers, Cheynes and the Animals are namechecked. Of the blues, Eric Burdon told Bickford: 'it's one of the greatest art forms . . . I put my heart and soul in it.'[36]

In April, *Melody Maker* covered the 'Massive Swing to R&B': 'In beat, the audience screams at the group . . . in R&B the group screamed at the audience.'[37] Despite the Animals' presence on the scene, Bob Dawbarn continued to describe R&B as the 'London sound'.[38] He quoted Bill Carey on the explosion of interest, who claimed that within a 64-kilometre (40 mi.) radius of central London, 300,000 people pay to hear R&B every week. He tripled not only the number of attendees notched up by Bickford, but the number of bands themselves: '300 groups in the country claiming to play R&B – 140 of them in Greater London area.'[39] Where did Bickford, Dawbarn and Carey get their figures from? Carey had written on the emerging scene back in January; now, he was manager of the 'Band and General Agency, recently formed by Ted Morton of Jazzshows'.[40] Hyperbole aside, he said that in the popularity stakes, the fight was between the Animals, the Pretty

Things and the Yardbirds, and he hoped to get the Tridents and Northampton's Apex on his books. Also earning a mention alongside pioneers Baldry, Jimmy Powell, Georgie Fame and Manfred Mann were the Who and Them (a first namecheck in the national music press for both bands, though which Them, from Hounslow or Belfast, is uncertain[41]), the Bluebottles (led by Mike Patto), the Groundhogs, Downliners Sect, the Cheynes and Alex Harvey.

In his weekly magazine column, Francis Hitching, the editor of *Ready Steady Go!*, wrote about the importance of the club scene for the television programme. He began with recalling the evening that the show's hosts took Dionne Warwick to the Scene Club, just off Piccadilly, and she was 'knocked out by the place. "We've got nothing like it in America," she said . . . above all, she got the feeling that kids over here had got themselves organized so that they could enjoy themselves the way *they* wanted to.'[42] Hitching then moved his attention from Soho's clubs the Ad Lib and the Saddle Room towards the suburbs:

> Just up the road from where I live is the Craw Daddy Club in Richmond – the place that found The Rolling Stones. About this time last year, only a few thousand kids who were members of the club had heard of The Stones, but already their following was noisy and enthusiastic enough to let any outsider know they were quickly going to make it in the big-time.[43]

The club scene is the incubator of teenage styles and trends, rapidly evolving and self-generating. Hitching told the story of the Stones, playing their usual Sunday night gig at the Crawdaddy Club during the summer 1963 National Jazz Festival, which was being held on the same grounds, and how they had become absorbed into the event. Their popularity was such that they had to be moved into the biggest marquee: 'Shake Kane, the great modernist trumpet player, couldn't believe it. "I've never seen anything like it, just never," he kept repeating.'[44] When the Stones moved on, the Crawdaddy fell into the doldrums for a while, but now, Hitching reported, it

> is back to its best form. And all because of the latest group they've got playing there, The Yardbirds. It strikes me that kids at the club rave even more about this group than they did for The Stones – if that's possible! They're not so wild-looking as The Stones, but most of the fans think the music is wilder.[45]

Supplemented by numerous company advertisements for R&B releases and from the artists' managers and agents, *Record Mirror* ran a four-page special on the boom that covered everything from the Rolling Stones' Bo Diddley beat on their latest disc, 'Not Fade Away', to blue-beat ingenue Millie, Solomon Burke, Island label's Sue Records and that label's director, Guy Stevens, who wrote about Larry Williams and interviewed Jimmy Reed and Chuck Berry:

> I asked Chuck if he would describe himself as a rhythm and blues artiste, telling him of the major controversy over here at the moment about what is authentic rhythm and blues. 'No,' he said firmly, 'I would like to think of myself as an artiste who can sell to any type of market.'[46]

In the United States, Chuck said, he was considered to be rock 'n' roll; R&B was performed by vocal groups like the Moonglows, the Flamingos and the Dells, while 'Muddy Waters or Howlin' Wolf are considered to be folk blues artistes.'[47]

In the first two issues of *Jazzbeat*, the Beatles and the Stones were interviewed about the emerging scene and for their take on just what defined R&B. The Beatles were perplexed by the whole idea of neatly pigeonholing artists, Paul said:

> Everything is in little categories. As soon as we started playing they said, 'Okay, what kind of music are you playing?' and we answered, 'You know, it's rock isn't it mister? Then they said 'It's not quite rock it's a little bit different'. So we said 'Well is it rhythm and blues then? Rhythm and Blues ... yeah man ... the new sound ... we really never were a rhythm and blues group, we just used to play numbers by R&B artists.[48]

What particularly annoyed the Beatles was the inverted snobbery that ensued when an artist had a hit and whatever type of music they played was now deemed to be 'pop' – a lesser form. Elvis Presley, said John, '[is] a better R&B singer than anyone in Britain ... it's just that people feel ashamed they collected his records'.[49] Besides, he continued, 'what I want to know is where all these R&B enthusiasts that know all about R&B were last year?'[50]

Despite having been ousted by the Stones as a potential manager, Gomelsky was still game enough to interview them for *Jazzbeat* and to take the opportunity to highlight his club's role in their success:

> Their liking for R&B grew out of practicing it, by getting to know it more and more. They are not 'purists', their concept of R&B is a 'popular' one in the best sense of the word and their appeal to the mass audience proves their claim. It so happens that even if their visual appearance is dead in line with present teenage fashions their music is fairly uncompromising and those who know them personally have often wondered at the incredible wealth of information they possess about their particular brand of R&B.
>
> They are – in a way – rebels, and this is perhaps why the surprisingly conservative jazz world at first snubbed them. But luckily for them the 'trend' was towards R&B and their very modest beginnings at the Richmond CRAWDADDY

CLUB soon turned into a fantastic success. After it was relatively easy: a record then another, both big sellers.[51]

Mick Jagger told Gomelsky about a group of south London R&B enthusiasts, different from those on the club scene, who considered Jimmy Reed, Bo Diddley and Chuck Berry to be like gods. R&B to these aficionados was like a religion and 'nobody else could do it. When a bunch of white kids like us came along and started producing something which came surprisingly close to it, they didn't like that either.'[52] Brian Jones added: 'It's really a matter for a sociologist, a psychiatrist, or something.'[53] Discussing R&B's appeal, Jones said, 'If you ask some people why they go for R&B you get pretentious answers. They say that in R&B they find "an honesty of expression, a sincerity of feeling", and so on, for me it is merely the sound'; Keith Richards agreed with him.[54] The key for Jagger was that the music held something 'wild', like Little Richard.[55] Jones concurred: 'My tastes are becoming more and more basic, really. I don't like pretentiousness.'[56] When asked if they consciously tried to create that effect in their own music, Jones replied: 'As soon as we get on stage things just become "one mood". Because we have strived so hard to get this integrated sound and integrated mood, as soon as we start to play we become the cells making up an organ.'[57]

The band discussed with Gomelsky their choice of material, its adaptation to their own sound and sometimes, to their surprise, their improving on the original: 'This music is essentially "alien" to us and we have to do a lot of listening . . . until we're completely drenched in it.'[58] That alienness led the discussion towards questions of how 'R&B is supposed to be more "ethnically" connected, more "racial" in a way'.[59] In his response to Gomelsky's observation, Jagger made a connection between Muddy Waters and Jerry Lee Lewis; 'There isn't really much difference between a good rocker or a white R&B singer and a Negro R&B artist.'[60] Jagger then took issue with the 'authenticity' said to be inherent in R&B when contrasted with 'manufactured' pop or rock. He considered R&B to be aimed at the Top 10 even if it didn't sell: 'R&B that gets into the hit parade – in America at least – needn't be "manufactured". It all depends on the artist and the number.'[61] Jones said he had 'read somewhere that whereas the content of pop songs is about life as the singer or the composer and for that matter, the audience, would *like* it to be, the blues – and R&B – are about life as it really *is*. At least generally speaking.'[62]

John Baldry added to the controversy regarding how R&B was to be defined and who should not be included in the scene; interviewed by Dawbarn, the band leader 'vehemently disagrees' with those who said his band played 'authentic R&B':

> I'd like to make it clear that we are a blues band and we dissociated ourselves from the current R&B scene . . . I am a blues singer with strong jazz influences, the band is a blues band and we don't play Chuck Berry or Bo Diddley stuff . . . There is so much terrible rubbish going under the guise of blues, when it really has nothing to do with it . . . Berry, Diddley and Jimmy Reed are so easy to emulate. We are the only blues group that improvises.[63]

In March, Mick Jagger wrote an open letter to *Melody Maker* to answer all those who kept writing to the paper about the 'desecration of the real thing'.[64] He hit back hard and fast, writing that no one could be more of an advocate of John Lee Hooker, Jimmy Reed, Chuck Berry and Bo Diddley than he was. Readers only had to ask those at Pye Records if they remembered the 'thousands of letters' from him asking that they release more recordings by these artists. To that point, the Stones made it something of a duty to announce from the stage who originally did the numbers they played. They were out to educate their listeners to the music they loved, and they were helping rather than hindering: 'If they put the original record out, it wouldn't sell much. But it's likely to spread more if we plug the song, isn't it? Can that be bad?'[65] One issue Jagger couldn't change was that 'girl fans, particularly, would rather have a copy by a British group than the original American version – mainly, I suppose, because they like the British blokes' faces, and they feel nearer to them.'[66] He concluded with 'a final, important point – will all the people who shout about R&B copyists please make sure first that they have bought the records by the original artists? I hope they see what I mean.'[67]

Towards the end of May, *Melody Maker*'s Bob Dawbarn and Ray Coleman debated the merits of the Rolling Stones. Dawbarn was the naysayer; he thought it was 'farcical to hear the accents, sentiments and experiences of an American Negro coming out of a white-faced London lad', but more than their inauthenticity or long unkempt hair, the biggest crime the Stones committed was that they didn't swing.[68] Coleman acknowledged that latter point but thought it didn't matter because they have 'drive and they generate'.[69] At their core, he wrote, 'The Stones' music is British rhythm and blues. It is crude, raw, earthy, and has plenty of spontaneity. It is sometimes happy, sometimes morose, always alive.'[70]

In June, *Ready Steady Go!* got in on the act and had Mick Jagger and Long John Baldry debate the matter. Baldry held to his line that 'there's no group playing in Britain today that can produce real R and B.'[71] Jagger countered: 'Well, John and I have argued about this for years. I just don't agree with him, and I probably never will.'[72] He was supported by Brian Jones: 'The basic sound we make is right. The point of rhythm and blues is that it's got soul. You've got to believe in what you're doing,' which the Stones undoubtedly did.[73] Keith Richards later added his thoughts to the debate: 'I'm fed up of people calling us non-authentic. Why can't we play what we like? Who's laying down the rules?'[74]

Chris Farlowe followed Baldry's line – 'We don't play any Chuck Berry or Bo Diddley. That has really been played out.'[75] Both bands defined themselves by what they were not as much as by what they were. For Farlowe, the Berry–Diddley R&B rave-up had become exhausted; for Baldry, it was simplistic musical fare, easily mastered and therefore of no value. Though the issue continued to be channelled through questions of authenticity, musical ability and the fall in the novelty value of R&B now played a part. The label of R&B, however, was still being claimed by all sorts of groups. If anyone was policing the debate, as Richards suggested, the regulations were remarkably anarchic.

Like rock and roll before it, rhythm and blues was never a specific musical form, readily defined, like ska in 1965; it was a sensibility that, at least initially, encompassed an uncertain schism with the jazz from which it was launched. To an extent, R&B was about polarities of musical taste, which were generational – from jazz to beat – but it also registered as a continuity with previous forms. The Animals had a take on this, which they shared with *Beat Instrumental*:

> 'Music today is a funny thing . . . Today it is called Rhythm and Blues. Yet, the same music of four or five years ago was called Rock 'n' Roll. I'm not sure if any group play R&B really.' 'R&B is just blues with a beat,' said Alan Price. 'Yes, it's kind of rocked up,' chirped in Chas. 'Nothing played today is genuine blues. Only the stuff played by the originals . . . Jimmy Witherspoon, Jimmy Reed and that lot.' 'We're not a R&B group at all,' said Hilton. 'I'd call it Rock 'n' Roll.' . . . 'Even Chuck Berry said so,' added Hilton Valentine.[76]

The musicians' union's block on giving work visas to Americans, unless there was a reciprocal engagement for British artists, eased somewhat in 1964, enabled by the greater number of British musicians travelling to the United States in the wake of the Beatles' success there. In September, *Melody Maker* carried the news that 'Eleven blues stars' were set to tour Britain, including Lightnin' Hopkins,

Howlin' Wolf, Sonny Boy Williamson, Sunnyland Slim, Sleepy John Estes, Willie Dixon and Sugar Pie DeSanto.[77] Independent of this package tour, an 'Evening with the Blues' was being held at the Marquee on 17 September, featuring Little Walter and Memphis Slim. The Chris Barber Band with Ottilie Patterson and Long John Baldry's Hoochie Coochie Men were also on the bill.[78] Around the same time, Rufus Thomas, Jimmy Reed and John Lee Hooker were playing the London clubs (T-Bone Walker and Muddy Waters were set for the new year). Tamla Motown stars Marvin Gaye, Martha and the Vandellas, the Miracles and Kim Weston were set to make television and personal appearances in November, a prelude to a major package tour being set up for spring 1965.[79]

In May, Stateside, EMI's leasing label for American recordings distributed the UK's first collection of Tamla Motown productions, *The 'Sound' of the R&B Hits*. Despite the title, none of the fourteen tracks had been big sellers in Britain, though three Motown covers had been included on *With the Beatles*, released the previous November. The anomalous inverted commas around 'sound' worked in two ways: they differentiated the company's recordings – 'The "sound" on this album is the sound that identifies a Tamla Motown production,' as the sleeve note explains – and made the claim, by implication, that it was *the* R&B form in a field overrun with competing bids to be just that. It was also pitted against Stateside's own absolutist sets *Authentic R&B* (1963) and *The Real R&B* (1964). In his sleeve notes for the Inez & Charlie Foxx LP *Mockingbird* (1964), Guy Stevens wrote about recent developments in Black American music; without mentioning Motown directly, though listing Mary Wells alongside Major Lance and the Soul Sisters, he said they belonged to a 'new wave of rhythm and blues'. This trend would soon be renamed 'soul', but until then it was just another part of R&B's rich and diverse panoply of sound.

In October, with some of the Mersey groups having failed to make the charts with their latest releases, *Melody Maker* reader

Bryan McComb from Wembley Park in Middlesex considered the Liverpool scene to be on the way out: 'The Rolling Stones will definitely take over from the Beatles as top group, and the Yardbirds and Pretty Things will gain ground.'[80] In the same 'Mailbag', B. Walker, Blackpool, posed the question, 'what will happen when the rhythm-and-blues boom goes bang?' 'Answer: the only people to suffer will be the commercial imitators. Real greats like Muddy Waters, Howlin' Wolf and Little Walter will go on making records just the same, boom or no boom.'[81] Replying to another letter of similar sentiments to these, C. Martin, London SW18, refuted the idea that R&B was an 'indigenous American music which does not transplant into other localities. It does not matter where R&B is performed, or by whom, as long as it is appreciated. Pompous "connoisseurs" . . . must learn to live and let live.'[82] Reader Christine Beck, London E1, was not concerned with issues of authenticity, or with whether R&B was played by pale mimics, but instead with what would happen when the Yardbirds followed the Stones and Manfred Mann and became famous, because then, 'their fans won't be able to chat to them when they are off stage'.[83] For much of 1964, the debate had been over defining R&B, but as the year moved to a close, the focus shifted to what happens when a club scene moves into the mainstream.

In *Melody Maker*, published the week after this debate in the paper's 'Mailbag', Bob Dawbarn wrote:

> Manfred Mann fixed me with an unwinking stare and said 'I'm bored with the whole thing – with the endless idiotic arguments about rhythm and blues.' The sudden attack of boredom had followed my asking whether he thought that when groups made the Top 10 it became a case of more rhythm and less blues . . . 'We don't even want to be mentioned in the arguments – especially all those ridiculous letters about R&B on the back page of *MM*.'[84]

The fact was that there was still a good deal of mileage left in exploiting the arguments; in the same issue, *Melody Maker* asked its readers 'Just how hip are you?' and offered the chance to win £150 worth of Marshall gear in an R&B quiz: '1. Which R&B star owns a guitar-shaped swimming pool? . . . 6. Graham Bond has a sensational drummer. Who? . . . 15. Which famous British R&B pioneer died recently?'[85] In December, *Melody Maker* ran the year out with a humorous 'ABC of R&B': '"A" is for Amplification, heart of the beat sound. Also for Mose Allison, who has his imitators, and Britain's Art Woods. It's also for the Audacity of those who steal hits by covering American blues records.'[86]

In a letter published in the September issue of *Rave*, Jenny Sharpe from Birmingham wrote in support of her favourite band: 'O.K., so the Beatles are top now. Pretty soon they will be ousted by the Stones. And then, the Stones will just have to make way for Mickey Finn and the Bluesmen [*sic*], the guv'nor r-and-b group in Britain.'[87] Though the letter might be a genuine fan's fantasy, it reads more like hype from the band's publicist; today, Mickey Finn are recalled for two reasons only, their 1967 freakbeat 45 'Garden of My Mind', which sold zilch and now commands high collector prices, and the fact that Jimmy Page played harmonica with them on early sessions and appeared in some of the band's 1964 promotional materials. Not contradicting Jenny's claim that they were the nation's leading R&B combo, they recorded blue-beat-inspired numbers, exploiting the interest in the Jamaican sound that Millie with 'My Boy Lollipop' (recorded in London and resting at the top of the charts in February) and which independent labels such as Island, Planetone, Rio, Blue Beat and R&B were licensing and recording. An Island Records advertisement in the *NME* from January 1964 lists 'Ten Great Rhythm & Blues and Beat Records'. It made no distinction between the releases by American artists Inez Foxx and Russell Byrd on Sue and Jamaican discs from the Vikings and Derrick Morgan on Island and Black Swan. It either presumed potential customers were aware of the distinctions, or it barely mattered – it was all R&B.

Mickey Finn and the Blue Men's first single was on the Blue Beat label, UK home of Prince Buster, who thought the 'lads [were] just great'.[88] Beyond loaning their name, the band had nothing to do with the disc.[89] They subsequently released a cover of Bo Diddley's 'Pills' in the same idiom, but returned to a more standard take on Chuck Berry's 'Reelin' and a Rockin''; its B-side was an original, 'I Still Want You', based on a generic Jimmy Reed riff and in the same mould of R&B ravers as the Downliners Sect. *Record Mirror* wrote that they had a unique image, 'East End Mod', and were the 'first all-white blue beat group in the country'.[90] In January 1964, Decca released a single by the Beazers – a shell band that acted as a front for Chris Farlowe – that aimed to exploit the fad. The disc was titled – what else – 'Blue Beat'. The Yardbirds brought 'Blue Beat' into their act, dropping Eric Morris's 'Humpty Dumpty' into their cover of the Isley Brothers 'Respectable'. Georgie Fame had also covered Morris's nursery rhyme on his live album *Rhythm and Blues at the Flamingo* (1964) and on his May 1964 EP *Rhythm and Blue Beat*, a compact title that said it all.

The white British adoption of blue beat was a further exploitation of Black musical forms, one which had the effect of broadening the base by effectively reimagining the Atlantic triangle of commerce that existed between the West Indies, the USA and Britain. From such old maps, trade continued to flow – sometimes to the benefit of all, but oftentimes only to those who owned the means of production and distribution.[91]

None of this was hidden from view; front and centre of the debate about the boom was the issue of race – R&B as 'African tribal music', as the *Daily Mail*'s Charles Greville described it – a continuation of that which started with jazz and became amplified with rock 'n' roll.[92] The March 1964 issue of *Beat Monthly* predicted that the Rolling Stones would make it in the States because,

> despite the knockers, the Stones are capable of getting right in the genuine Rhythm 'n' Blues field. Sometimes they stray away in the interests of commercialism but they get nearer to the 'coloured feel' than most other groups. If they stuck to their 'way-out' material, they would go the proverbial bomb in the States.[93]

One reason given was that 'racial problems in parts of the States could mean a big welcome mat out for a white group capable of getting the coloured way of music' – echoing Sam Phillips on his discovery of Elvis.[94]

In March, *Pop Weekly*, a predominantly photographic magazine aimed at teenage girls, dedicated its leader column, 'Pop Soapbox', to the issue of the day: 'What is Rhythm & Blues?':

> Our impression of pop and R&B records is that they were two different fields entirely. To us rhythm and blues meant muffled recordings by singers with strange names like Muddy Waters etc., singing songs with some kind of story behind them. On the other hand Americans are quick to point out that there is no such thing as an English R&B group, as the music was born and bred in America and only American groups can play it. Sounds slightly daft to us . . .
>
> To be honest, Chuck Berry's and Bo Diddley's records we like. But we do think that, as recordings, they can be done so much better by other groups. Yet if a British group does a Chuck Berry number, and away goes all that muffled background sound and you end up with a cleaner record, what happens? Everybody says it's not R&B.[95]

It was all utterly incomprehensible, the *Pop Weekly* editors decided, just as unfathomable as a Bo Diddley number. The 'muffled' sound, the 'strange' names and the perplexing nature of it all was, of course, what drew suburban acolytes to the form in the first place: it was an antidote to the anodyne, quotidian, polished pop products of the day, of the over-familiar, oppressive sounds of the wheels of commerce turning. To make the everyday marvellous, to transform the mundane, demanded that a catalyst of alien grease and grit be pumped into the machine to help *jazz* up the glaringly obvious and add colour and light to the banal. As R&B went mainstream, the editors of pop magazines, record producers, and radio and television programmers were intent on removing all that grinding noise to give the groups an appeal suitable for mass consumption.

The process of pop's deracination of the racket, the dirt in the machine, was cyclical. For the *NME*, Ian Dove traced things back to the beginnings of rock 'n' roll: 'Rhythm 'n' Blues got lost in the mid-1950s. And Elvis Presley helped it to lose its way.'[96] The premise was that Elvis created a 'confusion' and a sensation by imitating blues singers and recording their songs, but he didn't follow through on his promise. Dove quoted Alexis Korner: 'Elvis was one of the best white blues singers around – early Presley that is. It was damn good stuff.'[97] Of Elvis's more recent recordings, Korner is less impressed: 'I feel saddened that a number like "Good Luck Charm", which was rhythm 'n' blues in form, wasn't terribly exciting in treatment. It should have been exciting but Elvis now leaves something out.'[98] In 1956, Elvis was 'steeped in rhythm 'n' blues' and

> stood at the crossroads but rather than stick with the style he abandoned it for sentimental ballads. He infected others, the excitement died down, and as a result even the beat became blander . . . until now. The British public is in the grip of the first real revival of rhythm 'n' blues. And the whole scene is more healthy. One reason the British scene is more authentic is that it copies direct from the source, Muddy Waters, Bo Diddley, Ray Charles, Howlin' Wolf, Chuck Berry and Jimmy Reed, rather than imitate imitators.[99]

Booking agents Charlesworth Presentations promoted themselves as '*the* agency for real Rhythm and Blues', and two of their clients, the Graham Bond Organisation and the Bluebottles, as 'Authenticity in R&B'.[100] Whatever the over-hyping of the 'real' or 'authenticity' might actually represent, what mattered was the signalling of difference and values: sincere motives over commercial interests. But as the wheel of fortune spun, for some of these groups they discovered a counterweight that pulled away from the genuine towards the synthetic.

Bern Elliott and the Fenmen, who had been knocked for their anodyne covers of R&B songs (the autumn 1963 Top 20 hit with 'Money' and their eponymous January 1964 EP, which had three Motown covers on its A-side), struck back against their accusers:

> We do not NOT play R and B. We never said we did . . . R and B is basically a race music. It has to have a coloured feel to it. It's impossible for a British group to get anywhere near the true American coloured sort of performance . . . What I want to know is how British groups who claim to be playing Rhythm and Blues can justify themselves.[101]

The Fenmen's take was echoed by the Nashville Teens:

> Negroes sing from way down deep in their bodies, their voices express something that is completely innermost. They sing, in the blues field, about their way of life, their experiences. So it is just plain stupid for white performers, here in well-off Britain, to say they are producing REAL Rhythm 'n' Blues.[102]

In turn, this aroused the ire of Georgie Fame (who led a mixed-race group): 'White. Coloured. Rock, R. & B., American, British – all this labelling's a drag. The only label I'm interested in is the blues – and there are many, many different ways of playing the blues. We just play one way.'[103] For Fame and his band members, what mattered was the 'feel' you had for the music; authenticity lay within the performance, it was not extraneous: 'We are not phoney, we don't jump around like lunatics. We try to make the music jump. The blues is truthful music and we believe this kind of truth stands a chance of reaching the top.'[104]

Long John Baldry's bandmate Rod Stewart provided his thoughts on the matter for Decca's promotional campaign to support his debut single, 'Good Morning Little School Girl':

> A white person can sing the blues with just as much conviction as a negro . . . All these negro singers singing about 'Walking down the railroad track . . .' They've never walked down a railroad track in their lives. Nor have I. You've got more to sing the blues about in the Archway Road than on any railroad track I know.[105]

Jazzbeat quoted from the press release and concluded that Stewart had 'made one of the most valid contemporary blues justifications we've heard'.[106] All of which only confirmed just how twisted and solipsistic the debate had become.

The term 'rhythm and blues' gained currency in the United States in the immediate post-war period when it was used as a way of encompassing the myriad forms of small-band music played by Black musicians. In 1949 Jerry Wexler expropriated it as an alternative to 'race records', which was how the *Billboard*'s chart that documented sales in the Black market was named. In an article published in the *Saturday Review* in June 1950, Wexler explained the term's etymology and current use: 'In these more enlightened times, the word ["race"] has been abolished in favour of the more direct "rhythm and blues", after temporizing with such too-colorful substitutes as "sepia" and "ebony"'.[107] It was not just that sensibilities had changed and a more progressive identification of Black music was needed; the market also demanded it as artists crossed over and sold in increasing numbers to white customers. 'Rhythm and blues' replaced an unambiguously segregationist label, 'race', with a term that, while still recognizably racial in its delineation, provided a cloak of deniability. For Wexler, at least publicly, it was more about identifying the changes the market was undergoing and the wider acceptance of Black artists by white consumers. This trend, he thought, came at a cost to the truth and honesty of Black music: crossing over too often resulted in 'pseudo-sophistication, sentimentality', the 'commercial tinge of our poorer pop records have come to infect the blues'.[108] Wrexler wrote:

> The new urban and urbane manner . . . have left their influence and brought about a shift in emphasis. Where rhythm and blues records were once almost unfailingly stamped with honest sensuality, social identification, and strong, steady beat of the unadulterated Southern blues, they have more and more been vitiated by the prurience, fatuity, and lack of pulse of the bad Tin-Pan Alley products.[109]

For all that was positive about the increasing integration of Black and white pop forms, now represented by the R&B label, Wexler nevertheless also considered it to signify a loss of purity, a degradation of the truth that pre-war jazz and blues once held for him. But all was not lost: 'With a little investigation, however, the hot may be separated from the hoke . . . a core of honest blues records continues to find its way to market' that for the most part was produced by independent record companies like Atlantic, Aladdin and King.[110] R&B, then, marked the movement of 'race' music from segregation to integration. It could be as trite as any other Tin Pan Alley confection aimed at the pop market, but it could still follow a more honest path. In a related but distinct

LONDON GETS BLUES IN THE NIGHT

Keith Relf sings out for The Yardbirds

Go into any Liverpool club, and you'll hear the sound of Today crashing out from a web of dimly-lit cellars. But who are the personalities on the London scene?... the scene that belts out the sound of Tomorrow....

'London Gets Blues in the Night . . . the scene that belts out the sound of Tomorrow': clipping from *Fabulous* (27 June 1964).

way, R&B in the context of British popular music was as equally contested and confused, and though it set out to establish aesthetic and philosophical boundaries, defining itself originally by not being pop, it would eventually become, like its American forebear, inclusive of more commercial imperatives.

To the extent that there was some confusion in the distinctions between R&B and the beat scenes in Britain, *Melody Maker* attempted to enlighten its readers. Ray Coleman quoted one of its correspondents who helpfully had done the job for him: 'Rock is not new, but it should not be confused with rhythm-and-blues,' which 'has roots in the blues, and rock is just a form of pop.'[111] To provide some more clarity, Chris Barber outlined the historical development of the form that echoed Wexler's version, and then added his rider: 'The truth is that many of the newer groups using electric guitars and electric basses have the SOUND of real rhythm-and-blues, but they don't have the STYLE.' Barber could tell you what it wasn't, he could tell you who played it, but the question of 'just what is R&B?' would always come back to the indefinable, a feeling or a style.[112]

In its last edition in April, *Record Mirror* published its first ever R&B poll results, which were dominated by American acts, but the Stones, Manfreds and Yardbirds all competed for a place. Mary Wells won best female singer, the Miracles were voted best male group and the Shirelles, best female. Best all-time disc was Howlin' Wolf's 'Smokestack Lightning', and Booker T. and the MG's took top slot in the instrumental section. Best British artist was Georgie Fame. Still without a record release, the Yardbirds were voted into tenth position in best male group category – they received 31 votes – and the Rolling Stones came third, with 378 votes counted.[113] The poll confirmed *Record Mirror*'s interest in promoting the boom: 'After sifting through thousands of entries we came to the conclusion that R and B in Britain is much much bigger than anyone suspected.'[114]

At the beginning of July, with the Rolling Stones sitting on top of the charts with 'It's All Over Now', having usurped the Animals, who had fallen one spot below with 'House of the Rising Sun', confirmation of R&B as the most important scene in contemporary music seemed assured. Mick Jagger, however, wasn't convinced. *Melody Maker* asked him to pen his thoughts on the Animals:

> They're a rhythm-and-blues group all right, but I don't think 'House of the Rising Sun' is very R&B. I don't think the song is typical of the stuff the Animals play. Personally I like the Bob Dylan version.
>
> Don't think I'm putting the Animals down – they're a sensational hit with the song, and it's good for the scene to see them make it.
>
> But don't kid yourself there's rhythm-and-blues at the top of the chart with the Animals. It's no more R&B than how's-your-father![115]

But even if Jagger didn't think a pure form of R&B had conquered the charts, it had captured the creative impulses of bands now *bothering* the charts – though that too came at the cost of exhausting the form:

> When we started, we were trying something nobody had started on. It was all Shadows-type stuff – all the groups sounded like the Shadows and everybody tried to look like Hank Marvin. It was a drag scene.
>
> They don't now. They all want to get an R&B sound – harmonicas, rough sounds, the lot. So there's not a lot new to be done. It's all been tried.[116]

Jagger signed off with a list of his current pet hates: 'phoney beat groups who scream like mad to try to create excitement', who 'think they're being hip and with-it. Loathe that. It lacks any subtlety. I hate the record "I Can Tell", by the Zephyrs. It's unbelievable. They try hard to sound gassed and excited. They end up sounding like a load of rubbish. I hate "You're the One" by Kathy Kirby.'[117] He didn't hate Motown, but he disagreed with the Beatles' adoration of the Detroit sound: 'I like Marvin Gaye's "Can I Get A Witness", but otherwise I can't see what the Beatles rave about the other crowd for. The Temptations and the Marvelettes and the others are boring.'[118]

Confirmation that the scene had firmly established itself came in the form of a small booklet that a reader had to cut and fold for themselves, published in a July 1964 edition of the girl's magazine *Boyfriend*. *The Mod Book of R&B – A Boyfriend Extra!* featured the Rolling Stones on the front with colour pictures of Bo Diddley, Carl Perkins, the Animals, Howlin' Wolf, Manfred Mann, the Kinks, Chuck Berry and Georgie Fame, with band profiles, including the Yardbirds and the Pretty Things, inside. There was confirmation here too that the Yardbirds had an appeal to teenage girls that would eventually take the band away from the club scene. This point formed the core of a discussion between Bob Dawbarn and Klooks

Kleek club owner Dick Jordan; there were, they said, two distinct groups in the scene, one formed of adults, the other of fourteen- to seventeen-year-olds. 'Even if I could afford them, the Yardbirds would be no use to me,' Jordan told Dawbarn, 'They attract the youngster and my club is on licensed premises.'[119]

3

Moving Like a Crazy Caterpillar Fed on Pep Pills, 1964

The Yardbirds received their earliest national press coverage in March 1964, with a report in the *Daily Mail* about the 'Fab. gear'. Really swinging' scene at the 'Craw Daddy' Sunday night rave at Richmond Rugby Club, where the band whipped up a frenzy and reporter Charles Greville experienced 'the most incredible evening I have ever spent'.[1] Some of the Mods in the audience clung upside down to the steel beams that ran along the club's ceiling, holding on with their 'arms and legs, and moving like a crazy caterpillar fed on pep pills'.[2]

> What a sound! With kinky fluorescent blue and scarlet light picking them out the group unleash a throbbing explosion of sound which frequently blasts the electric bulb filaments. On the floor there is a shaking mass of flesh. It reminds you of an African tribal ritual. All inhibitions are released. Frenzied youths and girls clamber on to the beams to do the Shake. They do the skipping rope – a dangerous dance in which someone is swung around while others leap over his writhing body. When space gets short they climb on to each other's shoulders to Shake.[3]

New fashions could also be seen, 'girls in ankle-length tweed dresses; boys in jeans, bobby socks and anoraks'.[4] In one of the accompanying photographs, a boy hangs upside down above the crowd's heads; in the other, girls dance in front of the stage as Keith Relf wails into a microphone, the audience as transfixed on itself as it is on the band, with witnesses to the scene, like Greville, uncertain who was the main attraction.

On other nights and other days, when it was not hosting the Royal Horse Show, the pavilion was the headquarters of the 'haughtiest rugby club in the game', but on Sundays it was the southern equivalent of Liverpool's Cavern Club. The Rolling Stones started here, 'but now they've moved on to higher things. The Yardbirds will also be whisked away on the escalator of fame soon,' Greville reported.[5] But before that happened, the scene was owned by its participants, who summoned that band to play – not the other way around.

Rave magazine also produced a short account of the Yardbirds at the Crawdaddy: 'The Group has the same sort of appeal as the Rolling Stones, though they are closer to their audience. When excitement reaches fever pitch – usually during "Smokestack Lightning" – dancers shake from the rafters!'[6] Like Greville's, this piece concluded with a few fashion pointers, because the audience were the scene makers: 'Styles are way-out. The girls are specializing in white ankle socks and slippers, pleated skirts and initialled sweaters and pigtails.'[7]

In advance of the the media's interest a small coterie of blues fans produced specialist magazines that directly addressed the young scenesters at Yardbirds gigs. The initial issue of *Jazzbeat* led with a piece on Sonny Boy Williamson and his planned shows with Cyril Davies and Chris Barber. Issue 3 of *R&B Monthly* also covered Sonny Boy in Britain but, when interviewed by Neil E. Slaven, Davies had died and the Yardbirds were now his backing band. Slaven tried gamely to pick out the fact from the fiction in Williamson's tales, a thankless task, but a Saturday night at the Crawdaddy Club in Croydon with the Yardbirds, he wrote, was the best he'd seen from the man:

> His cheeks were working like the pistons of a locomotive, his tongue licking the sides of the harp, sweat pouring

The Yardbirds at Crawdaddy, Richmond Athletic Ground, 1964.

> from him, a distant look masking his face. To their lasting credit, the Yardbirds seem to have been the only group in this country to inspire Sonny Boy, and this night was no exception. All the boys worked like Trojans; Chris, Sam and Jim laying down a rock-solid rhythm and Eric contributing some extra fine guitarwork.[8]

Jazzbeat's first issue also pictured the Yardbirds illustrating Giorgio Gomelsky's report 'Is There a Rhythm & Blues Boom?' Alongside the first part of his article on the Rolling Stones, Gomelsky provided a story on Horst Lippmann, a German jazz promotor who would record the Yardbirds in the studio and on stage with Sonny Boy Williamson. Slaven, for *R&B Monthly*, profiled individual members of the Yardbirds across issues 3–6, throwing the spotlight on what he believed 'will be THE Rhythm and Blues group both South of the River and in the country – The Yardbirds'.[9] His first experience of the band was on the opening night of the Crawdaddy Club at the Star Hotel, Croydon. Not only were they liked by the local, 'exacting audience', but they impressed Sonny Boy, Lonnie Johnson and Matt Murphy, who were in attendance.[10] Since then, they have improved 'ten-fold', he wrote, especially Eric Clapton. The guitarist talked about his admiration for Murphy, T-Bone Walker, Otis Rush, Robert Lockwood Jr and Freddie King along with stories about playing with Manfred Mann's Tom McGuinness and his time at Kingston School of Art, from which he got kicked out because he had spent his time playing guitar and not learning about stained-glass design. He was proud of his expulsion, he said.

Slaven was taken with how Clapton used the Bo Diddley-inspired '"space" noises on faster numbers'; solos were 'improvised on the spot'. 'I use mostly my own ideas but I occasionally put in a little phrase I remember off some record or other,' said Clapton.[11] Slaven considered him among the best of the British blues guitarists playing today, 'a natural talent'.[12] The following issue featured an interview with Keith Relf, like Clapton a one-time student at Kingston who left before completing his studies. When the two were both in attendance they had played guitar together. They had attempted to organize a group, but that had come to nought. Relf then went on to form the Metropolis Blues Quartet with bass player Paul Samwell-Smith. After that band had folded, the duo got together with drummer Jim McCarty, rhythm guitarist Chris Dreja and lead guitarist Top Topham (replaced by Clapton in October 1963), the latter two also students at Kingston. After Gomelsky entered the picture, the band secured more regular bookings, a growing audience and expanding fanbase. The heart of Slaven's profile is concerned with Relf's vocals:

> His singing is individual, except a slight tendency to produce the lazy effect of a Reed number. More significant is the fact that Keith never tries to directly copy any singer whose song he may be singing. He probably realises that he can never sound like a Negro, so there is no point in

> trying. This, I think, is one of the things that will ensure that success comes to the Yardbirds. Whilst not being original in their material, they are original in their treatment and overall style.[13]

That original approach to the material they were auditioning was carried over into Relf's harmonica playing; if he had one influence, Slaven pointed out, it was Slim Harpo, but he thought Relf was moving to his own style, which he would soon refine.

Slaven continued his story of the Yardbirds over two further issues; the third episode was a potted biography of Chris Dreja, who told him that it was the *Bluesville Chicago* album that got him away from an infatuation with the classic blues singers like Blind Lemon Jefferson. That LP was a circa 1959 French release on the Top Rank label of licensed Vee Jay artists. The album featured three mainstays in the Yardbirds' set: Billy Boy's 'I Wish You Would' and 'I Ain't Got You', and Snooky Pryor's 'Someone to Love Me'. Of Dreja's playing, Slaven wrote:

> Rhythm guitar can sometime be a thankless task, but Chris has certainly developed an individual approach to his job. He has developed a fantastic nerve-beat which comes to the fore on the Bo Diddley numbers where he nearly out-Jeromes Jerome on maracas. This is also shown on the numbers where the group include their famous 'climax'. Both Chris and Sam set a fantastic rhythm, bent over their instruments, their hands a blur.[14]

Slaven thought the band's rhythm section so good that he would often find himself focusing his attention on Samwell-Smith, Dreja and McCarty at the expense of the two soloists, Clapton and Relf. Slaven's profile of the drummer and bass player doubled down on the latter's 'imaginative figures and patterns' and the former's 'hard-driving, relentless beat' – 'indispensable part of probably the greatest rhythm and blues group in the country'.[15]

On 6 April 1964, Gomelsky signed four members of the Yardbirds in a formal two-year agreement to 'sing dance act perform and exercise each and every talent as entertainers wherever and whenever required'.[16] In return for their services, Gomelsky agreed to pay them no less than £500 per week. Eric Clapton was not a signatory to the contract, which was witnessed by Keith Relf's father, the band's de facto tour manager.

Towards the end of April, the Crawdaddy co-promoted club events and the imminent release of the Yardbirds' debut single. The band's logo, designed by Hamish Grimes, and complementary hand-inked lettering was used. Subsequent ads in the same graphic style proclaimed that 'Yardbirds are not very good to eat, but they play R&B with good taste!', and in block type: 'It's a happening! Modybodys Mingling! Nodding! Modybirds Birdmerized by Yardifying Yardbirds! Massyfying Bodys of Modyfying Modybods Mobbyfying Record Slops to Buy "I Wish You Would".' Meanwhile, the band continued to headline at the Marquee on Friday nights, usually with the Authentics (a wholly apposite name for an R&B group) in support. In the 16 May edition of *Record Mirror*, again in Grimes's hand, the band touted its new fan club: 'Everymody loves Yardbirds. Everymody loves Crawdaddy. Every Yardbird loves Crawdaddy. Big Daddy Loves Crawdaddy loves Yardbirds. Everymody loves "I Wish You Would". In fact, everymody loves everymody! The official Yardbirds' Fan Club Opens Today!!'[17]

In May, *Melody Maker* put the Yardbirds in among a list of contenders – Mojos, Pretty Things, Georgie Fame, Animals, Interns, Paramounts, Gamblers, Migil Five and Cliff Bennett – headlined 'The Beat Battle Is On'. It described the Yardbirds as having a 'very clean sound, with bass and drums predominant – a highly rated lead guitarist. Ranges from current beat favourites to out-and-out R&B – "Five Long Years" and "A Certain Girl" are good opposites.'[18]

EVERYMODY KNOWS
MILLIONS OF IMMACULATE
MODYBODYS MINGLE, NOD
IN MEZMERIZING MASSES
AND NOMODY FORGETS
SUNDAY NIGHTS AT
RICHMOND ATHLETIC
GROUNDS, WHEN
YARDBIRDS
BIRDMERIZE
CRAWDADDY!

THE OFFICIAL
YARDBIRDS' FAN CLUB

S.A.E. to 18 Carlisle St.,
London, W.1.

'In mezmerizing masses': advertisement for Crawdaddy and the official Yardbirds fan club, 1964, designed by Hamish Grimes.

London's *Evening Standard*'s pop columnist, Maureen Cleave, who had given the Beatles their first feature outside of the north-west, turned to the Yardbirds as her lead story in the 23 May edition of the paper. She highlighted the band's exotic Russian manager – beard, dark glasses and owner of a Lancia sports car – and, with an insider's reference to Beatlemania, noted 'All five Yardbirds wear shoes. This is a major breakthrough for shoelaces. With all these boots around shoelaces haven't had any sort of deal for years.'[19] As nearly every other report on the band throughout the year would do, she noted that the Yardbirds were following the trail laid by the Rolling Stones by taking over their spot at the Crawdaddy Club. Like Greville before her, she then focused on the club's members:

> At five on a Sunday many people are to be seen at London Bridge boarding trains to go hear the Yardbirds. They see it as an outing: They like walking over the grass to get to the club room. 'Better,' say the Yardbirds, 'than getting on a bus and going to some stinking pub.'
>
> When the club members get there they listen to rhythm and blues. By and large they don't scream. The Yardbirds say they seem sort of *stunned*. 'When they dance they kind of stumble. The young ones at the front are so jam packed they can't move. The ones at the back are older and more intelligent and that go the most mad. They may want to kiss us but they don't scream.'[20]

A 'yardbird', Cleave explained, 'is an American Negro slang word for Hobo – a chap who hangs round railroad yards waiting to hitch a lift'.[21] It was also a term used to describe prison inmates or idlers and, for those deeply in the know, it was the nickname of saxophonist Charlie Parker, as the record reviewer of the *Warrington Guardian* noted:

> [the Yardbirds] bear an honourable name and a heavy responsibility. But jazz buffs will find no resemblance to Charlie 'Yardbird' Parker, greatest of all modern jazzmen . . . They look sprucer than the Stones, but have the same hapless, wooden-effigy stance. Like movie extras on the Marienbad set! The sound is basic Rhythm and Blues – primitive but not too concentrated. Their first disc sports the down-to-earth title, 'I Wish You Would'.[22]

The reporter fashioned a cultural put-down of the first order.

If the reference to Alain Resnais and Alain Robbe-Grillet's 1961 art-house hit *Last Year at Marienbad* may have played above the heads of some of the Yardbirds' menagerie of modybodys, it wouldn't have escaped the band. They namechecked the film alongside Michelangelo Antonioni's *La Notte* (1961) and *L'Eclisse* (1962) in a *Disc Weekly* personality profile that featured a list of things they liked.[23] Other R&B combos also enjoyed parlaying their intellectual side; according to an anonymous *Warrington Guardian* reviewer, the Pretty Things were 'an engaging, slightly eggheaded quintet who number among their favourite authors Henry Miller, Norman Mailer, William Burroughs and George Orwell. Their style is rudimentary R&B with a saving touch of humour. Their first disc – "Rosalyn" (Fontana).'[24] Five months later, the Pretties were selling a similar literary line to *Disc*.[25] Dick Taylor added Jean Genet to Burroughs and Mailer; Brian Pendleton added Albert Camus to Orwell. All the band loved Jimmy Reed, but they also rated the 'modern jazz' of Charlie Mingus, Thelonious Monk, Ornette Coleman and John Coltrane, their aesthetic tastes in modernism – film, literature and jazz – a counter to the perception of the band as cultural troglodytes. The Pretty Things and the Yardbirds may have reinvented themselves by stepping into the gutter with the blues, but they were also well-enough versed to employ some of the cultural capital that they had acquired at art school.

Cleave avoided any literary or filmic pretentions that the Yardbirds might have harboured, but their adherence to the blues was such that she suspected the band would 'quite like to be American Negroes and thus better musicians'.[26] Nineteen-year-old Eric Clapton, she wrote, 'so impressed Muddy Waters, the great Negro singer, that he asked him to play guitar for him on one of his records'.[27] Despite the accolade, Clapton was not above admitting to a bit of affectation in his self-presentation: 'Eric was wearing a Guards' tie. He likes to wear the sort of clothes, he says, that Americans would wear if they could. Not that he has any right to the Guards' tie either. "I'm a bit shallow", he says.'[28] Clapton's sartorial style often registered more directly than his guitar playing in his 1964 media appearances.

'Keith Relf', Cleave wrote, 'has a pale face and looks sensitive though the others say this is nonsense. He gets involved with his music, was once known to go on with "Smokestack Lightnin'" for half-an-hour. He worries a lot.'[29] The purpose behind all this hullabaloo is the promotion of 'I Wish You Would' – 'though they are not wholly satisfied with it, I am sure you will be,' Cleave signed off.[30]

The band had their first feature appearance in *Record Mirror* the week following Cleave's piece, headlined: 'The Blueswailers with Mod Appeal'. By then, the *Sunday Telegraph* had also got in on the act and reported on the band's appeal, but it had misnamed them 'The Yardsticks' (an error parodied in a Crawdaddy ad: '~~Yardsticks, Birdyards, Stickbirds, Birdsticks~~. Yardbirds at the Crawdaddy'); the Sunday paper also mistakenly claimed the band were public schoolboys. Norman Jopling's piece for *Record Mirror* corrected the errors, and noted, once more, that they are following in the steps of the Stones, playing at the Crawdaddy, but that attendance has considerably increased. Roughly a year earlier, Jopling had written his glowing report about the Stones playing at the club.[31] He profiled each Yardbird, highlighting the fact that Relf, Dreja and Clapton had all gone to art school. Clapton's dress sense was again a feature: 'The Yardbirds in general are regarded as the most fashionable group, but fashion leader Eric is often accosted by small mod girls who blandly accuse him of being "... one of the top faces".'[32]

Despite *Boyfriend*'s make-your-own R&B magazine, in the teen pop glossies, R&B was a fad that was barely worth a mention except as it related to the Rolling Stones. They were 'the most offbeat, the most wildly exciting group of the lot', which was how the editor of *Fabulous*, June Southworth, described the band she said she'd fallen in love with the previous year when she saw them play at an 'overcrowded rhythm 'n' blues club in Richmond, Surrey'.[33] *Fabulous* stayed cool on the rest of the scene until June, when it put the Stones on the cover and inside featured the 'new groups' including the Pretty Things, Manfred Mann, Georgie Fame and the Blues Flames, the Animals and the Yardbirds. The latter two pulled together to form a menagerie, Sam the Peacock, Chris the Pigeon, Eric the Parrot, Keith the Canary, Chas the Elephant, Alan the Camel, Eric the Mole, Hilton the Chipmunk and Johnny the Kangaroo.[34]

In a belated acknowledgement that the centre had moved from the northwest to London, Southworth wrote: 'go into any Liverpool club, and you'll hear the sound of Today crashing out from a web of dimly-lit cellars. But who are the personalities of the London scene? The scene that belts out the sound of Tomorrow ...'[35] At the end of June, the Yardbirds had a feature and a colour pin-up in *Fabulous*. The Rolling Stones had tipped June Southworth off about the band, but Brian Jones had not forewarned her that Relf looked a lot like him: 'from the back the difference is practically nil. From the front, he's not actually like Brian, but he has the same kind of pale sensitive face.'[36] She watched them at the Marquee:

> They look most like The Stones when Keith plays harmonica between vocals and Chris Dreja puts aside his guitar to do a Mick Jagger on maracas. They come off best when they look more like The Yardbirds, with Keith's foot stamping out a

> tempo with the effort of being part of it. The sound they make is indescribably exciting . . . Keith's foot taps faster, faster, faster until the guitarists' hands are just blurs over the strings. The drummer takes up the rhythm from Keith and spurs them all on until the whole scene is a hundred miles 'away'. I stood and looked along the rows of flushed, excited faces crowding up to the stand, and there wasn't one clubber who wasn't shouting with the group; who wasn't stamping and clapping them on. Great![37]

In the same week that the Rolling Stones appeared on *Juke Box Jury* (broadcast 27 June) and upset the nation with their surly, negative responses to that week's record releases, the man that gave them their first break, now manager of the Yardbirds, Giorgio Gomelsky spoke to *NME*'s Ian Dove about the Crawdaddy and his role with the two bands, most intriguingly about the short film he shot of the Stones at the club in which they perform Bo Diddley's 'Pretty Thing': 'I have a seven-minute documentary of the Rolling Stones still. It was supposed to be 20-minute film but we never got around to finishing it . . . It shows them arriving at the club and all that.'[38] He had named the club after the Bo Diddley song, which was then a mainstay of the Stones set. Jopling's report covered the move of location from the Station Hotel to the Athletic Ground, and how Gomelsky lost the band to Andrew Loog Oldham, but quickly found their replacement, the Yardbirds, 'and people kept coming in':

> 'But,' says Gorgio [*sic*], 'it's not the same audience. The audience the Rolling Stones brought in got up and shook, nodded, and moved around generally. This was the appeal of thc Stones music.'
>
> With the Yardbirds it is different. 'I've seen them at Crawdaddy playing to 400 people and it's a little like an

oil painting. Only the eyes are animated. There's no hysteria. I've seen people in a trance listening to them.

'They don't get up and dance. Only the solar plexus moves. If I had to sum it up briefly, the Stones' appeal is erotic, the Yardbirds are sensual. I think their music is less superficial – the cry is not on the surface.

'Most of the pop music is like a scream, but the Yardbirds and groups like this make their music come from inside.

'With the Yardbirds we want to make music less vulgar, with an image related to public need. The appeal of the Rolling Stones seems now to be based entirely on image. I don't agree with this. Music should come into it more.'[39]

He first encountered the band, he recalled, when they were the Metropolis Blues Quartet, 'playing folk blues. You know, no drummer.'[40] He had considered putting the band on to play in the interval between Stones performances, but he had doubts because 'This was a very peculiar time for the Stones. They had a very weird sense of humour: they would grow culture on rotten eggs and rotten bacon!'[41] But now, the Yardbirds were looking likely to enter the charts with their debut single: 'I thought it would be a sleeper,' Giorgio said, 'I'm glad I was wrong!' – which was, like much of Gomelsky's ballyhoo, part hype, part fantasy. 'I Wish You Would' scraped the bottom reaches of the Top 30.

Gomelsky did recognize, however, that he needed to distinguish his new charges from the Rolling Stones. The Yardbird audience responded differently – not convulsively, but in a trance-like manner; as Cleave described them, 'stunned'. Their observations appear at odds with Greville's or Southworth's image of the fans' frenzy, but as Cleave also noted, the audience members at the front of the stage were so jammed in they couldn't move, while Gomelsky was pushing the line that the Yardbirds were less superficial and instinctual than the Stones, more considered and calculated, less erotic more sensual, he claimed. The terms would change over time, but the basic idea of the Yardbirds parlaying a more musically creative and intellectually stimulating brand of R&B remained in play throughout their career. Talking to *Ready Steady Go!* editor Francis Hitching at around the same time as he had spoken to Ian Dove, Gomelsky said that the Yardbirds were a 'bit more thoughtful' about their music than the Stones: 'If they really *are* more perfectionist about their sound than The Stones', wrote Hitching, 'some poor recording manager is going to do his nut. Because The Stones are so fussy it takes them weeks to decide on which number they're going to record – let alone what the arrangement will be like.'[42] Prevarication, said Gomelsky, is one of the reasons why the Stones 'had only three singles on sale. Right now they're looking for a new one – but typically, they can't make up their minds.'[43] 'For the Yardbirds it is easier,' wrote Hitching, 'They're just waiting to see how high "I Wish You Would" gets in the charts.'[44] Hitching didn't want to make any predictions about the single's trajectory; he thought they would make better ones, but he did think that their fans at the Crawdaddy 'rave even more about this group than they did for The Stones – if that's possible! They're not so wild-looking as The Stones, but most of the fans think the music is wilder.'[45]

In early August, the Yardbirds were interviewed by Pete Goodman for *Beat Instrumental.* The emphasis of the piece was still very much on the scene that they were creating at the Crawdaddy – 'Richmond, Surrey, is a somewhat snooty sort of area. Thames-side beauty spot. But it certainly produces the steamiest, hottest sort of music' – and once again, the band were positioned as successors to the Stones, the audience members so crammed together that the only space available was above the crowd:

> It's a regular Sunday evening pilgrimage. At least a thousand fans make their way to the Richmond Athletic Ground, to a rugby club headquarters to worship at the feet of the

> Yardbirds. In a steamy atmosphere, with pictures of Rugger Internationals looking down from the walls, the fans pack in so tightly they literally hang from the oak beams and gyrate to the dance steps.[46]

Relf talked to Goodman about the band's history, the Metropolis Blues Quartet period and their move to electric instruments, which happened 'only late last year. But now we make a few concessions to the commercial "feel"', he said.[47] The group's dedication to the music of their American blues heroes, and the backing they'd been given by Muddy Waters and Sonny Boy Williamson, is a feature, but it is their live performances at the club that are emphasized:

> Highlight of the Yardbirds' stage performances now is the old Isley Brothers' 'Respectable'. They hammer out the R and B, then suddenly switch to a middle passage on a blue-beaty 'Humpty Dumpty', then leap back to the straight rhythm 'n' blues. The wilder the atmosphere, the longer the number. Probably it shows, more than most things, the ultra-violent approach of the furious fivesome.[48]

With 'I Wish You Would' only troubling the lower reaches of the charts, a new single was being prepared for a 4 September release, and a month later, an LP containing 'mostly material recorded "live" at the Marquee Club, London'.[49]

Even as late as July 1964, Yardbirds' shows outside of London were being advertised in relation to the Crawdaddy Club's reputation, as if it held more pull than the band itself: 'Direct From The Craw Daddy Rhythm and Blues Club, London' was how the Il Rondo in Leicester billed its Wednesday, 15 July, booking.[50] Preceding an August show at the Empire Ballroom, Torquay, the local *Herald Express* plugged the gig by noting that 'the Crawdaddy Club in Richmond is in a minor way doing for London groups what the Cavern did for Liverpool outfits. It produced the Rolling Stones, and now two other groups which have made a name for themselves there will be appearing at Torquay shortly' – the Yardbirds and the Pretty Things.[51] The show at Torquay Town Hall, sponsored by the Acorn Youth Club, was billed as a 'Late Nite Rave, Big R&B Dance' headlined by the Yardbirds 'Direct from the Crawdaddy Club (Richmond)'. But now listed under the band's name was the title of their debut single, 'I Wish You Would'.[52] With this and subsequent record releases to aid their promotion, the Yardbirds' direct affiliation with the Crawdaddy Club receded.

'The Pop World by Roger Bennett' in the *Evening Post* reviewed 'I Wish You Would' in an entirely routine manner: 'The Yardbirds followed the Stones into the Crawdaddy R&B club. Now they bid to follow them into the charts. It's rough, hairy stuff, and right in fashion. So maybe they will.'[53] Runcorn's *Weekly News* predicted the cover of the Billy Boy Arnold number would be a hit: '[it has] a fabulous instrumental break in which the boys demonstrate some high-speed strumming that is out of this world. Clever stuff throughout with a likeable second side too – "A Certain Girl".'[54] The *Thanet Times* also wrote about the single's hit potential: 'So much popularity as this group has gained without making a disc has made it all the more difficult to get the right material, but they have done it.'[55] Scotland's *Wishaw Press and Advertiser* agreed that the group had earned their reputation as 'The Stones' favourite British group': '[they have an] authentic blues sound, the sort of raw, rough sound that the Rolling Stones put in the charts.'[56] Lead singer Keith 'Relfe [*sic*] . . . has plenty of power', but the 'material is not strong enough for a hit, although their many fans could boost its chances'.[57]

Reviewing the disc for the national *Daily Mirror*, Patrick Doncaster wrote: 'On the rhythm-and-blues kick there are the Yardbirds, a group creating as much, or even more, excitement in my local area at Richmond, Surrey, than the Rolling Stones did when they were regulars there. Their new disc is "I Wish You Would". And

I think it has a chance of success.'[58] Hit or miss, it made the Top 30; the record was hyped on the back of a reputation established on the live circuit, especially their Crawdaddy residency, the ground broken by the Stones and the hip trend of 'authentic rhythm and blues' that they augured. With a picture of the band hanging on to a cast-iron fence pulling monkey faces, aping a similar image used by the Stones to advertise 'I Wanna Be Your Man', the music press advertisement for the single asked, 'Do *you* suffer from an incredible urge to let loose and shake away all your frustrations? Then listen to the most blueswailing Yardbirds record – "I Wish You Would".'[59] Like the Crawdaddy block ads, the use of humour was fairly unique. Most bands were advertised with a publicity shot and the record's title, label and catalogue number. The Yardbirds were aiming for something different.

Record Mirror's review ran in their 'Singles in Brief' column: 'An old Billy Boy Arnold number and this British group has a very good R&B sound. Plenty excitement all the way. Might be big.'[60] Yet by the time of the single's release, some critics were already a little jaded with the scene. *Disc*'s reviewer could find little to get excited about: 'Hoppity R 'n' B work with male lead chanting to rhythm and mouth organ accompaniment. Best thing is a building thirty-second solo by the mouth organ. Edgy vocal noise on the turnover becomes a bore.'[61] Ray Coleman in *Melody Maker* wrote that the band were 'on an authentic blues kick [with their debut single] . . . the sort of rough and raw sound that put the Rolling Stones in the charts. The lead singer has plenty of power, too. The song isn't strong enough for a hit, but their many fans might boost it enough.'[62]

The band's cover of 'I Wish You Would' did not lack in conviction. At a mid-way point, supported and cajoled by Samwell-Smith's bass runs, Relf's harp pushes their performance up a gear, overgunning to the point of stalling and then, on the edge of collapse, shifting down to return to the tune's popping rhythmic swagger. It was unadulterated, trademark Yardbirds. Energetic with focused aggression, ultra-violent even – as *Beat Instrumental* suggested in their unacknowledged borrowing from Anthony Burgess's novel *A Clockwork Orange* – the single was patently a calling card rather than an all-out tilt for a hit. The problem for the band was that there was already a good number of similarly intentioned discs on the market.

'Come back baby . . .' Five intense young men: 'I Wish You Would' sheet music, 1964.

The original Billy Boy cut had been released on Chicago's Vee Jay label in 1955. Swinging implacably over a Diddley-esque drum patter, the singer bewails his woman's attempt to love both himself and another man too. He wants her back. His appeal, given early in the morning at the break of day, like the echoing harmonica, lost in the void. The Yardbirds play their version almost at double-time, the Diddley-beat compressed in the rush with Relf jabbing an accusing finger at his wayward girl rather than swirling in a cold pool of dejection. The Yardbirds account is more brutal than blue.

The Yardbirds promoted the single on *Ready Steady Go!* on 22 May, the first of two appearances on the show that year.[63] The band wore dark suits, white shirts and ties. Relf had removed his jacket and Clapton, sporting a very Mod crew-cut, replaced his sports coat with an off-white Harrington buttoned up at the neck. In all, the Yardbirds would appear fifteen times on the television programme.

Bass player Paul Samwell-Smith spoke to *Beat Instrumental*'s Pete Goodman in broad terms about their recent television appearances; other than *RSG!*, the band had appeared on ITV's *Thank Your Lucky Stars* (27 June 1964), *Discs-a-Gogo* (1 and 29 June), *The Cool Spot* (7 July) and *Go Tell It to the Mountain* (27 July).[64] He mentioned that appearances 'could help us with the next discs, but TV is nothing for atmosphere compared with the club scene. We realize we'll eventually HAVE to get out to bigger audiences, but for the time being the Crawdaddy Club is a spiritual home.'[65] Samwell-Smith was not making an idle prediction about the band's move to larger venues; by the time he spoke to Goodman, the *NME* had already announced that the band would be joining Billy J. Kramer as part of an autumn package playing theatres and cinemas.[66] Concessions to the 'commercial feel' were the new imperative.

Part of the concession that the band needed to make was engaging with pop magazines, which had little or no interest in authenticity and blues purity but did want to tell their readers just what interested Keith and the boys: 'You'll find [Keith] shy at first. But you can get him going talk wise as a rule by asking about his days as an art student – or when he had a job doing up antique furniture.'[67] In June, the band was pictured in London Zoo petting a gazelle, which was perhaps as cute as they ever got.[68] In October, the Conservatives were ousted from power by the Harold Wilson-led Labour Party, and *Rave* joined in on the occasion by asking pop stars what policies they would pursue if in government. Eric Clapton answered for the Yardbirds: he wanted to appoint a Minister for Hot Rods to create dedicated tracks for bikers and hot-rodders so they could stay off the roads and have more fun.[69]

The B-side of 'I Wish You Would', Allen Toussaint's 'A Certain Girl', was first recorded by Ernie K-Doe and released on the Minit label in 1961. The Paramounts had coupled their version, also as a B-side, with 'Little Bitty Pretty One', released in February. The First Gear put the song, produced by Shel Talmy, on the top side of their disc, recorded in July and released in October, and the song also made an appearance on a Wayne Fontana and the Mindbenders album, distributed in December. Four covers of an admittedly infectious dance number, and one with impeccable New Orleans credentials, yet it was hardly an outstanding song deserving of such attention. All these versions suggest just how competitive the market for novel R&B compositions had become.

The search for song material was in the context of the wholesale exploitation of the Jimmy Reed, Chuck Berry and Bo Diddley songbooks, alongside the Chess label more generally, especially Howlin' Wolf's 'Smokestack Lightning', Sonny Boy Williamson's 'Bye Bye Bird' and seriously overworked items such as Muddy Waters's 'Got My Mojo Working', which was already a fixture in Chris Barber's set lists, and probably most working bands at the time, as well as being recorded by Manfred Mann, Chris Bennett and the Rebel Rousers, Alex Harvey and His Soul Band, Dave Berry and the Cruisers, the Sheffields and, of course, by the Mojos – all in 1964.

It's easy to appreciate how 'A Certain Girl' would work as a live highlight in the Yardbirds set, with its pulsing undulating rhythm, its call and response – 'what's her name?' The band added harmonica to the introduction, and Clapton provided a compressed and greasy solo (a showcase he was denied on the top slot), which adds texture to the dry treatment given to Relf's vocal. Production is credited to 'R&B Associates', but in its chirpy bonhomie it is more like Merseybeat than raving R&B, lacking the drive and resolve of its upper deck.

On 4 August, *Melody Maker*'s Chris Roberts went to watch the Yardbirds play at the Fender Club at Kenton Conservative Hall, Middlesex, to see for himself what was behind the letters that 'have poured into the paper's office from frenzified fans of the frenzifying Yardbirds'.[70] The hall, he reported, was crammed, and the band 'were loud' – the fault of the venue's acoustics, explained Dreja, 'rhythm guitarist . . . driving and powerful'.[71] Roberts then featured the other members of the band: 'McCarty broke a bass drum skin and the vocals from singer-harmonica-player Keith Relf were almost indistinguishable from the roar of the group – though at times he appeared to be swallowing the microphone. Lead guitarist Eric Clapton was very good, bass guitarist Paul Samwell-Smith . . . less so.'[72] He had some advice for the Yardbirds: 'Sonny Boy Williamson was right when he said British groups need to "cool it" to achieve a good blues sound. Volume doesn't heighten excitement – when it reaches the threshold of pain, you forget about the number and run away looking for a soundproof room and a record of "Whispering".'[73] He would not be the last critic to comment on the volume the band produced, but he did concede that 'none of the audience seemed to be running away . . . Criticism over. The group's overall instrumental sound, including Keith's excellent harmonica, gives them a deserved spot on the R&B map. Their treatment of numbers, timing and endings were worth hearing for their professionalism.'[74]

On Sunday, 9 August, the Yardbirds played on the final night of the fourth National Jazz and Blues Festival. The Rolling Stones headlined Friday's opening night, billed as 'Rhythm and Blues' and sold as 'a triumphant return for the conquering heroes . . . For on that night, the Rolling Stones will return to the now-famous Crawdaddy Club, where little more than a year ago they played every Sunday evening.'[75] The T-Bones, the Authentics and the Grebbels were the listed support acts. Saturday was 'Modern Jazz' with Ronnie Scott and 'Blues and Jazz' with Chris Barber. Long John Baldry and Manfred Mann were billed alongside American bluesmen Memphis Slim and Jimmy Witherspoon. On Sunday, 'Rhythm' was reattached to the 'Blues' for a day and night of 'Jazz and Rhythm and Blues' headlined by Mose Allison and Kenny Ball. Humphrey Lyttelton was billed alongside Graham Bond Group and Georgie Fame and the Blue Flames.

For the Yardbirds, the Richmond showcase was not a grand success. Keith Relf had been too ill to play and Mick O'Neill of the Authentics and blues aficionado and editor of *R&B Monthly* Mike Vernon were called on to deputize in his place. Relf had suffered from a collapsed lung after the first set at the Marquee on the preceding Friday night; he would spend approximately seven weeks in recovery. In the 12 September edition of *Melody Maker*, it was reported that 'Keith Relfe [*sic*], lead singer with the Yardbirds, left hospital on Friday after three weeks of treatment for a punctured lung. He hoped to re-join the group in two or three weeks.'[76] Gomelsky told the paper:

> Keith collapsed . . . and was ill at home for two weeks before going into hospital. We had to postpone the group's next Columbia single which was due on September 4. Their previous single has been released in America by Epic and they have been getting a lot of fan letters from the States.[77]

The report finished with a note that 'The Yardbirds' first LP, "The Five Live Yardbirds", recorded at London's Marquee, is released by Columbia at the end of October.'[78]

The little bits of business about record releases in the *Melody Maker* news item deflected attention away from just how seriously ill Relf had been. A week before the report, Maureen Cleave in the *Evening Standard* had relayed the information that he had left Richmond Hospital on Wednesday, 2 September. When he had collapsed, 'it was rumoured he had laryngitis. But today his manager, Giorgio Gomelsky, said Relf had nearly died. "To think that he had been playing and singing in smoky clubs and cellars with his lungs in that condition," he said.'[79] Relf was planning a month's convalescence in Cornwall, she reported, but eighteen days later, on Relf's return to live engagements, Cleave wrote that the '21-year-old had made a remarkable recovery from a collapsed lung that nearly killed him three weeks ago, and hopes to sing with the group at Maidstone tonight. His doctor advised him to rest for three months but admits that he's a lot better.'[80] Relf's near-death experience would be replayed in countless profiles to follow. As he returned to the fold, however, drummer Jim McCarty 'moved out. He has a stomach chill and won't be able to play tonight,' wrote Cleave.[81] *Rave* magazine covered the whole episode as if it were a melodrama: 'When a Yardbird collapsed. It was nearly the end. At first it was a racking cough. Then Keith Relf's voice grew weaker and he had to face every singer's secret fear.'[82]

Between his collapse on 7 August and his return to the stage on 21 September, the Yardbirds played around sixteen gigs with Mick O'Neill, Tony Carter from the Grebbels or Mike Vernon standing in – this despite cancelling the first three scheduled dates on the Billy J. Kramer package tour. On 9 October, the band played Grantham Granada Cinema alongside Kramer, the Kinks, Bill Black's Combo, Cliff Bennett and the Rebel Rousers and the Ronettes, each act playing two sets. 'Tears, sweat, screaming females and dazzling lights featured in the defining reception' that met them for a packed second house, reported the *Grantham Journal*.[83] After a sober opening with Bill Black, 'Things livened with the advent of the Yardbirds, this dedicated group showing why many people regard them as the Rolling Stones understudies. They produced that unmistakable rhythm-and-blues sound with the reminiscent staccato snatches at the harmonica and "mike" by vocalist Keith Relf.'[84]

On 23 October, the Yardbirds were back on home territory at the Marquee, and *Melody Maker* reported that 'The "most blues-wailing" Yardbirds made a welcome and power-packed return.'[85] A 'large and very enthusiastic audience supported them throughout, from their bluesy opener, "I Ain't Got You," to the marathon raver "Here It Is", which closed their first spell'.[86] In their second set, they featured 'I Wish You Would', which 'demonstrated the exciting work of harpist-vocalist Keith Relph [*sic*] and accomplished playing of lead guitarist Eric Clapton. The sheer quality and atmosphere – and volume – of their present performance must surely propel the Yardbirds to the top of the chart.'[87] Underneath the live review was a 5-centimetre (2 in.) block advertisement for Rod Stewart promoting his *Ready Steady Go!* appearance on 30 October and his single 'Good Morning Little School Girl'. The Yardbirds too were booked for that evening and would be performing their long-delayed follow-up single, the identically titled 'Good Morning Little School Girl'.

Rather than nullifying each other's effort, the duplication turned out to be somewhat beneficial for both parties, at least as far as producing publicity material. 'It's a Record! It's a Record', ran the repeated headline of Patrick Doncaster's 'Discs' column in the *Daily Mirror*.[88]

> Tin Pan Alley excels itself this week . . . As if you and I haven't enough song titles to cope with – eighty a week or 4,000 a year – here come two records with the SAME A-side

> title . . . but the songs are entirely different! . . . The rhythm 'n' blues-ey Yardbirds group bid for the spins with one version on Columbia. The rhythm 'n' blues-ey Rod Stewart, 19-year-old Londoner from Highgate, swings in with the other on Decca.[89]

Doncaster preferred Rod's effort, though he thought that the Yardbirds could still 'make some noise'.[90]

The repetitive nature of the scene was also picked up by the *Evening Post*'s Roger Bennett, who again put the two singles together for his review. The Yardbirds do a 'harmony vocal with a Stones-style backing, while Rod Stewart sings solo against rolling barrelhouse piano and guitar . . . Mr. Stewart has the distinction of having been shipped home third-class by the British Consul after sleeping rough in Barcelona Football Stadium.'[91] The promotional tag around the Yardbirds release was less romantically bohemian and told again the story of Relf's collapse.

Elsewhere in his column, Bennett noted that the Kinks' follow-up to 'You Really Got Me' was 'All Day and All Night'; he disliked both. Johnny Kidd and the Pirates had a 'bluesy version of 'Whole Lotta Woman' and the Cops 'n' Robbers (yet another R&B group named after a Bo Diddley song) had taken the 'jazz classic' 'St James Infirmary' and given it an 'Animals-type treatment, with an organ prelude like something out of Bach'.[92] He made a joke out of groups with 'grammar-wrecking' names like Belfast's 'Them', who had 'Baby Please Don't Go' on release: 'They sound a bit like the Stones, which is enough to send the Mountains of Mourne crashing down to the sea in horror.'[93] If all this repetition was suggestive of pop's superficiality, when it came to Lulu, repetition was precisely what Bennett wanted: 'Who on earth told Lulu to stop sounding like Lulu?'[94] After the 'sizzling' 'Shout', in 'Here Comes the Night' sixteen-year-old Lulu now sounded like Dionne Warwick.[95] Production and composition were by Bert Berns, who was working concurrently with Van Morrison's Them; the band had recorded the song for their next single.

Rod Stewart's 'Good Morning Little School Girl' was written and first recorded by John Lee 'Sonny Boy' Williamson, who had died in 1948 at the age of 34. Sometime thereafter, Rice Miller stole his name and had been running with it ever since, even bringing it to Britain when he was accompanied on stage by the Yardbirds and the Animals. The original Sonny Boy was just a month or so over 23 years old when, on the top floor of the Leland Hotel in Aurora, Illinois, on 5 May 1937, he recorded his song about the seduction of a schoolgirl for Bluebird Records. Rod Stewart was still two months shy of his twentieth birthday when his cocksure version was released. (The Paul Butterfield Blues Band recorded a more lascivious full-band version in 1964; produced prior to their first album sessions, it remained in the can until 1966.)

Though Williamson's blues is clearly the antecedent of the Yardbirds' recording, their version was based on Don and Bob's dance tune that added a jumping rhythm and a popping two-finger piano accompaniment and a chorus of 'hey, hey, hey'. The plea is from a boy to his girl to dance the hop at the soda shop. Recorded in 1961 for the Chess subsidiary Argo, the record is a classic cut of teenage popcorn. Long part of the Yardbirds' live set, the decision to release a version as a follow-up to the more roughhouse sounds of 'I Wish You Would' was self-evidently a commercial ploy.

Record Mirror reported on the record's imminent release, noting the number was included nightly in their stage act on the Billy J. Kramer tour and that it was an 'American tune with a catchy, commercial sound'.[96] The item concluded with a list of TV shows booked to promote the single: *Three Go Round*, *Ready Steady Go!*, *Discs-a-Gogo* and *Top Beat*.

Pop Weekly wrote that although '[the] boys give a good, clean-cut performance and there is some striking guitar work', it was likely to 'get lost through lack of overall distinction'.[97] *Disc* gave it

After a hard day's night: advertisement for the single 'Good Morning Little School Girl', *Record Mirror* (31 October 1964).

three out of five stars, described it as a 'group vocal' and thought it should add to their growing reputation with the R and B set. 'A brisk attacking production . . . Ought to prove to be commercial'.[98] The single was promoted with an advertising campaign that used a photograph of a column of girls in school uniform rushing towards the band, who are waving back at them – the girls at the rear are blurred and distorted, as if moving too fast to be caught by the camera. Hamish Grimes's typography is once more a feature, here incorporating a school crossing sign. The scene hijacks, even perhaps parodies, Beatlemania as seen in *A Hard Day's Night*, which was released a few months earlier, in July. The pop contract, fostered by magazines, radio and television, between teen-girl fans and the band is the logic (and alibi against accusations of a prurient interest in underage girls). *Boyfriend* magazine ran a full-page, full-colour article on the band and the single. It made much of Relf's recent illness and noted that he was recuperating at home, which was close to a girls' school: 'And all the time he was ill, the fans just kept on calling to find out how he was, sending him presents, and writing "Get well soon, Keith" on the wall. And that's why the record was released – as a sort of tribute to all those schoolgirls.'[99] Indeed.

Though it continued as a theme of pop songs well into the late 1970s, today's sensibilities render the schoolgirl as a figure of desire utterly unacceptable. None of this was registered at the time, however – except in one review, as something to be joked about: 'The lyric is a bit how's your father, because an obviously masculine-type geezer is stating his desire to hug and squeeze a little schoolgirl, which doubtless is a fine form of relaxation but fraught with danger because of the laws of this great country in which we all live.'[100] The critic was the predatory child abuser Jimmy Saville, which now leaves any excuse or alibi of innocent intent tainted. In a *Melody Maker* interview with Chris Welch, Relf countered Saville: 'I don't think they're suggestive at all . . . And I don't think the record could be banned or something like that. You can have an 18-year-old schoolgirl, don't forget.'[101] Besides, Relf might have added, the protagonists in the Yardbirds' recording were both self-evidently still at school.

The Yardbirds stayed fairly close to Don and Bob's blueprint, upping the tempo and exchanging the piano for Relf's harp. Double-tracked vocals made for a warmer sound than Relf had achieved on the debut, and this time Clapton got to burn on the top side. Keith Relf sets Clapton up for his showpiece with a hollered 'whoa' before the guitarist lets rip with a stripped-down, exuberantly economic set of repeating, strafing motifs; they were as greased and compressed as they were on 'A Certain Girl', but this time Clapton claimed the song for himself.

The flip side, 'I Ain't Got You', another cover of a Billy Boy Arnold cut on *Bluesville Chicago*, and a Calvin Carter composition also recorded by Vee Jay labelmate Jimmy Reed, returned the Yardbirds to the aggression of the debut single. It's a bragging blues: the singer has a flash car (Arnold a Cadillac, Relf a Maserati), a charge account, a tavern and a liquor store, with women to the left, to the right and all around him, but he ain't got the girl. Relf assumes Billy Boy's masculine posture and experience, though he sings 'hain't' rather than 'ain't', and – for the duration of his performance, at least – he makes you believe in the possibility that he possesses such potency. Like the adolescent he actually still was, Relf's all dressed up with no place to go – he's shaking with style while doing nothing much at a considerable pace. Once again, the tempo is double-time that of the original; Clapton's solo is less squeezed, less greasy, than on the top side, but it races from a standing start like a Maserati GT with snakeskin upholstery.

Record buyers ignored both the Rod Stewart and the Yardbirds singles, and neither much bothered the charts. *Pop Weekly* hoped that the Yardbirds would get a second chance, considering the band as one of the 'most popular groups going without a hit'. This idea was supported by *Rave* magazine's end-of-year poll for their readers' pick of the best of the new; the band came second to the Mojos, but four places ahead of the Pretty Things.[102] *Pop Weekly* felt that 'people in the business too often discard a group these days if they don't get a hit straight away. But the same happened with the Pretty Things, who are going to be worth a fortune if handled properly.'[103] The Pretties were riding high with 'Don't Bring Me Down', maximizing on their long-haired bad-boy image, which was the smarter move. The following week, *Pop Weekly* returned to its theme, writing that 'Good Morning Little School Girl'

> has hovered in between being a hit and a miss. Sales are good but it needs that extra few thousand to push it over into the Top Twenty. Say the lads, 'What about some help from the birds then'. Come on girls. One of the best-looking sets of men asking for your help. You can't ignore that.[104]

ON THEIR FIRST TWO SINGLES, the Yardbirds had delivered four covers of American blues in double-time, accelerating the original versions to a tempo that the band's amphetamine-enhanced fans could shake and rave along with. When *Five Live Yardbirds* was released in December, a performance captured back in March at the Marquee Club in its new Wardour Street location, the band and their producer, Gomelsky, chose to quicken things further still. The Yardbirds had delivered their set at full throttle, but even then, the tape was sped up to enhance the feeling of excitement and (artificial) energy – the Yardbirds over-caffeinated, playing at the sound of speed for an audience of crazed caterpillars.

'Good evening and welcome and now it is time for Birdmerizing, Yardmerizing, in fact most Blueswailing Yardbirds'; the evening's compére, Hamish Grimes, introduces each of the band members – 'Five Live Yardbirds'. Without further botheration, the band leap into Chuck Berry's 'Too Much Monkey Business'. Straight out of the traps, no pause, no let up, pumping adrenalin as they skid momentarily to a halt and then slam into Slim Harpo's 'Got Love If You Want It' – its shuffle beat frenzied and overwound – things moving so fast that spying and peeping neighbours hardly get a look at Relf's lovin' man; he's been and gone by the time it would have taken Slim to settle on his stool, tune his guitar and adjust his harp rack.

A pause, only long enough to introduce the next song, and then the band are off again with 'Smokestack Lightning', barely any change of pace, but with Samwell-Smith's bass booming like never before as the two guitars clang and ring down the lines. The Howlin' Wolf number is the first of the night to use the patented blueswailing rave-up; the band dropping behind Relf's pulled and teased harp squalls, blowing sweet and bitter, crashing into and bouncing off the thrashing guitars. When the playing gets back on track, it pushes and pulls along the straight, building momentum until it hits another incline. Slowed down, percussion taps and steel-sprung guitar licks hold time, the harp drawing air and then, when the rise is mounted, whiplashing round the bend, descending once more into a rave-up that hurtles through red lights and over the bluff to Skedaddle – thrilling, breathless music that has the audience screaming with delight.[105]

Relf fluffs his lines introducing 'Good Morning Little School Girl', on which he gives over the vocal duties to Samwell-Smith and Clapton so he can concentrate on the harp. Impossibly, the band play it even faster than the single version. Their blue-beat-ish cover of the Isley Brothers' 'Respectable' follows, with its bass runs played like rosary beads fed through fingers at speed, squeezed 'n' squirted guitar licks and the 'Humpty Dumpty' intervention. The band maintain the pace of the previous numbers; a rapid pursuit of a girl who has never been kissed in the moonlight. The end of the first set.

The album's top side is twenty minutes of the most over-stoked live sets to have been put down on record. Gomelsky and team perfectly captured a steam-heat ambience. Grimes returns to introduce the 'still alive . . . five live Yardbirds' for 'side two'. Pulling the pace back down to a fast stroll with the standard twelve-bar blues, Eddie Boyd's 'Five Long Years' that was as likely learned from a Muddy Waters 45 as from Boyd or any one of its countless covers, including those by John Lee Hooker and Junior Parker. Muddy's version was recorded in May 1963, accompanied by James Cotton on harmonica, Otis Spann on piano, Willie Dixon on bass and Luther Tucker on guitar. Clapton follows Tucker's blueprint of pinging tasteful yet libidinous licks in answer to the singer and the piano – the dominant instrument. The Yardbirds extend the song to twice the length of Muddy's 45 and grant themselves two solos; Relf takes the first, telling himself to 'go ahead now' and pulling and building his bluesy, modulating flattened sevenths across the break. The harp solo is but a prelude to Clapton's full entrance, centre stage, as he lays down the groundwork for the reputation he will build and capitalize on with John Mayall's Bluesbreakers.

After 'Five Long Years', 'Pretty Girl', the first of three Bo Diddley numbers, separated only by John Lee Hooker's 'Louise', are all taken at such a pace that the 'shave and a haircut, two bits' rhythm is buried in the rush to get to the end of one song and on to the next. Clapton tries out a wha-wha effect (the pedal won't be on the market until 1966), but otherwise has little time to show off. 'Louise' maintains the frantic pace but, like the two songs before, it is essentially support for the second set's showpiece, 'I'm a Man', which like 'Smokestack Lightning' is a rave-up, this time a strum-and-thud rhythm tied to a marching beat. Its own series of false climaxes prefiguring the fact that it too is but a prelude. 'Here 'Tis' is the final E. McDaniels composition and the last song of the night. Well, here is what 'tis: Relf loves his baby all day and all night but he's not at all happy, so he sings, 'ho oh ho'. The song decomposes into a percussive fit of pots being rattled, shuffled and hit. Clapton plays his lead as if answering Relf's harp, but that's still in the singer's pocket. Relf is finally rendered as breathless as his audience. After 21 minutes, side two ends where things had started, back with Hamish Grimes now intoning 'very hot, still alive, the Yardbirds . . .'

Relf doesn't sing the blues – certainly not on 'Five Long Years', where he barks and yelps out the words. There's no oil in his voice; it lacks sonority, not mimicking the mature resonance of Muddy's singing like Eric Burdon or Van Morrison. Instead, Relf sounds like the English adolescent he was. Relf was not an imitator, he couldn't simulate the urban blues that Chess traded in, his blues was more country – not Mississippi Delta but Nashville, with that cartilage-and-bone nasal sound produced by Jimmie Rodgers or Hank Williams. Relf couldn't fake a Rodger's blue yodel any more than he could Howlin' Wolf's eerie moans, but he is like the pair's rockabilly inheritors, not Elvis or Johnny Cash but maybe Carl Perkins, Gene Vincent or Eddie Cochran, and certainly he's in the mould of Dale Hawkins, Johnny Carroll or Johnny Burnette. Relf's true progenitor, however, is Ricky Nelson, a singer with a similarly limited range who also delivered the goods on his blues covers 'My Babe' and 'Milkcow Blues', the latter copped wholesale by the Kinks. Both singers are affectless, yet not artless in how they communicate, with an intimacy that does not preclude an element of vulnerability – 'Some people call me a teenage idol. Some people say they envy me. But I guess they got no way of knowing how lonesome I can be' – that many adolescent white blues singers worked so hard to conceal with a macho bluster.

Unlike Nelson's rockabilly peers, Relf is obviously not from south of the Mason–Dixon line (or California) but southwest London. He's a transpontine, as George Melly called those who lived over the bridge, more so even as Relf was from Kingston, Surrey. He's a young suburbanite – 'Baron's Court, All Change' – riding the Piccadilly line into Soho.[106] Relf's immediate influence on other vocalists could be heard with David Bowie, when he wasn't imitating Anthony Newley or Al Stewart, and with Syd Barrett and Kevin Ayers too. But his greater impact wouldn't be felt for another ten years when a new generation of vocalists, non-singers like Johnny Rotten, Billy Idol or Dave Vanian, had Relf as a model. Even more so with Vic Godard, vocalist in the Subway Sect, and the tranche of beating-heart Scottish post-punk bands that he in turn influenced – Fire Engines, Joseph K, Orange Juice, and Jesus and the Mary Chain among the many.

Relf sang in a pitch that matched his harp playing, a perfect pairing, pulling air from the top of his lungs, shallow, and exhaling in spasms and wails. He played directly into the vocal mic, which lacks the fuzzy warm reverberating valve sound that Little Walter harnessed. In contrast to Walter's overloaded amplification was Jimmy Reed's dry, high-pitched and throttled tones. Relf sat somewhere between the two, his style more like a horn blown on a Thames river barge, reedy but firm, and loud enough to punch through the smog. Relf wasn't trying to parse the sonorous descant of an American locomotive's whistle, as maybe Cyril Davies or Brian Jones had attempted. Both of these players may have been technically better than Relf, which is arguable, but their style was borrowed – Relf sounded like no one else. Discussing his and the

Stones' use of the harmonica, Mick Jagger said, in Britain, 'That bloke with the Yardbirds is just about the best.'[107] It was the truth even if, as some suggested, Jagger said it to disrespect Brian Jones, who had earlier put on record that he rated Eric Burdon as the country's best vocalist, to Jagger's obvious opprobrium.[108]

Five Live Yardbirds is excitement over refinement, passion over cool presentation, mistakes over tidy perfection, youthful spontaneity over staid rehearsal. The album was not given an American release either in Canada or the United States. Four tracks were culled from it for side 2 of the band's second album in those territories, *Having a Rave Up with the Yardbirds*: 'Smokestack Lightning', 'Respectable', 'I'm a Man' and 'Here 'Tis'. They were undoubted highlights from the Marquee set but, outside of the showcase of *Five Live*, and with track separation interrupting continuity between the numbers, the performances are rendered mundane. There is no sense of occasion, no shared interaction between band and audience, and the limitations of the recording are all too apparent, the weaknesses in delivery and audio fidelity amplified.

Reviewing *Five Live* for *Melody Maker*, Ray Coleman wrote that the band were worthy successors to the Stones crown, and it was an 'excellent example of the music of a young group that has absorbed the blues idiom, then given it a peculiar yet refreshing new slant of individuality. Their asset is instrumental prowess . . . it has atmosphere and powerful sounds that communicate.'[109]

In the new millennium, a second 1964 live performance was released, recorded at the Marquee in July (though some claim it was taped on the night Relf collapsed, 7 August).[110] The quality of the audio is an improvement (though the drums are more ambient than present), and the set is similar, but with the addition of Snooky Pryor's 'Someone to Love Me', and a loose approximation of Elmore James's 'The Sky Is Crying', which bookend 'Too Much Monkey Business', 'I Got Love If You Want It', 'Smokestack Lightning', 'Good Morning Little School Girl' and 'Respectable'/'Humpty Dumpty'.

The song arrangements are much the same, but as a portrait of the band and their audience it sounds sterile by comparison, a document rather than a manifesto of second-generation suburban-delinquent rock 'n' roll.

In the early 1970s, in a column for *The Listener* magazine, John Peel serially referenced *Five Live Yardbirds*, 'one of the ten or so LPs from which I would not be parted'.[111] Looking at the development of high-tech recording studios and the ability to capture and create extraordinary soundscapes and faultless musical performances, he bemoaned the fact that the 'live' LP can only then be considered as second best to studio productions. What is gained in the pursuit of perfection conversely implies a loss of spontaneity, the draining away of a 'great many of the essential energies from what is supposed to be music at least as physical as it is cerebral.' 'Listen', he wrote, 'to what could be the first and certainly is one of the very best live LPs ever made, *Five Live Yardbirds*, and you'll see what I mean':

> *Five Live Yardbirds* was recorded in 1964 at the Marquee Club in colourful Soho. The sound quality is fairly dire, but the atmosphere of a remarkable live set is captured with beautiful accuracy. You practically choke on the stale cigarette smoke in the privacy of your own home. The album is especially notable for the first appearance on LP of . . . Eric Clapton and, despite many recordings made in the wake of his successes with the Yardbirds, only his playing with Cream, on their own concert recordings, equals the drive and excitement of his playing at the Marquee. If you can't get the Yardbirds' LP – and it may prove difficult – then listen to the Stones' live *Get Yer YaYas Out* or the Who *Live at Leeds*, and you'll hear the best and the most exciting music those two pivotal groups ever recorded.[112]

He lists a few other favourite live albums, by Quicksilver, Hendrix, Grateful Dead and the Allman Brothers, but omits the MC5's *Kick Out the Jams* (1969) – an album surely made with the Yardbirds' Marquee performance in mind, the only live disc to come close to capturing the interaction between band and audience that *Five Live Yardbirds* did first and best and the perfect primer for third-generation rock 'n' roll devotees.

No doubt Gomelsky and the band were taking something of a risk in releasing a live album as opposed to an LP of studio recordings (or the confected collections released outside of the UK), but they weren't working in virgin territory. Alexis Korner's Blues Incorporated had released the well-received R&B *From the Marquee* in 1962; Georgie Fame and the Blues Flames had his album debut, *Rhythm and Blues at the Flamingo*, in the shops by March 1964 (*Record Mirror* wrote that the album had 'earthy and atmospheric performances, and the "feel" of this disc makes up for what is lost in recording quality'); and British jazz artists had a long history of releasing live recordings.[113] In the States, James Brown's big-selling *Live at the Apollo* was first delivered to stores in 1963, the same year Motown released Little Stevie Wonder's *The 12-Year-Old Genius – Recorded Live*. Chess Records followed suit that same year with *Bo Diddley's Beach Party – Recorded Live*, an album so raucous it might well have been the Yardbirds' sonic template for their own raw and unprocessed effort.[114]

Rexy Regan in *Boyfriend* began his review of *Five Live* by highlighting how little action the Yardbirds had garnered with their releases to date when compared to their peers, 'Yet their popularity is incredible,' and that was due to their live appearances: 'When they play, it's not genteel and phoney like some groups, who've climbed on the beat wagon. It's the real thing.'[115] Rexy thought the album captured the excitement of seeing the band live and 'rocks so much it nearly bounced my record spinner off the table'.[116] 'Yes, the Marquee has been a big help to us,' Relf told *Melody Maker*,

'But', added Clapton, 'we worry like hell that we'll lose R&B fans if we get a hit record . . . We like pop fans, but we want both. We would look upon it as our biggest achievement if we could be the best popular band in the country without a hit record.'[117] Clapton had summed up the dilemma he and the band were facing: how to maintain momentum without giving in to commercialism or driving down the dead end of authenticity. 'We're tired of snobs who say they don't like an artist anymore because he has a hit record,' Eric said, 'Why is it criminal to be successful?'[118] Despite protestations to the contrary, it was a question that he would continue to ask himself for the rest of the decade.

THE YEAR OF THE BEATLES: 1963. The following year, their appeal was consolidated and broadened, but 1964 rightly belonged to the Rolling Stones. In *Record Mirror*'s portrait of a year, Richard Green wrote: 'Rhythm and blues became what Trad was a couple of years ago, hundreds of new groups tried for the big time, and the comparatively new Tamla Motown sound hit the scene with a bang.'[119] A colleague of his at *Record Mirror*, David Griffith, also paid tribute to the Rolling Stones: 'To the five hopeful and dedicated R&B musicians who, in 1963, used to hang around the *Record Mirror* office listening to records, and who, in 1964, became the world's most famous R&B group – our heartiest and souliest congratulations.'[120] Looking forward to 1965, *Melody Maker* tipped the Yardbirds to emulate the Stones' success, or at least make their mark.[121]

The year finished in more auspicious surroundings than those it had begun in, with a 3 January gig at the Marquee in Oxford Street. On 7 December, the Yardbirds played the Royal Albert Hall alongside seven other acts for the 'Top Beat' event that was sponsored by BBC 2. Their final gigs of the year and the first of the New Year were as part of the Beatles' support package that ran throughout the Christmas holidays at the 3,000-seater Hammersmith Odeon (24 December to 16 January (except Sundays)). In between, they had played more than two hundred shows across the UK and over a week in Switzerland where they had played without Keith Relf.

Rave magazine gave a spot to the band's Hammersmith shows:

> New Look Yardbirds
>
> Yardbird guitarist Eric Clapton has designed the striking stage suits that the group is wearing in the Beatles' Christmas show currently at London's Hammersmith Odeon.
>
> Eric's keen eye for the unusual produced a jacket with a short lapel and a very wide collar. They have patch pockets with flaps.
>
> The group were so delighted with Eric's designs that they trooped into tailor Paul Keam's showrooms and ordered two suits each to this pattern! One set is straw-coloured, the other in direct contrast is diamond black barathea.[122]

From the Marquee to the Royal Albert Hall, from authentic purveyors of R&B to pop stars in matching suits. 'Can they break through soon?' asked *Melody Maker* in their end-of-year round-up of new faces.[123]

4

Maximum R&B: Selling (Out) the Authentic, 1965

In February 1965, Charles Greville, the *Daily Mail* journalist who had reported on the Yardbirds and their Crawdaddy audience a year earlier, dropped a reference to the band in a piece he wrote for the paper on debutants studying at the Heatherley School of Fine Art, 'Budding sculptress . . . Anne Napier, niece of Sir William Hayter, kinswoman of Lord Napier, who lives – so she tells me – at one end of the Rockingham Castle' and 'budding artist' Shara Berriman, also eighteen years old, 'daughter of Dr. John Berriman, one of George Brown's new advisers, was doing a dance called The Fox to a Yardbirds L.P. with a girl called Freddie': '"There's such a marvellous free and easy atmosphere here," said Miss Berriman. "Everybody is so sort of . . . at ease" . . . The fact that the school turns out more peers' wives than artists disturbs nobody.'[1] As the Yardbirds turned into the New Year, had this Chelsea set usurped their original fans, or were the band looking to capture the Beatles' audience that they had played for over the Christmas period? Did being true to their original coterie of R&B fans matter?

What was certain is that things were changing fast as winter moved towards spring:

> 'Rhythm and Blues is losing its grip,' say the Yardbirds. They feel the big bands in Britain don't do justice to real R&B. 'R&B has reached saturation point and we have set out to make a record with more commercial appeal,' they say about their latest release, 'For Your Love'. It was written for them by a lad from Manchester who has not met the group.[2]

'Yardbirds Breakthrough' was the headline in *Beat Instrumental* for a short piece on the band, who were enjoying the chart success of 'For Your Love', released in the first week of March. 'Looks very much as if the "most blueswailing" Yardbirds have finally broken through in a big way. But only after a lot of internal argument about policy – the boys have now moved away from the R'n'B scene. Which meant the departure of "purist" Eric "Slow Hand" Clapton.'[3] Speaking for the band, Paul Samwell-Smith explained:

> Eric helped us a lot. Fine. But we couldn't get him to bend his approach at all. He was all for authenticity. We all were . . . once. But it is useless having a tiny band of fans and failing to get through to the mass audience. Eric hated our hit single, 'For Your Love'. But look at the way it has sold.[4]

Clapton's departure from the Yardbirds was expertly stage-managed, an object lesson in how to deflect attention away from the real cause of his leaving – his personal behaviour and a falling out with management – and onto a story that has lasted down the years. The reason why the excuse given for Clapton fleeing the nest worked so effectively is that it dovetailed with the wider story of the schisms within the R&B scene as a whole. On the one side, you had the purists, the blues apostles, and on the other, the apostates, those selling out to Mammon – it created a simple binary.

The line given to the press was so appealing that even the daily nationals ran with it: 'Eric Clapton, the Yardbirds' lead guitarist, has left the group because he prefers pure rhythm and blues, while the others want to go commercial and play pop,' was the *Daily Mail*'s version.[5] In that same edition, the new single was made 'pick of the week': 'Most commercial the Yardbirds have yet produced, and a change from all that "pure R&B" bit.'[6] In its first March edition, *Disc Weekly* didn't mention anything about musical differences, just that Clapton was 'leaving the group to take up management of a record shop'.[7] It was announced that Jeff Beck would be Clapton's replacement, and that after the new boy's debut gig in Croydon they were holding a 'farewell party' for Clapton. At least on the surface, the split turned out to be a rather humdrum affair.[8] The *New Musical Express* didn't even carry news of Clapton's exit until 'For Your Love' was sitting at no. 12 in its charts, at which point they introduced the new line-up.[9]

Just before Clapton's departure was announced, Chris Welch in *Melody Maker* positioned the band against the wider schism:

> Now the record scene has been swamped with all the sounds that groups can produce, it is virtually impossible to break into the chart with pure unadulterated R&B. But their latest record, 'For Your Love', achieves a new sound and hit potential, without sacrificing the essential ingredients of Yardbirdery – soul and excitement.[10]

Welch spoke to Samwell-Smith and Relf in the pub during the interval of a recent Marquee session; the former told him, 'We added harpsichord, played by organist Brian Auger, and bongos. The recording gets much louder at the climax.'[11] They had augmented their sound with the two instruments 'because the R&B sound is a bit dated now – it really is', although on club sessions, Samwell-Smith said, 'you still can't beat R&B.'[12] Welch's report concluded on an upbeat note: 'Keith looked worried when I mentioned the record, which he sings in a very Lennonish style. "We need a hit badly. This might be it though," he added brightening up.'[13] The review of the single in the following week's *Melody Maker* predicted that it would 'hit big'.[14]

Melody Maker broke the news of Clapton quitting in the second week of March; he had left, he said, because 'They are going too commercial.'[15] As Relf explained,

> It's very sad because we are all friends. There was no bad feeling at all, but Eric did not get on well with business. He does not like commercialization. He loves the blues so much I suppose he did not like it being played badly by a white shower like us! Eric did not like our new record . . . He should have been featured, but he did not want to sing or anything and he only did that boogie bit in the middle.[16]

His replacement, Jeff Beck, was 'very good', said Relf: '[he] was recommended to us by session man Jimmy Page, who is the guv'nor'.[17] *Record Mirror* noted that Clapton's last gig had been at Bristol Corn Exchange (3 March), and that Beck's debut would be at Croydon Fairfield Hall tomorrow (5 March) 'in a Radio Caroline concert'.[18] Clapton, it was reported, was joining a new outfit, Mike O'Neil Jr and the Soul Brothers, put together by the Authentics' singer and keyboard player, and Relf's sometime stand-in.[19]

But the binary was never a simple opposition; after the declaration of 'I Wish You Would', the band made a transparent attempt at a pop song, 'Good Morning Little School Girl', albeit one with an R&B pedigree. It faired poorly, even when compared to their debut. Dropping the twelve-bar template for Graham Gouldman's baroque pop song 'For Your Love' not only made commercial sense but signalled that the band was not willing to remain a cultish pleasure for a small group of admirers. The Yardbirds were intent on grabbing the carousel's brass ring.

Taking over from Samwell-Smith in the interview with *Beat Instrumental*, Giorgio Gomelsky explained to the magazine that this labelling of groups is pure suicide. 'Groups have to realize that they are entertainers, not merely trendsetters . . . Why complicate something which is basically so simple.'[20] But don't worry, they told their readers, the Yardbirds 'still dig the raw blues . . . "it's a compromise," said Chris Dreja. A compromise to try and find real success at all levels. Which means that we'll always be trying to find brand-new ideas to add to our showmanship approach."'[21]

'The Yardbirds hop in . . .' Four of the five Yardbirds were the 'unexpected guests at the Carlton Tower tea party on Boxing Day for the prizewinners of . . . "It's A Woman's World" competition'. Eric Clapton was the missing 'Bird; he at least was not being a showman and playing the pop game.[22] But that was a new-found disinclination to join in. Only a few weeks earlier, he had been part of the adjudication committee for Porthcawl Council's Beat Competition at the Grand Pavilion on 14 December and was pictured with the rest of the band and three pretty Welsh fans, but he was absent without leave on 26 December.[23] He had not previously been adverse to playing the pop game for photo stories in the teen magazines, such as *Fabulous*, which ran a piece on the band messing about in boats in September 1964, and in February 1965 made up a story of them as cavemen.[24] The accompanying colour pin-up of the band was the fifth printed in the magazine to feature Clapton. However, a day or so before the release of 'For Your Love' on 5 March, he'd chucked in the towel completely, played his last gig with the band and Jeff Beck had taken his place.[25]

In its 17 April edition, *Record Mirror* announced that 'Ex-Yardbird' Eric Clapton was joining John Mayall, replacing Roger Dean.[26] The move could almost have been pre-planned, from leaving a group with pop ambitions to joining a band with certain blues bona fides, yet in the heated mix of early 1965, as the original R&B scene dissipated, was it really so unambiguous? The readiness with which the band and Gomelsky provided an alibi for Clapton's departure, alongside his complicity, might just as well suggest it was a ploy designed to provide a dignified public face to the parting of ways, a diplomatic explanation. Egos clashing was undoubtedly the soundtrack behind the break, Clapton's purism the given excuse.[27]

Talking to the *Evening Standard*'s Maureen Cleave, as the single was poised for the top spot, the Yardbirds said, 'We're just making it now . . . just grabbing it.'[28] They cynically discussed how the music business worked:

> A lot of ratting in it . . . but you learn to make the best of it. It's pretty grim. We've brainwashed ourselves to accept most of the things that go on; all you can do is laugh – otherwise you'd go potty. The normal office worker couldn't put up for two days with what we have to put up with. It's the tension that builds up; the travelling upsets your stomach and makes you tired. And then when you feel bloody awful, you're meant to get up on the stage and be the big extrovert.[29]

To survive, Cleave wrote, the band 'keep going on private jokes; fortunately they still like each other. "I don't even *know* anybody else," Chris Dreja said.'[30]

The travails of a working band come down to moans about 'one or two of their most violent fans' who carry scissors to scratch foul and vulgar things on the side of their van – 'an essay in filth'.[31] Working hard, they said, takes the fun out of things, 'but they reckon it's worth it'. 'I'd hate to be a has-been,' said Keith Relf, 'the lead singer who looks pale and interesting . . . "I think I'd miss the sensation of being slightly larger than life."'[32] Talking to the *Daily Mail*, Paul Samwell-Smith explained the change in direction: 'R&B is out', he said, 'it's basically club stuff. R and B just doesn't come over on disc.'[33] Clapton leaving was again put down to his purism and dislike for the single, but also his 'strong personality' and 'terrible bad moods'.[34] One-night stands were taking their toll too, said Relf, '"trying to whip up unenthusiastic audiences. Now we're aiming at the nation – not just fans." Purism, it seems, just doesn't pay.'[35]

While Clapton's fidelity to a blues purism might be seen as laudable as his old band were selling out any credibility they had banked, from the Yardbirds' point of view, the pursuit of the authentic was a drag, a block on creativity. Those who claimed the mantle of the real were also declaring a form of proprietary control – maintaining an exclusive club, setting out the criteria of who might or might not be granted membership. The Yardbirds saw that as an entrapment; they chose instead the freedom to go in any direction they wanted, to be open to new ideas, sounds and forms. Letting Clapton walk away with his reputation as a bluesman intact might not have been the gift some subsequently thought it to be.

Looking back at the break-up from the vantage point of July 1965, after having notched up two hit singles, Samwell-Smith told *Melody Maker*'s Nick Jones that the 'change was justifiable because we have become successful. We slogged away for years playing R&B and the general public just didn't want to know. Many people didn't feel there was enough in plain rhythm and blues. They need something of a little more substance.'[36] Asked if they had set out to make a 'commercial' record, he replied, 'Well, the group liked the number, except for Eric Clapton who was a bit doubtful, and we decided to record it. I don't think we were prostituting ourselves by doing it. It was our luck the record sold, NOT our fault!'[37]

The key issue for Samwell-Smith was the distinction between studio and stage work: the first two singles 'were made with the idea of getting our stage sound. It was a mistake, because trying to get a stage sound captured in a studio is very difficult. The Stones have tried, but they failed.'[38] With Jeff Beck, he said, the band had become 'more sophisticated and versatile'; their sound had 'tightened up'.[39] However good Clapton was, suggested Samwell-Smith, he imposed limits on the band; Beck opened things up:

> Surprisingly enough, our stage sound is less commercial than it was. We used to play, really, commercial R&B. Now Jeff is starting electronic sounds. Personally I don't find these sounds artistic, but Jeff is so fantastic – and the best at it in the country. On disc I like our sound to be tidy and

> neat – keeping the backing simple. 'For Your Love' was done only with bass and harpsichord playing the melody. The rest was like percussion, providing rhythms.[40]

Derek Johnson reviewed the single for the *New Musical Express*, catching its appeal: 'Strangely insistent minor-key item . . . Has strident chords, bongos and drum thumps – then suddenly changes tempo and breaks into an orthodox shaker. Lead singer of the Yardbirds handles the plaintive lyric, while the others chant the title phrase. Unusual, makes you sit up and take notice,' which is precisely what the reviewers for the local and regional papers did.[41]

'In the Groove', Bob Farmer's reviews of new releases, a column with wide syndication in local and regional papers, gave the Rolling Stones' 'The Last Time' a positive spin – 'should restore them to favour after that "Red Rooster" rubbish. Probably No. 1.'[42] The second disc reviewed was 'For Your Love': 'Throbbing, thrilling, eerie item that's going to give over-due Top 10 fame to the group that became replacements at the Richmond Club that discovered the Stones.'[43] Other press reviews basically repeated the same lines as Charles Fiske in his column for the *Newcastle Evening Chronicle*, 'Fiske's Discs': 'This new Columbia single is produced by Giorgio Gomelsky and, with an arrangement by bass guitarist Paul Samwell-Smith, boasts superb harmonies and some very effective harpsicord playing. Lower deck title is "Got to Hurry".'[44] The novel use of the plucked string keyboard captured the interest of reviewers: 'Whatever would old Mozart have said if he'd heard the harpsicord played on a pop record? Whatever would he have said about pop records for that matter!'[45] In its 'Spotlight on Modern Youth' column, the *Tewksbury Register* put emphasis on the percussion: 'It has a remarkable beginning, with bongo drums which I think I like best out of the whole record. After a slowish beginning, the group break into a beat which sounds uncannily like a Beatles' release.'[46]

The *Port Talbot Guardian* worried over how the band would reproduce the record on stage given that the 'harpischord and bongos were added after the initial tape was made'.[47] The absence of Eric Clapton from the line-up was also a problem to be managed: 'Eric is one of the most highly rated guitarists on the London R&B scene and was surely the biggest factor of the groups original success.'[48] The *Coventry Standard* invited members of the Sacred Hearts Youth Club to review the single along with other recent releases: 'This is too bitty to be a hit,' said Christine. Gillian agreed. Howard did not. 'This is the best of the ones played so far. The Yardbirds are under-estimated as a group, and I like their style.' Michael summed up his opinion on the record and the Yardbirds in two words: 'absolute rubbish'. But declared: 'With a sound like that it will be a hit and a very good seller. Just look at our members going wild over it.'[49]

And a hit it was, rising to the very top, where it battled it out with Cliff Richard, one chart putting Cliff on top, the other, the 'Birds. The confusion around the top spot gave the band a front-cover appearance in the national *Daily Mirror*: 'they celebrated with a bottle of champagne before going to play at Southampton last night.'[50] In *Disc Weekly*, Penny Valentine wrote that it was the band's best disc: 'A tremendous hit this and obviously a lot of thought has gone into the whole thing – especially the arrangement. Harpsichord and bongos start it with a sexy sound that gets faster and faster and sounds like a horror film . . . Enthralling. Flip written by – incredibly – C. Rasputin.'[51]

The single's B-side was a showcase for their soon-to-depart guitarist; on the record's label, under the band's name, was printed 'featuring Eric "Slowhand" Clapton'. On the A-side, on which Clapton barely featured, it highlighted 'musical director Paul Samwell-Smith' – the binary appeared to be inscribed into the disc and its labels. 'Got to Hurry' is a remarkable farewell card from Clapton. Recorded back in August at the original 'Good Morning Little School Girl' sessions, the band pull together a Booker T.

and the MGs' patented blues stroll – 'Green Onions'/'Home Grown'/'Jellybread' – the sort of thing the Rolling Stones had earlier attempted on 'Stoned', the flip of 'I Wanna Be Your Man' and the Nashville Teens, also on the B-side of their second single, with 'T.N.T.', which featured Jimmy Page on guitar. Clapton channelled Steve Cropper to maximum effect, holding a tight rein until the middle eight, at which point he and the band threaten an extended rave-up but instead keep things in a tense hold. Clapton fully earned the featured role, as did Samwell-Smith for his arrangement of Gouldman's number.

Relf summed the situation up for *Disc Weekly*:

> I personally feel it's doubtful that another R and B record will be a hit in our charts. As a music it's been flogged to death and the only real R and B record that was representative in this country, I think, was The Rolling Stones' 'Little Red Rooster'. This is the age of the good commercial pop disc and in a way its far more exciting because it's an adventure trying to evolve a hit record.[52]

An adventure for the ages.

'For Your Love' was a genuine leave-taking from the Most Blueswailing Yardbird days; it was most obviously distinctive because of the fugue-like state of lost time that the harpsichord and the echoing percussion provided, but also because of the shifting time signature that first occurs only a minute into the song, followed by the Beatle-esque break at the bridge. These moments of acceleration/deceleration had been rehearsed in their rave-ups, but the harmony vocals that provided a frame for Relf were entirely new to the band. This all gave the singer a context to play out a suggestion of vulnerability – Relf sings as if he's been hurt and can be hurt again. There is anguish in his voice. When Maureen Cleave described him as 'looking pale and interesting', knowingly or not, she was setting out the terms of the new contract that the singer would make between himself and his audience. No longer the blues shouter, if he was ever that, he was now more akin to a French café-concert singer, his straining against a limited vocal range keeping the emotion in the song earthbound, a street realism that was a very European form of the blues – Jacques Brel rather than Bobby Bland. More importantly, his group had earned a place in the hearts and on the garments of fans across land and sea.

> 'Flight to Gretna Ends in Deep Water'
> A boy and girl stowed away in a cargo ship at Warren Point, Northern Ireland, on Friday because they wanted to marry. But after being discovered at sea they found that the vessel, the Norwegian freighter Joselin, was bound for Poland.
>
> The pair . . . Lawrence Kell (17) . . . and Michele Seagrove (16) . . . admitted stowing away . . . Kell, who said that he wanted to go to his grandmother's home in Surrey, had the words 'Rolling Stones', 'Yardbirds' and 'Mod' printed on his khaki combat jacket.
>
> *THE GUARDIAN* (31 August 1965)

UNDOUBTEDLY, SOMEWHERE ON Lawrence's jacket he'd also scrawled 'The Who', a band that competed directly with the Yardbirds across the whole of 1965. 'The Who – Maximum R&B – Tuesday Nights at the Marquee' ran the tag line on the iconic monochrome poster, designed by Brian Pike and used during the band's 23-week Wardour Street residency – a cornerstone of the Who's foundation myth. Yet the preponderance of their gigs at the club were not advertised as such, but rather, and more enigmatically, as 'THE WHO – LONDON 1965'. Sometimes with the hyphen, sometimes not.

Following the Kit Lambert and Chris Stamp takeover, there was an ongoing debate over the band's name and how best to present it.

For their first show of the residency, 24 November 1964, they were billed as 'THE "WHO"', which continued until 5 January 1965, when the quotation marks were left off. The punctuation was back again the following week and stayed in place until the first gig in February, when it was dropped once more. From 9 February until 6 April, the shows were promoted as 'THE WHO – LONDON 1965'. For the final two Tuesday nights of the band's residency at the Marquee, 27 April being the last of the 23, they were simply 'THE WHO'.

On the Brunswick label for 'I Can't Explain', and in press advertisements and posters promoting the single, there was never any uncertainty over how their name was to be presented, they were just 'The Who'. The appendage 'LONDON 1965' for the Marquee (and Ealing Club dates in February) was a declaration, but more than that it was an agreement with their audience. 'The Who – London 1965' laid down the claim that the band not only were at the very centre of things in Soho and West London, but they were its entire focus – 'right here, right now, we are what's happening', 'join us' it said.

Introducing the band subsequent to 'I Can't Explain' hitting the charts in March, *Melody Maker*, under the heading of 'WHO – and why', confronted the issue of the band's name: 'Long before the present craze for group names like Them, Us and Themselves, the flat-mate of 19-year-old guitarist Pete Townshend thought of Who. When, nine months ago, drummer Keith Moon joined the group – then called the High Numbers, it changed its name to the Who.'[53] With the single sitting at no. 25 in the charts, the Who, *Melody Maker* decided, were no longer 'all that anonymous'.[54] Moon, Daltrey and Entwistle's names were correctly spelled but 'Townsend', ever the group's spokesman, had still to suffer such minor indignities. He explained that their follow-up single was likely to be 'You Don't Have to Jerk', because the group 'all dig jerking' . . . the Who: a bunch of tossers![55] The band also dug 'Bobby Bland, James Brown and the Tamla-Motown gear, particularly Marvin Gaye', he said. While on stage, the *Melody Maker* reported, 'the Who don't play many far-out numbers. But . . . all their numbers are given Who interpretation, which combines tremendous fire and aggression. Pete regards this as the aggression of the "mod" person, and believes that the Who is a group which appeals mainly to "mod" people.'[56]

Townshend linked the band's passion to their Mod followers, creating a solid symbiotic relationship; one as profoundly important in the band's mythology as the Marquee. In an April 1965 interview, published in the May edition of *Beat Instrumental*, Kevin Swift didn't refer directly to either the club or the band's audience, but he did anchor 'The spectacular Who' as a 'revolutionary group':

> You see, these boys have got something special . . . nerve! Watch their stage act and they will generate about six different sensations through the audience. Among them – excitement, frustration, wonder, even awe. But hang on, perhaps 'stage act' is an unfortunate choice of term – 'presentation' is probably better. Where does the nerve come in? All through the performance. The group's all 'go' and they do things anyone else would be nervous about.[57]

Moon is described as a 'nut', 'frantic': 'the way he waves those sticks about could easily earn him the title "The Male Shiva". Indeed to many of the Who's followers, he is a god.'[58]

> Townshend is the band member with the best opportunity to attract the audience's attention . . . His guitar has become his slave. He makes it moan, scream and mumble and, sometimes, in fact, it seems it can do quite well on its own. This illusion occurs when Pete is characteristically bringing his arm round in a wide arc above his head ready for the next stroke – usually up. The fingers on his left hand stop the required notes and the power in his set-up does the rest.[59]

Daltrey was Swift's third 'wildie' in the band: 'He has feeling plus, but keeps just within the bounds of reality,' belting his tambourine against the mike stand until it disintegrates.[60] 'Like Pete and Keith, Roger is completely unpredictable on stage.'[61] Predictably, Entwistle is described as 'the quiet one'.[62] Like Townshend, he used feedback and played his bass in an unconventional way, 'like a lead guitar at times, and that is a sin to most folk'.[63] Behind the 'three wildies and a quiety' is the duo of Chris Stamp and Kit Lambert, who 'look upon [the Who] as the embodiment of London's various characteristics'.[64] Swift wrote: 'It is quite a valid theory when you consider it for a moment. After all, their act contains an aggressiveness, humour, action and an overall indication of frustration. London – The Who. The Who – London. Even the name is representative of the anonymity of the big city.'[65] Tapping out the signifiers with which Lambert and Stamp had provided him, Swift acknowledged the London-centricity and aggressive image as being as important to the band's identity as their Mod followers and the Marquee residency.

When Pete Meaden managed the band, he had explained to *Record Mirror*'s Peter Jones that the 'Mod scene is a way of life. An exciting, quick-changing, way of life. The boys are totally immersed in the atmosphere. So they have direct contact with thousands of potential disc buyers.'[66] They wore all the right gear too: 'Their clothes are the hallmark of the much-criticized typical mod. Cycling jackets, tee shirts, turned-up Levi jeans, long white jackets, boxing boots, black and white brogues and so on to the mod-est limits.'[67] Pete Townshend, near 6 feet tall with 'cropped dark hair, piercing blue eyes', said, 'I admit to spending a fortune on bright and in-vogue clothes. I go for the *West Side Story* look and the Ivy League gear.'[68] Of the High Numbers single 'I'm the Face', backed with 'Zoot Suit', Jones wrote, 'one thing is for sure: the phraseology is good and authentic. Mod, in fact.'[69] In truth, the disc was a competent rewrite, competently played, of two blues tunes – Slim Harpo's 'Got Love If You Want It' and the Dynamics'

'Misery', but if the record was barely distinguishable from others, their smart, short-haired Mod style certainly did make them stand out; while every other band was wearing suits and ties, the Who looked unique. They had that Mod phraseology down pat.

Around the same time as the band were talking to Swift, they also spoke to Norrie Drummond at the *New Musical Express*. He misspelled 'Townsend', 'Daltry' and 'Entwhistle', but noted, anyhow, that the last preferred to be called 'John Browne' (he'd been 'John Allison' in the High Numbers).[70] Their individual identities may have not yet been fixed, but that flux was also part of the story the band wanted to tell about itself. Though Townshend didn't contradict what he told *Melody Maker* about his relationship with Mods, he did complicate things. Explaining the name change from the High Numbers to the Who, he said, 'at this time we had a fanatical mod manager who wanted us all to be complete mod. But this was contrived, artificial modness and we wanted to be ourselves.'[71] Finding one's authentic self within a cult of individuality in which the members all conform to the same notion of non-conformity would perplex Townshend for the next several years.

Townshend's search for a righteous identity and Lambert and Stamp's presentation of the Who as 'London 1965' was to be conducted not just on records and stages but in film and television too. The promotional line Lambert gave to the *NME* was that, despite only having had the one hit, the band had already made four film appearances. The most interesting of the four was for French television and had been promoted in *Record Mirror*, where it was noted that filming took place in three key locations: Soho, Shepherd's Bush and Hammersmith: 'Mods' – *Seize millions de jeunes* (Sixteen Million Teenagers) was broadcast on 18 March.[72] The thirty-minute programme covers London's new working-class youth. Shots of run-down Hammersmith and its empty streets introduce the city; it is a grey, desperate place without industry or a future. 'Great Britain' has become a world of old men with only the pub and television for entertainment. But look away and there is a youth explosion about to happen, and the Who and their Mod audience are its hidden, but soon-to-be public, face.

In front of French TV cameras at the Marquee Club, the band perform James Brown's 'Shout and Shimmy', Garnet Mimms's 'Tell Me Baby' (a cover version of its flip side, 'Anytime You Want Me', will fill out the lower deck of the Who's U.S. release of 'Anyway Anyhow Anywhere'), Martha and the Vandellas' 'Heatwave' and Howlin' Wolf's 'Spoonful' and 'Smokestack Lightning'. These segments are interspersed with a Mod boy and girl talking about parents, marriage, religion and race. Townshend adds his thoughts to these topics and Kit Lambert acts as the 'adult' interlocutor, explaining teenage London and their violent revolt against bourgeois conformity. The *New Musical Express* quoted the programme's producer, Alain de Sedouy, who said the Who were 'a logical musical expression of the bewilderment and anarchy of London's teenagers', which sounds like he's swallowed Lambert's hyperbole hook, line and sinker, though it was also undoubtedly the truth.[73] As Lambert had explained to *Music Echo*, the film would not be televised in Britain as it 'talks about purple hearts, and criticizes parents, God, the Queen and the Government!'[74]

Aside from the Who's appearance – especially their Yardbirds-styled rave-up on the Howlin' Wolf medley, which the band make entirely their own by running it down rather than building it up – the highlight of the documentary is the kids, smashed-blocked, and dancing like beautiful fools at the Goldhawk Club to some other band chopping away on Muddy Waters's 'I Just Want to Make Love to You' and Bo Diddley's 'Who Do You Love?'. At the centre of the dancers is a young lad who looks like Keith Relf, self-absorbed, manically chewing gum; another boy, head snapping back and forth, gurns into the camera; a third, on a mate's shoulders, shakes and claps emphatically. The boys and girls in their entirety create a single line of hedonistic pleasure that runs back through Lambert and

Stamps's documentary of the High Numbers and the audience at the Railway Hotel, from the previous year, to working-class kids jiving to the Chris Barber Band in *Momma Don't Allow* (1956).

At the beginning of April, the Who were profiled in *Record Mirror* with the headline 'The group that slaughters their amplifiers ...' Once again, they discussed the band's name; Daltrey explained that they had been the Who, then they were the High Numbers and now, 'we changed our name again and altered our style. We used to have long hair so we cut it short.'[75] They had played 'Jimmy Reedey stuff. Real R&B. But when everyone else started playing it we changed. We do James Brown stuff now, but if everyone else started doing it we'd change again. What to? I don't know, it's difficult to say what's to be next.'[76] Daltrey may have been uncertain about the band's next moves, but not so Townshend and Lambert.

The Who's 'Maximum R&B' slogan had impact in the autumn of 1964; it suggested the band went further, to greater extremes and with a more focused target, than their peers in the highly congested London club arena. But their stance was suggestive not only of pushing at the boundaries of the form but of its exhaustion. The Clique, who would record a couple of singles for Pye in 1965, advertised themselves as playing 'Raving R&B', which took them very close to the Yardbirds' patented appeal. West London's Muleskinners, who had among its members future Small Face Ian McLagan, trailed their Twickenham, Ealing and Eel Pie gigs as 'Knockout R+B here Tonight', with an award-winning poster designed by Colin Fulcher (later known as Barney Bubbles).[77] As for the Birds, they tagged themselves as playing the 'greatest R&B'. All four slogans suggested just how overcrowded the scene had become as much as they pointed to a band's self-proclaimed uniqueness. R&B at the tail end of 1964 and the beginning of 1965 remained a broad church, but one band after another had begun to put some distance between themselves and what they saw as the genre's limitations.

In February 1965, Billy Harrison, the leader of Them, told *Record Mirror*'s George Rooney that 'R&B won't last forever . . . We've been labelled as [an] R and B group, which we are basically, but let's face it . . . We'll be lucky to get a year out of it . . . At the moment we are just waiting – we don't know what for – just waiting to see what's going to happen I suppose.'[78] Other bands echoed those sentiments. Norman Jopling's profile in *Record Mirror* of the Artwoods, from late spring 1965, summed up the dilemma. The article defined the band as one of the 'most *realistic* groups on the scene', but they were also without a hit record.[79] They didn't mind 'pandering to commercial tastes, even though they have been hailed as one of the most authentic R&B groups in the land'.[80] The problem, said frontman Art Wood, was that

> authentic R&B just isn't pulling the crowds anymore. The audiences want to be excited not to be lectured on what is 'good' and what is 'bad'. Although there was a time when you could spend half an hour on one number with long solos by everybody. It didn't last long. And although there are some clubs like that still, most of them want something fresh and new.[81]

In a profile of Keith Moon for *Beat Instrumental*, Pete Goodman returned to an image purloined from *A Clockwork Orange* that he had first used to describe the Yardbirds, 'ultra-violence':

> It's when you talk about drumming that you realize just how extraordinary Moon really is. And how extraordinary the Who, as a group, are. They put on an all-round spectacle of ultra-violence. Keith leads the way, crashing his foot against his drum kit, smashing drum-stick against drum-stick . . . hurling the debris into the audience.[82]

'The most important thing', Moon told him, 'is to be yourself. I'm a Mod . . . If I change, I'm not being honest with myself.'[83] But the band were changing, 'The Who, with what is now described by their management as "Pop Art", have become a major force in the Pop scene. Keith is obviously glad to be a Pop Art-ist.'[84] The previous month, the magazine had reviewed 'Anyway Anyhow Anywhere': '"Pop Art". That's how the Who's new record is described. It's a sort of musical action painting. Everything happens where it's least expected. There are touches of "I Can't Explain", weird drum-breaks, and funny feedback noises, in fact it is just like The Who are on stage.'[85] Things were moving and shifting quickly with the Who, but apart from a few Townshend compositions, their live set was lagging seriously behind their ambitions.

'A Disturbing Group' was the headline of Richard Green's coverage of the Who after seeing and speaking with them at the Marquee at the end of February 1965: 'The best part of their appeal, I am convinced, lays [*sic*] in the antics of lead guitarist Pete Townshend. He is the first man I have seen who really shows that he understands what an electronic guitar means.'[86] In April, *Melody Maker*'s Nick Jones reviewed a Tuesday-night Marquee set by the Who; he had previously reported on the band following their last Soho gig of 1964. He remained entranced:

> Despite all that has been written about the Who, one of the latest groups to emerge from the club scene into the hit parade, their act has to be seen. For instance, when guitarist Peter Townshend wrecked his speaker last Tuesday [13 April] at London's Marquee, belting it with the end of his already battered guitar. Feedback screeched out of the remaining speaker and the rest of the group thundered away behind him. It sounds like a gimmick, but the audience loves it.[87]

The uniqueness of the performance chides, however, with the set list Jones provides: 'Heatwave' and 'Motoring' were covers of tunes first recorded by Martha Reeves and the Vandellas; 'Shout and Shimmy', 'Please, Please, Please' and 'I Don't Mind' were by 'the great James Brown, the inevitable "Smokestack Lighnin'" [Howlin' Wolf] and the tremendous "I'm a Man" [Bo Diddley]. The Who have to be seen!' Those final two numbers had been mainstays of the Yardbirds' set for the best part of two years – they as good as defined the band, yet they were stand-outs of the Who's set too.

Reviewing another Tuesday night of the band's residency in Soho, Richard Green wrote: 'It is true that "I Can't Explain" is not really typical of the Who's style. But then one number at the Marquee lasted for 26 minutes. These days, that would be the length of an average LP.'[88] Nick Jones had previously suggested that the Who should bill themselves 'not only as "Maximum R&B" but as "Far-out R&B"'.[89] Whichever of the two resonated, the set list and the R&B tab made them appear as Yardbirds imitators, and that was something they needed to avoid at all costs. Even if the Who had essentially built their whole act on the form, from this point on, 'R&B' didn't feature in the band's publicity.

The rhetoric that came out of the Who's camp suggested that they dealt exclusively in the novel, but the songs that made up their set lists and formed the core of the initial tracks they had laid down for their debut album with producer Shel Talmy did not carry the shock of the new. Though there were more than a few hangovers, the Who had pretty much left behind the Chess catalogue, Jimmy Reed and the like for James Brown and the emerging soul music of young America. 'Now we all prefer the Tamla-Motown and Zoot Money sound of music,' Entwistle told the *NME* in April: 'We went to see the Motown show and loved every minute of it! But we expected a far bigger audience. It's a pity support was lacking because they're great artists.'[90] Being a covers band, however, was not where the Who were heading.

In July, Lambert told *Melody Maker* the band had finished with 'Smokestack Lightning' and R&B; new original material would consist of what he called 'hard pop'.[91] That same month, Townshend told *Disc Weekly* about the new song that the Who would be recording – 'My Generation'. 'It's a more up-tempo number,' he said, 'and it talks about old people and young married people. The fellow who's telling the story can't really express himself properly and stutters.'[92] 'The Group', Rod Harrod wrote, 'are also starting a new approach in their stage act. "We're going to do a new kind of number – if I can churn them out. A New Orleans type thing. We're getting off the Tamla-Motown kick. The group sound has changed, we've got a rougher, more vicious approach now."'[93] Maximum R&B was dead. Long live hard pop, the sound of tomorrow: a future the Yardbirds claimed belonged to them alone.

5

The Futuristic Sound of the Yardbirds, (1975 in) 1965

The Two New Feet of the Yardbirds belong to JEFF BECK.

He measures from his Vidal Sassoon hair-cut to his second-hand shoes, 71 inches. I saw Jeff when they were recording 'Saturday Club' the other day and asked him what he thought about joining the Yardbirds. His insolent reply was 'It is the greatest thing since I stopped working for the South Clapham Mentally Handicapped Ear Hospital!'

And then I asked the Yardbirds for their comments.

Keith Yodbod: 'He's got the hairiest guitar sound and twiddliest left hand I've ever seen, heard or smelt.'

Sam Yodbod: 'Jeff? Oh, he's a shot of nerve gas at dawn!'

Jim Yodbod: 'Very funny. Yerst. Yerst. Mind you, his jaws are very useful for opening coke-bottles, beer bottles, nuts, bolts and assorted screws.'

Chris Yodbod: 'Well, he's got the sound of '75, but Jeff himself is a . . . . .! But not bad on the whole.'

MUSIC ECHO (March 1965)

For a March issue of *Music Echo*, Yardbirds insider Hamish Grimes deputized for an absent Michael Aldred, 'Aldred's Eye View' temporarily substituted for 'Hamish I View!', where in, in the first of many such references, Chris Dreja named Jeff Beck as the 'sound of '75' – ten years ahead of his time.[1]

'The Yardbirds were eating strawberry yoghurt when I told them. "It's jumped to No. 4,"' the *NME*'s Alan Smith wrote, '"and it looks like it might go higher next week!" Drummer Jim McCarty's mouth fell open and rhythm guitarist Chris Dreja sent his thin, gold-framed sun glasses clattering to the floor.'[2] After reminding readers that the Yardbirds were refugees from 'Rolling Stone land' and repeating the story of Clapton's exit, the profile concentrated on Jeff Beck and the band's ambition to keep changing and not make a repeat version of 'For Your Love'.[3] The point was echoed by *Ready Steady Go*'s presenter Cathy McGowan: 'The Yardbirds . . . are very intelligent – especially Sam . . . They are always trying for something new in the way of arrangements. I admire them for that.'[4]

For *Music Echo*, Michael Aldred watched Beck's Marquee debut on 8 March, the guitarist's third show: '[he] is great and had the audience up in arms yelling for more. This is pretty unusual for a Monday night crowd. I noticed T-Bone Walker in the audience, obviously digging what was happening.'[5] A week later, on 15 March at Advision Studios, the Yardbirds recorded 'Steeled Blues' and 'I Ain't Done Wrong'; on 13 April, they returned to the studio and laid down 'My Girl Sloopy' and 'I'm Not Talking', along with a first attempt at their next single, 'Heart Full of Soul'. 'Steeled Blues' would be placed on the flip of the single, and the other three tracks would comprise an EP.[6]

Club dates made up most of the band's bookings through late March and on into April. At the end of the month and then well into May, the band played second on the bill of a package tour headlined by the Kinks, supported by Goldie and the Gingerbreads, the Riot Squad and the Mickey Finn (and his Bluesmen), with the Walker Brothers a late addition to the line-up.[7] Penny Valentine reviewed the Kinks/Yardbirds package:

> The Yardbirds, in pale suits, were obviously the people that everyone had been waiting for. Over the noise, hardly any of Keith's vocal could be heard, but it was really new guitarist Jeff Beck who came off best. He's tremendously good and

Record Mirror

Largest selling colour pop weekly newspaper
No. 216 Week ending May 1, 1965
Every Thursday 6d. Registered at the G.P.O. as a newspaper

THIS WEEK
CILLA & BOB DYLAN
COLOUR. FEATURES ON
UNIT 4+2, DAVE BERRY

THE YARDBIRDS. Left to right—Paul Samwell-Smith, Jim McCarty, Chris Dreja, Geoff Beck and Keith Relf. (RM Pic by Keith Hammett).

The Barron Knights

The group now prove that not only can they hold a position in the top five of the 'best sellers' chart with parodic humour, but can equal the top groups, playing anything from Ballads to Rock.

Columbia
33SX1648 (mono LP)

The Supremes

The three lovely Supremes in their distinctive Motown style, have taken one after another the hits that brought the British Groups to the top. Their versatility has produced an all-star package of top entertainment.

Tamla Motown
TML11002

Latest single

Pop go the workers
Columbia DB7525

EMI
THE GREATEST RECORDING ORGANISATION IN THE WORLD

E·M·I RECORDS LTD · E·M·I HOUSE · 20 MANCHESTER SQUARE · LONDON W·1

Thumbs up from new recruit Jeff Beck: *Record Mirror*, 1 May 1965.

the by-play between him and Keith really had the audience on its feet. I'd personally say that the group's choice of material was more suited to their club appearances, but the audience was so happy in just having them there, that they couldn't have cared if they'd been singing 'Auld Lang Syne'.[8]

Beyond ticket sales, the package produced the usual media coverage about the tomfoolery and practical jokes involved with being on tour, especially Mick Avory's attempted decapitation of Dave Davies with one of his cymbals.[9]

Toward the end of April, the *NME* reported on the band's scheduled releases: 28 May for the single and sometime before that for the EP, which, in the event, was held back until August. An album was being prepared, *A Yardbirds View of Beat*, which would be a 'compendium of rhythm and blues, gospel and spiritual styles'.[10] The album never happened; instead, Gomelsky pulled together a ragbag of tracks for the North American market, *For Your Love* (Epic), which was in U.S. stores in July but remained unreleased in Britain. A series of Sunday concerts at summer resort locations was announced for July into September.[11] In the late summer, the band would fly to the States for television and live dates.

Following the chart run of 'For Your Love', the Yardbirds doubled down on promoting themselves in the teen magazines aimed at girls. In May, *Fabulous* conducted a shoot with house photographer Fiona Adam in Marylebone's Good Yards, posing the band in front of trains and rolling stock so as to illustrate the idea behind their name. Editor June Southworth reintroduced each of the band members to her readers: 'I took a long hard look at The Yardbirds. There's no doubt that Sam is the glamour boy. That Chris is the boy-next-door. That Jim is the bringer-upper of brought down Yardbirds. That Jeff is the down-to-earth one. That Keith is the most *interesting* of them all.'[12] You couldn't argue that the band were exceptionally handsome young men, but Southworth's characterizations were hard fought for. Excepting Relf as the most interesting among them, none of the other members had a character that the teen magazines found easily relatable, certainly not like the Beatles, the Stones or the Who. Describing Beck as 'down-to-earth' missed the mark entirely; Southworth was closer to the target when she discussed his unease at being costumed and groomed. During 1965, Beck's image as the band's refusenik, its rebel, would be refined. McCarty, Samwell-Smith and Dreja remained all but undefinable as far as the teen magazines were concerned. Relf justified his characterization by making himself available in the summer for a piece titled 'My Kind of Girl'.[13] He liked girls with long flowing brown hair that dressed simply and smartly, not too tall, slim, intelligent, not too chatty and little make-up. She would look a bit like Françoise Hardy. *Boyfriend* described him as a 'leading personality on the pop scene ... he's ultra-sensitive and not brash. He's quiet but has a lot worth saying. He retains your interest 'cos you feel you could do a lot of soul searching into him.'[14]

The band's anonymity played into the idea that they were not party-goers, preferring a night in to a night out. Nor were they scenesters or fashion mavens. In a profile in *Boyfriend*, the band were characterized as 'the way behind but way-out Yardbirds'; uncomfortable buying clothes in Carnaby Street for their upcoming North American tour, Jeff Beck 'a devoted denim-ite', was 'rarely seen out of jeans'.[15] He and Jim 'are what you could call the big ravers of the group. They go to about one party a year!'[16] The piece ends on the note that by 'preserving their individuality in a set-up where there is so much cadging and lack of originality, the Yardbirds will probably stay in step, out of the crowd, for some time yet!'[17] Few bands who courted the teen market looked as stiff and uncomfortable posing for publicity photographs as the Yardbirds. They always appeared as if they'd rather be someplace else and, given they were a group, with someone else.

With 'For Your Love' high in the charts, Columbia re-promoted *Five Live Yardbirds* to British record buyers and Gomelsky set about making a short film of the single for the overseas market. A harpsichord was carried onto a field in Windsor and then the five 'Birds were mustered together wearing costumes gleaned from a grand dressing up box – tricorn hats, suits of armour, Elizabethan ruffles and feathered caps, cavalier boots and swords: 'You might be excused for thinking the most modern group in Britain had gone out of its mind' wrote the *NME*'s Keith Altham about the shoot.[18] The takeaway image is not of Beck playing his guitar with an épée but Altham's description of them as 'the most modern group in Britain'.[19] It was an idea that would increasingly be played out across the rest of the year, and one that was most often associated with Beck's guitar technique, played with or without a duelling sword.

Again making the distinction between studio and live work, Relf told Altham about their 'wild' selection of material for club dates, 'We do a lot of Bo Diddley and Buddy Guy numbers, but you wouldn't recognize them after we have finished with them. We do all our own arrangements. Jeff Beck has probably more ideas about different effects produced from a guitar than any other guitarist in the country.'[20] On the 'tricky problem' of succeeding Clapton, Beck told *Beat Instrumental*:

> Eric was very popular. Now I honestly find I can't look directly at audiences. I've got this feeling, you know, that they're all there just waiting for me to make a mistake, so they can stand shouting out to get Eric back in the group. Maybe I'll get over it, but it's a very real problem right now.[21]

Alongside the first published colour photograph of the band and their new line-up, featuring a sulky-looking Beck, Richard Green, for *Record Mirror*, ran down what the changes would mean:

> 'Rhythm and blues is becoming what trad became and we are going to change some of our numbers.' Thus spake Keith Relf, the singer with the American footballer's shoulders who fronts the Yardbirds. 'We're getting away from the old twelve-bar bit and doing other things,' he added. 'We may include a Dylan number and more pop stuff.'[22]

Beck was central to the sense of change; he'd been bored in the Tridents, he told Green in a Soho pub: 'The blokes I was playing with cheesed me off and we did the same old numbers all the time.'[23] He had played recording sessions with Jimmy Page, which was how he had learned that the Yardbirds needed a guitarist and how his introduction had been facilitated. It was not Beck's ability to play the same lines as Clapton that scored him the gig, but what he did with the guitar and amplification that went beyond both the blues and what his predecessor had offered: 'During one number, Jeff produced noises like a violin, a musical saw and a chicken clucking from his guitar. I asked Keith about this strange sound and he replied that something similar to "the musique concrete" or "musique electronique" albums would suit him.'[24]

In July, Green again met with the band and picked up on his conversation about 'their experiment in sound':

> A couple of years ago when they were charging about in Richmond, the Yardbirds created a certain sound. Kids dressed like beatniks and hung from rafters. 'Smokestack Lightning' was heavily featured. So was 'Boom Boom' and the usual collection of r-n-b numbers. All with the most blueswailing treatment. Three hits later – two top tenners – the Yardbirds still play 'Smokestack Lightning' but it never sounds the same twice. 'When we go on stage, we don't plan anything. It's a kind of ad-libbing, if you like,' said Keith Relf . . . 'We do all this electronic bit. It's really an experiment in sound. "Pop art" is the wrong way to describe what the Who are doing. I think new wave pop music would have been better.'[25]

The shift from the old R&B scene was complete; the new lines were being laid down even as the band spoke to Green. But there was no wholly appropriate category or name within which it could be couched. The Who had offered 'hard pop' and now were throwing

'Pop art' into the mix, a term they were making an exclusive bid for, so Relf proposed 'new wave pop' as he questioned and competed with the Who. Green reported:

> Manager Giorgio Gomelsky seized upon this opportunity to launch into his own theory on the Who's method of playing. Very technical he can get when he likes, too ... In Paris [supporting the Beatles in front of 12,000 screamers], Jeff was the cause of much shouting from the fans by going on for about four minutes with the drummer in an improvised session of ravarama. 'Nobody's written a serious article yet saying what they're trying to do,' Giorgio complained. 'That's what you could do.'
>
> Obliging as ever, I asked Keith what exactly the Yardbirds were trying to do musically. Were they trying to educate the masses? Did they have a target at which they were aiming? ... 'People can see us two nights running and not see the same thing. We developed this using feedback years ago before the Who really. Jeff played with the Tridents, then the Deltones and he twirled his guitar round on top of the amplifier to get sounds when he was with them. I think the Who watched us and other groups and picked bits up from them all. Good luck to them, I'm not getting at them.'
>
> Could this mean, then, that the Yardbirds may in the future release a pop-artish record? 'Oh yes, we couldn't before, though, because we didn't think it was commercial. The public wasn't ready for it. I agree that "I Wish You Would" had a slight quality about it with raving and wailing harmonicas. Perhaps in two records time, we'll do something like that.' Should prove interesting.[26]

Gomelsky and Relf understood, or at least recognized, the theoretical terrain they were traversing alongside the Who, but they didn't have Kit Lambert's keen ear for the provocative high-art statement in a low-cultural form, or Pete Townshend to act as translator and realizer of ideas. Beck was clearing his own path, but when asked in July which group he liked best in the business? he said 'The Who'.[27]

In one of those moments of convergence, a contrived photograph of Pop's happy families, with friendly rivalry set aside, Keith Moon, John Entwistle, Roger Daltrey, alongside Keith Relf and Paul Samwell-Smith, were shown in *Disc Weekly* backstage of the Manchester *Top of the Pops* studio where both bands were promoting their latest singles.[28]

But changes on other fronts were also happening; two weeks earlier, at the beginning of April, *Melody Maker* reported on the Yardbirds' – followed by the Who's – emergence from the west London club scene and into a national arena. In its news pages, the two groups were coupled together beneath the headline 'Pace Hots Up for Who and Yardbirds': 'As they zoomed to the top half of the charts, two of London's top groups . . . faced their biggest crop of one-nighters,' as well as radio and television appearances.[29] They were tracking a path already trodden by the Stones and Georgie Fame, so were there 'any other groups in the darkness of the clubs knocking on the same door of fame?'[30]

> Says Yardbirds leader and vocalist Keith Relf: 'We owe a lot to the clubs, but after a few months, a residency gets a bit hard. I think the fans expect you to get a bit higher and they're a bit surprised to find you still playing at their local club a few weeks later. I suppose the real disadvantage of a residency is that you can't change your repertoire each week, and inevitably enthusiasm slackens.'
>
> Peter Townshend of the Who has a slightly different conception of the club scene. 'Most groups in clubs must really smash out into daylight otherwise they will be stuck

> in clubs for the rest of their lives,' he says . . . 'The Yardbirds have been doing the club circuit quite a while, and now they have made the charts everyone will say that they'll desert the club scene. Who'd blame them after three years.'[31]

The club scene formed these two bands; the fifteen-minute slot on a package tour brought them before bigger audiences, but it lacked intimacy and the room to improvise. As Zoot Money told *Melody Maker*: 'What can you give to those instant audiences in a quarter of an hour stint?'[32]

Early in July, the *NME*'s Keith Altham questioned the Yardbirds backstage at the *Ready Steady Go!* studios in Wembley Park: 'Keith Relf expressed the desire that they should be "the first group to tell the truth" and that he was tired of "watered down interviews which said nothing".'[33] Questions then followed about various pop television programmes, haircuts and playing with the Beatles in Paris before they turned towards the band's music:

> Q. How far do you think we can go before the machine takes over from the musician. For example, haven't the Who gone too far with electronic sounds rather than music?
>
> A. Keith: The Who are creating with sounds just as surely as an artist with brush strokes. What is more important, they are original. I've been listening to a symphony on the third programme where they used effects from steel sheets, slabs of marble and 15 speakers. It was wonderful. I also believe that the Who have been inspired by us. We were always seeing them in our audience at one time either at the Marquee or Crawdaddy.
>
> Jim: The Who and ourselves are the only groups doing anything new. I think that's far better than reviving old numbers like Peter and Gordon have. We all dislike that type of song.

> Sam: I would say that Bacharach's experiments with melody have been more successful than the Who's with sound.
>
> Jeff: I was experimenting with echo effects and feed-back years ago. Now it's become the thing. The Who's effects are drawing the crowds. I think they incorporate their own sound with some of the Beach Boys style, and they are very good.[34]

Relf's response to the question about machine music showed a willingness to go outside of the pop sphere, to the classical, to help explain the band's ideas. Samwell-Smith stayed on the inside with his comment about melody, Bacharach and the Who.[35] Relf was more generous in his acknowledgement of how the bands were aligned in their mutual experiments in sound, and Beck nailed the difference by making perhaps the first published link between the Who and the Beach Boys. Neither band had more than a couple of hits, but their solidarity around their sonic aesthetic was mutually affirming. The two groups would soon appear co-headlining the opening Friday night of the Fifth National Jazz and Blues Festival in Richmond.

In June, the *Melody Maker* picked up and continued the line of dialogue, introducing the Who once more – 'A new name is being hurled around in hip circles – the Who. They are four mods from Shepherds Bush . . . Like the Animals and the Yardbirds, the Who are the products of the club scene.'[36] The violence and aggression in their performances was highlighted:

> Their music is defiant, and so is their attitude. Their sound is vicious. This is no note-perfect 'showbiz' group singing in harmony and playing clean guitar runs . . . Moon thunders round the drums. Townshend swings full circles with his right arm. He bangs out morse code by switching

> the guitar's pick-ups on and off. Notes bend and whine. He turns suddenly and rams the end of his guitar into the speaker. A chord shudders on the impact. The speaker rocks. Townshend strikes again on the rebound. He rips the canvas covering, tears into the speaker cone, and the distorted solo sputters from a demolished speaker. The crowd watch this violent display spellbound.[37]

Moving away from the Mod idea, the Who linked 'their image with what they call pop-art'.[38] 'Anyway, Anyhow, Anywhere' was 'the first pop-art single', they told the reporter: 'pop-art is something society accepts, but we represent it to them in a different form.'[39] They were now 'designing their own pop-art clothes . . . The Who are modern, short-haired rebels with a cause. There's sadism in their characters and in their music. But at least what they're doing is something NEW to the pop world.'[40]

Aligning the Who with Pop art generated press coverage and wide interest, both negative and positive. In the last week of May, Richard Green in *Record Mirror* profiled the group under the heading 'The Who's Pop-Art Disc'. The piece was illustrated with a colour image of the band in front of a poster for the sexploitation film *Primitive London*; it was shot in Soho's Great Windmill Street. Disc jockey Tony Hall, Green reported, had said 'Anyway Anyhow Anywhere' was 'the most commercial uncommercial record' and 'the record people will love to hate'.[41] Green's piece (and the record) kicked up enough interest and controversy that he attempted to put it all into some kind of context and answer some of the questions it had raised:

> It now seems that whenever a solo singer, pop group, orchestra and what have you decides to do something a bit different, that it is taken as the signal for the 'Holier than thou' to start having a go. And they were in fine form when

> the Who had the effrontery to strike out against puerile pop and attempt a new form of pop music. Something they called pop art.[42]

Green looked to Kit Lambert to help him out; one correspondent had asked why, if the record was pop art, did it include 'orthodox vocal refrains at beginning and end'? Lambert responded: 'I think the beginning of the disc is like fly paper – designed to trap the unwary and hold them there while the "damage" is done. We're in a guerrilla role, so why complain about booby traps and fifth column tactics?'[43] Answering a query about the lack of originality in lyrics generally, and in the Who's record more specifically, Lambert countered that it had shunned the formulaic: 'Where are the sure-fire commercial references to love, happy or unhappy, the folk, the whimsy, homesick, crying, wonderful?'[44] The third issue raised with Lambert was about the integrity of the band's Pop-art credentials; he said: 'Jet planes, emergency signals, city traffic. What more do you want without going to the sound effects library? It's going to be very difficult to put pop art principles into lyrics.'[45] Lambert finished his spiel on Pop art by explaining how it was based on taking the everyday and placing it into a new context. Fundamentally, the 'statements it makes are very, very simple. One record, one idea.'[46] The self-imposed limits of the form mean there's only 'room for a few more records like ["Anyway Anyhow Anywhere"], but not many'.[47] He concluded:

> As far as I'm concerned, the Who have managed to get the attitude of kids into their record. Certainly their London fans have the 'if I want to do something, I'm going to do it' view. It's possible that others feel the same way. But at least kids can identify their feelings with the lyrics. And the sound is one that they like, which must be of some consequence.[48]

And on the story ran into the hot summer months, as it reached a kind of summit with a letter, 'Pop 'N' Who', from Flaubert in Stratford, which was no doubt composed by a member of *Record Mirror*'s editorial staff, or more than likely by Lambert himself:

> That controversy over the Who and their interpretation of pop music. I'd like to point out that even in serious music Stravinsky was booed and hissed at the first public performance of his 'Rite of Spring'. And today great composers like Berg, Ives and Schomberg are still not really accepted by the majority of so-called music lovers, simply because they have had the courage to break away from the old traditions. Although the Who cannot be classed as serious musicians (I don't mean this slighting, in their own style they are second to none), they are carrying the same wave of experimentation into the field of beat music as the above-named composers. Whatever one's opinion of pop-art, there is no doubt that the Who are the avant-garde of refreshing, unhackneyed popular music.[49]

When the Yardbirds were tentatively denied work visas to the United States on the grounds that they were not 'original', Relf responded by suggesting the band had jettisoned the 'most blueswailing' tag:

> Sonny Boy Williamson called us that. It stuck. But now we're not playing under the shadow of the Negro anymore, we have developed our own style. I don't consciously try to sing like a Negro, although I did in the early days. We have a lot of way-out sounds that we now use, like feedback and cross rhythms . . . A twelve-bar blues is great but not time and time again![50]

Rather than push towards a more aggressive declaration of novelty like the Who, the Yardbirds – at least on their recordings – followed the pattern of 'For Your Love' with another Graham Gouldman number, 'Heart Full of Soul'.[51] Samwell-Smith told *Melody Maker*:

> 'Heart Full of Soul' has really only 12-string guitar playing the melody, with six-string on the solo. Numbers with this type of arrangement cut out that continuous jangle sound of too many instruments playing the melody line. I feel a record swings more with few musicians. They can knit together more. That was partly due to Ron Prentice playing double bass – I was in the studio supervising![52]

Like most reviews of the single, the *NME* responded positively:

> 'Yardbirds – First Class.' After a dramatic crashing opening with reverberating twangs, the Yardbirds' 'Heart Full of Soul' (Columbia) settles into a medium pacer with crashing cymbals. As a backing to the soloist, the other boys indulge in wild flights of ethereal falsetto chanting. There are a few fascinating tempo changes, but generally the treatment is not so way out as 'For Your Love'. Performance is again first-class. A strong 'B' side, too. It's a slowly pounding blues instrumental with [an] accent on some intricate guitar work and harmonica solo. Good stuff.[53]

As Chris Dreja said, 'The Yardbirds are always trying to get hold of new advanced sounds.'[54]

In a side note, *Melody Maker* reported in August that Pete Townshend was 'keen to hear LPs by jazz avant-gardist Albert Ayler'.[55] Elsewhere in the same issue, Bob Dawbarn wrote a humorous guide to 'Jazz-upmanship', 'How to Fool the Cool . . .'[56] There were three types of jazz fans: the Traditionalists, who swot up on

DAILY MIRROR, Wednesday, November 10, 1965 PAGE 17

PICTURING: THE MARCH OF TIME DOWN MOD STREET

by
Dixon Scott

THEN Boaters and knickerbockers . . . top hats and flat hats and high stiff collars . . . an old cart . . . and The Shakespeare pub—the "Noted Whisky House"—that was Carnaby-street in Edwardian times.

NOW New faces in the old setting . . . long-haired, hatless and casual geared . . . the Yardbirds pop group—with "Mod King" John Stephen on the right—buy all their clothes" down Carnaby."

LOOK, man, that's how it used to be, that's what it was like in Carnaby-street, London, sixty years' ago.

Today it's the Kingdom of the Mods—and John Stephen, with his eight fashion boutiques for boys, is the Mod King of Carnaby.

Look . . . the street isn't all that much different.

The Shakespeare pub—the "noted whisky house" on the right—has had a face-lift. There's a lick of paint here and there on the shops on the left.

But the people. . . .

Back in the Edwardian era between 1901 and 1910—when the old picture was taken—the Boer War was ending, Income Tax was 1s. 2d. in the £, haircuts were threepence and music hall artistes like Marie Lloyd were the pop stars of the day.

Whistling

Those knickerbockered and flat-capped lads in the foreground would be whistling "Goodbye Dolly, I Must Leave You," or "My Old Man Said Follow the Van."

The chap with the clay pipe just leaving The Shakespeare and the fellow in the straw boater on the other side of the road were with-it kids, having recently adopted tailless coats for everyday wear.

And the ladies . . . well, they've got about fifteen years to wait before doing a Shrimpton with their skirts in the Roaring Twenties.

ANYWAY, time passed, as they say, and along came John Stephen.

A shop that would have cost £1 a week to rent when the old picture was taken cost Stephen £7 10s. a week in 1957—the year he opened his first boutique for boys.

Today you would have to pay an average of £100 a week for a medium-size shop "down Carnaby"—if you could get one.

But older shopkeepers are only just managing to hang on, it would seem.

Fantastic

A dry cleaners is sandwiched between Paul's Male Boutique and His Clothes. The ancient tobacconists, Inderwicks (Est. 1797) is hemmed in by Toppers Shoes and Domino Male. Male West One leans on an ironmongers.

John Stephen now has four boys' boutique competitors in the street and an estate agent who has handled several property deals is awed himself at the soaring shop values.

"It's fantastic," he said. "A back street has become one of London's hottest properties. It has come from nowhere . . ."

Well, not quite from nowhere. We know now it was there, pretty well the same, sixty years ago.

It's not so much the street has changed, as that the street has changed its people.

'Long-haired, hatless and casual geared' – personifying the Mod(ern), the Yardbirds posing in Carnaby Street, *Daily Mirror*, 10 November 1965.

'obscure Jabbo Smith numbers' and drink pints of bitter in a proletarian manner; the Modernists, who 'practice a knowing look for use during the more complex solos . . . It is permitted to like certain pop artists just to demonstrate that your tastes are really rather wide. Georgie Fame and the Animals are OK names. Never Donovan or the Stones.'[57] The last category was the Avant-Gardists, who

> Always carry a couple of ESP record sleeves. It's not essential to actually own the records – most shops will order the sleeves for you . . . Remember that nobody is likely to argue with your pronouncements on Avant Garde. A few well-rehearsed phrases like 'sounds of tomorrow', 'naked passion' or 'that Albert Ayler. Man . . .!' should see you through most conversations.[58]

The issue's jazz-and-pop theme was rounded out by the lead letter in that week's 'Mailbag'. Under the heading 'Roland Kirk – Man Behind the Who?', John Patience in Romford, Essex, wrote: 'After hearing several Roland Kirk records I think he is jazz's answer to the Who. Kirk's frantic solos and freak sound effects influenced Pete Townshend's electrical feedback and Roger Daltrey's wild cymbal smashing. We should see Roland Kirk in the chart soon!'[59]

Promoting his debut single, 'The Wizard', eighteen-year-old Marc Bölan was invited by *London Life* to review the new record releases, and in doing so showed a level of perception that was straight out of the Nik Cohn school of pop criticism. Bölan thought that Dylan had made his 'guitar sound like a motor-bike', while Nina Simone played her 'piano like a motor-bike'; as for the Who, he said the title track of their first LP 'really swings', but overall he thought *My Generation* was 'a bad LP' and then gave them a brilliant back-handed comment: Charlie Mingus's *Oh Yeah* album sounded to him like everyone who played on it was 'out of their heads' but 'after one track you know where the Who got their sound from'.[60]

Remarkably (or not, if it was Lambert and Stamp's New Action office who were penning the letters), *Melody Maker* published another high-cultural apologia for the band's antics:

> So the Who are over-amplified. So what? I thought that was the whole idea, and it comes off too. They are highly professional and they are not boring either. Visually they are

> today's most dynamic group and musically the most original since Edgar Vares [*sic*; Edgard Varése] wrote 'Ionization' and 'Poeme Electronique'. The Who provide a perfect break-away from the insipid world of Baez, Honeycombs, Reeves and Co. – A. G. Forrest, Farnborough, Hants.[61]

A letter writer to *Music Echo* was on the same track:

> Being a jazz and blues fanatic, I only listen abstractly to most of today's popular music. I must admit that The Who and the music they play generate a very exciting atmosphere which lights up something in everyone. Each of their records have been original and exciting and very good atmospherically. I am looking forward to their LP release.[62]

The letters were all pretentious, but there was something in this reaching for concepts that usually lay outside of the pop sphere. Able to pick up on what this was signifying, Gomelsky called what the Yardbirds purveyed 'freeform rock and roll'; it was as good a description of their self-concept as any that had been laid at their feet or in the music papers' letters pages.[63]

Townshend, however, was the rocker who said it was permissible to like modern jazz: 'I'm mad on it. My favourites are John Coltrane and Charlie Parker, their records number in the hundreds in my collection . . . I wrote our latest hit ["Anyway Anyhow Anywhere"] – and that was inspired by a Charlie Parker number.'[64] In January 1966, *Melody Maker* reported that the American avant-garde label ESP was promoting an 'impromptu happening at London's Marquee Club':

> This modern 'way out' Giant Mystery Happening is an evening of spontaneous avant garde music which will be provided by Pete Townshend (guitar and amplifier); Keith Rowe (electric sitar and guitar); Cornelius Cardew (electric

> piano and transistor radio); Graham Bond (Mellotron and alto); Ginger Baker (drums); Mike Taylor (piano): and it is also hoped that David Izenzon (bass) will be able to attend.[65]

As it turned out, the star attraction, Townshend with his guitar *and* amplifier, was unavailable; the Who were performing at the Beachcomber club in Leigh, Lancashire, on the night of the scheduled 'happening', 30 January.[66] In his place, a Who record was played ... *Melody Maker*'s reporter was less than impressed by the night's attractions: 'What little did happen at the Happening struck me as highly pretentious nonsense.'[67] Whatever the case, the compact of the avant-garde and pop was becoming less fantastical.

In a more considered piece than those usually found in *Rave* magazine, Alan Freeman interviewed the Yardbirds. He set the context of the day's music, which no longer went in for heroes:

> Dylan is the anti-hero ... the anti-star who rips away the glittering big time uniform to reveal one small person trying to make a living at the microphone. From anti-star it's an easy jump to the anti-group, a category in which I put the Who, the Stones ... and the Yardbirds. As far as anyone can make out, the five young men of the Yardbirds are the least groupy group on the entire pop scene.[68]

Gomelsky told him that when the band played Paris with the Beatles, French jazzmen were 'knocked out' by the Yardbirds because they were playing this futuristic rock 'n' roll, very original. 'But', he cautioned, 'you have to be careful about this futuristic thing, all the same. You can get too smart and try to use all the electronic noises and find yourself in a dark alley from which there's no return ... You get trapped when you cut down melody and depend on effects.'[69] Gomelsky again cited the Who as having fallen foul of this trap.

Snare or not, more and more bands turned to noise as an effective part of their repertoire.

The Small Faces' debut single, 'Whatcha Gonna Do about It', was reviewed in *Melody Maker* the same week as Ayler and Kirk were getting in on the action with the Who: 'Starts with that great Solomon Burke "Everybody Needs Somebody" beat, but it's a bit thin to come off. Not the Doris Troy version of the same title. Latest modern guitar solo using slides and feedback – a good disc but lacking in decisive punch.'[70] In *Disc Weekly*, Penny Valentine thought that the single had real promise but was 'a bit worried about that Who-type guitar break in the middle. An unnecessary resort really.'[71] Mike Chamberlain at *Music Echo* described the break as a 'supposedly Pop Art middle eight' that 'sounds like a disturbed beehive but no doubt is only a tortured electric guitar'.[72] All very third rate, he thought. Early coverage of the Small Faces hit on the comparison between them and the Who: 'It has been said, and fairly frequently lately at that, that Small Faces think they are the Who. That they copy their dress. That their playing is based on that of the Who.'[73] 'Forget it!' was Steve Marriott's response:

> We've only been together eight weeks, right? For that time, we're not bad. I'm not saying I can play the guitar, but I admire the playing of Pete Townshend and I admire the playing of Dave Davies and I admire the playing of Eric Clapton. The easiest of those styles for me to follow was Pete Townshend's, so I did. But we just don't copy the Who ... We don't use feedback now ... We did the record four or five weeks ago. I could kick myself for it now.[74]

Penny Valentine damned the 'Birds as mimicking the Shepherd's Bush quartet: 'I suppose all Who fans will love Birds' "No Good Without You Baby". Personally, I find these sort of records rather grim but it's well done enough with them fighting for sound under water and a foul guitar break.'[75] 'The Eyes', Valentine wrote, 'play a very strange sort of music . . . it's sort of nurtured Who music.'[76] She said much the same about Carnaby: 'a cross between the Who and the Kinks'.[77] The band posed for pictures in the West End location from which they were unimaginatively named. They were dressed by Carnaby Street's top retailer, John Stephen, who designed their 'Op Art gear . . . We reckon we've got a sound of our own,' said vocalist John Cahillane: 'We haven't deliberately gone after a special one. It just happened.'[78] Others looking for their 'own sound' included the Mark Four, the pre-Creation unit who hit the feedback switch on 'I'm Leaving', the flip of their August-released single for Decca. Before he was Bowie, Davy Jones (and the Lower Third), with 'You've Got a Habit of Leaving', had stretched his bid for novelty with a straight cop of the Who – that it was a Shel Talmy production can come as no surprise – also released in August. The following month, the Syndicats' 'Crawdaddy Simone' took Charlie Rich's 'Mohair Sam' into the Scene Club basement and got Joe Meek to create a spasmed, beautifully ugly climax. The Pink Floyd would read these runes as they played and visited London's clubs that autumn.

As the Yardbirds and the Who pulled out of the R&B scene and swerved into the pop concourse, they used sounds and tonalities, eclectic instruments and loud amplification to disabuse listeners of their received expectations – but they would not be alone for long, as the Small Faces' 'modern guitar' attack made patently clear. As did the fuzz-box featured on the Rolling Stones' latest, '(I Can't Get No) Satisfaction', which *Record Mirror* thought 'somewhat dirgy' but a hit nonetheless.[79] The Yardbirds, however, seemed to escape direct imitators on the London scene; in that respect, the Who took poll position. In 1966, in the North American market, the situation would be reversed – with free-form rock 'n' roll, the Yardbirds had the field to themselves.

Keeping up with the trends was a defining trait of the summer of 1965. The novelty of sonic explorations within an accelerating pop culture still held the attention of some but, within this niche, the Yardbirds registered a shift that moved things on from the sound of guitars mimicking an over-revving engine on to the drone beneath its reverberations.

PROMOTING THE FOLLOW-UP to 'For Your Love', in television appearances, Relf wore dark sunglasses straight out of the Roy Orbison style book and delivered the introductory lines of 'Heart Full of Soul' in fittingly abject desolation – he's sick in heart, lonely and in deep, dark despair. The initial reaction to the single rested on not its emotional punch but its instrumental hooks; *Record Mirror* noted the return of the guitar to the band's sound:

In the studio: 'Heart Full of Soul' sheet music, 1965.

> This time it's without Eric Clapton. But there's still that tremendously powerful sound that this group generate. A smooth, yet powerful beat and some rather interesting lyrics. Better probably than their last and not at all similar. Great guitar work and of course, a chart success. Flip is slow blues, with strained, almost tortuous guitar work and a pounding drumbeat – plus no vocal.[80]

A month earlier, in *Disc Weekly*, Relf had said that the new single would have a 'strangely oriental sound about it. We are using something called a sitar. It's a very long Indian gourd instrument with about 80 strings. You get a sort of drone sound.'[81]

Beat Instrumental carried news of the single's imminent release and continued the theme introduced by Relf:

> written, again, by Graham Gouldman, but this time has an 'Oriental' sound about it . . . taped at Advision Studios in New Bond Street and has Chris Dreja, rhythm guitarist, using an Indian sitar (dictionary definition: a guitar with a long neck and a varying number of strings) and a tabla, which apparently is a type of drum.[82]

The following month, the magazine expanded on this notice, describing how the guest players couldn't deliver on the band's demands, and how Beck

> opens the song with a unique 'Oriental' guitar figure which virtually makes the record. He did this with the aid of a fuzz-box borrowed from guitarist Jimmy Paige [*sic*]. This fuzz-box is similar to the one used to produce the whining guitar solo in P. J. Proby's 'Together' [1964]. The tabla sound was replaced by Keith playing bongos.[83]

The piece concluded with

> news for those who think The Who are the first group to come up with that 'distorted' sound. Apparently The Yardbirds have been doing this type of thing for some time – perhaps not to the same extent – and are still constantly experimenting with different effects that can be used on stage. Says Keith: 'I remember a good year ago, Eric Clapton (the group's former lead guitarist) was working with feedback and so on.'[84]

The *NME* described the Yardbirds single as having

> a distinct r-n-b flavour and a plaintive quality. A twangy strident riff opens the track, and underlines the vocal throughout. The midtempo rhythm is rather slower than many of the group's hits. The combination of that insidious, resonant guitar work, and the simple lyrics which requires no effort to memorize, is sure to mean another high chart placing.[85]

'The Yardbirds keep it strange,' wrote Penny Valentine in her review of the single.[86] She naturally compared it with its predecessor, finding it had the 'same sort of rather disjointed and highly uncatchy melody line. All of which makes it rather fascinating.'[87]

The oriental novelty had enough resonance to eventually invade the pages of *Ladies' Home Journal*:

> Have you heard . . . where the New Sound's next big twang is coming from? The folk and rock are both facing East – priming for an invasion of Indian sitars. The sitar, a magnificently complicated Oriental guitar, is already being fingered by such popstar strummers as England's Yardbirds and Beatle George Harrison.

> Actually, the Yardbirds haven't quite mastered the inscrutable sitar themselves – they recruited an Indian, one Diwan Motihar, to thwack if for their last hit record. Motihar, a regular with an Indian musical group led by John Mayer, can be spotted in a couple of background shots in *Help!*, the Beatles' latest flick. It was in *Help!* that Harrison got hooked on the Indian sound, decided to Beatle-ize it. (No word yet on the world's first electronic sitar, but it *must* be coming soon.)[88]

The Yardbirds demoed Graham Gouldman's composition during the session for 'My Girl Sloopy' and 'I'm Not Talking' on 13 April, the novelty of the harpsichord replaced with the sitar. The initial run-through used a player unfamiliar with pop time signatures, pinging on the off-beat, slowing things down, when it needed to be driving the theme home. On the fully realized version, recorded a week later, Beck substituted a twelve-string electric and amplified guitar for the sitar, and the contrast with the demo is striking. The recording has a propulsive energy undergirded by the rhythmic popping of the bongos and the percussive, reverb-less double bass played by session man Ron Prentice, a veteran of the Wood Green Stompers and various dance bands.

It was not only the exotic aspect in a pop context that Beck and the band were looking for from the sitar but its droning qualities, which matched Relf's mannered, flattened vocals; these querulously styled elements have the effect of creating an undertow, pulling back the careering rhythmic push of Jim McCarty's drums and all the additional percussion, producing a tension in the torque and release that underscores the song's theme of love lost. Cloaked in self-pity, Relf delivers a lament, a maudlin call to the realm of the dead to release the object of his grief. He is Orpheus descending into the underworld to reclaim his departed love, Eurydice. The couple can return to the world if he remains steadfast and does not look behind to ensure she is following him in his ascent. But his desire is too strong, his will too weak, and he turns. This time he loses her forever – where is she, tell me where?

The record shared thematic and sonic elements with the Kinks' 'See My Friends', released shortly after 'Heart Full of Soul' started its slow drop down the charts in the last week of July. The band's manager, Larry Page, had wanted 'Ring the Bells' as the band's single, but producer Shel Talmy won the argument.[89] Reviewing the Kinks disc for *Music Echo*, Mike Chamberlain wrote:

> Imagine four Kinks sitting cross-legged in an Indian curry house playing sitahs [*sic*] and you've got a rough picture of the Kinks' new record . . . Except perhaps that it's fantastic and is the best record the group have released. In this they have achieved a unique sound . . . Vocal matches perfectly the moody style of the disc.[90]

If the sitar version stayed in the vaults, knowledge of the attempt to entwine Western and Eastern forms was roundly discussed, especially Beck's ability to mimic the instrument. The attempt would be seen as a foundation for subsequent sonic experiments and assimilation of Indian music, most notably by the Beatles with 'Norwegian Wood' (1965) and the Stones with 'Paint It Black' (1966), which one wit, who'd written to the music press, described as the new 'Tabla-Motown sound'.[91]

Before his time in either Led Zeppelin or the Yardbirds, and like Brian Jones, Jimmy Page had understood the value of the sitar, if only as a prop for posing with (as did Donovan in 1966).[92] He had bought the instrument from Diwan Motihar, the player invited to guest on the initial session of 'Heart Full of Soul'.[93] When the Yardbirds promoted 'Over Under Sideways Down' on the BBC's *A Whole Scene Going* Ravi Shankar was also a guest on the show and Relf and Beck, sitting cross-legged alongside others, got to ask the man a few questions, all very respectful and entirely superficial.[94]

'Heart Full of Soul' entered the Top 10 at no. 9 on 3 July, the same week that 'For Your Love' also hit no. 9 in the States. The following week, in Britain, 'Heart Full of Soul' went to no. 4, then climbed to no. 2, where it stayed, held off the top spot by the Byrds' 'Mr Tambourine Man'. At month's end, the Beatles 'Help!' went straight in at no. 1, and the Yardbirds dropped to no. 6.

To maintain traction in the USA, while not touring there, the band were filmed alongside the Who and others at the Fifth National Jazz and Blues Festival, at Richmond Athletic Ground, on 6 August. Directed by American producers for the syndicated *Shindig!* television programme, two numbers were eventually broadcast in December: 'For Your Love' and 'My Girl Sloopy'. The latter had first appeared in the United States on the *For Your Love* LP in July, then in Britain on the *Five Yardbirds* EP, released on the same day as the festival. It should have remained in the vaults alongside their first stab at 'Heart Full of Soul'.[95]

'My Girl Sloopy' was a cover of a Bert Berns and Wes Farrell composition, first recorded by the Vibrations on Atlantic early in 1964.[96] In July 1965, retitled 'Hang on Sloopy', it was a hit for the studio band the McCoys on Berns's Bang Records and, as the first release on Andrew Loog Oldham's Immediate Records, it hit the charts in Britain in August. Reviewing the record for *Disc Weekly*, pop star Jonathan King predicted it wouldn't 'be a hit in 4,000,000 years. It's just another "Louie Louie".'[97] He was right about that last point at least. Reviewing the November charts for *Disc Weekly*, Relf said of 'Hang on Sloopy' that it was 'a bit near the "Twist and Shout" type. The Vibrations original is better. McCoys have done a good job – their harmonies are nice.'[98] Reviewing the Yardbirds EP, *Melody Maker*'s critic called 'My Girl Sloopy' 'a great number', but this version was 'lacking in presence'.[99]

That the song had earning potential was clearly why the Yardbirds recorded it back in April of the same year. The Vibrations version was foremost designed as a party record, indicated not only by the upbeat tempo but by having the sound of merrymakers overdubbed (just like the babbling voices on some copies of James Brown's 'Please Please Please' single, and those on a good few Beach Boys discs). Relf can rave with the best of them, but he doesn't do 'happy'. His vocals are typically joyless in affect, and the song drags on for just over five minutes. The chart placing that the McCoys achieved and the Yardbirds' live take, as the *Shindig!* footage suggests, was why the idea seemed like it might have had prospects, but it is best listed as a failed attempt at being 'commercial'. The EP's delayed release to make way for the far more in-character 'Heart Full of Soul' suggested band and management were somewhat in agreement with this assessment.

On the EP's flip, however, are two of the finest sides the Yardbirds recorded: a cover of Mose Allison's 'I'm Not Talking' and Keith Relf's rewrite of Elmore James's 'Done Somebody Wrong', retitled 'I Ain't Done Wrong'. The bell has tolled, and Elmore's baby has left him. He must have done somebody wrong, but who, and is it all his fault? James is all over confused. On the other hand, Relf accepts he's to blame but doesn't care anyway, he's gonna get a new doll and hope his luck changes. That lyrical shift and the Yardbirds' concussive approach turned James's pitching slide motif into a machine-hammered beat, guitar lashing with and between drum rolls. Beck duels with Relf's harp, crescendo follows lull, pause after acceleration: signature Elmore James transformed into signature Yardbirds. Such conversions justified the band's songwriting credit, so they would have argued.

What the Yardbirds did to Elmore James they also did to Mose Allison, though they left his songwriter credit alone – he was still alive, James was dead. Allison was a darling of art-school common rooms; his seemingly effortless bridging of rustic and sophisticated, country and city, black and white, modern and traditional styles was conjoined by a reserved cool that made him sound like no other, until Georgie Fame. The boys and girls in their art-school days looked to similarly cross the divides, most usually between home and exile, their time studying art also a time to figure out adult identities (or refuse them, to be forever adolescent). Part of the attraction of Allison's music was his undoubted authenticity, a white Southern man who played in a mixed-race trio and who had, it appeared, permission to play the blues, yet who vocalized without blatant imitation of Black voices. Allison seemed to take the blues into the modern age, an ambition that the Yardbirds shared. He was a model worth emulating, as Townshend surely comprehended with the Who's covers of 'Young Man Blues', 'Eyesight for the Blind' and 'One Room Country Shack'.

Allison played on the same bill as the Yardbirds at the fourth National Jazz and Blues Festival in August 1964; they had lifted 'I'm Not Talkin'' from that year's *The Word from Mose*, his third album for Atlantic. The Yardbirds kick his song in the head with two drum rolls under revving guitars before exploding down the straight, Beck riding the clutch into the corners, Dreja, McCarty and Samwell-Smith pumping full throttle, no let up. 'I'm Not Talking' is 100 per cent greased-up rock 'n' roll, the toughest number recorded in Britain in 1965, no question, no argument. It is a fulsome precursor to the Who's 'My Generation', scratching the same attitude and style into a Bentley's paintwork. Both numbers reached the same conclusion that talking only breeds confusion – things said at midnight might not be said in the morning.

Gomelsky wasted the two tracks by hiding them on the ragbag *For Your Love* album, squeezed between Clapton-era rejects of Major Lance's 'Sweet Music' and the Shirelles' 'Putty (In Your Hands)', both trite exercises in the Yardbirds' hands that fail as pop and anything else they might have aspired towards; the rest of the album included the six sides from the first three singles and 'Sloopy'. 'I'm Not Talking' and 'I Ain't Done Wrong' would have been better held in reserve to be coupled with subsequent singles and the numbers they would record in the States.

A problem the band had was finding time between incessant gigging, not just for recording but for developing new material. Everything appeared to be done on the run and, with Gomelsky having to cover recording expenses, time away from doing paying shows to time in the studio had a double cost factor for him. Penny Valentine attended a practice session at the Marquee Club one early summer afternoon:

> These sorts of rehearsals are rare in the group's busy life. They have a basic repertoire to which they usually add about one song every two months. This is because they have only a have few spare days to which they can devote to new numbers. They alternate these rehearsals between the Crawdaddy and the Marquee because they are the places they feel most at home. Even though they have to make it a 'quiet noise' at the Marquee because of the people working in the offices above. At midday on Thursday they were running through their latest addition – the Curtis Mayfield number 'I'm Trying' [actually 'I've Been Trying', the B-side of the Impressions' 'People Get Ready', which the Yardbirds first publicly performed on a BBC Radio *Top Gear* session recorded 21 June] – and eating sandwiches in between discussing arrangements.[100]

The band had tracked their third Graham Gouldman composition, 'Evil Hearted You', at the end of August. It would be coupled with Samwell-Smith and McCarty's 'Still I'm Sad', which was completed at the same session, having been part-recorded at the end of July. Of the latter, Samwell-Smith told *Disc Weekly*: 'It is certainly very weird – but not Who-like weird. It sounds a bit like a Gregorian monk's chant!'[101] The idea was to promote both tracks as 'As', though Gouldman's song received the greater interest and notices and led the flight up the charts. 'Evil Hearted You' entered the Top 10 on 16 October at no. 10, while 'Still I'm Sad' trailed at no. 20.

Scarecrow Keith Relf and his fellow 'Birds: 'Evil Hearted You' sheet music, 1965.

Beat Instrumental's Brian Clark attended the final recording session for the single, which mostly consisted of vocal takes (including a subsequently unreleased Italian version of 'Heart Full of Soul'). As a guide to the sound that they were after, McCarty and Samwell-Smith had brought with them an acetate of folk group the Silkie's cover of the Beatles' 'You've Got to Hide Your Love Away'. The Silkie's single had been produced by Lennon and was set for release in the second week of September, its echoic bottom-end to be recreated on 'Still I'm Sad'. It was a late-night session that began at 7 p.m. and ended at 3 a.m. Samwell-Smith took charge of 'Still I'm Sad', but Gomelsky was 'full of suggestions on how the vocal tracks should be sung. He was very meticulous because it's not a straightforward harmony or unison vocal.'[102] The 'unusual choir-type vocal work' was complemented by an 'organ sound from Jeff Beck's Telecaster, the effect is remarkable. Something like a Sunday morning church service on the Light programme.'[103] The session concluded with 'Evil Hearted You', 'a pounding up-tempo number completely in contrast to "Still I'm Sad"'.[104] The following day, they were off to the United States.

Rave magazine predicted the single, with its 'Gregorian chant', would storm up the chart, while the flip, 'reminiscent of "For Your Love"[,] is as invigorating as a gusty autumnal day'.[105] 'For Your Love' had been 'plaintive' and 'Heart Full of Soul' 'maudlin', and 'Evil Hearted You' continued to extend such mawkish themes; it had a 'suitably sinister' sound according to John Sandilands in the *Daily Mail*, and had hit him like a 'drum being beaten with a human head'.[106] Beyond the skull-on-snare-drum reverberations, Derek Johnson writing for the *NME* described some of the other sounds on the disc:

> Forceful Yardbirds. Strident twanging and cymbal crashing sets the mood for the medium-paced 'Evil Hearted You' (Columbia), the latest potential hit from the Yardbirds. Treatment is solo voice with falsetto chanting from the other boys with the minor key emphasising the plaintive effect. After a sudden break in the rhythm, there's a startling change of tempo, as in 'For Your Love'. It's extremely forceful, has a tremendous impact, and there's a great guitar interlude. This is a double-A disc, which means that the other side is regarded as equally important ... 'Still I'm Sad' opens with unison humming taking the melody line, and this continues as support for the soloist when he takes up the lyric. Effective![107]

Penny Valentine in *Disc Weekly* thought the idea of a double-A was just wrong 'when "Still I'm Sad" is so super and "Evil Hearted You" so dull': 'Keeping up with the reputation of turning out unusual discs, "Sad" sounds like a song to the Incas Sun God. Massive male chorus do humming bits and Keith sings wistfully about moonlight on hair. It's very way-out and very brave and I love it. Gives me the shivers.'[108] Sun gods, severed heads, Sunday church services and chanting may have accounted for the 'religious connotation' that Samwell-Smith said many listeners had found, but he didn't think there was any, and besides, he preferred to discuss his recording technique (Gomelsky is nowhere to be seen in this) with *Record Mirror*'s Richard Green:

> 'You start with a drum sound because that takes the longest. I use four or five mikes – one for the high hat, get the bass muffled, one for the snare and one for the tom tom. You get a good sound by equalizing. I put the drums and bass on the same track. The electric bass goes through a twelve-inch speaker, not a bass guitar amplifier, that gives you a very punchy sound,' he explained. 'The rhythm and lead you can do wherever you like. You should do backing with all four and maybe a guide voice. A good voice enables you to get the feel.'
>
> When they visited America, the Yardbirds did some recording with Sam Phillips who produced early Elvis Presley discs for Sun [Records]. 'He put drums, bass and rhythm on one track, then lead on another which left two tracks clear for vocals,' the Yardbird Sam told me. 'Everything is much simpler that way. But I would stick to our technique.'[109]

In pretty much all the band's encounters with the press they expressed their pleasure in the creative environment of the recording studio, a pride in their sonic experiments and their delight in producing pop records, but the reality of their existence was that relative to touring, little time was spent recording.

THE BAND'S DEPARTURE for the States had been delayed on a number of occasions and different excuses had been given each time – 'a lot of people being on holiday', for example.[110] The crucial reason was failure to gain the support of the American Federation of TV and Radio Artists, which had caused the cancellation of bookings for Hullabaloo, Shindig and the Ed Sullivan Show – they eventually flew out from London on Thursday, 2 September.[111] While in New York, it had earlier been reported, they hoped to set up an 'experiment in sound' at Columbia's recording studios with the idea of producing an EP.[112] *Record Mirror*'s Richard Green was with them in the hours before their flight. The visas allowed the band to make live appearances, they believed, but they couldn't perform before television cameras. Expectations, then, were not particularly high; no one anticipated being met by screaming fans: 'It's a kind of promotional tour for us with a view to returning for a proper tour later in the year. If we had gone out there on a Freddie and the Dreamers tour we would have been in their shadow.'[113] It was crucial, Samwell-Smith said, that the band was not seen as just another English pop import: 'We want to appear as an intelligent group, not a lot of long-haired people that can't do anything.'[114] Asked about what kind of show Americans might expect, Samwell-Smith replied,

> We'll have to cut out all the ravings. They can go on too long . . . I think the Who have made a slight mistake in doing too much. People go to see them expecting lots of things and they get them but it ends there. With us in America, we can't just foist things on them. I think they're more intelligent than British audiences, but it's got to be a gradual thing, a building up of our image.[115]

Keeping out of the shadows thrown by Freddie and the Dreamers was one thing, but leaving the Who behind was another.

For now, however, as the band told Green over the telephone from Los Angeles, they were having an 'English style rave-up' in a house owned by Bob Markley, a singer and songwriter, independently wealthy and friend of pop maven Kim Fowley.[116] His home was located more than 300 metres (1,000 ft) above the city. Fowley acted as Master of Ceremonies.[117] LA's weekly paper *The Beat* reported directly from the three-tiered modern house, which they erroneously wrote was owned by Fowley. The Yardbirds used borrowed equipment and 'gave us an hour of the most fantastic sound you've *ever* heard!' Singled out was Beck's use of feedback: 'the tremendous lead guitar of Jeff . . . Talk about working a guitar – well, Jeff *slaves* his!'[118] Gomelsky ran down the band's (and his) history for the paper. The previous week they had been the paper's cover stars; the inside story in this issue was how badly they had been received, not by fans but by the labour unions, hoteliers and Disneyland – unable to play for money, refused permission to appear on television, rejected from hotels and denied entrance to Fantasia . . .[119]

The band were in the States for the best part of the first three weeks of September, playing gigs in Oklahoma, Arizona, California, Tennessee, New York and Chicago, and avoiding or ignoring the union injunction. Cancelled dates in Pennsylvania, Kentucky and Texas suggest how poorly organized the jaunt had been. Like the Stones recording sessions in Chicago and Hollywood, the Yardbirds also booked time at Chess and RCA studios, as well as at Sam Phillips Recording Service (not Sun Studios) in Memphis. Unlike the Stones' well-planned dates, the Yardbirds' endeavours appear to have been smash-and-grab events: two days at RCA laying down unreleased versions of 'I'm a Man' and 'Steeled Blues', an overnight session in Memphis recording the backing tracks for 'The Train Kept a-Rollin'' and 'You're a Better Man than I' that followed two sets on the same day at different locations in the city two days earlier on 10 September and another in nearby Little Rock, the day before recording with Phillips (a fact that puts Gomelsky's much-told story of the band pensively hanging around waiting for Phillips, who was supposedly on a fishing trip, in some doubt).[120] A further day at Chess for the backing track to 'I'm a Man' followed, and one final day at Columbia to put the finishing overdubs and vocals and record a new number, 'New York City Blues'. *Rave*'s American correspondent summed up the trip:

> Despite a catastrophic American tour where everything happened to them from having their instruments pinched to their equipment blowing up, the Yardbirds did have some highlights during their trip. In Memphis, they recorded the backtracks for a new single at Sun Studios in a twelve-hour

KRLA BEAT

Volume 1, Number 29 LOS ANGELES, CALIFORNIA 15 Cents October 2, 1965

Was Yardbirds' Ordeal In Vain?

Cover of *KRLA Beat* (2 October 1965).

> session which ran through the clock from night 'til morning. And in California, they hosted a party attended by Peter and Gordon, the Byrds, Phil Spector and Jackie de Shannon [*sic*].[121]

Talking to *Beat Instrumental* sometime after the band's return to Britain, Beck described Phillips's studio as 'massive', which

> gave an overall sound that we've never achieved in an English studio. It was so much wilder. And we didn't use any special effects – just a bit of echo on Keith's voice to give it a bit of lift. The thing that made a big difference I'm sure was the placing of the microphones. Each one was a good two feet away from the amplifier so you could really belt it out.[122]

Other than covering 'some of the late Johnny Burnette's songs', Beck said he was keen to record some early Gene Vincent, especially 'Cat Man' and 'Red Blue Jeans and a Pony Tail', both songs that featured on his second album. *Beat Instrumental*'s John Emery concluded with the observation that 'if you remember these songs, just imagine them adapted to the weird sound effects and way-out arrangements used by the Yardbirds.'[123] Indeed. After Hank Marvin, Beck had been voted by readers of *Beat Instrumental* as second favourite lead guitarist in the magazine's 1965 Gold Star Awards.[124]

Neither 'The Train Kept a-Rollin'' nor 'I'm a Man' received a British release during the band's lifetime, though both tracks were uniquely coupled on a German single in November. The Bo Diddley number had been released in the States in October, combined with one-half of their latest British two-sider, 'Still I'm Sad' – rising as high as no. 21 in the *Cashbox* chart in December. In his 'Hollywood Calling!' column, publicist Derek Taylor wrote: 'Yardbirds are getting very hot – they're already No. 1 in Los Angeles and in the Top 30 in the nation after only four weeks.'[125] With 'Still I'm Sad' and 'Evil Hearted You' (recorded at sessions in July and August) ready for release on the band's return from the American tour on 1 October, holding back 'I'm a Man' made sense – besides, it was already overfamiliar, with a version on *Five Live Yardbirds*, and no doubt felt to be a little too anachronistic for the domestic market when held up alongside the Gouldman-penned hit singles. Gomelsky was still heavily promoting the idea of an imminent LP release; a news item in the music press at the end of September reported that it would include 'some recently recorded tracks', and 'within the next few weeks they will be in the studio cutting more songs.'[126] The following month, *Beat Instrumental* noted that the album was finished and had been 'tailored' by Giorgio Gomelsky to show 'the versatility of the boys'.[127] It never happened, at least not in Britain.

In the North American market, a second jumble sale of album tracks was released in November, *Having a Rave-Up with the Yardbirds*. Side one was compiled from studio sessions with Beck, while side two was made up of four tracks from *Five Live Yardbirds*, its scrapbook incoherence amplified by the inclusion of a live and a studio version of 'I'm a Man'. The top deck suggests just how strong an album could have been produced from the year's recording sessions, beginning with the otherwise unreleased 'You're a Better Man Than I', followed by 'Evil Hearted You' (not on a single in the United States), 'I'm a Man', 'Still I'm Sad', 'Heart Full of Soul' and with 'The Train Kept a-Rollin'' rounding off the side. It was as good a collection of tracks as had been released by any group in 1965, and it doesn't contradict the Canadian sleeve note that 'The Yardbirds RAVE UP is a futuristic sound . . . aimed at originality and pointed at YOU!' But it all looked like meagre pickings when the Rolling Stones had released two albums of new material in the UK and three in the States that year. The Kinks had also released two albums domestically, while the Animals had three out in North America and two in Britain. The Pretty Things had two LPs in the stores by year's end, and Them had their second effort released in the first month of the New Year. For the Yardbirds, who would end 1965 as the eighth best-selling artist in Britain, this was a sorry state of affairs.

With 'Shapes of Things' in the can early in January 1966, Gomelsky could have pulled together a sterling debut studio album for the New Year, which might have run something like this:

1 Shapes of Things
2 I'm Not Talking
3 I Ain't Done Wrong
4 New York City Blues
5 Train Kept a-Rollin'
6 Heart Full of Soul
7 You're a Better Man than I
8 Evil Hearted You
9 Still I'm Sad
10 Steeled Blues
11 I'm a Man

This imaginary set stays clear of the band's first three singles and, from 1965, leaves out only 'My Girl Sloopy'. Gomelsky had made a slightly better effort for a 1965 Scandinavian collection, but it mixed Clapton-era tracks with those recorded with Beck, which sat poorly together. At least the cover image showed some imagination, using a Dezo Hoffman photograph of the band taken in a television studio. At the centre of the quintet, Relf is seated on a high stool with his hands crossed on top of bongos; to his far right, Samwell-Smith is holding a double bass; Beck and Dreja stand immediately on each side of the singer, holding their guitars; and McCarty is to his far left. The colour image shows five young hipsters, looking more like jazz modernists than long-haired R&B ravers. The U.S. *Rave-Up* sleeve was comparatively awful, the band in black suits each surrounded by an ocean of white space, looking like a 1963 Merseybeat combo. The Canadian version improved on this by using a photograph of the band posed as if supporting the arch of the mock Tudor gardener's hut in Soho Square (a location to which the band would return for subsequent promotional shoots); it at least pulled the band together, but it still left a lot to be desired and wasn't nearly as striking as the Swedish sleeve. When it came to marketing the group, Gomelsky had clearly lost sight of the plot – he should have been looking to what Andrew Loog Oldham was doing with his charges. The cover of *Out of Our Heads* made the Rolling Stones style leaders, so far in front of the Yardbirds that Gomelsky couldn't even read their name on the tails of their shirts.

In a mid-October *Melody Maker* profile of the band, they were described as 'Britain's most experimental group. While other groups talk about trying to be "different", the Yardbirds are quietly doing it.'[128] But for all that, the band felt that they were not getting the acclaim they deserved: 'things are happening for them too quietly. They appreciate the occasional pin-up, but they feel they are not getting due credit for their music.'[129] Upset with the overall lack of exposure that highlighted their sense of musical adventurism, Relf said, 'Something very drastic is going to happen . . . The present mood of the group is one of frustration. But it's a calculated period of frustration.'[130] With no new album in immediate sight and no recording sessions booked to realize one, coupled with the debacle of their first trip to the States – 'we've just come back from America, where they didn't really know us . . . and we should have had a tour there by now, or something' – their frustration was almost certainly aimed at their management.[131]

At the end of October, it was announced in *Melody Maker* that a new album would be out for Christmas to support their 'Marquee Show' tour with Manfred Mann, scheduled to start on 18 November. In any event, they planned to have it released by the time they went to the States at the end of December. The album was to be called *Yardbirds, I View*: 'one side will contain five original numbers, one from each of the group, while the other side will be typical Yardbirds arrangements of classic numbers.'[132] The problem with this plan, however, as the news item conceded, was that the band was 'so busy that they have little time to record'.[133] The idea of each band member contributing a song apiece also sounded like Gomelsky was looking to negotiate a publishing deal similar to that which Lambert and Stamp had pulled together for the Who in 1966, prior to the recording of *A Quick One*, with each band member getting a generous advance on publishing, rather than just main songwriter Townshend. Regardless, did the Yardbirds even have five original numbers between them to record? The album remained no more than a rumour, and the recording sessions never happened. The *Melody Maker* did, however, give them the kind of coverage they desired:

> 'Sound Seekers . . . Now the Searchers after the Pop Truth Are about to Launch the Pop Avant Garde'
>
> Talk of free form improvisation has been floating round the jazz world for some time, but as yet has never been applied to pop music. Not until the Yardbirds that is . . .
>
> Keith said, 'It's important . . . to be able to play your instrument to its limit. Many expert musicians who are brilliant technically wouldn't play like us or do the sort of things we do with our instruments to create emotion – like prolonged feedback, for instance. But I'm sure they'd appreciate what we are experimenting with and trying to achieve.
>
> We are applying the principles of free form improvisation and extemporization to pop music. I feel we've left behind R&B school that we used to belong to. We just use R&B numbers – and a lot of others too – as raw material for our experiments.'[134]

The band played *Melody Maker*'s Alan Walsh an acetate of 'You're a Better Man than I', which they'd recorded in Memphis:

> [It's] almost certain to be their next single release. 'It utilises some of the principles we've been talking about,' said Keith,

> 'with the free improvisation of the guitar in the middle' . . . The number certainly has some experimental noises, though there's a strain of the Gregorian chant feel about it too. And it's certainly a new sound for the Yardbirds.[135]

In parallel, Townshend and the Who pushed on in their own uniquely antithetical manner: 'Who are the Who? What do they stand for? What do they hate?' asked *Disc Weekly* of Pete Townshend:

> In this age of the anti-song, the group that makes more out of anti-ness than any other is the Who. There is, they say, a hatred in the group stronger than any other group. They hate each other. They used to make great play of breaking guitars onstage in a positive fury of hatred . . . What is the group anti, exactly. And with all this hatred around is there nothing they actually like?[136]

They were the band with built-in hate, and at the heart of their antipathy was their 'protest' single, 'My Generation'.[137] It was, Townshend said, a throwback to when Mods got pilled-up; 'now they got drunk or other things.' Pills were a phase, Townshend told Richard Green. The song's character is 'supposed to be blocked' or 'he just can't form words.'[138] Like the anachronistic Mod, Pop art too had fallen away; it was the 'one subject strangely missing' from Townshend's conversation with Green: 'Not so long ago The Who couldn't open their mouths without extolling its virtues. What has happened to it now?'[139]

The Pop-art tag may have been abandoned, but Townshend still had a sharp sense of competition, and the Yardbirds got it in the neck from him once more: '"That Yardbirds thing doesn't deserve to be a hit" he opined suddenly. "The recording technique is no good. That idea of a Gregorian war chant is useless, who wants to know

Mutual tormentors: the Who and the Yardbirds in *Rave* magazine (January 1966).

about that?"'[140] Samwell-Smith leapt to the bait that Townshend had dangled and issued a statement published in the following edition of *Record Mirror*: 'Perhaps Pete Townshend of the Who could restrict his criticisms to subjects he knows something about. He made reference to a Gregorian war chant, does he think Gregorians were just a tribe of Indians or was it just a slip of his over-stimulated tongue?'[141] Daltrey followed up with more of the same, with 'Still I'm Sad' also as his target; he told *Disc Weekly*, 'the hit parade's getting to be like a hymn sheet.'[142]

Rave magazine visually summed up the symbiosis between the Who and the Yardbirds when it split a photographic spread between them: sliced on a diagonal, the Who sat on top, and the Yardbirds formed the foundation.[143] The overstimulated tongue was back at it in the first week of December, helping (or hindering) the marketing of the Who's debut album. He hated it, rubbishing track after track:

> 'I'm a Man'. We recorded this years ago. I hate this as well. I don't actually like the LP, it strikes me as kind of weird the way there are so many numbers from different stages of our career. I only hope they don't expect us to do it on stage. It's great how I get that piano sound out of my guitar. This is probably our best recorded feedback.[144]

Facetious as ever, the Who's version of 'I'm a Man' was a dud and was duly left off the American release.[145] In its studio version, the Yardbirds' 'I'm a Man' was, by contrast, fast, hard-hitting, dynamic and beautifully concise and compact in its immediacy, a minute shorter than the Who's effort. It begins with a quickstep marching beat and then, a little before the halfway mark, turns in a false rave-up, a tease that quickly returns to the dominant rhythm for a chorus length before delivering on the promise of the provocation. The mouth harp and guitar joust with each other as the band build into the rave-up proper, leaving behind a template that a thousand garage bands so willingly followed.

Alongside the news in *Record Mirror* that another Yardbird was hitched – 'A spokesman for Giorgio Gomelsky Associates confirmed on Monday that lead guitarist Jeff Beck was married before he joined the group earlier this year' – was a report of a second trip to the States, 10 December to 25 January, which would include ten days as part of the Murray the K show at the Brooklyn Fox; a week in California was scheduled, and management intended to avoid the visa problems that had soured the previous visit.[146] Before the trip across the Atlantic, the band was teamed up with Manfred Mann for a major British tour that ran from 19 November until 5 December under the title of the 'Marquee Show'. Gomelsky was producing, and it was co-promoted by the George Cooper Organisation and Marquee Productions. Also on the bill were the Mark Leeman Five, Paul and Barry Ryan, the Scaffold and the Summer Set.[147] The Scaffold would link together the various acts: 'We're setting out to channel the audience's energy usually devoted to screaming into laughter,' group spokesman Mike McGear, Paul McCartney's brother, told *Music Echo* before the tour started.[148]

The *NME*'s reporter Alan Smith interviewed the Yardbirds as the tour got underway; 'It could be the flop of the year – or it could be the biggest thing in package shows since the invention of the electric guitar. I'm talking about the controversially different tour of Britain that Manfred Mann and the Yardbirds will make together next month.'[149] A 'Pop Satirical Revue' was promised, but Smith thought it a huge gamble: 'Even promotors who have tried to "produce" pop shows have not gone this far.'[150] Chris Dreja hoped that it would attract a more intelligent and sophisticated audience than that which usually attended package shows. 'One thing that would spoil it would be screams,' said Relf, 'You can't get away with gags and comedy if people can't hear for the noise.'[151] The Yardbirds, Smith wrote,

> place a lot of importance on doing something different. They have a contempt for groups which turn out the same stuff time after time. Says Keith: 'like the so-called way-out groups that you go along to see, and they're just doing "I'm a Hog for You Baby", like everybody else.'[152]

The concept was to break away from the standard package tour and to integrate live performance with films and comedy skits. The tour programme laid it all out:

> DON'T EXPECT THIS SHOW TO BE LIKE ANY YOU HAVE EVER SEEN BEFORE. We mean, you probably think there will be a compére – curtain – act – applause – compére – curtain – act – applause compére onononon. You've got another think coming.
>
> We think Pop Shows have stopped 'popping' but this one is going to bang. (BANG.)
>
> Take this programme – take it and hang it on the wall when you get home. Or throw it in the bathtub. Or cut it up for sandwiches. Do whatever your imagination tells you because that's what we want to do at this scene. Moaners have always said pop people are morons. We know and you know this is not so and we think we have devised a show which allows the artists to let their hair down (?) and use their talents and imagination to the fullest extent.
>
> And if they don't perform as we say, we shall 'beat' the artists until they feel absolutely free to do whatever we (they) want.

The idea was sufficiently different from standard tours of musical acts that the organizers had to get clearance from the Lord Chamberlain Office, the official censor since 1737 for theatrical performances (the law was eventually abolished in 1968).[153] The *NME* reported on the second night in Chesterfield:

> The show opened with a film featuring Manfred Mann and the Yardbirds while a taped medley of the groups' hits was played. Suddenly the cast appeared on stage out of the blackness, leaving the Mark Leeman Five to rocket their way

through three numbers. Guest stars Paul and Barry Ryan got things cracking with 'Long Tall Sally'. Then they took things calmly with 'Don't Bring Me Your Heartaches' and 'Yesterday', ending with 'Money'. They were followed by satirists the Scaffold who the audience lapped up.

It was film time again with the Yardbirds dressing in all sorts of way-out clothing. At the end of the film, the group dashed onto the stage for a fantastic reception with 'For Your Love'. Their six number stint included all their hits.

Gary Farr and the T-Bones opened the second half and their next single, 'Together', went down a bomb. The Marty Wilde Three replaced Goldie and the Vagabonds for the first three nights. With Paul Jones leaping about all over the stage. Manfred Mann with its new band sound crashed in with 'The One in the Middle' and followed with a couple of tracks from their new EP, before featuring 'Why Bother', 'With God on Our Side' and 'Do Wah Diddy'.[154]

The show at the Odeon Theatre in Derby, on Saturday, 20 November, was enthusiastically reviewed in the *Derby Evening Telegraph*:

> Anyone who went to the 'Marquee Show' at the Odeon, Derby, on Saturday night, must have wondered, at first, if they were in the right place. To say that the show was unusual is the understatement of the year. Never before in Derby has there been a 'pop' show like it, and what a mad, zany change it was.
>
> Gone were the smartly dressed singers and groups trooping on one after the other. Nearly everyone involved in this show was onstage at the same time – most of them in tee-shirts and hipster slacks.
>
> It was a show full of surprises, and you can imagine the surprise of the audience when the curtains drew apart to

> show a film of the antics of Manfred Mann. It certainly was a novel start.[155]

Disc Weekly covered the opening show of the tour in Stockton-on-Tees where Manfred Mann held the audience 'spellbound and hushed' for 'God Rest Ye Merry Gentlemen' and then, when they got too lively, asked them to 'quieten down while he sang Bob Dylan's "With God on Our Side"'.[156] The rest of their set was 'wild and energetic'. The Yardbirds' appearance was preceded by a short film of the group that 'worked the house into a frenzy even before they came on stage. Keith Relf and Chris Dreja had the crowd on their feet and rushing the stage . . . all in all, it was a successful night'. *Melody Maker* reported on a Saturday night show at the Granada East Ham and made almost exactly the same points as *Disc*'s reporter.[157] The reviewer for the Bristol *Evening Post* for the show at Colston Hall on Tuesday, 3 December, was much less impressed: 'The show which was supposed to be so different turned out to be a big disappointment. The girls screamed, the boys whistled and a lot of them threw bits of paper and sweets at the various groups.'[158] The Yardbirds, it was reported, 'were mediocre', but Paul and Barry Ryan were 'superb'.[159]

Two nights after the end of the 'Marquee Show' tour on 8 December, the Yardbirds were topping the bill at the Tower Ballroom in New Brighton. The event, called 'Zowie One', had been organized by Radio Caroline and had twelve other acts playing fifteen-minute sets. As headliners, the Yardbirds had 22 minutes to put themselves over to the half-full room of Merseysiders. Joining the band and the other artists in two reserved carriages on a train from Euston to Liverpool was British journalist Caroline Silver and her photographer husband, Nathan Silver. Their report would be published towards the end of the following year in a delightful American paperback, *The Pop Makers: British Rock 'n' Roll: The Sound, the Scene, the Action*.

The train left London just after midday, one coach given over to singing and music making, the other for quieter pastimes: 'For most of the journey rain dribbled down the coach windows. Outside, the winter Lancashire countryside, sooty with the ashes of industrial towns, raced backward.'[160] The caravan of acts arrived at Lime Street Station nearly four hours after it had set off. Met by local and national press, they posed for photographs before getting on buses to take them via the Mersey Tunnels to the other side of the river. The event began at 7 p.m. with the Yardbirds on stage at 10:50, when –

> A great roar burst from the crowd, who rushed the barriers and began to climb them. Stewards moved quickly in to hold them back as the Yardbirds went straight into 'Still I'm Sad', a slow number by Sam based on a Gregorian chant. Blink, drummer with the Mark Leeman Five, stood in the wings watching the eyes of the fans going glassy as they gazed at the Yardbirds. Almost immediately a girl fell over the railings in a faint, was picked up by a steward and carried backstage with the groups. Blink made experienced guesses as to which girl would be next over the barrier. 'Look at that one!' he'd exclaim, pointing to a girl with a fixed, moon-struck expression who was yelling 'Keith!' and 'Jeff!' and screaming between yells . . .
>
> On the higher stage the Yardbirds went into a series of fast numbers, Keith frequently doubling over the microphone with blonde hair tossing, drawing extra screams from the crowd every time he did so; Jeff doing a series of very clever imitations on his guitar, somehow getting his instrument to sound successively like a chicken, a steam roller, a car's tires squealing and an explosion.
>
> Suddenly it was over . . .[161]

Outside the venue it was still raining. The acts caught the 12:20, the last train back to London that stopped at every station and took over six hours to reach its final destination. The artists hadn't eaten dinner and there was nothing to be had on the train – not even drinking water. Two back-to-back Welsh gigs followed the next evening, and then two nights later, the same doubling-up with gigs in Illinois: Chicago and Rockford. The band's itinerary was utterly relentless.

In *The Pop Makers*, Silver titled the chapter devoted to the Yardbirds as 'Not All Roses'; she had wanted to de-emphasize the usual starry-eyed story of a pop group, to instead stress the boredom and drudgery of life on the road:

> At 6:45 a.m. the train arrived at London. A hungry, thirsty, stiff, and haggard-looking party got off into the gray morning, the fortunate to crawl off home to bed, the less fortunate onto more work, such as Jeff, Keith, Sam, Jim and Chris, who had to take a morning flight to America to start a six-week tour there. Successive days provided no newspaper coverage of the *Zowie One* show, despite the journalists and photographers who had been present. The organization and effort that had gone into the whole tiring day resulted in no financial or spiritual reward for the performers save for a few record plugs on the radio and the attention of a dishearteningly small audience.[162]

Even though they attracted the screamers and worked the crowd into a frenzy, wore hip gear and had hit records, the message the authors wanted to get across was that the Yardbirds were the era's anti-glamour band – but in such shadowed places, romance lurked.

When talking to the *NME*, Relf relayed a story of a letter from 'a girl who said one of our records made her think of autumn leaves and soft, green meadows. This is what we want. We like to feel we're producing an emotional experience in sound.'[163] Relf had started 1965 with a view of making his band commercial; by year's end, he'd achieved it, but it came at the cost of appealing to a split audience of sophisticates and screamers and playing the game of a pop star with profiles that testified to his love of puppy dogs, his own experience of courtly love and his protective zeal when it comes to his sister and the boys who fancy her.[164] Dawn James for *Rave* magazine caught the contradictions the band were plying:

> The empty club was dark except for one white spotlight shining on stage. A loud, soulful noise came from the five young men up there. The lead singer's cream suede shoes, padded shouldered jacket and skin-tight silk pants moved with him, merging cream and brown and black. The red and chrome guitarist stared at the floor in concentration and a crude, sweet sound twanged from his electric strings. The tall, thin boy with the aristocratic face stood erect . . . 'Ok let's take a break,' said the singer, and jumped down and came towards me. Keith Relf, Yardbird leader, has long fair hair and piercing blue eyes. He is frail like a sparrow and strangely, surely masculine.[165]

Relf's vulnerability, his frail heath, marked him as different from other group singers like Jagger and Daltrey. He did not pose as a threat to *Rave*'s readers. Talking, once more, of their desire to spark a synaesthetic response to the band's music, Samwell-Smith said, 'Keith and I reckon that if we could make a record that made people think they could smell damp grass or sea air when they heard it, we'd be getting somewhere.'[166] Speaking about how the non-pictorial can evoke strong emotional responses, more so than the figurative, Relf said 'Pop music is like abstract painting.'[167] Such was the intangible sensibility he was after in the band's music, but then, as if he'd gone too far in his use of pastoral imagery, he switched the scene away

Richmond Park pastoral: 'For Your Love' sheet music, 1964.

from the English countryside to the United States and his recent experience of American culture:

> 'It's a fast country,' Keith said. 'Everything is bigger and brighter and better than anything I've ever seen anywhere else. Everyone seems to have their minds fully occupied. I got in a taxi and it was sweltering hot and I said to the driver, "Gosh it's hot!" and he said. "Yer." So I said, "This is my first trip. Do you know anywhere good to go at night?" and he said, "No." So I gave up talking. But everyone struck me like that taxi driver did: they only spoke if necessary.'
>
> Chris got up, shook himself, and flopped down again. 'America was like Jeff,' he said, 'like the noise he is making now. He is like it. He only talks when it is necessary. He

> is 1975, like America is. Me, I'm in between.' 'I'm happier in an English churchyard than in a New York boulevard,' Keith said, 'but there is something to be learned from the Americans.'[168]

The band returned to work; for James, the new number they played conjured images of 'mists and mellow moorlands, and smells of dew and damp grass', and then the spell was broken: 'A red chrome guitar screamed like a New York subway train.'[169] Like 1975, in 1965 the tomorrow was NOW.

What the Yardbirds were attempting was a delicate balancing act, expressed in the tentative bridge between Relf's pastoralism and Beck's hyper-modernity. In his own inimitable way, Andrew Loog Oldham summed up this tension in an advertising tagline for 'Get Off of My Cloud', which he described as playing on 'the dividing line between art and commerce . . . in other words the rolling stones have a great new single'. As a statement of fact, it was rather more appreciable then the abstract concoction he had used to sell '(I Can't Get No) Satisfaction':

> faces of today: sounds of tomorrow
> spots, not gauze, and peepers of truth
> an audience in a sea of fear
> for big daddy doesn't relate any more
> this does: so float into tomorrow

Moving on, at a press reception for the launch of Immediate Records, Oldham laid down another manifesto:

> We believe that success lies in dispensing with accepted tradition and going against the current trend, which is to deal with pop merchandise in a stiff and unimaginative manner. We want to give an aura of youth. There's no room in the

> business for an old-club atmosphere . . . one must adopt streamlined American methods of selling and promotion.[170]

Just around the corner was 1966, and the Yardbirds with Jeff Beck, who already sounded like he was straight out of the 1970s, were in for the ride – America was their future, Britain's churchyards their past.

6

Going Way-Out (and Then Further Still), 1966

Faster than a speeding harmonica. More powerful than an amplified guitar. Able to leap high notes in a single bound.

'Look! Up there in the sky! It's a Rolling Stone!'

'It's Bob Dylan!'

'No! It's The Yardbirds!!'

Yes, it's The Yardbirds, long-haired visitors from across the sea who came to America with powers and abilities far beyond those of ordinary musicians.

The Yardbirds, disguised as mild-mannered recording artists for Epic Records, are fighting a never-ending battle for the searing harmonica sound that explodes over relentless drum and bass figurations . . . lonely dramatic guitar chords that echo in the night and the frantic pulsating freight train beat that builds till it blows your mind.

HIT PARADER (April 1966)

Two days after playing the Empire Ballroom, Neath, on 9 December, the band were in Chicago delivering a show with the Lovin' Spoonful and the Turtles, among others. They spent the final three weeks of December and most of January in the States before returning – via the Sanremo song festival in Italy, two Paris gigs and a short respite – to the British club and ballroom circuit with a show at Baths Hall, Scunthorpe, on 19 February.

The band were well received on their second visit to Los Angeles, where they were based for part of January. On 4 and

8 January, they recorded performances of 'I'm a Man' for the *9th Street West* and *Shivaree* television shows, respectively; for the latter they also played 'Heart Full of Soul'. They made two appearances on *The Lloyd Thaxton Show*, recording on 2 and 11 January, miming to 'Shapes of Things' and 'For Your Love'. They had planned to film more, but 'there was union trouble again,' Samwell-Smith told a reporter on the band's return to London: 'We were only allowed to do three TV shows. We had all the visas lined up before we went, but when a man came back from being ill, he didn't agree and cancelled a lot of things. The visas had been issued by his deputy.'[1]

'Hollywood is an extraordinary place,' Relf told *Music Echo*:

> It's not a bit like any of the other American cities. People there seem to be living for kicks all the time. Some of them are genuine, but there are a lot of what we call weekend beatniks around, too. You know, hangers-on who dress up for the part in between being bank clerks or something... We heard Paul Butterfield's Blues band there, and it's really something. It's a rather strange scene in America at the moment for music. The white groups seem to be playing rhythm and blues like we used to here two years ago. But in Hollywood there's a sort of rock and country mixture with blues thrown in, and it's great to hear.[2]

Had Relf been listening to the country blues of the Rising Sons? Taj Mahal and Ry Cooder's band were playing at the Trip around the time the 'Birds were in town and would, according to the *Los Angeles Times*, open their set, just as the Yardbirds often did, with 'Train Kept a-Rollin'.[3]

On New Year's Eve, the Yardbirds played in Tacoma, Washington, with the Beach Boys and others. On a trip to Britain in May, Brian Wilson's stand-in, Bruce Johnson, recalled that the 'Birds amplifiers had 'blown up' so they used the Beach Boys' set-up:

> Dennis plays drums, so he doesn't understand amps, and Mike just sings, so he doesn't understand what's going on with amps either. Jeff Beck turns his guitar towards the amps to get feedback and Dennis and Mike were going to pull the plugs out, they thought the Yardbirds were harming the equipment. I had to stop them and explain what was happening. They were getting really mad.[4]

The anecdote, like *Hit Parader*'s parody of Superman, underscored how alien, yet exciting, the Yardbirds appeared to those who first encountered their early North American shows.

The LA weekly music paper *The BEAT* introduced the band to its readers by first trying to explain 'rave-up' – a new sound – 'an English expression, coined expressly for use in speaking about the Yardbirds and their kind of music': 'The thing is – it's just about as hard to explain the word as it is to describe their music! To "rave" is to be really excited about something, to really pour your heart and soul – mostly *soul* – into something, to really break it up and have a great time.'[5] The paper's reporter joined the band at Markley's house, their second visit to his abode, which 'could probably hold – *uncomfortably* – about, oh . . . 75 or 80 people. Well, there were about *five hundred* and seventy five people present.'[6] The band gave an impromptu show and 'let out with some of the wildest sounding music heard in a long, long time':

> Theirs is the music which you will feel in every muscle of your body, not only during the performance, but for hours afterward. It is an emotional experience in which you become completely involved, and it's for certain that you won't soon afterwards be able to uninvolve yourself. Nor will you want to . . . They are funny, they are serious, they are five musicians working together as one to come up with one of the most fantastic sounds ever.[7]

The contrast with Caroline Silver's report of the dowdy times in New Brighton could not be more stark.

The rave at Markley's place was reported by Harrison Carroll, in his syndicated column 'Behind the Scenes in Hollywood', to be the 'Wildest scene of the year'.[8] It 'happened when a mob of screaming teenagers converged on the party given in a private home in the Hollywood Hills for the newly arrived English rock 'n' roll group, the Yardbirds'. Hundreds of kids, he wrote, 'tried to crash the affair . . . some of the kids got in, some were driven away by police and bodyguards at the door. There were several fights, but no serious injuries. And at midnight when the Yardbirds entertained, the teen mob danced in the street outside the house.'[9]

Back in London, the music press reported on the band's Hollywood partying: 'Natalie Wood, Sonny and Cher, Phil Spector, the Fortunes and Marlon Brando got turned away from a party by the Yardbirds in a private home on Hollywood Boulevard. "I feel so embarrassed about it. It was a complete accident," said Paul Samwell-Smith on the transatlantic phone at 4.30 am.'[10] Fowley said, 'It's been quite a party,' adding that 'The Yardbirds are quite a group' and have 'paved the way in America for groups like the Who. Their clothes and manner are the first ideas of pop art the West Coast has been given. They look like becoming the corner-stone for pop art here in 1966.'[11] To keep the rivalry with the Who alive, Relf noted that the U.S. scene was still occupied by Beatles, Stones and Kinks copyists, 'But the Who just haven't caught on here yet.'[12] The report ended on the note that they'd cut 'Shapes of Things' in Chicago as a U.S. single and a British album or EP track. While in the city, Jeff Beck recalled for *Beat Instrumental* that he'd jammed in clubs with Howlin' Wolf and Hubert Sumlin and in another venue with James Cotton: 'I just couldn't get over it. They all seem to live their music. There's a jukebox in nearly every joint that sells anything to drink – but you won't find Dave Clark on them!'[13]

Throughout 1966, in his *Disc* column, 'Hollywood Calling', publicist Derek Taylor kept up a steady stream of positive notices about the Yardbirds' impact on the West Coast scene, noting the band's appearance in the audience for a double bill of the Byrds and Paul Butterfield 'and his beautiful' Blues Band at the Trip. He thought the Yardbirds 'an exciting group', who Hollywood had grown 'very fond of'.[14] In April, he reported that 'In brief... Yardbirds very hot here. Very "in".'[15]

Unlike their initial house-rocking performance at Markley's back in the late summer, the Yardbirds followed up with some less spontaneous gigs; this time they played an exclusive LA engagement at Dave Hull's Hullabaloo on Sunset Strip on 5, 6, 7 and 9 January. Originally called the Moulin Rouge, the club had been a major Hollywood attraction in the 1930s and '40s, 'but all that was long ago', according to New York's *Hit Parader*,

> when movies were dreams and no one needed LSD ... It is possibly the poshest teenage nightclub anywhere, including posh Hollywood. In fact, it's posher than most adult clubs. Bigger, too. And it's managed as a 'class' establishment for young people ... It's like a concert hall with tables and the floor is built on levels just like a theatre, leading down to eye-level with the stage itself. It has a revolving section in the centre so that entertainment is continuous ... The basic philosophy behind the Hullabaloo is simple and direct ... The club is used to present big name acts and local talent in a clean, healthy atmosphere. No dimly lit, smoke-filled den of iniquity, the Hullabaloo serves no liquor and discourages scruffy clothing ... Capacity is 960, but it can hold as many as 1,400 ... about $100,000 was invested in repairs and equipment, with about $20,000 for the sound system alone.[16]

'The sound was immaculate,' said Samwell-Smith of the club's set-up, 'the best sound we've ever had, except for the Marquee Club, London. One night we had three thousand people in.'[17] This was something of an exaggeration, as Tracy Thomas, the *NME*'s Hollywood correspondent, reported.[18] The Yardbirds did, however, prove to be a bigger draw than either the Everly Brothers or Gary Lewis and the Playboys, 'even though the admission fee was doubled'.[19] The band 'whipped up a commotion', and later three of them joined the Paul Butterfield Blues Band for an 'informal session', which then fell foul of their visa permissions, leading to 'threatened deportation', Thomas wrote.[20]

A teenage correspondent for the *Los Angeles Times*, Marilyn Caldwell, gave them a fulsome write-up under the heading 'Yardbirds Find Own Style in the Far Out':

> Still another English group has sung, swung and vibrated its way onto the pop scene. But the Yardbirds have proved themselves to be anything but another lot of stereotyped long-haired 'yeah-yeah' singers. The boys have labelled their particular sound product 'abstract expressionism' or 'futuristic rock 'n' roll'.
>
> 'We started with the usual sort of folk blues stuff,' said Keith Relf . . . 'Then the numbers started to take on their own feelings. The solos got longer, became more abstract. They lost their original format. Now we even change it night to night. And it's developed like that over the two years we've been together. The numbers were just copies of somebody else; now they are us.'[21]

The band's far-out sound owed much to Jeff Beck, Caldwell wrote: 'He works with three amplifiers and can produce an incredible range of sounds. His speciality is feedback, all kinds of weird, echoing effects. Other top guitarists call Jeff "a fantastic cat".'[22]

KRLA the Beat also gave the band a warm reception (and send-off). The report of dressing-room conversations with various members emphasized their finer feelings:

> Jeff is emotional . . . perhaps a little more so than the others. But it is *because* of this sensitivity that he is capable of creating the unique and beautiful sound which he does . . . More people milling about, and then – in the middle of the room, perched on the dressing table – was Yardbird Keith Relf. Keith of the deep blue eyes, and deep thoughts of many things.[23]

When not romanticizing the band, the reporter asked about their music. Relf qualified the tag 'pop art', which he was said to have used on stage, by renaming their sonic approach as a form of 'abstract expressionism'.[24] McCarty was a little more circumspect: 'I asked him to describe the sound as it is now. He wrinkled his forehead in thought, then began: "I don't really know – it's a very *atmospheric* type of thing. Futuristic rock 'n' roll, if you like. It *could* be termed 'pop art' – I never thought of that. It depends what a person *wants* to call it."'[25] Samwell-Smith was less guarded: 'It's *not* pop art; it's futuristic sort of music. It's experimental futuristic – essentially electronic music.'[26] The prevarication about what they played was an indication of a band not entirely confident negotiating the publicity machine (especially when compared to how the Who spoke about their act).

It was the last night of the band's residency and the report's conclusion is tenderly sentimental:

> They had brought to us some music – music that was new and exciting. They had added a little thing called *life* to our existences, and soon they would fly away. Back to England, back to their world, back to – perhaps – some other crowded

> dressing room in a night club somewhere . . . Good-night Yardbirds – and thank you.[27]

Before Christmas, during a two-day stop-over in Chicago to cut 'Shapes of Things', Dreja found time to talk to Carol Sincak, who wrote for *Hit Parader*. The interview, with her 'ideal of what a teenage idol should be', formed the core of a two-page profile that covered the usual ground of the band's history, their desire to be a 'different group with different sounds and different music' that Dreja dubbed 'futuristic rock 'n' roll' and, for a good half of the allotted space, characterized them as gentle pranksters, practical jokers.[28] The impression left is of a band of dedicated musicians, sincere and intelligent but also accessible, knowable and out for a lark: teen idols with an edge. One correspondent to the magazine congratulated them on the coverage given to a band with a 'sound unequalled by any other group'.[29] It was, Richard Spaete wrote, a 'driving' 'wailing' noise, a 'razor' and a 'punchy sound all at once'. The band in the United States had crossover appeal, enhanced by the fact that the majority of journalists who wrote about them in American magazines were female; in Britain, Maureen Cleave, June Southworth, Dawn James and Penny Valentine were the exceptions.

The sonic adventurism of the Yardbirds (and the Who) kept them ahead of the pack of R&B-scene graduates, but others in their cohort were keen to join them on their journey. Echoing the debate around commercialism and experimentation, the Small Faces explained to *Melody Maker* that their 'Sha-La-La-Lee' single was a necessary commercial ploy so that they can make some 'bread' and establish their name.[30] Steve Marriott said, 'If we can score two or three big hits, then we'll start making the kind of records we want to.'[31] They were intentionally parlaying a kind of schizophrenic approach to their music, a personality split between creating contained hit records and the wild abandon of their stage act. The ambition was to bring the two sides together: 'We want to get the full force of our stage numbers on record,' Ronnie Lane said.[32] With the recruitment of ex-Muleskinner Ian McLagan on keys, the band had made a musical step change, according to Marriott. After a period of being taken aback by his playing where the band 'just sort of stood about on stage and watched him go', they now had McLagan 'under control' and '[used] him as a carpet'.[33] Marriott was not demeaning McLagan's role, as the keyboardist clarified: 'What he means is that I'm a bass sound underneath the guitar, bass and drums, keeping a steady rhythm and melody so that the vocal, bass and guitar can loon about on top.'[34] Marriott had the last word: 'At present we only do this free form stuff on stage and sometimes on our B-sides of records . . . I know "Sha-La-La-Lee" is a long haul from it, but one day we hope to be doing right weird, far-out stuff.'[35]

Among the best of the Who impersonators, the Eyes had taken yet another lead from Townshend and proclaimed they were jumping off the sonic bandwagon that the Small Faces were riding, as *Beat Instrumental* in March 1966 elucidated:

> The group have always been bang up-to-date with trends and were one of the first outfits to swing away from contemporary sounds into the fields of feedback and distortion. But rather than lamming it out in wild style they made it more of a delicate art form creating identifiable sounds such as police sirens, clocks striking, cars skidding. After a while, of course, it became played out. Everybody had stated this kind of thing. Now The Eyes only feature it once or twice in their stage act. They won't put it on records ever again, although their previous recording, 'When the Night Falls', made use of it.[36]

While some, like the Small Faces, developed the 'free form' side of their acts, others more directly mimicked Yardbirds records.

Without prior knowledge of what he would hear, Mick Jagger, taking part in *Melody Maker*'s 'Blind Date', was played Walker Brother Gary Leeds's solo single, 'You Don't Love Me', a cover of a 1960 Willie Cobbs number. 'I've heard that riff before,' said Jagger. 'Is it the Yardbirds?'[37] A month later, in another 'Blind Date' column, Dave Dee hit the same problem as Jagger when responding to the Fleur De Lys cover of Pete Townshend's 'Circles': 'Guitar sounds like the Yardbirds . . . It's half Yardbirds and half the Who on the solo, and I think perhaps there's no room for another group doing that sort of sound.'[38] Wayne Fontana, when presented with an actual Yardbirds single – 'Over Under Sideways Down' – said, 'It's not the Yardbirds, is it? It's weird, but it's not a good weird sound . . . It's got the old Indian bit going.'[39] The issue that the band had to resolve was how to exploit their established identity and yet not sound like they were impersonating themselves. Their next disc would be a masterclass in resolving that problem.

'Shapes of Things', backed with 'You're a Better Man Than I', was announced as the new Yardbirds single by *Record Mirror* at the end of January, just prior to the band's return from the USA and Europe. Written by Manfred Mann's Mike Hugg, the flip had been recorded as long ago as the autumn trip to the United States. The top side had initially been tracked at Chess recording studios, Chicago, on 21–22 December and completed in Hollywood with sessions at Columbia on 7 January, and mastering at RCA, 10 January. Samwell-Smith gave the *NME* the background to the song's composition:

> We lifted about eight notes from a Dave Brubeck figure ['Pick up Sticks'] for a part of the number . . . It's essentially a marching tempo and Jim worked out the basis of the idea long before I got around to writing the lyric. I actually composed it in a bar while we were in Chicago. I was not exactly inspired – just sat down and worked hard at it. The idea of the lyric is just my impression of things.

> Things like 'trees that are still green and will they still be seen?' Well, that's just a hope that some fool is not going to reduce the world to an asphalt-flattened plain by tomorrow. It's really an observation song. Along the lines of the type of things Bob Lind is writing, which I admire very much.[40]

The *NME*'s singles reviewer, Derek Johnson, caught the impact of 'Shapes of Things' – great fun, but you can't hum the tune:

> Drum-break opening explodes into a stamping thumper, with cymbal crashes and underlying rasping guitar. The lyric is philosophic and worldly wise. There's not a great deal of melody – nothing you can really whistle – but the disc has tremendous impact, with characteristic breaks in tempo and startling effects. And in the instrumental passage, it suddenly switches to double-time shuffle pace with falsetto chanting. A gas![41]

Record Mirror described the single as having a 'chugging opening' as a prelude to a heavy, stomping beat and group vocal . . . 'Curious guitar figures later on' concluding in a 'semi-Indian sort of attitude towards the end': 'Commercial sound but isn't the best yet from this chart-busting group.'[42] Another reporter for the paper, Richard Green, asked Samwell-Smith if the 'sitar sound towards the end' of the recording 'had been intentional'. He replied, 'it's just Jeff's feedback, that's all.'[43] In *Disc Weekly*, Penny Valentine wrote that the single was 'very unusual . . . "almost a protest" (sorry!) – about not knowing what to expect next. Rather frightening, really. It's done with a fuzz box sort of effort that makes it sound as though it was recorded in a shoebox. Has a very solid beat, and a terrifically angry break in the middle.'[44] Ex-Animal Alan Price was less impressed: 'I'm very much against the sort of sound the Yardbirds get. It's a jigsaw puzzle record,' by which he presumably meant that it was less

Uniformity – a quick step into the future in matching suits and ties: 'Shapes of Things' sheet music, 1966.

than the sum of its parts – a collage of time changes, mood shifts, melodic pauses and a recording in which the edits could be heard.[45]

Relf had described Beck's playing as 'sort of Arabic . . . He really produced a weird, vicious sound.'[46] In big bold typeface, *Melody Maker* led its review of the single with the headline 'Great Beck Guitar Means a Big, Big Yardbirds Hit'.[47] It really was all about Beck and his 'sitar-like' effects. In a rant to *Melody Maker*'s Nick Jones about fakery and insincerity in the British scene, Eric Clapton said he wanted to get out and go to America – to Chicago, 'his spiritual home'; he was excited

> because Jeff said they [Chicago's bluesmen] dig what he plays, and that he dug the whole scene like mad. I gather that it became Jeff Beck with the Yardbirds. The white

> Americans over there, who know what they're on about, dug Jeff a lot more than Keith Relf's half-hearted singing.[48]

Cheap shots at his old bandmate aside, the elevation of Beck to star role was indisputable. Nobody needed to tell that to the Yardbirds audience; the evidence was all over the band's post-Clapton run of singles. Beck's solos on 'Shapes of Things' and 'You're a Better Man Than I' are the loudest element in the mix, compressed to the point of overload. Jabbing away like a boxer in front of a mirror, Beck demands attention – 'listen, you've not heard this before,' he seems to say to himself as much as to another.

In March 1966, Paul Williams in his recently launched fanzine, *Crawdaddy* (named after the Richmond club), which aimed to address the day's doting and female-aimed fan magazines, took one of his favourite bands to task.[49] His review of 'Shapes of Things' called it 'flawed', sounding like a 'marching song for the Indian army'.[50] It was 'protesty' but 'meaningless'. He then highlighted its structural inadequacies before ending on a kicker: 'it's not R'n'R, or any other kind of integrated sound. This isn't a song – it's an experiment.'[51] Admiration for the band's audacious experimentation was balanced by a counterweight of scepticism about its impact on song craft that would become a defining element of the critical reception the Yardbirds attracted in 1966.

While the borrowed bass figure from Brubeck's 'Pick up Sticks' in 'Shapes of Things' is readily apparent, the more interesting connection between the piano man's Quartet and the Yardbirds is how each defined their push against their respective chosen musical forms. Steve Race's sleeve note for Brubeck's *Time Out* (1959) goes to great lengths to note the originality of their time signatures: 'should some cool-minded Martian come to earth and check on the state of our music, he might play through 10,000 jazz records before he found one that wasn't in common 4/4 time.' While Ellington, Hawkins, Bird, Diz and Monk had broadened jazz's harmonic horizon, conjuring up more complex structures and providing a palette of more diverse colours, according to Race, they were still all bound by the time of marching feet. Brubeck, however, had 'gone further, finding still more exotic time signatures, and even laying one rhythm in counterpoint over another'. On the use of 6/4 time on 'Pick up Sticks', he wrote:

> it is the bass part which supplies the anchor for the listener. This time Eugene Wright plays a regular pattern of six notes: a *passacaglia* on which is built the whole structure of this closing number.
>
> The highspot of 'Pick up Sticks' comes near the close, in a session of commanding piano. This is Brubeck in the grand manner, as exciting as eight brass, but with that feeling of urgent discovery which can never be captured by the arranger's pen.
>
> In short: *Time Out* is a first experiment with time, which may well come to be regarded as more than an arrow pointing to the future. Something great has been attempted . . . and achieved. The very first arrow has found its mark.

When Samwell-Smith made use of that bass line was he also thinking about how the Yardbirds' rave-ups carried a similar sense of 'urgent discovery' and how, in pop music, they were now marching to a new time step and shooting their own arrows into the future?

WHILE FINALIZING 'Shapes of Things' in Hollywood, the band also recorded the backing tracks for 'Questa Volta' and 'Paff . . . Bum', which had vocals added in New York on 17–18 January, two tracks that are, unquestionably, the direst efforts in the Yardbirds catalogue. They had to be taped prior to the band appearing at the Italian Sanremo Song Festival on 28–29 January. The song choice was made for the band, and foreign competitors were paired with an Italian – in the Yardbirds' case, Bobby Solo.[52] The format was to have them both sing the same song in Italian. Françoise Hardy, P. J. Proby, Gene Pitney, Pat Boone and Chad and Jeremy were among the other foreigners.[53] Of the two songs, Samwell-Smith said they were all 'wrong' for the band.

> We played badly and it just didn't go down well. The Italian people gave us just one mike apart from the one for the singer. The second night, 'Paff Bum' was much better. It was very much the same riff as 'Sloopy'. We did quite well I think and we very nearly got into the final with it. The chap who did it with us was very tiny, about four feet nothing . . . He came on and sang his heart out.[54]

A short, fat singer with a beard was how they disparagingly described Solo. He was neither fat nor bearded, but the point was made: the band and singer were ill-matched.

The Yardbirds were a poor fit with the festival's audience too, which was made up of moral guardians – Catholic parents – who didn't like long-haired groups and were 'very middle-class and very wealthy'.[55] As Leonard Levesley wrote in his overview of the festival for *The Tatler*,

> nobody under 20 could afford to get in – best seats on the final night cost about £40, and £25 buys you a hard chair half behind a pillar. The 700 or so people who pay these prices come mainly from the world's publishers and recording companies, who treat the affair as an essential expense. This odd and rather depressing collection of people is the main reason why Italian pop music is still stuck around 1950. As an experiment, the organizers introduced three beat groups this year, including the Yardbirds. They were all

> looked upon with unconcealed scorn, and the experiment almost certainly won't be repeated.[56]

Even if, via television, the Yardbirds managed to get through to a younger, more responsive audience, 'the contest was unfortunate,' Samwell-Smith said.[57] *Melody Maker*'s correspondent wrote that the band's first number made him 'shudder, but they restored some lost prestige with their performance of "Riff, Boom" [*sic*]'.[58] *Disc Weekly* ran a picture of the band being fitted for dinner suits for the event at John Stephen's boutique: 'They feel very funny', said Keith, 'after what we usually wear on stage.'[59] Such was the lot of the pop star.

Whether or not the contest expanded the band's Italian fanbase, it clearly had the effect of further distancing them from Gomelsky, who had arranged for them to take part in the event and wasted recording time on the two songs, which Beck had refused to play on anyway. The long-promised album was no nearer to completion. Gomelsky's plan, perhaps to quieten the disgruntlement in the ranks, was to get the members to record solo singles, Keith Relf with Bob Lind's 'Mr Zero', the singer-songwriter's 'Elusive Butterfly' was just then competing with Val Doonican's cover version, both chart features in the latter part of March. In the hope of boosting the composer's profile, against the highly popular Doonican, the Yardbirds, Larry Page and Gomelsky paid for an advert in *Record Mirror*, proclaiming Lind's 'Elusive Butterfly' to be 'Authentic, Original, Valid!!'[60] Samwell-Smith was to record a song given to him by Jackie DeShannon, 'Green Trees'; Dreja and McCarty were working on a humorous set piece; and Beck was expected to record an instrumental.[61] As if writing the guitarist and drummer's comedy skit, Gomelsky said of the Relf disc: 'We have an idea that neo-Elizabethan romantic folk might happen.'[62] The hoped-for release date for these ideas, depending on things working to plan, was in April or early May, and Gomelsky added a new ambition to the mix: 'We are writing a rock and roll symphony as well. This is part of the expansion of the group and pop music. We have progressed beyond r-and-b and are always experimenting with new ideas.'[63] Meanwhile, they had dates in Denmark, Germany and Belgium to play – or at least that was what was reported. In fact, they first set off on another round of club and ballroom dates. On playing British ballrooms, Mick Jagger had an opinion, as he did on much else:

> Never went into one until we played them. I'd hate going to one, I don't like the atmosphere. I prefer little clubs. I don't like these glittering Ernies' Paradises. Glittering, flashing, revolving lights hanging from the ceiling. Horrible. Guys in evening dress announcing: 'And now from Grimsdyke the fantastic Falcons!' It's a horrible ritual you read about.[64]

Rave's Mark Grant caught up with the Yardbirds at the Locarno Ballroom, Streatham, on 24 March, and later in Gomelsky's apartment. 'You can't stand still in this business,' Beck told him:

> You've got to be ahead of the times. We're convinced that people are tired of seeing the same old stage presentations. We're working on a completely new idea now which will take things along at a faster pace. No announcements or breaks in numbers. For example, 'Heart Full of Soul' would run straight into 'Still I'm Sad' with just a few words said over the intro. We want to cut an LP the same way – no tracks – one continuous album. We're working on a symphonic arrangement along those lines and really hope to bring out an album that will make every pop-conscious fan sit up and take notice.[65]

Was Beck's concept a version of Gomelsky's rock 'n' roll symphony?

Four days after the Locarno gig, the band were finally in Advision Studios, cutting tracks for the proposed album, but the session lasted barely a day, producing some perfunctory blues jams and unrealized covers of songs long part of their live set. The tapes stayed in the vault until the 1980s; they sound like a band out of ideas, no indication whatsoever of the symphony or of 'super-pop and images in sound' that they had earlier discussed with Mike Grant, certainly nothing that suggested the experiments with 'electronic sounds and tapes' that so interested Samwell-Smith: 'You produce the required noises and sounds by loops – making your own music by electricity,' Samwell-Smith told Grant – 'Although I still regard us as musicians rather than electricians.'[66] Samwell-Smith's ambitions echoed Gomelsky's and Beck's: 'Future plans for the group include writing a symphony,' the *NME* reported, or 'At least, the writing of a number along symphonic lines. The classical construction of music is something which particularly influences Paul.'[67] A month or so later, Samwell-Smith expanded on these ideas for the U.S. magazine *Hit Parader*: 'We want to have the classical attitude in mind of starting with a statement, improvising on that and then going into a final statement which is a combination of these two parts. "For Your Love" was a bit like this.'[68] Much of this was just thinking out loud, laying down vague ideas that somehow expressed both ambition and progression. The band were never literally moving towards symphonic music, but they were keen to explore the limits of the pop format, to push against the two-and-a-half-minute duration of a standard single and its verse, chorus, middle eight, repeat structure. But to do that, they needed both studio time and the right sort of songs. They had neither to hand and were on the verge of breaking with Gomelsky.

In mid-April, *Disc Weekly* reported that Beck was seriously ill with meningitis, which would necessitate an 'enforced two months complete rest.'[69] The news broke as the band were travelling back from concerts on the continent; they were seeking a temporary replacement, it was reported.[70] British booking commitments would be fulfilled, but album recording sessions were likely to be cancelled.[71] A week later, Beck was back in harness: 'Doctors decided his illness was not so serious.'[72] However, he was now due to enter hospital to have his tonsils out. Was the illness feigned or real? Was it a ploy on the part of the band to delay recording commitments with Gomelsky until new management was in place or was the issue Beck's mental well-being? The rumour mill was turning on these questions, which were being mulled over not only in London but in Los Angeles – was Jeff looking for a way out?[73]

In a footnote, without context, on the back page of *Record Mirror*'s 16 April edition, mention is made that there was 'still no new LP from the Yardbirds'.[74] A week later, in the same gossipy column, 'The Face', the paper asked if Jeff Beck was 'looking for an exit from the Yardbirds?'[75] By the month's end, the news was out that the band had split from Gomelsky, and Keith Relf wasn't talking 'about the reasons for the Yardbirds' change of managers'.[76] Except that he did have a good deal to say about it to *Record Mirror*'s Richard Green, who paraphrased his thoughts: 'The Yardbirds would much rather be recording than continually travelling to foreign countries to entertain. Making records, to them, is a far more satisfactory medium – both for establishing a name for themselves and for earning money.'[77] Their new manager, Simon Napier-Bell, had secured them a better deal: 'We were being paid a wage each week. Now we'll be able to see exactly where the money is going,' said Relf.[78]

As of October 1965, according to one of Chris Dreja's payslips, the band members were each being paid a basic £27 per week.[79] (Adjusted for inflation in 2024, that amount would be approximately £23,000 per annum.) An interim bonus payment of £500 (£8,225 in 2024) for the year was paid out as well that month, but given all the touring, and with three hit singles, it was not at all a generous return and, bonus aside, had not changed much from the contract they had signed two years earlier.[80] In April, the 1964 agreement ended, though Gomelsky had the right to extend for a further two years with a raise to £750 a month for the band. Poor remuneration, then, was clearly a motive to sack Gomelsky and break the contract, but so too was bad decision-making like participating in the Sanremo Festival, which Dreja railed against: 'It was a waste of time going out there. We could have been recording. People are always asking when we're going to do another LP. We've only had one and that was years ago. If we [had] waited until we'd finished travelling round the world, we'd be old men.'[81] Napier-Bell 'was a man with ideas', Relf and Dreja said, and had 'success written all over him'.[82] The break came at a significant cost, however, as they signed over to Gomelsky the rights to their recorded output up and until that point. But the band were looking forward, not back.[83]

> It's a shame the Yardbirds have no image because they would be the Number One group in England.
>
> PETER NOONE, HERMAN'S HERMITS, 1966[84]

AT THE END OF FEBRUARY, the Yardbirds had talked to *Record Mirror*'s Richard Green about their imminent plans, though they kept the disquiet with Gomelsky, which had been long brewing, out of the discussion. A year on from the band's embrace of the commercial, Samwell-Smith and Relf, at least, were intent on forging a more folk-orientated path. For his part, Beck was putting a break on that venture – he '[didn't] like folk numbers' – and as a singularly important member of the group, his tastes and interests were not to be ignored.[85] Still, the singer and bassist thought at least two folk songs might be included on the ever-elusive album. Jackie DeShannon's song 'Green Trees' was still on the agenda for Samwell-Smith; DeShannon, like him, 'adored Dylan', or at least the 'simplicity and beauty of things like "Song For Woody"'.[86] Samwell-Smith was not a fan of Dylan's recent turn to electricity and the amphetamine-surreal, but he had found what he thought the man had lost in the songs of Bob Lind.

Samwell-Smith had brought back from the States a fair number of the singer-songwriter's demos: '"Elusive Butterfly" is very beautiful,' he said. '"Mr Zero" is very good. It's not been recorded by anyone yet, not even by him, unless he's put in on his LP [the two songs would appear on Lind's debut album, *Don't Be Concerned*, released in April]. He's been playing in clubs quite a while now.'[87] The 'mournful' quality of the demos registered with Richard Green, who 'wondered how a boy so young could write such sad lyrics. The mood was very sad and taken at almost a funeral pace.'[88] But how, Samwell-Smith had wondered aloud to the journalist, would it be possible for the Yardbirds to cover such wistful tunes without sounding like the Byrds? That was also a problem he would have had to confront with DeShannon's 'Green Trees', if he ever recorded the tune. A version was given air later in the year, sung by Johnny Walsh on CBS; it was a jangly twelve-string affair, and rather maudlin, not unlike something by Lee Hazlewood.

All the discussion of solo ventures had been sparked by what the band members themselves perceived as their own lack of personality, nevermind what Peter Noone thought of them: 'We've realised during the last two or three weeks that the poor Yardbirds are imageless,' said Relf to *Disc* in March, 'And it is all a bit worrying.'[89] As the others explained:

> People are apt to nod their heads knowingly when the name of the Yardbirds is mentioned. 'Ah yes,' they say, 'A very good group.' But show them a picture of a cheery-faced tall boy in a £10 furry coat and it's doubtful whether they would recognise him as Chris Dreja.
>
> 'Keith and Jeff,' said Chris thoughtfully as they sat with Paul Samwell-Smith in a Kensington pub last week, 'yes – they have got images. But the rest of us aren't really known as personalities' . . . This dreadful searching for separate identification is one thing that has led the Yardbirds to split

> up on records. 'People are being very peculiar about this separate recording thing,' said Chris. 'All it means is that if we do a date we'll do Keith's song, or Paul's, as part of the act.'[90]

Part of Gomelsky's thinking with regard to the solo projects was undoubtedly to do with maximizing the band's earning potential, as he explained to the *NME*: 'We are not sure which label Keith will record for as he is not contracted as an individual to EMI – only as a member of the Yardbirds. We'll see who is going to make the best offer.'[91] Whether or not the image problem was resolvable on these terms was up for debate, but there was no way the Yardbirds were going to conjure up the type of individualism within a collective that a band like the Who enjoyed.

The big news, however, was Keith Relf's marriage to April Liversidge. From backstage at a *Ready Steady Go!* engagement, the *NME* reported on the shock felt by fans, and described the bride as a

> pretty, petite 19-year-old with dark attractive shoulderlength hair. She too was in the dressing room, dutifully being seen but not heard, it was reported. 'I hope the marriage will not affect the group's popularity,' said Keith. 'I don't see why it should. I never had the Romeo image – I was never the raver type. I had a nice image. The type of boy they could take home to tea on Sunday.' April showed just a trace of a smile at this![92]

Meanwhile, the album was no nearer being recorded, a problem they conceded was as great as the personality deficit, while Paul Samwell-Smith was still moaning about Pete Townshend and the Who stealing their tricks and the Yardbirds not getting the credit they deserved – though it was all fairly good-natured.[93] The Who, in turn, had nicknamed Samwell-Smith the 'Screaming Skull' – 'They just can't believe anyone can have a face like mine.' The two bands were appearing together on a special edition of *Ready Steady Go!* filmed in Paris.[94]

Under Napier-Bell, Relf had finally recorded 'Mr Zero' – 'It got held up because again there wasn't time,' said Relf. 'Now we've done it with orchestral backing. The "B" side is something I wrote myself.'[95] The same line used under Gomelsky about the band being 'faceless' was still in play under their new management. Jeff's solo might now be a cover of 'Alfie' (earlier it had been publicized that his solo would be an original instrumental with 'an orchestrated introduction', suggesting that things were still very much in flux).[96] Whatever the status of the solo projects, the band had recorded both sides of their next single, 'Over Under Sideways Down', which Relf said they rated as 'our most commercial disc yet. It's an uptempo rocker with some surprising breaks.'[97] Its flip was 'Jeff's Boogie'. A slot for the album session had been booked for the end of March/beginning of April.

Samwell-Smith and Napier-Bell doubled up on production duties for Relf's solo single, Penny Valentine wrote that she was 'very fond of dear Keith Relf with his starved face, and I too thought that this would have been just the sort of sad song cut out for him. BUT', says Valentine, Relf's version was too fast, and hence it lost 'a lot of the impact of loneliness' of Lind's original.[98] Derek Johnson in the *NME* gave the single 'full marks . . . This Bob Lind number isn't easy at all to sing, largely because there's little melody you can get your teeth into, but Keith copes admirably and his diction is perfect.'[99] Relf may have had a limited vocal range, but his phrasing was always precise, rarely – if ever – slurring across lines. Norman Jopling in *Record Mirror* reviewed 'Mr Zero' more positively: sung 'with haunting tones, building the drama well. Should be a hit.'[100] He also favourably reviewed Susie Klee's version, released in the same week as Relf's effort: 'don't overlook this one by a sweet-toned Swiss girl – because the song could be even stronger for a girl.'[101] Those sentiments were echoed in *Melody Maker*'s dual review of the two singles, which had Relf sounding 'like a cross between Tom Lehrer and Paul McCartney', capturing the 'poetic mood of the song', but Klee giving a 'better interpretation' – 'the lyrics definitely suit a girl more.'[102] Here was the rub, however: Klee's version of 'Mr Zero' was produced by Giorgio Gomelsky.[103] With Doonican and Lind's own version of 'Elusive Butterfly' riding high in the charts, the singer-songwriter, with his orchestral folk style, was the man of the moment.[104] Cover versions flowed out of pop's factory doors, and Relf had missed his opportunity – the single peaked at no. 50 in *Record Retailer*'s chart in the last week of May. Gomelsky's spoiler made nary a dent in the hit parade, but perhaps his point had already been made. Despite what is often reported, this shot at solo stardom was not simply an attempt by Napier-Bell to make Relf into a pop star at the expense of the band; it was a project carried over from the Gomelsky era, and one Relf and his fellow 'Birds were keen for him to pursue.

Whatever Relf's chances of becoming the next Scott Walker, he had an image to match, even if his singing couldn't compete. In *Fabulous*, June Southworth further forged Relf's Romantic profile:

> Keith Relf was waiting for me in his manager's flat. As he had been every time we had met before, he was neither friendly nor unfriendly. He asked what I wanted to talk about, and when I said Keith Relf not a flicker crossed his face.
>
> We walked down the road for a drink and made polite conversation on the way. It was beginning to rain and the wind was bitterly cold. Keith strode along with his hands in his pockets and his shoulders hunched. The wind tore his long fair hair back from his face, leaving it more defenceless-looking than ever. He looked like some fragile bird battling against the elements.[105]

For the pop magazines, the image of Relf as vulnerable to not only the elements but the vicissitudes of love and life was drawn to elicit maternal, protective feelings from their teen female readers, even as they conceived of him as alone, preoccupied with his thoughts, a Romance poet for the pop age.

Under the name of the Paul Samwell-Smith Orchestra, the 'Birds bassist expounded a little on his planned solo project to *Beat Instrumental*. He intended to make a 'fully instrumental EP', with the Kinks' 'See My Friends' alongside three originals: 'He stresses that he won't be using brass, strings or any gimmickry . . . [and is] very fond of what he describes as "That tinkly sound".'[106] He expected to record at CTC studios, with sessionists to include Art Greenslade, Big Jim Sullivan and Jimmy Page. Like so many touted Yardbird projects, it never materialized – a shame, since a cover of Ray Davies's drone tune would have been worth hearing.[107]

Discussing why he felt that Relf's solo venture had failed, Walker Brother John Maus told *Disc*:

> The Yardbirds are this whole thing. If Jeff Beck was to leave the group they would have to find someone who played just like him. The two most important people in the Yardbirds are Jeff and Keith. And when Keith made that record on his own he was stepping out of the thing that he does with the group. Jeff Beck could play as well anywhere else but he still would have that certain Yardbirds thing, and still play a sound that was connected with them.[108]

Beck would play lead guitar on John Maus's 1967 solo single 'I See Love in You', the B-side of 'If I Promise', and you can hear what Walker meant by the 'connected' sound.

American pop journalists were a lot less reticent about working on the band's identity, developing a more refined sense of who they were collectively – as five highly sensitive, thoughtful, intelligent

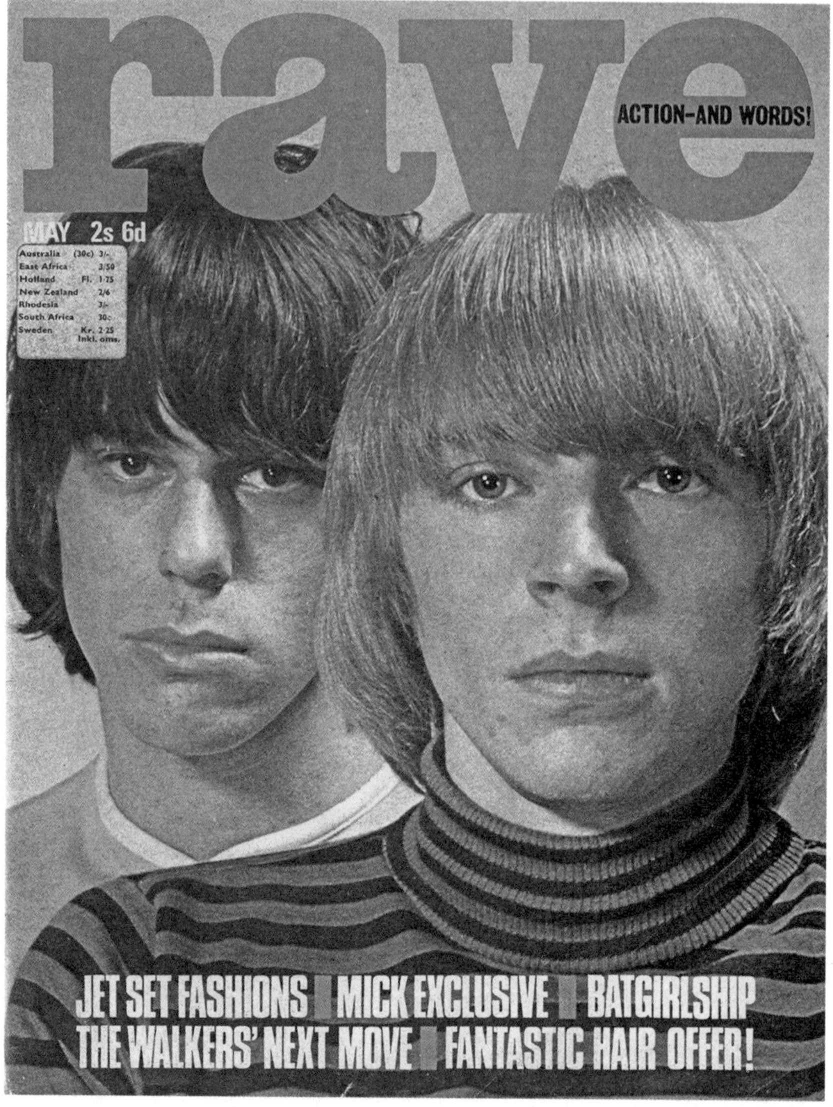

Upfront: Relf and Beck, *Rave* magazine cover (May 1966).

and talented musicians – and individually, though Relf and Beck still held the centre ground. In a long profile of Relf for *The Beat*, Eden wrote:

> He is a sensitive person, and yet strong enough to stand up to the pressures placed upon him by the world in which he

> lives. He is strong enough to understand the burdens which he has taken as his own, and to accept them as a necessary part of his life: a life which he has chosen.[109]

Such an intimate portrait could also be carried over to others in the band, yet it tended to stretch credulity; on Chris Dreja, *The Beat* reported,

> [his] fair hair compliments [*sic*] Keith's stark whiteness and the others' deep darkness. He stands the far opposite of Jeff and his light hair is cropped close for a Yardbird. It behaves and so does Chris. Perhaps it's afraid to move out of place but now it seems to have lost that initial shyness just as Chris has overcome his urge to remain in the background.[110]

Compared to the way that the Beatles or the Stones were characterized, and certainly next to the easily identifiable four members of the Who, the Yardbirds presented a resistance, albeit passive, to such caricatures. Regardless of the depth and reach of their contributions to going further out, which were multifaceted, McCarty and Dreja would remain in the background.

> The Yardbirds were a miserable lot. They really were.
>
> SIMON NAPIER-BELL[111]

SIMON NAPIER-BELL was profiled in May 1966 in the *Evening Standard*'s pop pages by Maureen Cleave: 27 years old and handsome, 'he owns, or part-owns, five companies (one of which employs his father), manages the Yardbirds, directly employs eight people, and lives in a large, expensive flat high over Gorringes with a splendid view of the garden of Buckingham Palace'.

> His looks, his manner, his habit of travelling first class on aeroplanes, his fairly well-substantiated claim to earn £20,000 a year, have convinced his colleagues in the record industry (many of whom dislike him intensely) that his family is rich, or that he has money behind him. This is not so: he is where he is entirely by his own efforts over the last three years. Before that he did nothing, or worse than nothing. 'I was virtually delinquent,' he says, looking back on it . . .
>
> One wondered what egged him on. 'Not the money,' he said. 'That's not security: I'm too much of a socialist to believe that. Security is the ability to survive life, to work another day, another week. The whole of one's life is dedicated to avoiding the boredom that would make one commit suicide.'[112]

The contrast in style and attitude with Gomelsky could not be more striking: Napier-Bell was from the Andrew Loog Oldham school of management, though more financially sharp.[113] In a profile later that year by Nik Cohn, the critic thought Napier-Bell to be 'the most successful, most interesting arrival on the managerial scene since Andrew Oldham, and also the sharpest analytical intelligence that British pop has produced'.[114]

Gomelsky had acted as an independent producer-manager, financing then licensing the Yardbirds' recordings; he was their effective employer, which surely created a whole raft-load of conflicting interests, and one reason that he toured the band relentlessly at the expense of their health and recording opportunities. Napier-Bell turned that around and completed a deal with EMI for the band to record exclusively for the company, with *Melody Maker* reporting the sign-on fee as £25,000.[115] 'In addition,' *Billboard* related, 'members will produce other artists for EMI release.'[116] EMI then struck continuity deals with Barclay for France and Belgium and with CBS for Epic in the United States, Germany and Austria.[117] A new publishing deal was also done with the Big 3 Music Corporation for all territories outside Britain.[118] Napier-Bell scheduled in a holiday break for the band, their first, it was reported, for two and a half years – Relf to Corsica, McCarty to St Tropez and Samwell-Smith to Dublin, while Dreja stayed home – 'But where Jeff Beck has gone I don't know. He just wasn't saying.'[119] Queried about his health, Relf told *Disc*: 'The whole group's been suffering from nervous tension . . . Jeff actually had a nervous breakdown recently.'[120] Was that a reference to the meningitis episode? Whatever the case, Corsica's sun would do himself some good, Relf said.

After their holidays, the first job was to record a new single; like Gomelsky before him, Napier-Bell worked alongside Samwell-Smith in the studio and, at the very least, provided them with the top side's title, 'Over Under Sideways Down'.[121] In a short profile of the entrepreneur in the *Financial Times*, he explained that he was after something new in pop, which was 'not a word he likes. "I am trying to think in terms of sound. At the moment people imagine there are only two sorts of records – pop or serious. There is no reason why this should be so."'[122] In this matter, however glibly Napier-Bell dismissed them in later years, he was in lockstep with the Yardbirds' ambitions.

Two weeks after the release of 'Mr Zero', 'Over Under Sideways Down' was in the shops. *Record Mirror* gave it unconditional support: immediately catchy, not too ambitious, excellently recorded and undoubtedly 'a very big hit'. [123] The reviewer made a note of the 'odd lyrics' and 'those odd guitar-stimulated sitar sounds again'.[124] In her critique, Penny Valentine wrote: 'I can only suppose that on their next record the Yardies will have the entire Dagenham Girl Pipers playing pick and shovels . . . things have got to quite a pitch in their search for new sounds. On this they have great clappings and Russian-type "Heys", Indian rave-ups and a part that sounds like the Arabic call to prayer.'[125] The *NME*'s Derek Johnson opened his review with 'Here comes that sitar sound again – and very effective it is too, on this fast-moving toe-tapper.'[126] In his column for *Disc*, Jonathan King, in his usual snarky manner, summed things up: 'The scene is terribly stagnant again, isn't it? All we have got to live with is the Yardbirds and they are fifteen centuries ahead of us poor normal people.'[127] Being 'further out' than anyone else was becoming a dead end, a novelty that had all but played itself out.

Jeff Beck's mimicry of the Indian instrument was raised, once more, when Richard Green visited the band during the recording of the LP. Beck repeated that although he could play the instrument, he was not sufficiently proficient to use it on recordings, nor would it play 'sharply' enough for his needs: 'We've been using the sound about two years now,' Beck said. 'I didn't listen to Indian music or anything to get the idea. I got it when I was out of my head with the music in Chicago.'[128] Writing to *Melody Maker*, one wit (or sage) considered Beck's effects to owe more to Joe Venturi, pioneer jazz violinist, than to Ravi Shankar – everyone had their finger on the repeat button.[129]

While Samwell-Smith and Napier Bell were in their producers' chairs, Beck said he was 'playing lead, bass and rhythm'.[130] Dreja was singing with Keith, and everyone was contributing ideas on how to get the songs to sound different – as Green reported, the 'African ice cream song' (aka 'Hot House of Omagararshid') used a wobble board and teacup-and-spoon percussion.

Samwell-Smith told *Melody Maker*:

> We're doing some pretty unusual stuff on the album . . . it's difficult to describe so you'll have to wait to hear it. There aren't any unusual instruments – except Jim McCarty imitating a French horn with his voice. Our approach is exactly the same in making an album as for a single, in fact we look on [the album] as 12 singles.[131]

No symphonic arrangements, then . . . Asked whether there was a danger of leaving the public behind with their experiments, Samwell-Smith said, 'we do have to be careful, although in fact, I think we have become more commercial. "Shapes of Things" was perhaps a bit ahead of tastes, but the new one, "Over Under Sideways Down", isn't. It's just a different section of music – happy rock-'n'-roll with a few Russian undertones.'[132] Or Bill Haley's 'Rock Around the Clock' sped up and refashioned, Yardbirds style. Last, he was asked if his negative opinion of British recording studios had changed: 'I must say we are all raving about the sound that Roger, the engineer at Advision, has been getting on the LP.'[133]

With the album finished, Napier-Bell had organized a truly ambitious tour of the USA, '36-day coast to coast', from 1 August. Before then, the band would headline at the Olympia, Paris, and Beck's solo single was scheduled for release at the end of June – 'he sings as well as plays guitar on the track.'[134] And then news broke that Paul Samwell-Smith had quit.[135]

Samwell-Smith's disillusionment with the pop merry-go-round had been apparent for some time; in March, he had told *Disc Weekly*: 'I thought it meant that the audiences knew what you were trying to do and appreciated it. But all they want you to do is leap around and smile. I won't leap about and smile.'[136] 'I don't really care what happens to five-piece groups and the last thing I want to be [doing] in ten years time is playing in a group,' he told *Melody Maker*: I'd like to go into films and be a director.'[137] In June, while recording the album, he expanded on his disillusionment to *Melody Maker*:

> 'The real trouble with success is that you aren't given time to do what you want to do. We have five days to do this LP, writing all the numbers ourselves. We almost write them in the studio. If we could only have the studio for a month it would be fantastic. Instead we have to rush all over the

> world. And all we are doing is standing in front of a lot of kids when, personally, I'd rather be writing songs and recording them.'
>
> 'You have to go on, though.' Why? 'Because I haven't earned enough yet to do what I want . . . Am I a bit disenchanted?' Yes! 'We must have made around 600 personal appearances over the last two years. And, really, that's enough! You aren't creating, just doing the rounds. And frankly it bores me stiff!'
>
> 'I can't see myself doing it all that much longer. I won't be standing up there in five years or so. If we could produce two albums of really great tracks and five singles a year – that would be Utopia.'[138]

After the announcement of his leaving, he told the *NME*'s Keith Altham:

> I'm a bit too old at twenty-three for all those screaming kids leaping about. I really don't think I'll be missed in the group – no one really noticed me on stage. I might just as well have been a dummy. A robot could have done what was required of me. Keith and Jeff are really the only two faces that matter in the Yardbirds.[139]

He would miss the 'companionship and humour of the group', and he had fond memories of the early days: 'there was a lot of excitement to begin with, but now it's gone, and I've got to find a new baby.'[140] Intriguingly, the *NME* announced that Samwell-Smith was to be part of a new studio group featuring Animal Hilton Valentine and Mockingbird Graham Gouldman. They were looking for a vocalist and would be under the management of Harvey Lisberg, who also represented Herman's Hermits and Wayne Fontana.[141] Nothing came of the venture.

Record Mirror

Largest selling colour pop weekly newspaper 6d No. 277 Every Thursday Week ending July 2, 1966

THE YARDBIRDS (R.M. pic)

Jimmy Page replaces Paul Samwell-Smith, *Record Mirror* (2 July 1966).

Subsequently, the reason given for Samwell-Smith quitting the band was the drunken antics of Keith Relf during the May Ball at Queen's College, Oxford. The story is much told – especially by Jimmy Page, who thoroughly enjoyed watching Relf berate the stuck-up audience and blow raspberries into the microphone. No doubt the whole escapade did rile with Samwell-Smith, but as this gig was on 18 June, and, just three days later, Page had taken his place in the band for his debut at the Marquee, it seems more likely that the break had been planned well in advance.[142] As Relf had said before the band's much-needed holiday, Samwell-Smith, like Beck, had been feeling a 'bit nervy'.[143]

Meanwhile, Beck's solo single, recorded at IBC studios in May, was now re-scheduled for release at the end of July, according to a news item in *Melody Maker*.[144] Playing alongside him in the studio was a disgruntled Keith Moon on drums and session men John Paul Jones on bass, Nicky Hopkins on piano and Jimmy Page on second guitar. That the last had a considerable reputation was confirmed when, on its front page, *Melody Maker* led with not Samwell-Smith leaving the Yardbirds, but Page joining them.[145]

Typed as a long-time friend of the band, 'New Yardbird Jimmy Page is the original Mr Tall, Dark and Handsome. He has sleepy eyes, long curly dark hair and elegant sideburns more befitting an actor in a Victorian melodrama,' wrote *Disc*'s Mike Ledgerwood, who had talked with Page right after his debut with the band at the Marquee.[146] 'Frankly,' Page explained, 'I felt I was getting stale doing sessions. I was restricted – and it was beginning to [show].'[147] He was looking forward to exploring the ideas he'd been storing up: 'after playing for two years at muted volume, I was a little uncertain about playing live and loud. I thought I would fluff it up. I only had a couple of hours rehearsal – and when I got up on stage I gave everything I had. I got very excited.'[148] Though brought in to play bass, it was clear from the outset that this would not be the limit of his contribution; he told *Melody Maker*:

> maybe I'll do a few things with a second guitar. Jeff Beck and I have had a lot of very interesting talks about using two lead guitars. In fact we've even experimented with them ourselves but not with the group. On the free form parts of the numbers, twin lead guitars will be absolutely great. The whole trouble with feedback is that there is never enough power or backing to carry the sound itself. I was using bass guitar feedback the other night which was very good – a whole wall of sound – I got a ridiculous droning sound. On 'Mister You're a Better Man', the overall sound was fantastic.[149]

His arrival, it was reported, had perked up the band; their depressed state could be measured by an account Beck gave to *Disc* about his disgruntlement with unenthusiastic British audiences: 'we're cheesed off with fans. Fans who stand expressionless in front of the stage showing about as much reaction to the Yardbirds' music as a herd of Friesian cows.'[150] Page was looking forward to going to the States, especially the West Coast; as the article's author noted, 'You can probably imagine the Californians' shattered surprise if Page does make it with the group. Two electronic fanatics both raving away could well do the Americans in. We'll be seeing the Beach Boys in Union Jack jackets next!'[151] As the *NME*'s Keith Altham wrote: 'One thing is certain, and that is with Jeff and Jimmy in the same group, the Yardbirds have, with the exception of Eric Clapton (himself an ex-Yardbird), the two most creative guitarists around the group scene today.'[152] For Page, the appeal of playing with the Yardbirds was that they 'have begun something with their new sounds and unusual techniques which is by no means over, and I would like to contribute and help develop their ideas'.[153]

Hit Parader's 'Gal in London!', Miranda Ward, watched the Yardbirds prepare for their appearance on *Ready Steady Go!*:

> It was the first time I'd seen them with Jimmy Page, and it was interesting to see how well he fitted in visually as well as musically. The Yardbird he replaced – Sam – was also there. In his new capacity as co-producer of their records he was helping the sound men get a good balance. It was weird seeing him wander around unhustled by autograph hunters.[154]

Beat Instrumental wondered whether Page's recruitment would change the band's sound. It was expected that by the time they were in the States, he would have moved from bass to second guitar, swapping roles with Dreja. Again, the fact of the two guitarists routinely using set twin-guitar pieces in rehearsal suggests that this was planned from the get-go. He and Beck, Page said, had copied Freddie King solos note for note, with the two guitars playing in 'unison or in harmony'.[155] Would it become the Jeff and Jimmy show? Kevin Swift asked. Page didn't think so.

As a session man, Page, it was noted, had played with just about everyone, the Beatles excepted. He'd also had an aborted solo career: 'I was pressurised into doing a single of my own once. Nothing fantastic. A song called "She Just Satisfies" which Jackie [DeShannon] persuaded me to record. Still I got a great advance for it and was able to go to the States.'[156] Though a guitar for hire, Page had received his fair share of publicity over the last two years. Earlier in 1966, he had been featured in a *Sunday Times Magazine* article that profiled the people behind the day's pop stars. He was called the 'king' of the session men, and it was noted he was still only 21 years old (they had added a year to his actual birth date – January 1944 – and then Page took another year off his age when he joined the Yardbirds).[157] He was pictured sitting cross-legged among guitars, playing the sitar: 'Session men are moody because hardly any of them want to play pop. The strings are classicals who can't find orchestras; the horns are jazzmen who need extra cash. The only pop players are the rhythm section.'[158] He was described as 'softly-spoken, shy and a bit fey'. His ambition, he said, was to save enough 'to get out and buy a place where the climate is good, like the Greek islands. I'll just bum around and paint and think about music.'[159]

Before Page helped shift the Yardbirds' direction of travel, there was their first studio album proper to promote. The *NME* gave the Yardbirds star-billing in its 22 July edition, running individually through each of the twelve tracks on the eponymous LP that would acquire the nickname 'Roger the Engineer' due to the cartoon figure of Roger Cameron drawn by Chris Dreja on the album's sleeve: 'Someone listening to the first few numbers asked me: "Is this a Chinese group?" Not without cause. Oriental sounds predominate to start with,' wrote Allen Evans.[160] The theme continued with 'Lost Woman', which had Relf wailing on his 'harmonica through a fuzz box' – producing a 'breath of the Orient'.[161] 'Over Under Sideways Down' had a 'swinging Arabic sound'; 'Nazz are Blue' had a 'jazzy blues sound'; 'I Can't Make Your Way' was 'folksy' and 'Eastern'; 'Rack My Mind' was 'Chicago styled r-and-b'; 'Farewell' was a 'sick', 'Dylan-influenced . . . nursery rhyme'; and 'Hot House of Omagararshid' featured 'exotic jungle percussion' and Beck's 'snake-charmer music'.[162] The guitarist's show piece, 'Jeff's Boogie', used snippets of other tunes including 'Alfie'.[163] 'He's Always There' had the 'cricket-like sound' of a guiro; 'Turn to Earth' was a 'slow, low-key blues' written by Samwell-Smith and his girlfriend, Rosemary Simon; 'What Do You Want' was a 'raver' with 'jangle guitar'.[164] The album finished with 'Ever Since the World Began', a 'dirge' with a 'gospel tinge' that 'snaps out of it to a swinging pace' before a 'quick ending': 'Simon Napier-Bell and bass player Paul Samwell-Smith (who says Mick of the Triangle played bass on half the tracks) have produced a clever set. You'll find new things about this album each time you play it, which should keep you playing it often.'[165]

With the album, the Yardbirds' 'orientalism' had reached a peak, at least as implied by this review, but their exoticism was located no further than Soho's burgeoning Chinatown – itself a transplant from Limehouse, not the Far East – or with the Indian diaspora then making a home for themselves in the East End of London. The 'oriental' had become a shorthand for the band's experiments in sound, which were no more ethnic than a paisley print Nehru jacket bought in the King's Road. If anything, it was an ethnicity of their own devising, a foreignness conjured wholesale with comic-book renditions of the British Empire such as *Zulu* (1964), the adaptation of H. Rider Haggard's *She* (1965) or any of the James Bond overseas adventures. But the alien strangeness of their sonic experiments did adequately signify just how mutated and mongrel the band's most blueswailing roots had become.

'Yardbirds: All Our Own Work' ran the heading for *Disc and Music Echo*'s review of the long-delayed album:

> In their own quiet and highly individual way the Yardbirds have sprung something of a mini-Beatles on us with this album. All the tracks are well-written, played and produced, and what with their frequent Indian sound, their Gregorian chants plus pure blues the boys prove themselves one of our best AND most original groups.[166]

Even the sleeve design was praised. *Melody Maker*'s critic thought the overall result was 'an interesting and often exciting album', enhanced by the inclusion of 'Over Under Sideways Down' – 'surely one of the best pop records of the year'.[167] Jeff Beck's contribution is highlighted. Richard Green dutifully reviewed the album for *Record Mirror*, pronouncing on each track in turn. He thought it a 'definite hit' – good original numbers and well produced, 'there's nothing I can think to fault them on.'[168] But that hardly sounded like a ringing endorsement either.

Richard Green did ask Eric Clapton what he thought of the LP: '"I just don't want to know," he said after a short snort. "One of those numbers I gave to them two years ago and arranged it and everything."'[169] Having established his authority, he then slammed the Yardbirds for not appearing at the sixth National Jazz and Blues Festival in Windsor: 'They do this thing about Keith Relf collapsing five minutes before they go on stage, then they pull the whole band out [It was Beck who had taken ill; Relf apologized for their no-show from the festival's stage]. Clapton's new band, the Cream, debuted that day.'[170] 'Everyone's waiting for the big split,' he told Green.[171]

In his column in *Queen*, Nik Cohn reviewed the Yardbirds' album, which came sandwiched between the Beatles' *Revolver* and *Live! The Ike and Tina Turner Show*. He thought the former album

Plumb line abstraction: posing in a modern art gallery, promotional picture for 'Over Under Sideways Down', 1966.

Renewed potential: Beck–Page line-up, promotional picture, 1966.

to be the band's 'most complex', and that it could sit alongside the Beach Boys' *Pet Sounds* 'as the most progressive record of the year'.[172] Cohn was generally positive about what the Beatles had achieved collectively, but harsh in his criticism of the individuals involved. McCartney dominated the album, which gave full rein to his Romantic inclinations, Cohn wrote. Lennon had taken a step back and Harrison had filled in, though Cohn found him 'a bit of a bore':

'The Indian bit is half-baked and his tunes are monotonous. His guitar playing, on the other hand, is less limited than it used to be ... Other LPs this month fade into insignificance by comparison.'[173] He then turned to the Yardbirds:

> Good in well-spread-out patches. Jeff Beck is an excellent guitarist and there are some inventive arrangements. But most of the songs are nothings and it's unbelievable that such an instrumentally gifted group should use a vocalist of Keith Relf's monumental drabness. This is a group whose imagination stretches just nicely to cutting three or four well-produced hits a year, but quite clearly don't have the staying power for a full album.[174]

Up against the Beatles, the band's shortcomings were always going to be magnified.

EMI plugged the album in their in-house journal, *Record Mail*, but had a hard time figuring out just what it was that they were selling. They came up with 'more than just another LP – it's a mood put on record. A mood that hits you right from the opening track, vital and alert.'[175] Mood music? Well, perhaps, depending on your disposition. For the copywriter, what stood out was 'the use of the sitar', which 'gives an extra emphasis to the instrumental breaks'.[176] While in the band, it would be ever thus for Beck and his virtual sitar dexterity.

Contributing to the fifth issue of *Crawdaddy*, Michael Kac was as frustrated with the U.S. version of the new album as his editor had been with 'Shapes of Things'. Kac's review was also not that distinct from what Cohn had written: 'Perhaps the most persistent problem the Yardbirds have is that their songs are not unified by discernible beginnings and ends; they have a tendency to start – and leave off – in the middle.'[177] For these listeners, the Yardbirds were, it seemed, less than the sum of their parts.

The sense of things being pulled in different directions, with the centre collapsing in on itself from competing tensions, defined the second half of 1966 for the band. When Beck and Page found themselves on common ground (and with a suitable sound system to project their dual guitar attack) the band was without peer as a live attraction. But on too many occasions Beck's propensity to either not show up for a gig or to put in a half-hearted performance told on his bandmates, whose patience with him had limits. The Yardbirds also had to contend with Clapton having put himself back in the frame with his new band the Cream; and he had something to prove.

7

Stock Explosions and the Perversion of Sound, 1966

> I play an old Gibson Les Paul guitar and use a Marshall 100-watt system which goes through eight 12 in. speakers. I designed the strap myself in an impulsive moment! Before the Yardbirds, I was with the Roosters and Casey Jones. I intend to stay with John unless I get the chance to form my own group sometime. Some artists I have worked with are not widely known as being great and are to many people obscure. Jack Bruce is definitely one of them. He's the best bass player I know. My favourites are all American and cover a very wide field. The most significant are BB King, Otis Redding and Paul Butterfield.
>
> ERIC CLAPTON (1966)[1]

In the spring of 1965, after he left the Yardbirds, Eric Clapton's profile in the music papers became negligible to non-existent. He was a shadow figure, his currency summed up by two members of the Mark Leeman Five chatting twelve months later to Christine Osbourne for *Music Echo*: '"Everyone wants to make money. Anyone who says they're dedicated – well, that's a load of rubbish. No one is dedicated." "That bloke who left the Yardbirds is," chipped in Blink, "That Eric Clapton," they agreed, "He gave up a lot."'[2] A year later 'that bloke' re-emerged and, by the end of 1966, Clapton and his new band, the Cream, could hardly be ignored.

Talking to *Melody Maker* as he ate a plate of spaghetti, Jeff Beck bemoaned the fan that demands and demands:

> A pop star is made to feel terribly obliged to his audience. This may be hard to understand, but we, the group, feel obliged to bring out a new record – you realize fans are waiting and asking of a new disc. Most people think it doesn't work that way, but we get all tied up with making a good commercial record.[3]

The complaint was a prelude to why he so admired Clapton:

> He didn't bend to what the public wants. The kids were digging and buying commercial stuff but he refused to play it. He is against images as well. He once complained to me about modelling clothes – because he's a kind of purist and we're suede jacket and jeans boys at heart.[4]

In 1966, Clapton would run with the dedicated purist tag, making his anti-commercial pitch right into the heart of the pop music machine, the contradictions in his careerism barely acknowledged.

Gigging with the Bluesbreakers had enhanced Clapton's standing with his peers, confirmed by *Melody Maker*'s poll of musicians for contenders in their 'Group's Group'. Clapton came top as lead guitar to be supported by Bruce Welch on rhythm, John Entwistle on bass, Brian Auger on organ, Ginger Baker on drums and Steve Winwood on vocals. Clapton received nominations from Mick Jagger, Eric Burdon, Spencer Davis, Steve Marriott and Paul Jones.[5] Back in the real world, John Mayall's Bluesbreakers were playing to house-full notices at the Marquee, billed as 'featuring Eric Clapton'. *Melody Maker*'s readers fed the paper's mailbag with a steady flow of fawning letters about the man's pre-eminence – 'I agree with Jeff Beck, Eric "Slowhand" Clapton is the best guitarist Britain has. When he plays blues he really plays blues.'[6]

Running alongside a spoof interview with Fred Scuttle, leading light of the Rhythm and Spoons phenomenon then trending in London's clubs, *Melody Maker* profiled Clapton:

> Eric Clapton stands at the back of the stage, almost behind the drummer. His legs are slightly apart and his clothes are reasonably casual. When John Mayall finishes his solo he looks towards Clapton who flicks a switch and takes off into a whirlwind of bending notes. He looks like a bobbing puppet as he literally twists and turns the notes out of his guitar.[7]

At every gig, Nick Jones wrote, there are 'the Clapton-idolising contingent who shout things like: "Give God a solo", or "We want more God"'.[8] The deity compliantly provided Jones with an account of his time with the Yardbirds – it was spiked with animus:

> They were playing things like 'Can't Judge a Book', sort of everyday R&B. Like R&B puppets. I don't know why but I thought what a cushy job this would be so I joined them. Eventually I got brainwashed with commercial R&B . . . it was only when I got on stage away from all the hubble bubble, that I suddenly realised I didn't really like what the group did or played . . . the whole thing got so business-like with finances, companies, promotion and all that, we became machines instead of human beings. I thought, 'If I'm going to become a money-making musical factory, I'll pull out.' So I did.[9]

He belittles Relf's singing and just about everyone else on the scene:

> The stuff coming out of England now, makes me puke. I'll be the first to put Chris Farlowe down . . . He can't hope

> to simulate what the American Negroes do. The Miracles, Ray Charles, everybody, make their records commercial for the American white public to buy. Therefore by the time Farlowe and all have got the numbers, they're about third hand. Anyway, I think the only way is to go to America.[10]

He planned to go to Chicago; 'I deal in realism. Nothing but realism, and the nastier the better. The buyers and sellers of records are not concerned with it, this is why I'm being driven out.'[11] Clapton played from the heart: 'This is blues. Expression. I am contacting myself through the guitar and telling myself I have a power.'[12] Eric Clapton – victim, outsider and saviour.

Clapton had been recording with Mayall since April 1965, when they played together on a *Saturday Club* session (they would tape two further engagements for the BBC show, the next in October and then again in March the following year). These radio sessions filled in time while issues were resolved with Mayall's company, Decca. In the meantime, Jimmy Page produced 'I'm Your Witchdoctor' and 'Telephone Blues' for Immediate Records, released in October 1965, which captured the band at their most howling and coruscating. On the top deck, Clapton laid down a minimalist solo with sustain and feedback straight out of the Beck school. Since profiling the Yardbirds in 1964, *R&B Monthly* broke its tacit rule to review only Black American records; it gave the single some space, describing the top side as a 'fast number with some haunting guitar phrases from Eric Clapton and excellent vocal from Mayall himself . . . Excellent value for the not-so-ethnic collector.'[13]

Despite a growing fanbase, Clapton had taken a leave of absence from the Bluesbreakers' ranks and went travelling for two months.[14] On his return, with Decca still showing a reluctance to work with Mayall, the band's producer, Mike Vernon, and not coincidently editor of *R&B Monthly*, paid for an October 1965 session. They cut 'The Lonely Years' and 'Bernard Jenkins', which resulted in a single on Vernon's Purdah label, released ten months later. In December, before the ever-hesitant Decca committed to an LP, a further session for Immediate was undertaken, again with Page at the deck. In March 1966, nearly a year after Clapton had joined them, the sessions for the album were underway.[15]

The purist approach that the Bluesbreakers maintained was justified when they continued to receive reviews in journals that normally locked out commercial pop discs. *Jazzbeat* applauded the Bluesbreakers' authenticity:

> The greatest compliment I can pay this set is to say that had I come across it in a blindfold test, I would have guessed that it came from one of the many blues bands playing clubs in Chicago. In this showing, Clapton is one of the best of our blues guitarists, his understanding of the idiom is quite astounding.[16]

The reviewer for *Beat Instrumental* concurred, and underscored the impression that it was 'Clapton who steals the limelight . . . Since he has left the Yardbirds he has become almost a legend.'[17]

In the first week of August, *Melody Maker*'s review of the album caught the general consensus about its merits and virtues:

> John Mayall refuses to be sidetracked with minor issues like pop music or commercialism and is about the only group left in the country who ever claimed to play blues still actually playing that much abused music . . . It's all played relentlessly, bitingly and with feeling. But it is all one feeling. There isn't a spark of humour in anybody's playing . . . It's joyless and savage and gives a grim satisfaction. No British musicians have ever sounded like this before on record. It is a giant step.[18]

But a month before the album was in distribution, Clapton had moved on, taking with him that aggression and obstinacy he'd so briefly loaned to the Bluesbreakers.

In its 11 June issue, *Melody Maker* echoed its fictional story from three months earlier of a supergroup, which was now fact:

> A sensational new 'Group's Group' starring Eric Clapton, Jack Bruce and Ginger Baker is being formed. Top groups will be losing star instrumentalists as a result. Manfred Mann will lose bassist, harmonica player, pianist and singer Jack Bruce; John Mayall will lose brilliant blues guitarist Eric Clapton, and Graham Bond's Organisation will lose incredible drummer Ginger Baker. The group say they hope to start playing at clubs, ballrooms and theatres in a month's time.[19]

Two weeks later, *Melody Maker* carried the exclusive that the new group's name was the Cream, and they were to be represented by Robert Stigwood as agent and management. They would also record for the impresario's Reaction label.[20] Later, Clapton explained that they took their name because they were a 'group's group': 'I didn't mean it like we are the cream of groups . . . Just like thick rich cream.'[21]

Before they played clubs, ballrooms and theatres, the Cream gave a showcase debut performance at the sixth National Jazz and Blues Festival, now relocated from its old Richmond base to Windsor. *Melody Maker*'s Chris Welch attended the band's rehearsals for the show that were taking place at a church hall: 'with the eyes of thousands of fans, and rival groups upon them, and the burning of boats behind them, how does the Cream feel now? '"Nervous, very nervous," said Eric Clapton, sideboards bristling, guitar slung at hip.'[22] Bruce and Clapton are pictured wearing military dress tunics, the former supplementing his costume with a Scottish regiment's forage cap. Baker stands behind his bandmates looking like a Baptist preacher, the look visually rhyming with Clapton's declaration that they were to play 'Blues Ancient and Modern', to which Bruce added, 'We call it sweet and sour Rock and Roll.'[23] Eric approved:

> Yes, that's a good headline . . . What we want to do is anything that people haven't done before. Pete Townshend is enthusiastic and he may write a number for us . . . Most people have formed the impression of us as three solo musicians clashing with each other. We want to cancel that idea and be a group that plays together.[24]

Parodying the vogue for bands tying their music and image to a modern art movement, the Cream would deliver a 'Dada-esque performance' that would include turkeys and stuffed bears on stage while Eric intended to wear a hat with a 'cage on top and a live frog inside'.[25] Whatever their costumes and stage props, the overriding promise was that the show would be loud.

Despite the heavy rain across the weekend of the festival, *Record Mirror* reported that 'hundreds of people had arrived purely to see Eric Clapton and the Cream . . . The newly-formed trio proved to be as good as was hoped and look set for a big future.'[26] Jimmy James and the Vagabonds, the Spencer Davis Group and the Small Faces played the Friday night. On Saturday evening, after the afternoon jazz programme, Jimmy James was back, followed by Gary Farr and the T-Bones, Julian Covey and the Machine and the Move. The last impressed with their 'incredible Indian excursion via Bombay, Calcutta and Birmingham, England'.[27] The Move also staged some mock fisticuffs as prelude to headliners the Who's act – a raucous performance that was the 'utmost in pop violence'; Townshend wore a bow-tie and dinner suit.[28] By Sunday evening, the rain had turned Windsor's field into a sea of mud, but coming on before the Action was the act 'thousands had been waiting for'.[29] The Cream 'kicked off with "Spoonful", "Sleepy Time" and Jack Bruce's harmonica and vocal feature "Train Time". Eric's incredible guitar induced the audience to shout and scream for more, even while he was playing more!' Ginger Baker's 'Toad' also received rapturous applause. Clapton looked resplendent with mutton-chop whiskers, white trousers and shirt with oversized penny collars worn under a golden floral-print jacket. Old Slowhand's authentic Mod-austere had been stowed away.

Following Windsor, the Cream played their first club night to a packed turnout at Cook's Ferry Inn in north London – an old jazz hangout. They opened with 'Laudie Miss Claudie' ('Lawdy Miss Clawdy') followed by Buddy Guy's 'First Time I Met the Blues' and 'Train Time', Jack Bruce's harmonica showpiece. *Melody Maker* reported:

> Enthusiastic shouting and cheering were reserved for the second half of their act when they dropped their nerves and reduced the gap between numbers. Solos from Eric, Ginger and Jack had the audience in raptures, calling for more. Although the Cream are still in the experimental stage, they are striving for a perfection which, when it does come, will be little short of sensational.[30]

One member of the audience wrote in to *Melody Maker*'s 'Expert Advice' column: 'When I saw Eric Clapton at Cook's Ferry a few weeks ago, he seemed to turn and face directly into his Marshall amplifier. Would this create the "continuous" note that he produced?'[31] Clapton generously provided an answer:

> The effect is at first achieved by just hitting the note and holding it, with finger vibrato. From then on it depends on the acoustics of the hall. If these are not satisfactory, it is necessary to turn round and face the amplifier, so that

> the pick-ups on the guitar are as near as possible to the speaker. I have everything turned full on, causing a lot of distortion.[32]

As much as this was a technical explanation of what he was doing, it was also an aesthetic declaration, a manifesto of noise. *Disc and Music Echo* described Clapton as 'tight trousered and evil-faced with straggly sides to his hair and frilled shirts worn with careless abandon . . . a drifter who when he first joined the Cream signed his first contract' (as he did with the Yardbirds, Clapton opted out of signing an agreement with John Mayall).[33]

For interviews, Clapton donned a clock of humility: 'I'm not a great guitarist,' he insisted to *Beat Instrumental*, who went 'face-to-face with the guy who is acknowledged to be the god of British blues guitar in his own small heaven – the top flat of an apartment block high above Notting Hill Gate'.[34] 'Clapton is god' was the shout from those who followed him from gig to gig; Kevin Swift asked the guitarist 'if he thought he deserved such acclaim':

> It's all very encouraging . . . but I'm not sure that people are interpreting the whole thing properly. I am not a great guitarist, it's just that they enjoy the style of guitar I play. It's rare, if not unique, in Britain. The acclaim puts a great weight on my shoulders and I feel a great deal of responsibility to the audience because I am supposed to be the greatest. I am expected to play better all the time, and this is hard.[35]

Asked if there was anyone on the scene 'who he felt inferior to, Clapton answered forthwith, "Jeff Beck"': 'He's more of a musician than I am. I do things the longest way round, and I'm shoddy, but Jeff knows exactly what he wants and how to get it. There's a lot of difference in our styles, and I should say that he is much more deliberate.'[36] Clapton's view of the differences in approach and style between himself and Beck was perceptive and on point; unlike his disparagement of the rest of his old bandmates, Clapton showed friendship towards Beck, as Beck did in return.

Clapton's modesty had not been felt by John Mayall, still smarting from his leaving. To Decca's surprise, the Bluesbreakers' album went Top 10; when asked how much of these sales were due to Clapton's involvement, Mayall told *Beat Instrumental*:

> Eric has always been associated with some kind of hero-worship since he left the Yardbirds . . . They used to play blues then, although I thought they were appalling. At one time all he wanted was to play blues, but now he seems to play for the admiration. We were quite well established when Eric came to me. Fans of the Yardbirds came over with him and we gained a whole new set of followers. I'd never found anyone who could play this kind of guitar, and when he left there was a danger of people attributing our power or structure as a group to this, and thinking the sound they liked would go with him.
>
> However, in Peter Green we have a replacement who is a young genius. He's better than Eric was when he joined, and for my money he'll be better than Eric . . . Peter is more interested in playing the blues than being a star. Eric's gone all 'showbiz'.[37]

There was the whiff of hypocricy in Clapton's move that jarred with his puritanical reputation. Clapton, however, sailed on: 'I'm tired of being called a specialist musician. People thought the Cream was going to be a blues band, but it's not. It's a pop group really. We were a bit ragged at Windsor, it'll take about two months before we are okay. We've got four good numbers and a few standards.'[38]

'The first is last and the last is first but the first, the second and the last are the Cream' was how one publicity handout described the band, according to the *NME*'s Keith Altham. In a short interview with the trio, he touched on all the usual bases but added: 'the group has a predominantly male following – although messrs. Baker, Clapton and Bruce are working on that one – and this is largely due to their reputations as musicians.'[39] That the Cream had wider (potential) appeal than a specialist blues audience was confirmed by a profile in *Rave* magazine written by Dawn James. In the accompanying picture, Jack Bruce wears the baroque jacket that Clapton had sported on stage in Windsor, and Baker looks like he has borrowed Eric's white penny-collar shirt – pop stars in the making: 'In a world where one hit record can earn an artiste of no exceptional musical ability up to ten thousand pounds, it is surely time the outrageous talent of guitarist Eric Clapton made some big money.'[40] Clapton concurred:

> I know I'm a well thought of guitarist, and Ginger is a well thought of drummer, and Jack a well thought of singer, but we are tired of having talent that doesn't make any big money. Personally, I'd like some big money. I've lived in dingy rooms long enough. I've given all I've had to my music. Now I want something back.[41]

It had taken him just over eighteen months to get to where the Yardbirds had earlier arrived, if indeed he ever did truthfully identify as a purist: 'I never wanted to make money from the wrong kind of music . . . and I was so sure about that, that I almost didn't want to make money. I was right to leave the Yardbirds, but I'd like to make some money now.'[42] He'd shucked off the hairshirt; the golden jacket was a better fit. But, in return, his acolytes now had an improved offer: 'The fans are ready to hear something more genuine, they are looking for depth and truth. They want to be given something with substance, that has more to it than just a nice noise.'[43] Jack Bruce added, 'We are in fact doing more and more complicated pieces . . . I'm writing a lot of them. I won't write a song unless it has a difficult pattern because there is no enjoyment playing it.'[44] Clapton summed it up: 'We don't want to be idolised as boys, we want to be listened to.'[45] Dawn James concluded, 'If there is any justice in the music business, the Cream must have a hit. Music must give them back something material at last.'[46]

And a hit was what the Cream were aiming for with their first single, 'Wrapping Paper', released on 7 October. It was, however, by any measure a strange choice, something more suited to Lovin' Spoonful – the New York band's spring 1966 hit 'Daydream' was its obvious precursor. Fans were puzzled by this initial excursion: 'We did it because we didn't want people to put us into a category straight away. We play soft numbers on stage, maybe we'll change it next time,' Bruce told *Record Mirror*'s Richard Green.[47] He continued: 'You shouldn't be limited by only recording material that you can play on stage . . . People who come to see us in clubs may not buy records and record-buyers may not only go to clubs, so we please them both.'[48] If fans remained perplexed by the single, *Record Mirror* reviewed it more positively as a 'gentle rippling, and excellently performed little number . . . All rather breathy, on the vocal side, and a compulsive but unobtrusive beat. Good words – almost a hark back in vocal group style. Effective and surely commercial.'[49] *Melody Maker* suggested that the single would 'astound their fans – possibly even drive them to suicide! . . . in the group's attempt at ultra-hipness, and shock treatment they may have outsmarted themselves . . . Most disappointing is the musical content of the number, which is nil.'[50]

The definitive before their name now dropped, Cream were consistent in making the case for releasing 'Wrapping Paper'; Clapton told *Disc*, 'we didn't think it would harm the image and personally I haven't had any real protests. We knew some people would like it and some wouldn't.'[51] It was a defence that could just as easily have been made about 'For Your Love'. 'Anyway,' he said,

'I don't think it is a betrayal of the fans because I don't think it is a bad pop record. If people have enough intelligence, they can accept pop records if they're good.'[52] Bruce told *Beat Instrumental*:

> When we each started to play we took set paths, went to blues or to jazz. We didn't listen to anything which was remotely connected with 'pop'. I suppose in a way we were like those maniacs who won't listen to jazz unless it was recorded before 1927. I wouldn't say that we were purists but we were musically set in our ways. Now there's so much more going on in 'pop' I think we would like to be part of it.[53]

Pop's terrain had changed in no small part because of the Yardbirds' interventions and contributions; Clapton may have forsaken his old band, but he was beholden to them nonetheless.

The link back to the old days continued in other, more obscure ways; publicity for Cream's single and album was organized by Paragon, a company set up by Giorgio Gomelsky and contracted by Polydor to work on their activities. Many of the employees at Paragon had cooperated closely with the Yardbirds, including publicists Gaby Sturmer and Roger Cowles, designer Hamish Grimes and copywriter Eddy Jenkins.[54]

The issues around the first single quickly fell away as Cream established themselves on the club circuit, their bona fides confirmed when they went head-to-head with the visiting Paul Butterfield Blues Band playing Blaises on the same evening as they played at the Marquee. There were packed houses for both shows, with Cream in attendance at the Chelsea and Kensington club after their Wardour Street engagement. *Disc*'s Hugh Nolan wrote up the evening. Despite not sharing 'an authentic blues background' like the six-piece mixed-race Chicagoans, Nolan thought that 'the second-hand British version sounded better if not louder.' Cream 'produced enough noise – good noise – to blast out everyone's ear-drums down at the Marquee, London. Some of their material came from their new album, including one they'd written themselves – ten times better than their current first hit "Wrapping Paper". Clapton's guitar-work is unbelievable, at times sounding like a horn.'[55]

Whatever the pop merits of 'Wrapping Paper', Cream said, 'for the fans who know us and what we do we made the "B" side "Cat's Squirrel"'.[56] The relentlessly driven cover of Doctor Ross's song, which he'd first recorded for Sam Phillips in Memphis in 1951 and later for Fortune in Detroit in 1959, was credited to 'Trad. arr. S. Splurge'. Plagiarism aside – though to be fair, the band did contribute the possessive to the title – the track opened side two of *Fresh Cream*. 'Wrapping Paper' was a notable absentee; as a pop entrée, its time had quickly passed, though the equally whimsical 'Dreaming' made a suitable substitute. Half of the album's ten tracks were blues covers: Robert Johnson, Willie Dixon, Muddy Waters and Skip James. The band's approach, its manifesto, on the Ross and Waters numbers was to do away with the Yardbirds-style rave-up or the Bluesbreakers rhythmic modulations and instead pile in full throttle with amps overheating and percussion cascading. The sonic model here was not the urban Chicago blues on which Clapton's reputation had been established and displayed on 'Sleepy Time Time' and 'Spoonful', but Shel Talmy-era Who. On 'Cat's Squirrel' and 'Rollin' and Tumblin'', Cream's template was the Shepherd's Bush quartet's closing number on *My Generation*, 'The Ox' – a tidal wave of surf guitar, exploding drums all riding over a bottom end as deep as the Mariana Trench.

Comparisons between the Who and Cream had been rumbling throughout the autumn, especially in the letters to *Melody Maker*'s 'Mailbag', which hit a kind of frenzy in the first week of October.[57] 'The Cream play their instruments – rather than bash the living daylights out of them to make people listen,' wrote Pam Atkins from Rutland.[58] 'The only similarity between the Who and the Cream is in their instruments, their sounds are worlds apart, so the Cream can hardly be accused of jumping on the Who's bandwagon,' wrote M. J. Bishop from Middlesex.[59] 'The Cream are perfectionists, and just about the most remarkable three people in this very dismal-sounding country,' was Miss B. M. Deane's opinion.[60] 'Ask the fans why they prefer the Who and most would reply – "because of their fantastic stage act"', wrote Miss Rozalind Beevor, Chiswick.[61] Others added their thoughts, but the week's LP Winner was Peter Warren from Sheffield:

> There can be no comparison between the Cream and the Who and to describe three of Britain's best musicians as 'just another noisy blues group' is, to say the least, bigoted. 'Let's hear some decent melody for a change' is what people were saying at the birth of bebop and modern jazz.[62]

Warren was a worthy recipient of the prize, neatly summing up what was now at stake as pop became rock; in the heat of debates over musical progression, the link between bands like Cream and the Who to avant-jazz no longer seemed parodic.

Clapton told *Melody Maker*'s Nick Jones:

> I'm no longer trying to play anything [*sic*] but like a white man. The time is overdue when people should play like they are and what colour they are. I don't believe I've ever played so well in my life. More is expected of me in the Cream – I have to play rhythm guitar as well as lead. People have been saying I'm like Pete Townshend, but he doesn't play much lead.[63]

Cream don't so much cover Muddy Water's 'Rollin' and Tumblin'' as pummel it without restraint – no submission. Not one of the three participants concedes any ground; there's no torque held in reserve, it just explodes over the quarter mile and then keeps going. Bruce's harmonica playing is an endurance exercise, avoiding the interplay with Clapton that Relf had mastered and then developed with Beck. With a breakneck bravado, Clapton raves on, countering the cool collectivity he had once shown with Mayall, while Baker knocks down one door after another. Such displays of muscular stamina awe and appal in equal measure; it is ugly and frightening, splenetic and ill-tempered, quite brilliant but unsustainable – though Blue Cheer would give it their best.

Bruce's own numbers, like 'N.S.U.', one of the great car songs of the London scene along with the Who's 'Jaguar', offered a more melodic and structured approach. On Johnson's 'Four until Late' and James's 'I'm So Glad', things are sufficiently slowed down; the propulsive desire paused, a respite established, and Bruce gets to show his range, his singing a tuneful alternative to the instrumental onslaught of 'Cat's Squirrel' or 'Rollin' and Tumblin''. Where Relf is familiar, close quartered, almost conspiratorial and certainly restrained in his delivery, Bruce is declarative – like a trained actor projecting, without amplification, to the rear of an auditorium. Bruce sings with the rounded vowels of a Scottish thespian rather than the Surrey accent of a guttersnipe with Romantic inclinations.

Cream had arrived, and all around, things were about to get louder.

THE YARDBIRDS HAD BEEN BILLED as part of the Jazz and Blues Festival that served for Cream's debut but pulled out at the last moment due to Beck's ill-health. On 2 August, however, they took off for their third visit to the United States. The opening gig of the tour was at Dayton's department store in Minneapolis, where they were to take part in a 'Smash Fashion Bash'. They hit the stage as a five-piece. Other than showcase gigs like those at the start of the year at Hullabaloo, most of their U.S. appearances in 1966 were part of

'Soopah Fashion Show': Dayton's Super Youthquake, *Star Tribune* (31 July 1966).

larger affairs in which the Yardbirds were not the main attraction. At Dayton's, they were just one event in a month-long series that under the banner 'Super Youthquake' sold teen gear in the weeks before the target audience went back to school.[64] The Yardbirds were participating in the 'Soopah Fashion Show', a tie-in with August's edition of *Seventeen* magazine. (The Yardbirds would, coincidentally or not, take part as supporting figures in a Mary Quant fashion shoot that was featured in *Seventeen* the following year.)[65]

Dayton's was a massive building, twelve storeys high with a parking ramp for 650 cars. The Yardbirds played two shows, at 1 p.m. and 3 p.m., in the auditorium on the eighth floor that had a capacity of 5,000. It must have been an alienating experience to move from the Pier Ballroom in Hastings or London's Ram Jam Club to a vast seated space inside a department store that made Oxford Street's Selfridges seem like a local corner shop. Before the shows, the band held a press conference and were asked the usual questions, to which they gave more-or-less stock answers: 'The Yardbirds regard all their records as "experiments", says vocalist Relf. "We've never really been pleased with any of them," he says. "they don't really represent what we feel."' Page livened things up a little by pushing Relf's idea a bit further, however: '"We have no plan or policy for our music," says bass guitarist Page . . . "It just happens."'[66] Fearing where this might lead, the interviewer noted that Page was the only member of the group who can read music and therefore labels him their 'arranger', contradicting his pronouncement on the band's spontaneous, improvisational, anarchic intent.[67] *The Tribune* ran a feature on the young people who attended the gig, with 'girl watchers' Larry Johnson, eighteen, and Scott Stein, sixteen, passing comment on what the young pretty things were wearing, but not a word on the show they ostensibly had gone to see.[68] That, it was implied, was a lot less important than selling clothes.

The next day, the Yardbirds were playing the Col Ballroom in Davenport, Iowa, and then on to Chicago. They would be touring for just over a month, with extra dates being added before their return to Britain on 10 September.[69] Publicity that circulated prior to the Davenport gig emphasized their uniqueness: 'This is a group that does not play for their audience – but WITH them!' wrote a Quad City *Times-Democrat* reporter, who also quoted Napier-Bell: 'The Yardbirds are not phoneys. They are not interested in an idol image. They play because they feel the need to do it, and believe that singing releases them from all the everyday pressure young people experience.'[70] The Dayton gig would surely have left the band feeling the absolute opposite.

They were back plugging teen sedition for their third engagement of the tour, Chicago's Civic Opera house, where 'about 300 girls' welcomed them, handing over gifts that included 'imported caviar and kumquats to instant psychiatric kits, 69 sweatshirts, stuffed animals and incense. One girl was on crutches and took moving pictures. Another brought along her plaster kit to get a mold of Jeff Beck's leg forever!' – she would be Cynthia 'Plaster Caster' Albritton, undertaking an early exercise in her singular art. Her sculptures would not be sold in Dayton's.[71]

The insanity of the Yardbirds' tour schedule is illustrated by being in Hamilton, Indiana, on Friday, 12 August; Amarillo, Texas, the following day; and then Great Falls, Montana, on the Sunday, where they were photographed disembarking from a DC-3. Arriving just two hours before showtime at the fairgrounds, they were met by around one hundred young fans.[72] Wichita, Kansas; Colorado; Santa Fe, New Mexico; Tulsa, Oklahoma, and Tucson in Arizona were covered in six days. Approximately 3,000 teenagers turned out at Thrift City, Tucson, where the band were met by screams and fist fights – 'the five-man group sang over a restless crowd as police escorted the apparent fight instigators from the former discount store, although stifling heat and a broken guitar string only added to the troubles.'[73] The Yardbirds cut through the anxiety following the fights, and the right kind of screams followed: 'the group is known

8 Great Falls Tribune Monday, August 15, 1966

LET THERE BE SCREAMS—But there weren't screams and nobody even fainted as London's Yardbirds snuck into Great Falls in relative obscurity Sunday evening at the airport, about two hours before a concert at the 4-H Building at the Fairgrounds. About 100 young fans turned out to meet the singing group, who rank just below the Beatles in international fame, but did their greeting quietly and from afar. The fourth member of the group is just leaving the plane at far right.

'Let there be screams': *Great Falls Tribune*, Montana (15 August 1966).

for feeling the audience's reaction,' wrote Carol Crane, 'and, on one occasion, Beck turned to drummer McCarty with a nod and a smile on his face.'[74] Crane reported that they all 'expressed a desire to buy Indian clothes while here. Their attire at the show swung away from the straight British styles into blue jeans, sweatshirts and sandals.'[75] Style leaders as they were.

Between 23 August and 7 September, the Yardbirds played the southern and northern extremes of the West Coast and points in between, including a jaunt to Hawaii. But Beck's increasingly regular no-shows were felt by fans; the sense of loss, of rejection, was palpable. In an 'open letter to five Yardbirds', unsigned but no doubt from *The Beat*'s editorial team, it was written:

> Once upon there was this bird, a girl type one, really. Down deep she was a normal everyday kid. Except, she had fallen victim to a dread disease, known as 'Yardbird' to laymen. Yardbird is a thing that starts in your ears, vibrates down to scruffy feet, and up, to resound somewhere in the general vicinity of the heart and comes out the soul.[76]

At a gig to see the 'disease' – 'Pow, Bang, Shezam' – the Yardbirds blew her mind, but something, or rather someone, was missing: 'with tears in her eyes. And her soul, where the music should be, is empty, vacant. Why, says she, why go without the most fantastic guitarist in the world? Why, Y-birds?'[77] New York's *Hit Parader* also published a forlorn letter from a fan, 'Nina Roberts, Venice, Calif.': 'This just can't be true can it? How can this terrible thing happen to the grooviest group going? No one can duplicate Jeff's sound. He is their sound. His weird feedback sound has become their trademark. If he leaves the group, I'll die.'[78] She was reassured that Jeff was still with the band. Relf, meanwhile, cut his second solo single at Sunset Sound Recorders in Hollywood, a move planned before the flight from London.[79]

Initially, news on the tour sent back to London suggested everything was hunky-dory, but the trouble with Beck's health later dominated.[80] Tonsillitis was again the given explanation for his absences.[81] News soon flowed back to Britain about Beck's hospitalization in Los Angeles, where, according to Relf, his tonsils had been removed (some news items had the surgery being performed in San Francisco).[82] *Melody Maker* gave the cost of the operation at $500, a huge sum that no doubt was intended to suggest how serious it all was.[83] In Beck's absence, the band were reported to be firing as a quartet, with Dreja and Page switching instruments. 'Jimmy Stars on First Big Date' ran the headline in *Disc and Music Echo*; speaking from San Mateo, near San Francisco, Relf said: 'Jeff's missed about seven dates so far – but Jimmy has been doing great

... leaping about all over the place. It's the first time I have seen him really blow out on stage.'[84]

Other news from Relf in America was his impression of the

> cult of psychedelic* music that has sprung up among the hippies of America's West Coast (*'Far-out' music). They keep coming up to us and asking: 'Where do you get those crazy sounds? You must be really high.' And 'What sort of a trip are you on?' [said Keith.] We've been playing along. But the whole thing's fairly degenerate. The big idea is 'Freak Out' records where you blow yourself out on anything available – music, LSD and things like that![85]

In her 17 July 1966 column from New York for *Sydney Morning Herald* readers, Lillian Roxon introduced the latest pop fad of psychedelic discotheques. She compared the effect of taking LSD with a drug-free environment made trippy by music, pictures, lights and smells. It started, she wrote, when 'Timothy Leary, father of the LSD revolution, wanted to give an interested section of the general public an idea of the "psychedelic experience" associated with the drug'.[86] Roxon attended one of these sessions, where 'lights flickered on and off. A rapid succession of images flashed on a series of screens. Eight or ten tape recorders bombarded our ears with a variety of sounds. Someone burnt an incense-like substance.'[87] The event 'succeeded ... in lifting us off the chessboard of life'.[88] Then, the previous April, Andy Warhol appropriated these experiments in image, smell, light and sound and created the 'first psychedelic discotheque', the Exploding Plastic Inevitable.[89] Others followed his lead, like the New World, 'which . . . went one better with eye-numbing Op art walls and a moving floor. In the wake of the psychedelic fad has come a whole new industry and language which has put the whole of Pop Art into the strictly square category.'[90] The British music press and Fleet Street lagged four to six months behind in its coverage of the new scene. In the States, the Yardbirds found themselves at the very centre of things.

Record Mirror reported on the concept of 'freaking out' in an October interview with Kim Fowley (in London to direct some recording sessions) and by reference to the Mothers of Invention LP *Freak Out*: '"Freaking Out" is a term which is being thrown about with gay abandon on the West Coast (California, not Cornwall), and like all successful movements there are plans afoot to introduce the concept on this side of the Atlantic.'[91] The movement was still 'underground' and had not been 'concocted by Madison Avenue. In fact, U.S. big business is only just beginning to realise that there are dollars to be made from this cult.'[92]

Among the underground bands listed that record labels were battling each other to put under contract were the Fugs, Blues Project and, in the band's earliest listing in the British music press, the Velvet Underground: 'this group is handled by film-maker Andy Warhol, who is responsible for many major "happenings" in the U.S.':

> The connection between Freaking Out and psychodelic [*sic*] music is not as strong as supposed. And the equally tenuous connection between both of them and LSD is more of an enigma than a tie-up. The leaders of the Freak Out movement claim to have never taken LSD – Frank Zappa of the Mothers of Invention and the omnipresent Kim Fowley.[93]

Back in March, the *San Francisco Examiner* had covered 'The Big Beat' on the local scene and noted how the 'English style prevails in the Bay area, each group usually taking a reigning professional band as its mentor. Thus one group will play "out of a Stones' bag", another out of a Beatles bag, a third out of the Yardbirds' bag.'[94] Texas band the 13th Floor Elevators had been heavily influenced by the Yardbirds, each member of the band having cited them as their favourites. The Yardbirds patented rave-up provided the

Elevators with a navigation chart to help guide them on their piratical voyage.[95] Roky Erickson's band had been described as 'psychedelic rock' as early as February 1966, and as that term gained in international currency and new bands appeared on the scene, the Yardbirds standing as the future of rock 'n' roll began its slow slip into the past tense.[96]

'Teen Writer' for the *Detroit Free Press*, Loraine Alterman, travelled out of town to see the Yardbirds at play.[97] Beck was present for the show, and Page had shifted back to bass:

> Watching them on stage, it hit me that the Yardbirds really look like they're having a ball. They're alive and you can feel them musically clicking with each other and the audience. Too many groups make it look like an ordeal but not the Yardbirds . . . On-stage Keith is very outgoing, but off-stage he is quiet and soft spoken. He's the kind of man who looks beneath the surface to find out why, and he's not content with pat answers. Just as his music isn't stuck in one groove, neither is his mind.[98]

If the Yardbirds were pretty much a known entity in Britain, over-familiar and easily taken for granted, in the States, they were still an endlessly creative novelty, full of surprises and hidden depths. Relf willingly played along: 'When Keith discusses his background, you can see what kind of person he is,' wrote Alterman:

> I was part of a scene in Richmond and Kingston just outside London that was like a creative upsurge and occurred about six years ago and numbered about 60. There were all sorts of people who were thinking. You could call us beatniks. All creative – painting, writing music, writing. I just became interested in music of the Dylan variety. We were pacifists too. It was one big family that roamed all over England and

> the continent to see how the world was beginning to shape up. Out of that I got into pop music . . . If I can't be with people I like, I like to be on my own. I call the other people nowhere people, zeroes.[99]

On his return to London, Relf was again among the zeroes.

Less than two weeks after getting back to Britain, the Yardbirds finished recording their next single, which they'd begun back in July, 'Happenings Ten Years Time Ago', and its B-side, 'Psycho Daisies'. The Yardbirds joined the Rolling Stones and Ike and Tina Turner on a short twelve-date tour that opened at the Royal Albert Hall.

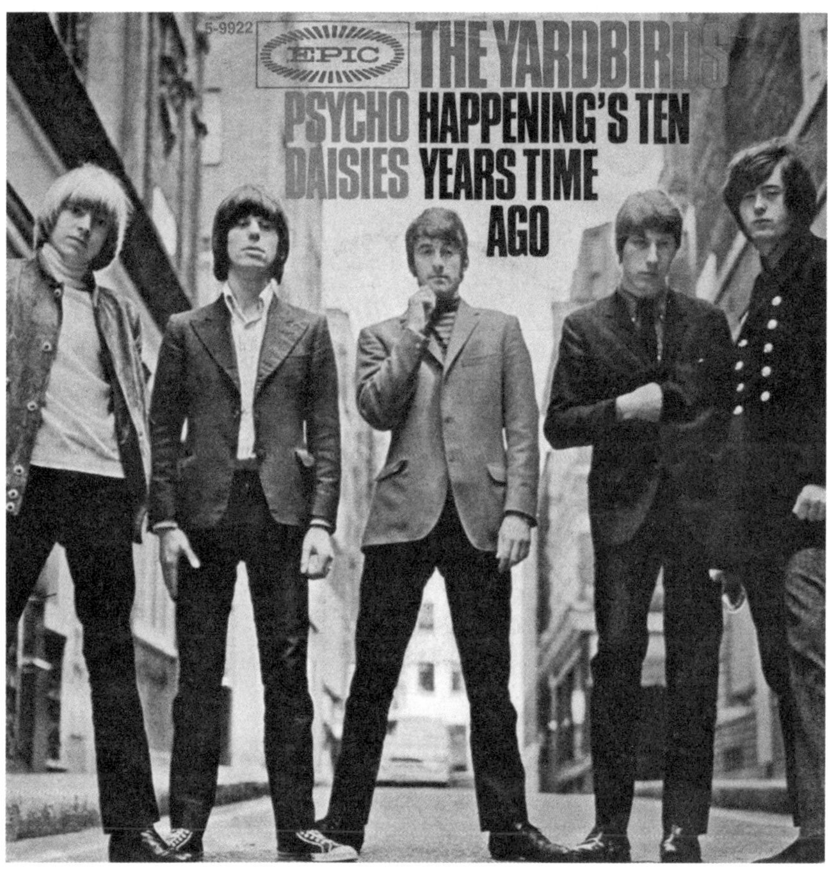

German picture sleeve (with misused apostrophe) for 'Happenings Ten Years Time Ago' alongside 'Psycho Daisies' single, 1966.

Page takes a pot shot at the band's critics, *Teen Beat* annual, 1966.

Their contribution was not well received: 'For the most part the Yardbirds' act . . . was an outrageous cacophony which completely drowned Keith Relf's voice . . . Perhaps if Jeff Beck cut out the gymnastics with his guitar, the group might find some semblance of music.'[100] While rating highly the Stones and Ike and Tina, *Disc*'s review of the Yardbirds was also less than flattering:

> The Yardbirds? Well, I am afraid they are just the Yardbirds. They're a fine group and turn out some sensational songs. They have also become exceedingly colourful lately. Jimmy Page's wardrobe must be fairly bursting with outrageous outfits. But the poor Yardbirds appeared rather stifled by the rest of the stars. And following the Turner team and preceding the Stones wasn't easy.[101]

Melody Maker concurred that the challenge of following the Turners and appearing before the Stones was a tough act, but also added that the Albert Hall acoustics were poor; even so, the band pulled off 'a surprisingly good reproduction of their disc hit "Over Under Sideways Down"'.[102] A reviewer for the *International Times* confirmed the awful sound: 'the voices of all the acts were almost entirely inaudible, due to an ineffective mike system, and most of the instrumental sound was lost or distorted in the vastness of the hall itself.'[103] For the Leeds gig, *Melody Maker* reported that the Yardbirds were 'good enough to fill the unenviable part of the show – just before the Stones. Keith Relf backed by guitarists Jeff Beck, Chris Dreja, and Jimmy Page set up a huge wall of sound and there were plenty of screams.'[104] *Melody Maker* concluded that the tour was 'worth seeing for [the] Ike and Tina revue alone. Add the Stones and the Yardbirds and you can't afford to miss it.'[105] Such positive press aside, the band was dogged throughout the tour with rumours of their imminent implosion.

Relf spent much of his time denying that they were splitting, as well as expressing his exasperation with British audiences and asserting the band's intention to spend more time in the States: 'The whole ratty scene here stinks!' said Relf:

> 'And our general unrest stems from the frustrated feeling of not getting any credit for the things due to us. Things like the introduction of the sitar into pop and our being played down on the recent Stones tour. Despite what you might have heard, we've been going down very well on it . . . In the States at least you get credit for the things you do.' . . . Keith feels pop has reached saturation point here. There isn't anything left for the go-ahead groups.[106]

But the new single, 'Happenings', is 'set to give the scene quite a jolt', said Keith:

> It's a rather revolutionary record even for us. There are one or two odd 'in' jokes in the song and a fantastic bomb

> explosion about half-way through. Jeff Beck does some ridiculous guitar noises like you've never heard in your life before. Actually, I suppose it's about on the verge of being psychedelic-inspired. Like all that stuff we picked up in the States on our last trip.[107]

In the society magazine *The Tatler*, Radio Caroline DJ Rick Dane, in his review of 'Happenings Ten Years Time Ago', echoed Relf's thoughts:

> Exciting new disc from the Yardbirds which will shake the record scene. It shows just how much this talented group has progressed musically. Jeff Beck handles the guitar breaks with some fantastic new approaches and the overall sound is almost psychedelic-inspired. This type of music is becoming very popular in the USA and I don't see why it shouldn't catch on here.[108]

Record Mirror wasn't so easily convinced of the single's revolutionary impact. 'Not quite so way out, but way out enough' was how Norman Jopling's review kicked off: 'An unusual song, presented jerkily but with big beat. Needs close attention to get the full gist. Instrumental break is alarmingly fierce . . . commended for originality.'[109] The *NME*'s Derek Johnson was just 'perplexed': 'It has a pronounced Eastern flavour, a storming rhythm, some really startling reverberating guitar, and some of the weirdest sounds on disc. It's hypnotic, wild and different. But what's it all about?'[110]

Jonathan King had obviously smelt blood; the following week, in his column, he laid into the band:

> Groans, complaints, knocks and grumbles from the Yardbirds. 'We have been going down very well on tour' boasts Keith Relf. Keith is a nice person, and so are the rest of

> the Yardbirds, but own up! At the Albert Hall we heard a ghastly cacophony of tearing chords; permanent distortion making Beck's first-rate guitar work sound boring and monotonous; too much volume drowning Keith's toneless – tuneless voice. Every record they put out is as dull as the last in its ponderous effort to achieve contrived originality. You were all very well in 1965, Yardbirds, but how about giving up in 1966?[111]

King was hardly the voice of a hip young constituency; he offered the 'purist soul' and 'professional image' of Cliff Bennett and the pop of Dave Dee as a counter to the Yardbirds 'contrived originality', but his voice added to the idea that the once sound of the future appeared to be going into reverse, to which long-time supporter Penny Valentine contributed her view when she also knocked 'Happenings':

> The time has come, the walrus said, to have a go. Well, he didn't actually say that, but I am going to have a go. I have always thought that a record should give, to each individually, it should impart something musically nice. This does not give. It takes. I have had enough of this sort of excuse for music. It is not clever, it is not entertaining, it is not informative. It is boring and pretentious. I am tired of people like the Yardbirds thinking this sort of thing is clever when people like the Spoonful and the Beach Boys are putting real thought into their music. And if I hear the word psychedelic mentioned I will go nuts.[112]

Her negative reaction was as much driven by the emerging lysergic scene as it was by the Yardbirds' complicity in the pretensions she and King disowned.

Beat Instrumental stayed on the fence about the single, but highlighted its deranged emanations:

> Disc . . . catches on to this American 'psychedelic' scene with many weird and wonderful, if not entirely coherent, vocal and instrumental sounds. 'Psychedelic' music has been kept underground in the States because the disc jockeys who claim that it is really music to 'loon' by. They contend that these songs are written and recorded while the artists are under the influence of drugs.[113]

Elsewhere in the magazine, Brian Wilson had what it all meant down pat: 'Psychedelic music will cover the face of the world and colour the whole music scene. Anybody happening is psychedelic – you just burn all the roots of old-style popular music.'[114] The Lords of Misrule were out and about, and 'Happenings Ten Years Time Ago' was a fitting soundtrack to their escapades.

It was the least pop formulaic of all their singles that had, anyway, made a point of not following the rules. 'Happenings Ten Years Time Ago' captures the sound of a roomful of pinball machines all being played simultaneously. It is a manifesto of sound that reaches out and swirls back in on itself, random audio clips laced together with controlled feedback over a strobing guitar riff that trips forward in fast-step time, momentarily recovering its poise before once more lurching into the threat of tilting the machine to a standstill.

That psychedelic music was a thing, something that had currency and could be marketed, was picked up in the pages of *Record Mail*, EMI's journal aimed at record retailers, in the November issue:

> Psychedelic music – this is the name of a new musical form that is currently the rage of America and looks like crossing the Atlantic to England. It involves an effect produced on the audience by the sounds of psychotic music and by unusual lighting effects intended to reproduce hallucinations experienced by scientists while under certain drugs.[115]

While the short piece was aimed to enlighten it was also primed to sell product:

> One of the first groups practising this new art form in this country are Southend sextet The Fingers. They also take with them on stage a monkey called 'Freak-out', which they claim to produce psychotic smells. They made their 'new sound' disc debut with 'I'll Take You Where The Music's Playing'.[116]

The synaesthetic side of psychedelic music was no doubt enabled by the freak-out monkey's aroma, but the single was an utterly square bit of pop-pabulum, old rope sold as new.

Record Mail columnist John Castle returned to the subject the following month, and this time made a rather more game effort to link the cultural happening with 'mind-manifesting' bands such as the Mothers of Invention and, in EMI's catalogue, Kim Fowley and his new 'freak-out' disc 'Lights'.[117] Leading British bands delving into the idiom were the Yardbirds and John's Children, Castle wrote.

Writing for the *Sunday Times*, Hunter Davies considered psychedelia to represent a shift in the location of the epicentre of the contemporary music scene: 'The American pop world has had a bit of an inferiority complex these last few years, ever since the Liverpool lads got going. Recent reports show that they've got onto something new, all by themselves; it's called, as you may have guessed, Psychedelic.'[118] Reproducing the effect of LSD in a musical form, making a performance into a 'happening, with strange noises, lights movement and action paintings' was the intent. Davies calculated – or plucked a figure from the air – that 'there are now over fifty psychedelic groups in the States . . . The leading group is called Mothers of Invention. They've got the flashing lights business down to a fine art so that members of the audience pass out through dizziness.'[119] If America was leading the way in pop's derangement of the senses, London was not lagging behind. For his contribution to the scene, elsewhere Jonathan King declared that he drank 'psychedelic milk'.[120]

Davies focused in on the Creation, whom he'd seen at the Flamingo Club on Wardour Street. The band's Shel Talmy-produced second single, 'Painter Man', was 31 in the hit parade:

> As they played, a series of paint bombs exploded on to a screen behind them. When the painting was complete the lead guitar rolled it up, used it as a violin bow for a few bars and then threw it to the fans. The Creation say they're not on drugs and there's nothing really psychedelic about them. 'It's just different and it amuses the kids.'

Too late for Pop art rave-ups and too straight to get on board the lysergic express: a circumstance that might explain why the Creation never took centre stage. Less reticent about their place in the emerging scene were the Pink Floyd:

> At the launching of the new magazine *IT* the other night a pop group called the Pink Floyd played throbbing music while a series of bizarre coloured shapes flashed on a huge screen behind them. Someone had made a mountain of jelly which people ate at midnight and another person had parked his motor-bike in the middle of the room. All apparently very psychedelic. The Pink Floyd's joint manager Andrew King says, 'We don't call ourselves psychedelic. But we don't deny it. We don't confirm it, either. People who want to make up slogans can do it.'
>
> The group's bass guitarist, a twenty-two-year-old architect called Roge Waters, was a bit less non-committal. 'It's totally anarchistic. But it is co-operative anarchy if you see what I mean. It's definitely a complete realization of the aims of psychedelia. But if you take LSD what you

> experience depends on who you are. Our music may give you the screaming horrors or throw you into screaming ecstasy. Mostly it's the latter. We find our audiences stop dancing now. We tend to get them standing there totally grooved with their mouths open.'[121]

'Hmm,' was Davies's response.

Davies's piece had been inspired by a two-page article on the growing phenomenon in *Melody Maker*: 'Psychedelic – the new word . . . and what it really adds up to is the great American comeback.' The magazine aimed to give readers the 'run down on the freaking out scene': 'Stick your fingers in your ears! Count five and wait for the bang. There's an American group explosion coming! – A wave of powerful new groups heavily armed with hits are saturation bombing the American chart front, and threaten to start shooting down British groups on home ground.'[122] The military/Vietnam metaphors persisted throughout the article's opening paragraphs; bands listed as being in the front line included Question Mark and the Mysterians, the Association, the Left Banke, Young Rascals, the 13th Floor Elevators, the Monkees (the television programme was yet to be screened in Britain, which partly helps to explain their inclusion), Positively Thirteen O'Clock, the Fugs and Love, among others. There was a shift from folk rock to 'really peculiar hot rhythm organizations', like the Mothers of Invention, who 'represent the freak brigade apparently . . . The group look more frightening than the Rolling Stones did when they were children of Richmond.'[123] With the exception of the Monkees, the Mothers and the Fugs, a case could be made that the key influence on these bands was not drugs but having listened long and hard to the Yardbirds. The Count Five most certainly, with their cribbing from "I'm a Man' for 'Psychotic Reaction', which *Hit Parader* described as a 'driving pulsing sound that is the most flagrant copy of the Yardbirds we've ever heard'.[124] Jerry McGeorge of the Shadows of Knight described his band as sounding 'vaguely like a cross between The Yardbirds and the Rolling Stones'.[125] But the Left Banke and the Association also owed a debt, with their borrowings from 'For Your Love' and 'Heart Full of Soul', and Love with the rave-up-styled stop-start racing pulse rhythms that were a mark of their early singles 'My Little Red Book' and 'Seven and Seven Is'.

Arvel Stricklin Jr, the Sir Douglas Quintet's lead guitarist, was asked by the *Witchita Beacon*'s 'Young Ideas' editor, Carol Dunlop, to define psychedelic music:

> To answer, Stricklin put on an LP by the Yardbirds, ranking masters of the Quintet's goal and a group greatly admired by the members. A Yardbird specialty is an almost perfect handling of their high-powered amplification – an ability best demonstrated by the imaginative lead guitarist. It creates an eerie, wailing, emotional quality in the music. At this point, Jake Dyer, the Quintet's road manager, summed it up as 'sounds of the mind'. Stricklin agreed that the foundation is that each musician plays what he hears in his own mind, and if the group works well as a unit it comes out harmoniously.[126]

With the new music in mind, the band were considering a name change.

The Yardbirds had earlier played the Cotillion Ballroom in Wichita on 15 August in front of more than '1,700 local hipsters' and had also been interviewed by the *Beacon*. The reporter was less interested in 'sounds of the mind' than hearing about the technique behind such ideas:

> In response to a question about the wailing bass violin sound prevalent in many of the group's numbers, 23-year-old Jim McCarty commented that it was 'produced by a

> normal guitar. It (the guitar) is played very loud . . . you sort of press it against the amplifier and the amplifier magnifies the sound. The violin sound is produced by a "fast unit" amplifier,' McCarty explained. 'The unit compresses the notes, making them thin so they will have a lot of volume.'[127]

Whether discussing technique or affect, at least in American media, the Yardbirds' sonic dissonance became a shorthand for psychedelic.[128]

According to *Melody Maker*, the term 'psychedelic' had already, 'without much justification', been used in publicity for 'Happenings Ten Years Time Ago', but to get a more nuanced appreciation, the Hollies' Graham Nash was asked to contribute, because he had actually 'attended psychedelic pop sessions in the States recently'.[129] Nash said,

> It's a question of trying to expand the consciousness to the limits. The theory is that you only use 20 percent of your brain but under LSD you use 80 percent. They aim to achieve the same thing by using combinations of sounds and lighting. It's wild. You think you're going daft.[130]

The same issue of *Melody Maker* reviewed 'Happenings Ten Years Time Ago', marking it as a 'Stateside influenced' track that some had 'tried to label . . . as psychedelic music . . . but it is not. Ad lib crescendos, weird noises, strange voices, backward running tapes, and anything else you want to chuck in doesn't make a psychedelic disc.'[131] But what else would? 'More thought is needed,' was the critic's answer. Still, 'the unsubtle approach is exciting, and Jeff Beck's guitar wings along on a well-constructed record. Should hit quite big.'[132] Was the Yardbirds' freak-out record inauthentic because it was London- not Los Angeles-born? Were the Monkees or Kim Fowley a more credible manifestation?

> 'Kim Fowley; "Lights" (Parlophone)'
>
> Holy dynamic duos it's a freak out disc, Suzy Creamcheese. Wowie zowie – blow your mind, with Kim Fowley's naughty, head-in-the-sand, chunder wonder! Strong influences from Zappa, Dave Dee, Freud, Frank Ifield, and de Sade. A switched-on, happening, hippie, phisyiokalidelic record of yesterday. And the day before that and the day before that! Everybody must Freak On![133]

Melody Maker's review of this cash-in single felt no obligation to take the latest fad seriously, not when, via Zappa, it was in good part defined by the self-parodic. *Melody Maker*'s Bob Dawbarn and artist and media figure Barry Fantoni followed through:

> Strummy Wart and the Haemorrhoids being the latest in rave, far out, avant garde psychedelic group we felt it was time to clear up a few misconceptions about the music. So we put the following questions to Strummy.
>
> What is the origin of psychedelic pop?
>
> It comes from Latin – psycho meaning loud and delic meaning out of tune. It was given birth mainly by LSD – the London School of Dancing. Unfortunately a lot of the boys have got on to the more way out stuff – like salmon – and – shrimp – and paste injections.[134]

Whatever its joke potential, and it was always an easy shot, psychedelia had traction, which was especially evident when the teen magazines took to describing the emerging scene for their readers.

'It's a weird new world, a strange new scene. And it's IN. The psychedelic cult. They said it couldn't happen here, but it is happening in the big cities. And here is where it's at,' wrote June Southworth in *Fab 208*.[135] Like so many of the scene's initial primers, Kim Fowley played a leading role in Southworth's account. He was both court jester and

Master of Ceremonies – someone not to be taken too seriously, but unavoidable, a bit like the scene itself. To her, the music 'sounded like the Who in the most advanced stages of nightmare . . . with feed-back-gone-mad sounds, flashing eye-boggling lights, stroboscopes, and all the fun (?) of blowing your mind without actually taking LSD. Which is something, I suppose.'[136] Following the Mothers of Invention, Question Mark and the Mysterians, the Association and Love are highlighted as the scene's leading practitioners, but a solid walk-on part is granted to the displaced West Coast band the Misunderstood, then in exile in London. Southworth wrote:

> The Misunderstood try to create moods on stage. They organized their feedback effects so efficiently that they have a ping-pong arrangement. They can leave their instruments on the stage, and walk off; the instruments will merrily play by themselves. They also use red, yellow and blue lights which are fixed to flash ever brighter according to the volume of the music. They are usually extremely bright. Leader Glenn Campbell meets opposition with comments like: 'We feel like Christopher Columbus when he tried to tell everyone the world was round. Everyone could see it was flat, so they wouldn't believe him. We're giving people more in music than they can hear on the surface. We're giving them a flying carpet.'[137]

To a land of enchantment, no doubt.

Derek Johnson reviewed the Misunderstood's single 'I Can Take You to the Sun' for the *NME*, alongside Jim [*sic*] Hendrix's 'Hey Joe' – 'guttural, earthy, convincing and authentic' – David Bowie's 'Rubber Band', which he described as 'a gimmick disc' but its flip, 'London Boys', 'really digs beneath the surface of the so-called in-crowd. Very perceptive!'[138] Inadvertently, he contrasted the real against novelty, with 'London Boys' as commentary. The

Misunderstood fell somewhere in-between: 'I suppose you'd call this psychedelic, with all its strange sounds, oscillations and reverberations. But it's extremely well done of its kind. A really penetrating performance that grips from start to finish – with pounding drums and weird effects from the slide guitar. Absorbing lyric and tempo change.'[139] The terms of description are the same as those used to describe the Yardbirds' most recent releases.[140]

At a press conference in New York, the Yardbirds described the British music scene as 'reactionary'; it was all happening in America, they said: '"Our music was the first psychedelic music to be heard, two years ago" . . . The group said they wanted to attend a "freak out" and hoped to catch the Mothers of Invention in San Francisco.'[141] Psychedelic before the fact, but still freak-out virgins. When *Hit Parader* reviewed the album *Having a Rave-Up*, they wrote that it was 'definite mind-blowing music. Long before anyone coined the term "psychodelic music" the Yardbirds were tripping everyone out with their frantic other-world instrumental explorations.'[142] For the present, *psych-o-delia* for the Yardbirds was also B-side material, embraced and parodied with 'Psycho Daisies'. It was the flip of 'Happenings Ten Years Time Ago', which was described by the *NME* as 'another tear-up at an even faster tempo [than the top side] in the so called psychodelic [*sic*] style. Very off beat, but with a tremendous beat that'll keep the toes tapping.'[143] The track was a love letter to not only Jeff Beck's Californian beach-movie starlet girlfriend, Mary Hughes, but the hippie lysergic dream scene itself, here sketched out as a punk tune that the Count Five or Shadows of Knight might have thrown back at the Yardbirds in homage. The track was withheld from release in the States and instead the B-side of 'Happenings', released a month after its launch in Britain in the first week of November, had the equally punkish 'The Nazz Are Blue' on its reverse, which had not been included on the U.S. album.

Talking to *KRLA the Beat* about what psychedelia meant to him, Jimmy Page got a little lost: 'Pop music can be psychedelic but not necessarily electronic. Electronic music *helps* – it's a much easier way of getting a psychedelic theme. But you can do this – get over a psychedelic point – without being necessarily electronic.'[144] Relf helped out, 'Dylan's lyrics are psychedelic; he's *lyrically* psychedelic. And *our sound* is psychedelic. There are several mediums of putting it across. I mean you could be psychedelic and have brass band playing.'[145] He wasn't getting any closer to the nub of the matter – perhaps that was impossible – still, he valiantly carried on: 'What we're trying to do with our music is trying to induce the same thing in the audience, the same feeling, the same sort of experiences that LSD does – it's very hard to do!'[146] When asked to explain what that kind of experience was, he offered, 'Well, to induce a state of timelessness and destroy the awareness of where you are. You just go inside your head – blow-your-mind, sort of thing!'[147]

Jeff Beck qualified what they meant by 'electronic':

> The original concept of our music was just to play what was inside us, and the best way of putting it over was by making 'electronic' sounds. You see, it's not like electronic music – if anybody thinks it is, go out and buy an album of electronic music and see how much different it is. I mean one or two bits might remind them of electronic music, but it really isn't – the idea isn't. It's just a means of using a guitar to put over a different sound, a different feel.[148]

And then Beck expounded on psychedelia: 'I've heard an example of "psychedelic" music, but it was just *rubbish*. It was just a noise – it was somebody just having what they call a "freak-out". It sounded like *me* giving my guitar to *Mum* and saying "Mum – play it!"'

After the Stones tour, still dogged by break-up rumours, the Yardbirds returned to the USA for scattered independent gigs and as a headline attraction on Dick Clark's Caravan of Stars.[149]

On 23 October, the Yardbirds played San Francisco's Fillmore Auditorium; Ed Denson reviewed the gig for the *Berkeley Barb*:

> 'Eleven amplifiers, eleven amplifiers, the Yardbirds have 11 amplifiers, Jesus Christ' – the words seemed to spring from the air in the Fillmore last Sunday as the other groups on the afternoon show waited for the Yardbirds, the stars, and the amplifiers, and their equipment, to arrive.
>
> We bounced a large balloon towards the ceiling, playing catch and I was thinking 'Eleven amplifiers . . . Standel advertises that 10 of theirs have the power to kill anyone standing in front of them . . . I hope these cats know what they're doing with that stuff . . .'[150]

The show was scheduled to begin at 2 p.m.; at 1.30, the stage was being set, and the band's equipment had arrived:

> They stack [the amplifiers] on the stage, forming an almost solid wall . . . Everyone runs about checking last minute details, asking if there will be time for them to check their levels and balance after two hours of waiting. No one has seen a Yardbird yet. The show starts, the other groups do their thing.[151]

Denson had seen the Yardbirds the last time they played in the area (possibly Civic Auditorium in Stockton, California, on 1 September 1966), when Beck had pulled out sick and Page had switched from bass to guitar and 'played all of his leads note for note. They were really mediocre, and we walked out in the middle of the set after not being able to hear a word they sang':

> Upstairs in the dressing room the Yardbirds have arrived and are talking with the other bands trying to find out what

> they can about the acoustics of the room, and the type of audience. They look like hippy bands all over the country do, beads and mod shirts, innocent clear faces. I remember listening to one of their LPs and sort of liking some of the things on it, some weird moments on it too, the kind that make you look up and say a little off-center of the person you are talking to 'those cats drop acid, listen to that' and then you settle down again wondering if you aren't projecting – who would dare to think that the English all take acid too. They all sure talk funny, those English.[152]

The band then moved through the audience towards the stage, instruments held above their heads. There was no eye contact between crowd and group, which happened when local bands play: 'nothing but a hall full of expectations, dark and surging, yielding to pressure like an amoeba, a body wanting rhythm with many voices, and glazed eyes not seeing anything except a form on stage with slots filled by the Yardbirds where a few minutes ago some other group was standing'.

> Their first note reveals the meaning of the eleven amplifiers. The guitar has power, a fullness of tone, a depth, that has not been often heard outside a recording studio. The sound moves out of the three amplifiers and possesses you, driving the normal impulses out of your nervous system and replacing them with music. But not a music that you've ever heard before. It has the textures and rhythms of Chicago blues, like almost all rock now, but as they play the bass player turns his body so that his instrument is facing the 27 square feet of amplifier and speakers that stand behind him, taller than he, and the feedback tones fill the room with a sound more powerful than anything before it, and touching more on what is happening, and then the lead

> guitarist goes into an incredible distorted run with notes and feedback blending into a beautiful new sound.[153]

Denson was sitting in the dressing rooms that face the stage overlooking the dance floor, a wall of windows between him and the music. 'The Yardbirds look possessed, filling the room with a field of their energy, jerking around, spinning into their amps, making hand motions that must be somehow connected to the music.'[154] He then moved down into the audience, where he could 'really feel the impact of this music. The air is hot and almost motionless, and most of the people are just standing and swaying, and the sound is so loud. Beneath all this hippy music, under the new electric music, inside the young projecting performers, there is a new music struggling to burst forth and take over'.

> We are in a period of musical chaos, a primitive boiling, and if the culture can just hang together long enough, if no child in the whitehouse kills us, or ruins the economy, for electric music is expensive, it will spring forth full-formed from someone's head. No other group has ever been as close to it as The Yardbirds – Beatles, Stones, forget it. They are still standing with cold teeth chattering in their cave wondering why these people are running around holding fire in their hands . . . I am convinced, I am converted, the Yardbirds are the best group in the world.[155]

Denson's review was a testament to the Yardbirds' capacity, on the day, to go way-out. The day after, when his mind had calmed down, Denson granted that they had a weakness – a lack of variety, or they didn't choose to show their true range on stage that day: 'Like Butterfield they did one thing, and really well.' The 13th Floor Elevators had also been in the audience; it was the third documented time they had paid to see the Yardbirds – these Texans the most dedicated of all the Yardbirds apostles in going further and then further still.[156]

Two days after the Fillmore show, the band, with Page and Beck on guitars and Dreja on bass, were filmed for *The Milton Berle Show* in Los Angeles, miming along to 'Happenings Ten Years Time Ago'. Four days later, they had joined Dick Clark's Caravan of Stars; Beck would last only for three of the shows after travelling through Texas, Louisiana, Arkansas, Alabama, Kansas and Oklahoma, and on 8 November, the band played in Davenport, Iowa. Shirley Davis reported on the show for the *Quad City Times-Democrat*. It was, she felt, 'one of the best rock 'n' roll shows to hit the Quad-Cities in recent years'.[157] She judged its success by the screaming kids who the ushers tried to keep in order:

> It was absolute bedlam when the Yardbirds came on; the English group sang 'Heart Full of Soul' and lots of others, apologizing for the fact that one member was missing. This reviewer's favorite in the group was the guitarist in the purple bellbottoms and the navy coat with medals on his lapels. Part of his charm was that his dark hair fell completely over his face . . . as he practically attacked the guitar, played it with a bow and then did something that made it seem like bagpipes.[158]

Davis's observation of Page is among the earliest published accounts of him playing his guitar with a bow, making his use of the technique contemporaneous with Eddie Phillips in the Creation, Roy Wood in the Move and Syd Barrett in the Pink Floyd.[159] Davis was also part of the growing chorus of female onlookers who found Page not just attractive, as they found Beck or Relf, but someone with an added sex appeal. Page's female admirers feminized him, fetishizing his long dark curly hair and flouncy dandy costumes, setting him off against the cocksure Beck.

Dick Clark's package tour must have seemed light years away from the psychedelic club scenes of Los Angeles and London, but the two worlds would briefly collide when the Caravan hitched up in Detroit for the Carnaby Street Fun Festival at the Michigan State Fair Coliseum for three days, 18–20 November. The event was sponsored by Food Fair Markets and heavily advertised across Michigan: 'See & Hear Top "Mod" Set Stars – In Person'. Dick Clark, Gary Lewis and the Playboys, Sam the Sham and the Pharaohs, Brian Hyland and a host of others featured, alongside headliners the Yardbirds, but what made this event just a little different from other stops on the Cavalcade was the promise of the added attraction of a Mod wedding:

> the bride will speak her vows in a mini-skirt, the groom in high-mod styles. WKNR disc jockey Scott Regan will be best man. Nico will sing the wedding song, played by pop artist Andy Warhol's Velvet Underground. Warhol will give the bride away. Judge George D. Kent officiating. Warhol calls the whole happening 'The Exploding Plastic Inevitable'.[160]

Detroit Free Press's teen correspondent Loraine Alterman had set the scene just a few weeks earlier with a visit to the recently reappointed Grande Ballroom in Grand River, one block south of Joy Road – 'a teen club that's absolutely Wow. . . Pow! Wham! Bang! Zow!':

> No doubt about it – it's the grooviest, most exciting teen night spot in town. If you're 17 or over and don't hit the Grande on Friday or Saturday nights, you are out of your skull . . . Dig the scene. You enter by walking up a wide staircase. On the landing the ticket taker is perched on a motorcycle. Next to him are pots of phosphorescent make up. Paint a big flower on your face or stripes on your

> hands. When you get inside, they'll glow in alive pinks, greens, blues.
>
> Step up a few more stairs. The wild vibrant sounds of today's music hits you. To borrow a phrase from Murray the K, it's what's happening baby. Then you're inside the big ballroom lined with fluted marble columns. There in a past era your parents danced to the big bands. But now it's today and today hits with the force of a blast furnace. Take the walls on either side of the stage where the MC-5 might be holding forth. The walls are a light show projected from the rear of the ballroom. Huge multi-colored bubbles and amoeba-like shapes are changing, rolling, dancing on the walls. Maybe an old Clark Gable flick is flashed over it. Fantastic!
>
> OK. That's the walls. Suspended from the ceiling are two movie screens. On them are old-time silent films, new-time artsy films, slides on top of films. Like wow! Step into another area of the ballroom and you'll be flickering just like you are in one of these ancient silent movies. What is it? A strobe light area and the strobe produces these zany effects. Naturally there's dancing and if you just want to sit and dig the sounds, you can do that too.[161]

The 'op art' multimedia happening was echoed in the same edition of Alterman's column, 'Where the Action Is', by news that Warhol was promising 'to bring his movie camera and equipment' to film the Mod wedding, so 'that the couple will have their own Andy Warhol movie. And if you've ever seen a Warhol film, you know how unbelievable it is.'[162]

In the media, the build-up towards the event was insistent:

> Pop artist Andy Warhol will make his first appearance in Detroit during the Carnaby Street Festival... Warhol's entourage will include the Velvet Underground, an instrumental

> group; Nico, girl of the year, and Gerald Malango [*sic*], the Super-Star . . . Warhol (of the eight-hour epic 'sleep' famer) intends to film the wedding and the newlywed mod couple will also receive a screen test for Underground Movies from Warhol during their honeymoon.[163]

Everything was going to plan, except for the need to find a willing couple; still, 'that could be right down the alley of non-movieman Andy Warhol, who's supposed to give the bride away. He can shoot a movie of a non-wedding.'[164] By the following week, that problem had been resolved, and the likely couple were pictured on the front page of the *Detroit Free Press*; 'It's the grooviest thing in the world. Getting married like this is out of sight,' said James Silver, who was set to marry Susan Bassett. They had been chosen from fifty other likely couples.[165]

When asked about Warhol, Silver said that he'd 'met him at a party in Ann Arbor after a film festival. The Velvet Underground, too.' The interviewing journalist intervened – 'Isn't the Velvet Underground the way-out psychedelic music outfit that makes weird noises with electronic amplifiers and all that? "They said they're going to play traditional wedding music." You know. "Here comes the . . . ."'[166] Despite the hype, Silver and Bassett pulled out and were replaced by Gary Norris and Randi Rossi; he was an unemployed artist, she was an unemployed go-go dancer who went by the name 'Cupcake'.

Against this backdrop, the Yardbirds barely registered; still, Alterman was a fan and duly interviewed the band once more, noting that Beck had left at mid-point in the tour, and illness had forced his departure. He'd played his last engagement at the Memorial Coliseum in Corpus Christi, Texas, on 30 October. The *NME*'s New York correspondent, June Harris, reported that 'mental exhaustion is the reason behind the non-appearance of Jeff Beck on the current Yardbirds tour. He has been unable to appear with the group on practically all their dates and has remained in California trying to recuperate.'[167] Jimmy Page had now permanently switched instruments with Chris Dreja. The band's popularity remained undiminished: 'such is the demand over here, that the 'Birds are already scheduled to play another eight day tour opening on December 26 in Tampa, Florida and winding up the trip in Chicago on January 2.'[168] The Syndicate of Sound and Question Mark and the Mysterions were expected to play support, and manager Napier-Bell was 'hoping to get clearance for his other English group, John's Children, whose "Smashed! Blocked" has broken out big all over the West Coast and is soon expected to reach the California best sellers'.[169]

The wedding did go ahead, the happy couple pictured on the front page of the *Free Press* alongside Warhol, who wore dark glasses, black jeans and a leather jacket:

> – A burly, bearded refugee from a motorcycle gang stood on the hood of a dilapidated DeSoto and banged in the roof with a sledge hammer.
> – A lithe young man slithered about the stage doing a dance in which he alternately used a bullwhip and two-high-powered flashlights for props.
> – A cute young girl wearing a white dress served as a canvas for an artist who decorated her with mustard and catsup squeezed from plastic dispensers.
> – A young man paraded about the stage carrying above his head a five-foot-long candy bar.
> – About 20 young dancers, dressed in mod attire and resembling a flock of birds of paradise in the molting season – did the latest dances.[170]

'"Oooooh", sighed a girl in the crowd of 4,500, "it's the first wedding I've ever been to."'[171] Warhol, who sat on 'a carton of Campbell's soup, beamed approvingly'.[172] Meanwhile,

> Nico sang a bizarre and totally unintelligible song accompanied by the electronic tones of the Velvet Underground, a rock 'n' roll group. Nico, a tall, lanky girl with straight blond hair and a gaunt face, began to sing just as the microphone went haywire. As a result, she sounded like a Bedouin woman singing a funeral dirge in Arabic while accompanied by an off-key air raid siren.[173]

Detroit's premier poster artist, Gary Grimshaw, reviewed the happening for the *Fifth Estate*; he'd been introduced to Loraine Alterman, who 'was bored', he wrote. He thought the whole thing a sham: 'Andy Warhol brought the supermarket to the art gallery. Now your friendly local supermarket (Food Fair) brings you Andy Warhol. Works out nice.'[174] The emptiness of spectacle was its meaning:

> The mod couple walked down the aisle of the Coliseum to the accompaniment of the throbbing pulsative improvised musical sounds of the Velvet Underground, the light and glare of the television cameras and the popping of flashbulbs. As they reached the stage, vocalist Nico briefly sang two numbers in keeping with the spirit of the ceremony.[175]

The sensational impact of the EPI was caught by a copywriter for the Vox company's promotional paper, *Teen Beat*, which placed an MGM promotional image of the Velvet Underground, leaning up against one of their amplifiers, just below a picture of Herman's Hermits, with an alliterative headline – 'The Velvet Underground Vibrates' – and then threw together some of the more choice quotations used inside the gatefold of the band's debut album:

> The Velvet Underground is a group whose howling, throbbing beat is amplified and extended by electronic dial-twiddling, has a sound hard to describe, even harder

> to duplicate, but haunting in its uniqueness. And with the Velvets comes the blonde, bland, beautiful Nico, another cooler Dietrich for another cooler generation. Art has come to the discotheque and it will never be the same again.
>
> Not since the Titanic ran into the iceberg has there been such a collision as when Andy Warhol's Exploding Plastic Inevitable burst upon the audiences at The Trip recently. For once a Happening really happened, and it took Warhol to come out from New York to show how it is done. The Velvet Underground is so far out that it makes the tremendous thumping beat of the great, groovy group [Mothers of Invention] which opened the program sound passé.
>
> Shatteringly contemporary – the electronic music, loud enough to make room and the mind vibrate in unison – Nico, the beautiful flaxen-haired girl, the noise, the lights, the film and the dances build to a screeching crescendo . . . The sound is a savage series of atonal thrusts and electronic feedback. The lyrics combine Sado-Masochistic frenzy with free-association imagery. The whole sound seems to be the product of a secret marriage between Bob Dylan and the Marquis de Sade.
>
> In other words – They'll 'BLOW YOUR MIND!'[176]

Strip out Warhol and the darker sensuality on offer, switch Nico's name for Relf and the Velvets for the Yardbirds, and the synthesis between the two bands – both playing 'electronic music, loud enough to make room and the mind vibrate in unison' – is manifest. Even though developed autonomously, the overlaps are especially discernible in the analogue between Page's bowing of the guitar with Cale's amplified viola and their respective roles in each band's sonic landscapes. The Velvets had a master songwriter among their number and took things a stage further, from evil-hearted lovers to *les fleurs du mal*, but they would not have been the band they were without that transatlantic crossing that began its journey at the Crawdaddy Club on Eel Pie Island before flowing down the Thames and out into the world. In late 1967 into 1968, the Yardbirds would return the gift by sometimes incorporating 'I'm Waiting for the Man' as part of their 'Smokestack Lightning' or 'I'm a Man' rave-ups, banging on their ding dong, just like Sister Ray said.

While in New York with the Yardbirds, Page had watched the Velvet Underground at Steve Paul's Scene during their twelve-day residency in January 1967.[177] The club, he said, was empty, perhaps because the band was 'too challenging for people who had got used to seeing regular bands . . . I think I saw the Velvets twice, three times in a row at the Scene. I went back to see them because I thought people would catch on, and the place would be full, but it never was . . . It was too cool and people didn't pick up on it.'[178]

For Jimmy Page, the occasion of the Mod wedding must have marked an unexpected reunion with Nico, whose single 'I'm Not Sayin' b/w 'Last Mile' he co-produced with Andrew Loog Oldham for the latter's Immediate label back in the summer of 1965. Jonathan King reviewed the single twice, once for *Disc Weekly*, where he wrote 'she's not my type really. The opposite of Gene Pitney. A girl singing low, and not a boy singing high,' and then again for *Melody Maker*'s 'Blind Date' column: 'she sings so flat she's almost in the next key.'[179] One friend of Nico's advised a pop columnist that the single was best played 'at night in a darkened room.'[180] *Record Mirror*'s Peter Jones was, however, smitten by her offering of an 'antidote to the current rash of girls who whisper fearfully through folksy lyrics. But then there are lots of things about Nico which are different.'[181] Nico told Jones that she had a 'habit of leaving places at the wrong time . . . just when something big might have happened for me. I did that in New York. But this time I'm determined to stay put in Earls Court until I know exactly what is happening over the record.'[182]

Despite an appearance on *Ready Steady Go!* to promote the single, nothing much happened with 'I'm Not Sayin'', and Nico was soon off back to New York, where Warhol matched her with the Velvet Underground. A year later, Andrew Loog Oldham was asked what had happened to her? 'Ah yes, I was glad I was right about Nico ... She's working for a group called the Underground Movement for about $11,000 for eight days in clubs like Hollywood's The Trip.'[183] No mention of Warhol, and the Velvets misnamed, but the venue – the Trip: 'the new shrine of pop culture' – where the Exploding Plastic Inevitable performed between 3 and 18 May, he got right; he probably remembered her pay out correctly too.

Chris Dreja caught some scenes from the Mod wedding in photographs he took of the event – backstage shots of Warhol and Lou Reed, shots of Page in the audience speaking to a blonde woman, perhaps Nico, and the Velvets on stage backing her as a figure with the giant inflatable Baby Ruth candy bar stalks to the side. The Yardbirds had crossed paths with Warhol on their first visit to New York, around the time that Nico was promoting her single in London, when he attended a party organized by their label, Epic, at Scott Muni's Rolling Stone discotheque, 17 September 1965, at which they played.[184] Their paths crossed again a year later on 8 September 1966 at another New York reception for the band given by Epic, where Warhol was photographed in the company of Relf and Page.[185]

When rumour was rife that the pop artist, the Velvets and the EPI would visit Britain and appear as part of the concert titled 14-Hour Technicolor Dream (a benefit in aid of *International Times*) at Alexandra Palace at the end of April 1967, *Melody Maker* ran a news story with a photograph of Warhol supplied by Chris Dreja. In a leather jacket and wildly oversized bug-eyed wraparound sunglasses, the artist looked the epitome of an East Side street punk. Said Chris: 'Andy came to see us. He said he wanted to be in the presence of the Yardbirds. He hardly ever talks in public, and communicates through an interpreter.'[186]

The Exploding Plastic Inevitable's multimedia mix, its status as happening and freak-out psychedelic extravaganza, was being

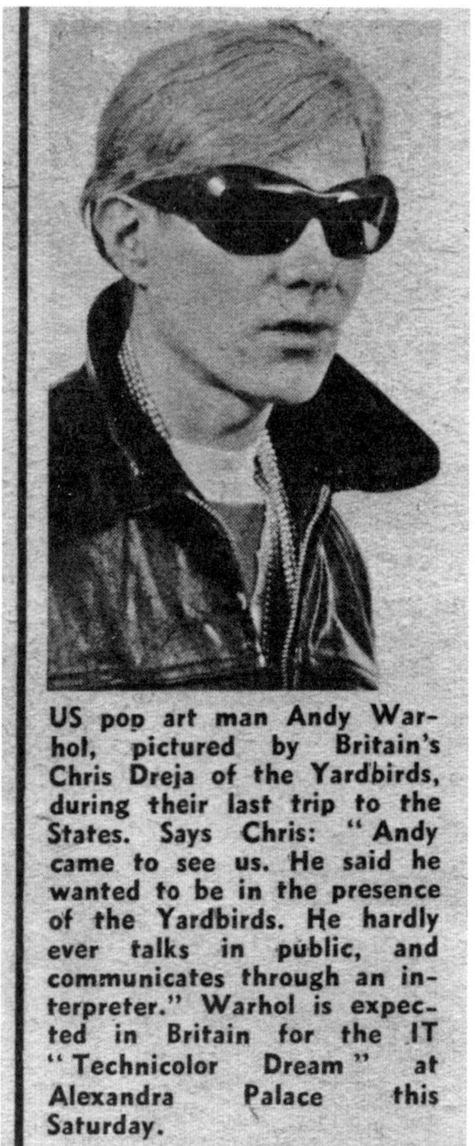

US pop art man Andy Warhol, pictured by Britain's Chris Dreja of the Yardbirds, during their last trip to the States. Says Chris: "Andy came to see us. He said he wanted to be in the presence of the Yardbirds. He hardly ever talks in public, and communicates through an interpreter." Warhol is expected in Britain for the IT "Technicolor Dream" at Alexandra Palace this Saturday.

Andy Warhol by Chris Dreja in *Melody Maker* (29 April 1967).

re-enacted on a slightly smaller scale in London's clubs. In October, *Melody Maker* covered the Move's Thursday-night residency at the Marquee: 'Psychedelic sounds came to London in a new – and explosive – dimension ... Finishing their act in an ear-splitting and conscious-shattering blaze of celluloid and sound ... The first set was fairly straight forward, hard hitting, crude Move music,' then later,

> A projector flicked colours, contrasts, textures and atmosphere onto the group who – as if incensed – jumped, swirled, dived, and thundered in front of the dancing backcloth. Then a giant explosion. They ripped the film screen off the wall and put a lot of weird smiles on the faces of the audience.[187]

By mid-December, the London psychedelic scene was wherever you cared to find it; a 'Double Giant Freak-Out Ball' was announced for 30 and 31 December, 'Psychodelphia'.[188] Friday night's attractions were Cream, Geno Washington and the Alan Bown Set; Saturday's were the Who, the Move and 'supporting groups'. Also promised were late-licensed bars, central heating, newly improved entrance facilities and 'psychedelic lighting effects'. A week before the show, it had changed its name to 'Psychedelicamania', and the Pink Floyd had been added to the bill. They were already being advertised as the 'Psychedelic Pink Floyd' for their gigs at All Saints Church Hall, Powis Gardens: 'Cream – Kaleidoscope Freak Out Zap!' were part of the promised attractions.[189]

The adverts also helpfully explained what a freak-out was all about: 'Come and watch the pretty lights': 'WHAT IS A FREAK-OUT? When a large number of individuals gather and express themselves creatively through music, dance, light patterns and electronic sound. The participants, already emancipated from our national social slavery, dressed in their most inspired apparel, realise as a group whatever potential they possess for free expression.' The night before they played the Roundhouse, the Pink Floyd were due to perform at the UFO – Night Tripper, located under Berkeley cinema, Tottenham Court Road, fresh from Thursday's Marquee bash. It would not have been hard to miss just who were the arrivistes on the scene. *Melody Maker* thought that their Saturday night performance had a 'promising sound, and some very groovy picture slides which attract far more attention than the group, as they merge, blossom, burst, grow, divide and die'.[190] Both the Who and the Move smashed things up, and the promise of getting high, expanding one's consciousness, freaking out while senses were 'bombarded with kinetics and sound', was tempered by the horrible condition of the venue, which caused Nick Jones 'to suffer frostbite, malnutrition and nausea'.[191]

If there was some uncertainty over the status of 'Happenings Ten Years Time Ago' and whether it could be branded as a legitimate freak-out disc, there should have been less ambivalence about Keith Relf's second solo single, 'Shapes in My Mind'. It had been tracked and mixed in Los Angeles and New York in August and September and was written and produced by Simon Napier-Bell. At the same session, Napier-Bell had also overseen the recording of the backing track for the John's Children debut single, 'Smashed Blocked'. Ostensibly a song about a lost love, Relf's disc is also about the derangement of the senses, the shifting shapes in the mind's eye, where colours cry, the brain explodes and the body shrinks inside the singer's head. 'Help!' Relf cries, 'Or I'll be dead,' an echo of the cry at the start of 'Smashed Blocked' – 'Please! I'm losing my mind.' But few were paying much attention to either disc, though *NME*'s Derek Johnson liked the John's Children's single, retitled 'The Love I Thought I'd Found' for the British market: 'A spoken intro leads into this stormer, which suddenly lapses into ballad tempo. Unusual in the extreme!'[192]

Norman Jopling and Peter Jones in *Record Mirror* described Relf's single as having a 'curious instrumental opening . . . Changes of tempo, powerful chords, rather unusual song,' but they didn't link it to psychedelia.[193] Neither did Derek Johnson in the *NME*: 'Sung on deep echo, with an enveloping organ sound and plucking bass well to the fore, plus a pounding beat – it has a nagging, insidious effect in keeping with the bemused lyric. Full marks to Simon Napier-Bell on his very startling production, and to Yardbird Keith.'[194] In *Disc and Music Echo*, Penny Valentine reviewed it under a pre-release title of 'Make Me Break This Spell', she too avoided any reference to the happening scene, but better caught its strange effect:

> Simon Napier-Bell has been groping around in the dark – in the musical sense – for a long time and may at last be coming into the light. This is as strange and weird as some of his other efforts (that includes the last Yardbirds' monstrosity) but unlike the others this actually works. Here then we have Keith's off-beat, sad, echoey voice in a desperate state at losing his girl. Once you've got over the shock of everything stopping and starting and feeling that somewhere lurks the phantom of the opera at his organ keyboard, you'll like it. It may even move you. It did me.[195]

With the image of Napier-Bell fumbling in the gloom, Valentine was most likely referring to his efforts with John's Children. The following week she was more direct in what she was indicating when she reviewed Marc Bolan's 'Hippy Gumbo', another Napier-Bell production. He hadn't let her down, she wrote: 'he never disappoints . . . I expected therefore surprise . . . but even I was stunned by the way the perfectly normal sounding gentleman from "The Wizard" now sounds like a crazed mixture of a bad female Negro blues singer and Larry the Lamb.'[196]

BACK IN EARLY OCTOBER, Bolan had accompanied his producer to Sound Techniques Studios in Chelsea to witness and, some say, to provide some ad-hoc backing vocals on the Yardbirds recording sessions for tracks that might potentially be used on the soundtrack of Michelangelo Antonioni's swinging London art-house picture *Blow-Up*.[197] The film opened in December 1966 in the United States and March 1967 in Britain. The last sequence of the movie to be shot, the Yardbirds' contribution was filmed in mid-October at Elstree Studios in a mock-up of the Ricky-Tick club where, in front of an over-lit zombie audience, they let go with 'Stroll On' – a faint rewrite of the 1956 Johnny Burnette Trio's arrangement of Tiny Bradshaw's R&B romp 'Train Kept a-Rollin'', which the band had previously recorded in Memphis.

Outside of small cliques of record collectors and nascent rock 'n' roll revivalists, much of the Trio's catalogue was unknown territory in Britain in the early to mid-1960s; little had been borrowed from it and refracted by British beat groups. The 12-track 10-inch British release of the Rock 'n' Roll Trio's sole album was so rare that, when found, it was being exchanged at the then astronomical price of £10 (today you would not get any change from £1,000 and that's if you could even find a copy for sale).[198] Such demand had led to it being reissued later that year as a full-blown 12-inch Long Player, a copy of which Bolan acquired. If he absorbed nothing else watching the Yardbirds record, he learned how to cannibalize the Rock 'n' Roll Trio, later transforming the stuttered guitar riff of 'Honey Hush' and 'Train Kept a-Rollin'' into 'Jewel', featured on the first T. Rex album (1970). It would be a fairly safe bet to assume Jeff Beck brought the Trio's record to the Yardbirds' attention, which, once recorded, remained in their set until the very end before becoming one of the key songs to make the transition into Led Zeppelin's song book. What's certain is that the Trio's album moved within a highly circumscribed group of musicians, all of whom were linked to Jimmy Page.

Four months before the Yardbirds were in Memphis, in May 1965, Screaming Lord Sutch released his cover of 'Train Kept a-Rollin'', produced by Joe Meek, with his take of the Trio's version of Big Joe Turner's 'Honey Hush' on its flip – replicating the original 1956 coupling on the U.S. Coral label. Just over a month after his single's release in Britain, where it had not bothered the charts, Sutch announced he was off to the States to promote the disc. *Music Echo* reported that 'His Lordship, who recently captured both France and

Australia after going to those countries "unknown", says that he'll shake the States in the same way the Beatles and Herman did.'[199] No such thing happened, and the single is now pretty much forgotten, except by Meek collectors. 'Passable British beat' is about the kindest thing that can be said about it. The best *Music Echo* could muster in its review was to note that 'it's still possible to have a diabolical singer with a good group.'[200] That it is such an anodyne version is perplexing because Sutch had recorded a blistering take the previous year, also with Meek at the controls. It was released as the underside of 'Dracula's Daughter'; as with 'Stroll On', it was hidden beneath a pseudonym, 'Come Back Baby'. Both Beck and Page are variously credited with playing on the session, which is entirely possible and probable (Page was also on Christian's Crusaders' version of 'Honey Hush', released a year prior to Sutch's effort and five months before 'Come Back Baby'). Mid-way through the Sutch B-side, a fuzzbox-driven lead guitar leaps out of the mix; it is outrageously overamped, a screaming sonic blister unequalled in Meek's catalogue until the Syndicats' 'Crawdaddy Simone', though not bettered.

Talking to an American reporter at the tail end of 1966, Beck explained that before joining the Yardbirds he 'was playing on records whenever I could. I was lucky enough to be known. Whenever they needed a rock and roll guitar break, I'd play it . . . I met Jimmy Page at these sessions.'[201]

By the time Beck had claimed the song for the Yardbirds, he'd tamed Meek's audio appliqué by applying new levels of skill, amplification and effects and was now supported by a band that could make good on the Trio's model of rhythmically violent paroxysm. With Beck backed by Page, 'Stroll On' ratcheted up the previous year's Memphis recording and turned the torque to breaking point. The tension in the song is a corollary with the film's compelling dive into combustible paranoiac delusions.

During a stay in London while accompanying Monica Vitti, who was filming Joseph Losey's *Modesty Blaise*, on 3 December 1965,

Antonioni had watched the Who play at what was their last time around in front of their home audience at the Goldhawk Club. He initially wanted Lambert's charges for *Blow-Up*, but terms or egos could not be agreed or stroked.[202] For the film, the Yardbirds more statically charged and controlled release was a style that anyway better fitted Antonioni's needs. The reason the director reportedly gave to Chris Stamp for not using his band was that 'What the Who do is too meaningful. I wanted something utterly meaningless, so I couldn't use them.'[203] Regardless, Relf's tendency to a self-effacing recital ripped with explosive bouts of emotion made a better onstage surrogate for David Hemmings's character than Daltrey's pugilistic stances would have delivered. There is little credibility in Sterling Morrison's 1982 claim, since much repeated, that the

'Five 'birds, one chick, four hits': the Yardbirds in their Simon Napier-Bell-approved white suits advertising Miss Disc cosmetics, *Rave* magazine (December 1966).

Velvet Underground were in contention for the role. Why would the film's producers cast an unknown American band, even with Warhol's imprimatur, in a film about Swinging London?[204] Finding home-grown British talent was hardly a problem. Antonioni and Vitti were next seen attending the Rave-Up at the Roundhouse, an October launch event for *International Times* that featured the Pink Floyd and Soft Machine.[205]

Like Antonioni, American singer Scotty McKay was also taken with 'Train Kept a-Rollin''; he released, in early 1967, his souped-up cut of the song, which he credited to 'The Yardbirds'. McKay had briefly been in Gene Vincent & His Blue Caps, had recorded a number of sides for Ace Records earlier in the decade and been on the scene long enough to catch a ride on the Dick Clark Caravan, where he hooked up with the 'Birds. They obviously hit it off because Jim McCarty produced two sides for him in Nashville that had a British-only release on Columbia in March 1967 – the top deck was a cover of the Yardbirds' 'I Can't Make Your Way', which moves with an easy sway but lacks the unbridled spirit of his version of 'Train Kept a-Rollin'' that, contrary to rumour, Jimmy Page doesn't play on.[206]

AT LEAST IN PLAYING their part in the promotion of Miss Disc cosmetics and toiletries through the autumn of 1966, the five-piece, white-suited Yardbirds looked every bit the together band, exuding a darker mien than usually found in their publicity images, though less dissolute in appearance than their performance for *Blow-Up*. Fronted by a healthy, young, smiling model, 'The Yardbirds' bird', ran one advert, 'doesn't sing. She doesn't play. But she does know a guitar from a sitar.' Another, with Beck in the front, had the tagline for the ages: 'Five 'birds, one chick, four hits.'[207] That the Yardbirds had sex appeal was especially apparent in the United States. A non-believer – an older male reporter, undoubtedly – reviewed the band's 18 August show at the Tulsa Assembly Center's exhibit hall. He was facetiously dismissive, linking the 'English rock 'n roll group' with George Orwell and a 'world taken over by Big Brother', but 'Orwell was wrong. The world is taken over by Little Sister.'[208] The sound is 'terrible', the band are 'awful' and the 'songs are all the same', but Little Sister doesn't care:

> She in her bell-bottom pants, a few of them the low-slung 'navel-knockers'. She in her trim little suits. She in her straight, slim dresses. She looking world-weary, dead-eyed and old, except for her pretty, little-girl knobby knees.
>
> Little Sister was happy Thursday night. She was being serenaded in the dulcet tones she understands, or thinks she understands. The whole evening . . . the soft drinks, the hall, the plenitude of boys, the band . . . obviously was ordained just for her convenience.
>
> Little Sister indubitable was in command.[209]

Patronizing, misogynistic and prurient in his interest, he is a fearful witness to a world he can't control.

For the most part, reviews of the Yardbirds tended to be written by members of their audience. Sixteen-year-old Vicki Boles wrote up of one of the final nights of Dick Clark's Caravan of Stars at the Memorial Coliseum in Winston-Salem on 25 November. In the 'Teen Pages' of the *Twin City Sentinel* Boles described the event as being 'like some imaginary world' where she got to meet and talk to all the groups and performers; local bands as well as Sam the Sham and the Pharoahs, Brian Hyland, Dino, Desi and Billy. But she gave her particular attention to the group from England:

> Then, as if they had appeared from nowhere, the Yardbirds surrounded me. Contrary to the rumors that they are a rowdy, unreasonable quintet from the suburbs of London,

> I found them to be extremely polite and a dedicated group of performers.
>
> We discussed their 'new sound'. Lead Yardbird Keith Relf commented, 'We use the feedback from our amplifiers to develop the strange twangy vibration that backs our music.' Jimmy Page, the newest Yardbird and the most wildly dressed, said he feels adults really understand today's music. 'They dig it secretly,' he added in a very distinctive British accent.[210]

Technical hitches caused problems at the start of the band's set; while things were being fixed, 'Keith Relf entertained everyone with a harmonica tune he had written for "just such an occasion"'.[211] By taking the incidents in stride, 'the Yardbirds overcame their bad luck and really "grabbed" the audience.'[212] And 'girls from 10 to 16 squealed in delight.'[213]

The band's final show of the U.S. tour at the Springbrook Teen Club in Lima, Ohio, on 4 December had been held over from 16 October. The original show was cancelled, according to reports in the *Lima News*, because one of the band had been taken ill.[214] In truth, the start of the latest U.S. jaunt, of which this gig would have been the first, was delayed due to filming their scene for *Blow-Up*. Expectations were high for Lima's weekend 'Breakouts'; the *Lima News* 'Woman's Writer', Chris Guagenti, covered the band's arrival in town and preparations for the show for the following Sunday's 'Mostly for Women' pages. The article was generously illustrated with four portraits of the individual group members tuning up, playing harp and looking 'handsome', which sat below four images of the teenage audience, one of 'an enraptured brunette', another of Connie Jones smiling while holding a drumstick given to her by McCarty after the show, and next to her is 'long-haired friend' Joe Lewis Perez.[215] In the caption for the third picture, readers are asked if they can tell the boys from the girls, while the main photograph, with girls to the front, is captioned, 'Enthusiastic teens are listening to internationally famed Yardbirds.'[216] The two afternoon performances were in front of capacity crowds.

Guagenti met the band at their hotel and was welcomed into their rooms, she mentioned that on one of the beds

> was what looked like the hide of some shaggy mammal or the hair of its owner. 'Oh, that . . . it's from Afghanistan . . . bought it in Chicago in some second-hand ditty,' Jim Page the guitar player said in a 'vetty' British accent. 'If you'll excuse me please I will just run some bath water,' Mr. Page said. 'I never perform before I have my bath.'[217]

She talked to Dreja, who mentioned *Blow-Up*, the length of the tour and another journalist's confusion over Leema and Lima. She noted that Relf's wife, April, is in the room: '"I don't always follow my husband around" . . . [she said,] through clouds of cigarette smoke which she created.'[218] Talk again turned to clothes and where they buy them – McCarty's favourite shops are Hung on You and Dandy. 'Sound like hit records, don't they?', he said.[219] At lunch, the issue of Beck's absence was raised; Dreja told Guagenti that he'd had 'what they call a nervous breakdown' – an end-of-tour moment of honesty, his guard down, unmediated by the Yardbirds management.[220] Perhaps aware of his faux pas, Dreja turned it into a joke: 'Basically he's a nervous guy but he was pushed over the brink when he found out that Brian was our new road manager in the States.'[221] The same explanation for his absence was given in a review of the Alexandria, Louisiana, gig on 1 November, though here it was not attributed to anyone in the band. But, even without Beck, the act was described as 'sensational.'[222] (During the 1967 tour of the United States, in Colorado Springs, Relf said simply that Beck was 'dispensable'; in such moments of candour, all the political politeness of excuses that usually surrounded Beck fell away.[223]) The conversation turned once more to fashion and what's being worn by women in London, trouser suits, mini-skirts or 'bikini-skirts' as Dreja called them. 'I dig the robot look. You know – the silver dress, silver shoes, silver stockings,' said Page.[224]

After lunch, Guagenti drove with them to the show: 'Because the Yardbirds' schedule is tight they haven't any time for practice before a performance. "We'll do our hit numbers 'Over Under Sideways Down' and 'Heart Full of Soul' and then our new release called 'Happenings Ten Years Time Ago'. You might have heard it", Keith said.'[225] The article ended when Relf explained, 'We do not have a pat name for our music. If anything, it's music for the mind . . . We leave it all up to the listener.'[226] And that listener, in 1966 USA, was more often than not female.

At the beginning of December, *NME*'s Hollywood correspondent, Tracy Thomas, reported on the continuing difficulties the Yardbirds faced, not only from Beck's absence but now from Dreja having fallen ill from tonsillitis, the band had missed three shows; 'With all the problems the Yardbirds have been having, it's no wonder there'll be some big changes very soon within the group. And if Jeff should leave, don't be surprised to find him going to California, where he's the darling of many West Coast groups which would grab him like a shot if he were free.'[227] Two weeks later, the split with Beck was confirmed by Napier-Bell: 'Beck has not been playing with the Yardbirds during their tour of the U.S., due to ill-health, and it has been agreed that he should leave. There will be only four members of the group in future.'[228] The last word was given to McCarty: 'Beck is out, no matter what he says.'[229] He was, according to the *NME*, 'referring to reports that Beck was still a member of the group'.[230] Rumours were rife, *Disc and Music Echo* even reported that Jimmy Page was set to leave and that Beck was to be replaced by an organist.[231]

Beginning with the September issue, Beck had been writing a regular column for *Beat Instrumental*. It was mostly anecdotal and inconsequential, but the column published in the first New Year edition laid things out from his perspective just before the split. Much of it was concerned with the smashing of his Gibson Les Paul at what was to be his third-from-final gig with the band in Dallas: 'I picked it up, swung it by the neck above my head, and smashed it on the floor. The neck came away and the pick-ups flew in two directions. Jimmy Page was horrified, but so was I when I realised what I'd done a bit later.'[232] He outlined the multiple reasons for why he had lost control; much of it was to do with the terrible conditions on the tour: more than 600 kilometres (400 mi.) travelled, no air-conditioning, crammed into the Greyhound with other groups endlessly 'singing Beatle songs in an American accent' – 'can you imagine?' – and the food was awful and made him ill.[233] (For the previous tour, back in the summer, the band had travelled in a DC3 that Napier-Bell had hired to get around striking American airline personnel.[234]) In Dallas, they were scheduled to do two slots, 6:30 and 8:30 p.m. Without a return to their hotel, the band had to sit around in their sweaty stage gear between sets: 'It was all wrong. At the end of the second spot we were all pretty depressed; then someone said something to me which made me blow up. Hence the smashed guitar.'[235] All was not lost, however; he'd seen Barney Kessel play at Shelly Manne's Manne-Hole Club in Los Angeles, and he thought his own technique was improving and that he and Page 'were getting a much closer sound':

> Each of us would play separate solos and then, when one of us started a phrase the other would slide into it, so that in the end we got a sort of stereo-sound effect between the two guitars. Now I'm just hoping that we can stay on form through our long-awaited rest period.[236]

His hope, and the promise of the dual guitar line-up, fell to the side, though he had won the magazine's poll for 1966's best lead guitarist – Clapton came third. Page and Dreja came fifth and seventh, respectively, for best rhythm guitarist, and Relf sixth for best vocalist. The Who topped best group on stage, and the Yardbirds came fifth, one place above Cream.[237] By the end of December, it was announced that Beck had signed to Mickie Most (sixth in *Beat Instrumental*'s poll of best 'recording manager') and would henceforth be jointly looked after by Napier-Bell and Most's partner, Peter Grant.[238]

Just before Beck's split from the band, *Hit Parader*'s Don Paulsen wrote that 'of all the British guitarists, [he] seems to have made the greatest impact on American audiences. His incredibly fluid and dynamic sound is a mind-blowing pleasure to listen to and a challenge to imitate.'[239] In turn, Beck had been held in thrall by Les Paul, 'who was able to get any sound out of a guitar'; he told Paulsen, 'I was fascinated by . . . I suppose it was a perversion of the sound. If a sax could sound like a piano, I suppose I'd start playing the sax.'[240] He discussed his admiration for T. Bone Walker, Buddy Guy and B. B. King. About King, Beck said, 'He has such great expression. He plays a lot of phrases that are the same, but they ring home every time. He's learned his "stock explosions". That's what I call them. He knows exactly how to tap the audience.'[241]

Beck's own perversion of sound and his stock explosions, his fluid, dynamic playing, defined the Yardbirds; for all his personal faults, his unreliability, while Beck was piloting the show, innovation was written into the script. As Beck's replacement, Page would first build on his predecessor's accomplishments and then push the envelope one more time.

8

Electrorock Therapy and the 14-Hour Technicolor Dream Machine, 1967

In the third week of the New Year, the Monkees were number one in the charts with 'I'm a Believer'. Across the early months of 1967, Hollywood's Beatle-esque confection dominated Britain's pop magazines and papers. *Disc and Music Echo* asked the Move's Roy Wood to comment on this and muse awhile on the current Top 10. He thought the Monkees were a 'bit of a fiddle . . . The thing we're annoyed about is that the British pop scene has let America walk in.'[1] He had nothing to say about Tom Jones at no. 2 with 'Green, Green Grass of Home', but he thought the Who, at no. 3, were 'a great group' and that their single 'Happy Jack' was 'simple, yet so commercial. And they always come up with something different.'[2] The Troggs with 'Anyway That You Want Me' were one place below the Who, and Wood thought it was 'tremendous'.[3] Cat Stevens's 'Matthew and Son' he also liked. The Four Tops' 'Standing in the Shadow of Love', however, at no. 6, was 'too like the last one'.[4] Next down, Cliff Richard, he ignored. The Move's 'Night of Fear' had risen that week into the Top 10 at no. 8, and Donovan with 'Sunshine Superman' was at no. 9 – Wood ignored it too. Jimi Hendrix with 'Hey Joe' had jumped five places to no. 10; Wood was surprised that he had 'sold so many – though he's just ridiculous. I don't think it will be a big hit.'[5] Cream were at no. 15 that week with 'I Feel Free'; Wood didn't 'blame them for going Commercial. People who go to watch you like what you play, but people who buy your records like you for your image' – the genuine and the projection.[6]

The configuration of the pop scene was up for grabs, oscillating wildly between the commercial and the authentic, the real and image: Donovan as sincere 'psychedelic troubadour' or bandwagon jumper, Hendrix as 'ridiculous' or the future face of pop. What wasn't in doubt was that an American rear-guard action now posed a threat to Britain's chart dominance on both sides of the Atlantic. Just where the Yardbirds fitted into this scheme of things was uncertain (and to a good few, irrelevant). After Beck's departure, it was as if the band had fallen through a crack in the pavement; against the coverage given to the Who, Cream, Jimi Hendrix and the Pink Floyd, they might as well have no longer existed. Compared to the blanket attention given to the Monkees, they didn't figure at all.

The band began the New Year in the States, followed by a tour of Australia and New Zealand. February saw them play gigs in Britain and Europe, and March was fairly free of live commitments but featured some studio work with Mickie Most at the beginning and the end of the month. In April, they were in Scandinavia. May was a mix of French and British shows, June was a series of domestic dates, and then July through to November was spent in North America. The band's ceaseless touring of Europe and North America with only a sole disc, 'Little Games', released in the British and European markets (with limited exceptions), meant that they were all but invisible in the British music press throughout the year. Most notices were therefore in forums like the *NME*'s 'America Calling' column. In January, the paper's New York reporter, June Harris, relayed to readers the news that there were 'riots at a Yardbirds concert last weekend [2 January], when the group played Long Island ice rink. Not only did the 2,500-strong crowd converge on the group, who were whisked off the stage after two numbers for fear of injury, but the ice melted due to a water pipe burst!'[7] *Blow-Up* had opened in New York, and Jimmy Page told her that they were now no longer looking to replace Beck – 'Really we've noticed no difference.'[8] In their absence, British press reports that mentioned the Yardbirds were nearly all to do with Beck's solo career.

In the February 1967 edition of *Beat Instrumental*, Beck gave his account of the split. You can feel the rancour rising as you read down the six column inches. He professed to not knowing why he hadn't left earlier; he could not talk about money, and what he did have to say about the group excluded Jimmy Page: 'you wouldn't believe the stupid bickering which went on between some of us.'[9] The smashed-guitar-in-Dallas incident arose due to something Keith Relf had said to him: 'you see I was never really accepted into the group and when things got a little rough, as they did on the last American tour, most of the moans were directed at me. Trouble was it never worked the other way round.'[10] His opinion on things was not sought or held in regard, yet 'all modesty apart, I feel that Keith Relf and myself were the main figures in that group. I was looking through back copies of *Beat Instrumental* and other papers a couple of months ago and it struck me that the others were never mentioned.'[11] Despite all that he had contributed, 'stage-wise and record-wise', the band just didn't care that he'd been ill: 'they came back to me and said that they had been OK on their own; they'd got by. Evidently they didn't think that they needed me, they certainly don't want a good guitarist with them.'[12] His last column for the magazine was in the March edition, where he discussed future plans and noted that his Gibson Les Paul was fixed; he was moving on.[13]

In an interview with the *Sunday Mirror*'s Jack Bentley, Beck changed tack and found a new target to blame for his split from the band – groupies. 'Pop Groups, Sex-Mad Girls and Don't-Care Parents', ran the headline:

> If it doesn't kill you physically, it's almost bound to professionally. I'm twenty-two, I've been in the pop business three years and I can't count the chicks I've had affairs with . . . This is no personal whack at the Yardbirds or any other group. This discussion is about me. The ravers only

> get their way if they're encouraged. You don't have to fall for the bait. I admit I did.[14]

For now, Beck was pulling out of that scene: 'I've a beautiful American actress girl friend called Mary Hughes who is coming over here soon. I am hoping it will develop into something more, and I am going to be blagged – she's favourite.'[15] The fact that Beck was already married didn't seem to bother him, though by November news of his imminent divorce had made the papers: 'Pop Star Sued By His Secret Wife' ran the *Daily Mirror* headline.[16] Two months earlier, he'd told *Record Mirror* that music to him was like marriage, 'which is almost the ultimate to most men, music is my ultimate. It's not that I'm queer or anything, but I don't suppose I'll get married. All I want is my music.'[17]

Unlike the Yardbirds, Beck maintained a presence in the pop press, both in Britain and the States. Recording with Mickie Most, Beck's first solo single, 'Hi Ho Silver Lining', written by Americans Scott English and Larry Weiss, was given a 3 March release date.[18] It was, at base, another Lovin' Spoonful pastiche. The Attack had also found their way to the song and released their single in the first week of March, reviewed positively by Penny Valentine:

> What I really like about this record is the song. Certainly of its novelty light lollipop type the best written this year by far. The words are really blissful – although somewhat incomprehensible – about her sitting in the sun under her umbrella watching TV and wearing her hippy hat. But the real joy is the chorus. There's some funny little spacey sounds and high wood wind. The lead singer pounces on the words like a spiteful cat and the whole thing moves well. Enough plays turned up loudly and this could be a nice round hit.[19]

Beck's version was released a week or so after the Attack, reviewed in *Record Mirror* at the end of the month:

> I'm sure this is a hit song – and I'm pretty sure this is a hit treatment by the new solo figure on the scene. Curious sound effects early on, then into a commercially staccato beating number, with a catchy chorus phrase. And Jeff's guitar gets a fair amount of space too.[20]

Valentine didn't review it for *Disc*, but it entered their chart at no. 20 in the last week of April. Beck told the paper that he was 'delighted': 'This is really one in the eye for those who knocked me down.'[21] He was obviously referring to his ex-bandmates, but also to his disastrous debut solo appearance on the opening night of the Roy Orbison/ Small Faces package tour that Peter Grant had signed him up for.

Licking his wounds after being ousted from the band, Beck was photographed and interviewed by Val Wilmer in the late spring of 1967. He was clearly still bitter, but also looking forward. In a last-minute despatch appended to the piece that ran in *Hit Parader*, Wilmer listed the new band members, noting the date of the band's debut. Beck had pulled together Ron Wood from the Birds, who switched from guitar to bass, Ray Cook on drums, who'd briefly played with Beck in the Tridents, and Rod Stewart from Shotgun Express on vocals. Wilmer was not impressed by Beck's choice of singer; 'All I can say is God help him with Stewart aboard, a class Z-singer!'[22] Whatever Stewart's strengths and limitations, by all accounts the group was woefully unprepared for the appearance at the Finsbury Park Astoria on 3 March. According to *Disc*'s Mike Ledgerwood, 'Beck looked unhappy and sounded diabolical. It is hard to believe he is a guitarist praised to the heavens for his talent. And audience reaction to his solo debut must have more than disheartened him.'[23] *Melody Maker* put the story on its front page; Chris Welch reported that

> [the] group were obviously under-rehearsed and in the first house on opening night Jeff walked off stage when the power failed. Rod Stewart attempted to salvage what remained of the act. In the second house they played badly and created a very poor impression. It was a sad occasion and an object lesson relying too heavily on past reputations.[24]

'A lot of reasons contributed to my calling off the tour,' Beck told *Disc*: 'All these things seem to come to a head on the opening night. First, the power for my amplifier was switched off. People may not have noticed it – but I did. Then some person damaged it – and I have to pay for it.'[25] Anyway, the whole set-up was wrong, he said:

> it's not worth appearing on a bill starring such names as Roy Orbison and the Small Faces. You're playing to fans of these acts. It's a waste of time trying to get across. Frankly, I would never tour with such artists again, and play low down on the bill. I'd rather top on a ballroom tour.[26]

His bruised ego also played its part: 'It was quite a comedown after appearing with the Yardbirds and topping an act like the Small Faces. I also understood my record "Hi Ho Silver Lining" was being released to coincide with the tour. But it was held up through some technical hitch. So that was a waste.'[27] The poor show then the no-show for the rest of the tour appeared like a reprise of his final American go-around with the Yardbirds. *Disc* quoted a spokesman for Harold Davidson's office, co-promoter of the tour: 'Jeff requested that he should leave so he did not appear on Saturday. I understand he wasn't too happy with his act, and he doesn't seem very keen on touring – he didn't care much for tours when he was a member of the Yardbirds.'[28]

The Monday after the gig, Rod Stewart told *Melody Maker*: 'We shouldn't have gone on the tour without enough rehearsal. We didn't have enough numbers and it was a real let down. But we will carry on and do club appearances. We'll have a new drummer. Micky Waller is joining us.'[29] Beck put part of the blame for the fiasco on Ray Cook, who had 'lost his timing'.[30] Chris Welch talked to the drummer's mum, Winifred Cook, who was unsurprisingly upset about the treatment her boy had received:

> Ray has had such a raw deal. He was brought out of the group he was playing with, Sands, and asked to join Jeff's group for the tour. He was promised a bright future and now he faces a very grim one with no job, no prospects and a very heavy debt incurred by a new drum kit costing £400 which he was told he would need for the new group. His father traded in his own set of drums to help raise part of the money.
>
> After the first disastrous night of the tour Jeff left another member of the group to tell Ray he was out. Now my husband and I have to support Ray, who has a wife and child, until he can find another group. I can't understand why Jeff should [*sic*] do this to Ray. We've known him a long time and Jeff and Ray played together before in a group called the Tridents. Jeff was a friend of the family. Ray had his nineteenth birthday the day after the tour opened. What a marvellous birthday present. I don't know how or where he'll pick up again.[31]

In a longer interview with Welch, Beck explained what he felt had gone wrong. Principally, he'd been rushed into getting a group together to deliver on the contract to play the tour. 'I broke every rule in the book,' he said, and he had done this to counter his 'reputation for being unreliable, which came about when I was ill in America and nobody believed me here'.[32] Now with drummer Micky Waller on board, he challenged 'any group to compete with us in a group battle'.[33]

Beck switched promoters, leaving Davidson and signing with Brian Epstein's NEMS Enterprises, who arranged club and ballroom dates; he also taped a half-hour phone conversation with Dick Clark for inclusion on his programme.[34] For his return to live performances, he headlined at the Marquee.

With 'Silver Lining' high in the charts, Beck talked to *Record Mirror* about the recent past and his ambitions. He'd rewritten the debut fiasco as press exaggeration and given it a positive spin on the angle that all publicity is good publicity. Besides, they'd followed up with a sell-out gig at the Marquee, and the single was a hit. The latter wasn't representative, he said; 'it was aimed at the people that don't know me.'[35] He'd recently returned from a trip to the States where he'd put things right with the press over there: 'You know how it is, you do a long show as happened when I was there last, and you're towelling yourself off afterwards and someone comes in and asks you some embarrassing questions. You are caught on the hop and the wrong sort of answers happen. Just happen.'[36] Speaking to Alan Jones of the *Lincolnshire Echo*, Beck said: 'That night didn't make all that difference. I'm not a cardboard pop star relying on floral shirts, silk ties and kinky gear.'[37]

His band was now settled, with Ron Wood on bass, Rod Stewart on vocals and Aynsley Dunbar on drums, who

> lays something down and I follow it. Then somebody else follows me. We're really going in a lot of different directions but the important thing is we must be different. The drummer is fantastic. He has this strange technique. It's like the rhythm of the chain-gang workers in the deep Southern States in America . . . that sort of thing. Could be very good.[38]

He'd recently been to see Iron Butterfly play at the Galaxy on Sunset Strip; their second set had impressed him, as it was 'devoted to just ONE NUMBER. It was an original for the group and they spun it out for around thirty-five minutes. That's why I liked them so much. Just for being able to do that.'[39] A chilling augury of the excesses to come.

Pretty much all the reviews of Beck's single made a point of acknowledging its B-side, 'Beck's Bolero' – 'a virtuoso (and noisy) guitar instrumental', according to *Record Mirror*, and from the *NME*: 'A showcase for Jeff's prowess as a guitarist . . . and he certainly pulls out all the technical and psychedelic tricks.'[40] The *Daily Mail*'s pop columnist, Virginia Ironside, wrote, 'First solo by the grooviest ex-Yardbird not bad, and listen to the B-side where his guitar comes into its own.'[41] Beck told *Melody Maker*, 'The B side is more my cup of tea. It's an instrumental bolero based on Ravel.'[42] It also happened to be among Jimi Hendrix's favourite sides of the moment – 'beautiful guitar', he commented.[43]

'Beck's Bolero' had been recorded back in May 1966, ostensibly as his solo single. Around that time, he was asked by *The Beat* what future plans he had; he said he wanted to produce, but not the Yardbirds, as they effectively produced themselves – 'it just happens. The record is built from the ground and no *one* person can take credit for it at the end. It's everybody's combined efforts.'[44] But as an example of what he can do, he offered the unreleased and yet unnamed 'Beck's Bolero':

> I've got an example of my production together with Jimmy Page and it's an instrumental. It's very stirring and it's got an intensive pulsating beat, which goes on and on and on, and it just explodes at the end. We designed it to affect a man's mind – or to make it sound as if the man was affected when he wrote it. I think we'll release it in an album, but it's going to be put out as a single by me. It's been finished three months, and there's no name for it![45]

Playing with him on the track were Jimmy Page, John Paul Jones, Keith Moon (AWOL from the Who) and Nicky Hopkins.[46]

Discussing how he wanted to achieve the same feeling, not an imitation of the 'coloured sound' on contemporary soul records, Beck turned to 'Bolero' as his point of comparison:

> I was really feeling that guitar. The idea of the record was to get a basic thudding rhythm, with a sad bit on top, suddenly breaking into anger. And the engineers were really trying to pick out the sad sounds, but I don't think they quite made it. If I'd recorded 'Bolero' in the States with coloured guys producing, it would have been so much better.[47]

Touring with the Yardbirds in September 1966, Jimmy Page discussed the recording of 'Bolero', describing it as 'exciting and strange'; released as a single cut, he thought it could be either a 'monster or a bomb'.[48] He was using it to talk about what a framework for exploiting electric solo guitar might be like, but he wasn't sure that the public would accept such a concept: 'You either make a commercial record or a musicians' record. You've got to draw the line somewhere.'

Back from the States at the beginning of December, followed by shows in Bristol, Aberystwyth and Hull, the Yardbirds recrossed the Atlantic for Christmas and New Year's dates in the United States before flying out on 15 January, with a stop and a gig in Singapore, to Australia and New Zealand, where they played with Roy Orbison and the Walker Brothers.[49] A short news stub has the band immediately going into the studio between the U.S. and Australasian dates, but the key reference book lists only a recording of a commercial for Macleans toothpaste at the Marquee studios in January.[50] *Melody Maker* reported that the band, just four days back from the United States, were flying out again on Sunday (22 January) and 'were frantically recording new material' in the week's gap (15–21 January) between this visit and their trip to the Antipodes, but they were due to play Singapore on 17 January and Sydney four days later.

'Thousands of Sydney teenagers, most of them girls, packed into Sydney Stadium last night for the "Big Show"'. Keith Relf 'clutches the microphone and[,] gleaming in a shirt of pink silk, seems to reflect the hysterical excitement of the evening'. *Sydney Morning Herald* (24 January 1967).

Whatever time was spent in the studio, the rushed nature of things was indicative of the problems that were besetting the band (and had done in the past). Jimmy Page said: 'The trouble is we aren't allowed to record in the States and that means we must do everything in a terrible rush when we are here.'[51]

It had been announced in January that they would undertake a three-day recording session in February, which would be filmed for television.[52] Whether or not that happened, on the band's return from their Australasian tour, one of the compositions said to be under consideration was the title song for a European movie co-production, a horror starring Vincent Price and helmed by exploitation maestro Harry Alan Towers, *House of 1,000 Dolls*.[53] If that song, written by Don Black and Mark London, was ever recorded by the Yardbirds, it has been lost – no doubt to the gratitude of all involved. A version would be released by Cliff Bennett and his band in February 1968; it is awful.

The last time that the band had been together in a studio was a couple of days before Christmas. They had convened at Olympic Sound Studios in Barnes and, with Samwell-Smith producing, had laid down the backing tracks for two songs. Principal work was carried out on another Graham Gouldman composition, 'You Stole My Love'. Working with Gomelsky, Samwell-Smith had produced a take of the song for Gouldman's group, the Mockingbirds, released by Immediate in October 1965. Given its structural similarities to his earlier compositions for the band, Gouldman probably wrote the song with the Yardbirds in mind. It has a strong melody and a dynamic arrangement. Its expansive sonic texture is deftly captured and enhanced by Samwell-Smith. The recording opens with a chiming guitar figure preceding the verse/chorus, which segues into a bridge that radically alters the song's direction, flipping it into a 3/4 waltz time arrangement. The song then returns to the opening guitar figure before launching into a rave-up section that heads back to the verse, ending with a final go around for the chorus and a fade out on the solo guitar. The backing track that the Yardbirds put on tape at Olympic follows this structure to the letter, but after the experiments of 'Happenings Ten Years Time Ago' it sounds redundant or, at the very least, a retrograde step, which was perhaps why the tapes were left unfinished. But if the band didn't want to go backwards, where were they now heading?

After traipsing around the Southern Hemisphere, the Yardbirds returned to play two dates in France. They then performed a short season of British ballroom dates in mid-February before venturing back to Europe for mostly Scandinavian dates throughout April. At the beginning of February, *Disc* announced that Peter Grant would be co-managing not only Jeff Beck with Simon Napier-Bell but the Yardbirds.[54] *Blow-Up* was scheduled for its British release at the end of March.[55] Recording sessions for a new single and album tracks with Mickie Most producing were held on 5 and 27–28 March and 23–25 April.[56]

While British attention was turned elsewhere, and the band were overseas, Columbia released an EP of four tracks from their last album; it was nothing more than a place-filler, kitted out in an inverted white-on-black image of the album sleeve and with a photograph of the band with Beck and Page on the rear. *Record Mirror* published a damning review – 'Four self-penned songs from the Yardbirds, who aren't doing as well as they used to' – and added some advice: 'They should get away from this droning sound on this EP.'[57] It sold poorly, if its high value in the contemporary collector's market is a guide. In the States, Epic released a *Greatest Hits* album, all but two of the ten tracks featuring Beck. But none of the band, from whatever line-up, featured on the front cover. As if this was a blues or soul album aimed at the white market, the artist was absent, and in his or her place was an overlapping set of images of golden-haired young women shot as if caught in the lights at a discotheque.

In its 'Raver's Weekly Tonic' column, *Melody Maker* ran one of its occasional snarky posts about the band: 'Why do the Yardbirds always claim to have done everything first?'[58] Their acerbic remark was in response to Keith Relf's assertion, in that week's edition, that the band had experimented with light shows as far back as their Crawdaddy days; always part of the advance guard but never honoured in despatches, was his contention. In his defence, Relf was trying to make a valid point about the band's longevity and what that meant in today's scene. He told Dawbarn, 'The Yardbirds are stale to British fans – like the Animals and the other groups we came up with.'[59] He was adding a dose of realism to their situation, even as he claimed a significance for the present. Jimmy Page added, 'We are still going down very well in America, it's still all fresh to them. Over here the scene is in a funny way at the moment.'[60] Keith agreed, and then positioned himself as an elder statesman:

> In Britain, unless you get to the level of the Beatles or the Stones you all become stale to the kids after a year or two. The new generation are followers of the Cream, the Move or the Action, I suppose. But I don't think there is the excitement that there was three years ago.[61]

Like Roy Wood, he thought American groups were now making advances. Page agreed:

> I've been on three American tours. On the first two there was nothing happening there at all. I was shocked by the groups we played with. Now you find good guitarists and good ideas everywhere – especially on the West Coast. They aren't just reproducing Beatles or Stones things anymore.[62]

Relf continued that line of thought:

> It's a very exciting scene at the moment. There's a whole undercurrent of youthful revolution that isn't apparent until you talk to people. When we were in Hollywood there were riots against the police. Kids were passing leaflets round saying when and where to turn up to protest against police brutality. I'm not condoning it but it's indicative of a whole revolution among the younger people in America.
>
> And musically it's all beginning to happen there, with the Monkees at the commercial end of the product and at the other end the Mothers of Invention. And we're in the middle trying to bridge the gap.[63]

Trying to bridge the gap was as fair a summation of the band at this point in time, but it was also a recognition of defeat. Where once the band led, now they followed. Relf had been predicting the end of days for a good while; back in August 1966, he had told an American reporter that he expected the band's 'popularity to fade in about one year'.[64] He explained that 'the distinctive quality of our music is that we feature our instruments more than ourselves.'[65] In this, they were on trend with many of the emerging psychedelic bands – certainly with the Pink Floyd, who were often hidden by their light show – but it also suggested the Yardbirds' growing invisibility in the pop market place.

Recorded on 5 March in London at Olympic Sound Studios, 'Little Games' backed with the band composition 'Puzzles' was released on 21 April. In her review for *Disc*, Penny Valentine noted Most's involvement and considered it to be

> an odd cross between new Yardbirds and old Yardbirds with a snatch of their guitar sound just to prove they don't miss Jeff Beck. Written partly by Phil Wainman, who a long time ago had a record himself called 'Hear Me a Drummer Man' that I liked, it has an odd insistence and the words of social significance and some nice 'cellos – I do like 'cellos. I rather like it.[66]

In the *NME*, Derek Johnson gave the single its most fulsome boost:

> Gee whiz, what a shattering beat from the Yardbirds! A heavy-handed walloping drive all the way – and this, coupled with raucous twanging and sitar effect, creates a completely insidious and nagging wall of sound. Psychedelic it may well be but not of a distasteful nature . . . I found it compulsive and intriguing, and it should do better than the Yardbirds' last one.[67]

The *Evening Standard*'s pop reviewer also liked it, though he was grudging in his praise: 'there's a wailing wall of sound behind the Yardbirds for their new one. But the lyrics are hard to catch and the whole thing is rather messy. Could be protest. Could be anything.'[68] Given the drubbing that *Record Mirror* had laid on the EP released in February, they were much more positive about the single:

> So okay, the Yardbirds don't always make it. But this is a clever song idea and the arrangement is first straightforward, though with a shove-along beat, and there's an instrumental spasm of high excitement. A hymn of praise to the big games

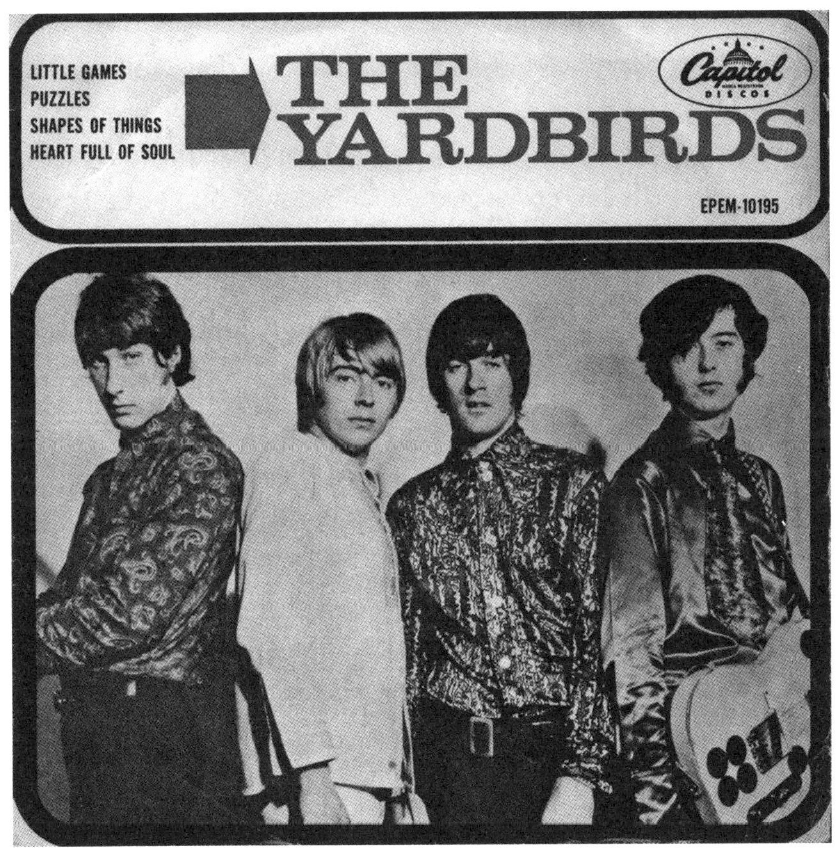

Satin, paisley and appliqué – debut as a four piece: 'Little Games' (Mexican picture sleeve), 1967.

> that big boys play! Flip: Not far short of the top deck for commercial quality.[69]

Cat Stevens reviewed the single for *Melody Maker*'s 'Blind Date': 'Fantastic song. Tremendous beat. It's great the way they put *the wrong inflection* on the words . . . Is Jeff Beck on this one? It's a beautiful record. A hit.'[70] He then caught the drift of the band's intention: 'It's directed at the American market. It could be one of those things that doesn't happen here, but I think it might.'[71] Maybe Relf self-aligning with kinky cats in Chelsea flats in the song's lyrics would play well in the American heartlands, but in 1967 Britain, was there a triter lyric delivered by a major band?

One of the few interviews the band gave to the British music press around the time of the single's release was a piece conducted by Bill Harry for *Record Mirror*. The disc and their plans were not mentioned; instead, the band used it as a forum to complain against police overreach and government clamp-downs on young people, picking up especially on the hypocrisy of politicians putting down pop culture as they gladly pocketed the economic benefits it created.[72] Two weeks or so later, on 1 July, the Yardbirds performed at the Roundhouse in Chalk Farm as part of the Angry Arts event – 'a demonstration by the Artistic Community against the War in Vietnam'. A dance troupe, literary, political and religious figures, theatre pieces and rock groups appeared. It was one of the rare moments when the Yardbirds put themselves at the centre of the British counterculture.

While there were any number of positive reviews of the single, it was the more negatively inclined that seemed to catch the zeitgeist, such as that in the *Runcorn Weekly News*: 'first disc under the supervision of ace producer Mickie Most, and he has made a superb job of this number. It's rather off-beat, with fantastic use of the lead guitar in the middle and towards the end. Keith Relf's distinctive vocal style is well suited to the number,' but:

> Of all the British pop groups who came to fame quickly and then faded, none were so disappointing as The Yardbirds. They made a fine start with three big hits on the run, then came the illness of their lead guitarist Jeff Beck. His replacement never quite fitted in, and the group went back to their early uncommercial style, the sort of music they played when Eric Clapton was with them. They maintain the pattern on their new single, 'Little Games', which must be the most unimpressive thing they have ever done. Meanwhile, their two ex-lead guitarists, Beck and Clapton, have made big names for themselves with their own groups.[73]

A month after the single's release, the *NME* ran a line in 'Tailpieces' expressing surprise that it had been a 'chart failure'.[74] In his column for *Disc*, 'Our Man in America', Derek Taylor wrote that '[the] Yardbirds' new single was admired by the best of the people in the trade here but it isn't selling at the moment.'[75] The issue was that 'it's fatal not to publicize discs,' Dreja told Val Wilmer: 'The Beatles are the only people who can get away without doing this. Even the Stones have suffered quite a bit from being out of the public eye. It's even dicey for the "untouchables", you see!'[76]

In a profile of Mickie Most, the producer conceded that the band had 'slipped in Britain recently', and that 'it might be because their records have been too way-out. "Little Games" is half and half . . . A good number, with some of the Yardbirds' style thrown in as well.'[77] He made the point to Bill Harry in *Record Mirror* that his work with an 'artiste' did not stop with the cutting of the disc:

> To make money you've got to help the artiste and promote the record and make sure that the shops have got their copies . . . I definitely choose all the material the artistes record. I play it to them and if they like it, good. If they don't . . . They still do it anyway. They trust my judgement. Herman,

> for instance, has sometimes not been too happy with material I've chosen for him – but he acknowledges that I've been right... and he's got 40,000,000 record sales behind him to prove it. After all, most artistes don't know what's good for them, unless they're songwriters. Donovan plays me several numbers and I choose which ones to record.[78]

By not generating their own material, the Yardbirds were beholden to Most; such deference may have been worth the cost of a lack of creative control over their records if hits had followed, but they didn't, so they were twice diminished by the relationship.

With the break-up of the Yardbirds still fresh, Page explained from his point of view the band's relationship with Most. After successfully self-producing 'Happenings', their manager, he said, had decided to turn them over to Most.

> We thought it was a great idea because the producer had tremendous success with 'Sunshine Superman'. We had tremendous confidence in him. So we did 'Little Games' and it didn't do very well, but that was all right. It was a reasonable number to do. Then he gave us 'Ha Ha Said the Clown', which we didn't like, but we still had confidence in him. Over a period of time, his ideas started to kill us off ... On the B sides he just put blues cuts from our albums and I knew something was wrong because the radio stations were playing the B sides.
>
> Another thing that bugged us about this producer [he didn't name Most] was he never once came to see us perform live. He had recorded us for two years and never came to see us. If we were a good selling commodity, you'd think he's come and join us just once to see what we were like on stage.[79]

For Page and Yardbird fans who subsequently felt Most ignored the innovations of the band's live show, the producer may well have been answering them in advance when he told Harry:

> I never go to see my artistes perform on stage. I have a set plan in mind with each artiste and I know in which direction I want them to go. If I heard them on stage they might play a number which might prejudice me. I might think 'that's nice' and it might throw me and alter the particular plan I've set out.[80]

After the release of 'Tally Man', Beck set out his understanding of the role of a producer:

> People don't realise how easy it is to produce records. Anyone with just a modicum of talent could do it. Ninety percent of the work in the studios is done by the recording engineer, and he's really the king pin of the whole operation. We didn't have a producer at all when I did 'Shapes of Things' with the Yardbirds, and that, in my opinion, was one of the best pop records ever. But everyone has forgotten it now [which no doubt was why he chose to re-record it for his debut solo album] – you know, we only used three instruments on that. On 'I'm a Man', again with the Yardbirds, the producer, Sam Phillips, was in fact an engineer.[81]

He had come to hate 'Hi Ho Silver Lining': 'that was a terrible record, and it only came out because it was commercial – not my decision to record that song, by the way.'[82] Even when he was wrong, Mickie Most was right – except when it came to the Yardbirds.[83]

Just how out of touch the Yardbirds had become with the British scene was symbolized in the biggest piece that the daily press put out on the band in 1967; 'My Lost Date with Pop Star by Roberta' was the headline that ran in the *Daily Mail* on 19 May. Roberta Martin, fifteen, had won a poetry competition organized by the band's fan club, and the prize was lunch with Keith Relf at the London Hilton. Despite writing letters telling of her availability, she'd been waiting over three months for her promised date. Apologizing, the new fan club secretary, Marilyn Marsh, 24, said she had been nagging and nagging Keith, who had now promised to get in touch with Roberta.[84] Except for Roberta's disappointment, it was a nothing story, yet it suggested a band and its handlers who were not in control of media management.

The Yardbirds were undoubtedly of the same mind as Jeff Beck about the British and U.S. scenes and where their efforts were best targeted. 'Let's face it,' Beck told *NME*'s Keith Altham in May,

> there's no glory to be made out of pop now in Britain . . . You have to go to America to find kids who are going to see you as entertainment and not as a necessity. I get the impression in Britain that young people feel they must go to a club every night – they're saturated with groups and pop music.[85]

At the beginning of July, it was announced that the Yardbirds were starting a six-week U.S. tour and had been booked for a five-week Far Eastern visit, including a week in Australia, beginning in January (it didn't take place). Ready for immediate release upon their arrival in America was their version of the recent Manfred Mann British hit single, 'Ha! Ha! Said the Clown', which had missed in the States. That miss justified Most pushing the tune on the Yardbirds in the hope they could do what the Manfreds hadn't (while that band's hit explained why the 'Birds' version was not released in Britain). No other new Yardbirds disc was planned for the domestic market until September.[86]

Recorded in Columbia's New York studio in June and finished a few days later in Abbey Road, other than Relf none of the band played on the 'Clown' session (if Page was present, the recording itself marked him absent). It was regressive and the worst kind of pop: cynical and joyless. If the band were floundering in the commercial void of Most's production and his choice of material, as a gigging band, they were nevertheless continuing to consider new avenues of sonic experiments. After the release of the 'Little Games' single, Val Wilmer reported that

> For the moment the Yardbirds are playing around with arrangements in the recording studio and starting to use taped sound effects during their act. 'The tapes will be switched on and timed,' said Jimmy, 'So that you'll have a train going across the stage in the middle of a song or suddenly Hitler will speak. It's not like John Cage's thing: this is completely our idea. We try to think widely and incorporate as many things in our music as we can.'[87]

Beat Instrumental also covered this story:

> New idea from the Yardbirds is to play some tape recordings on stage when they are changing over guitars. The idea comes from Jimmy Page. He has fixed up a tape recorder so that it plays over the PA system (the 'Batman' theme is the current favourite) and gives him time to change from ordinary guitar to six-string bass, sitar, 12-string guitar or an ordinary bass.[88]

As much as Page's guitar playing and creative ideas were admired, it was his showmanship that caught the eye of one female pop correspondent after another. Over a two-page, picture-heavy spread that featured photographs of each Yardbird and the image of a

A Yardbird Is a Wandering Bum, Is a Hobo, Is a Group Of Fun-Loving Musicians . . .

By CATHERINE BARNETT
Gazette Telegraph Staff Wrker

A yardbird is a hobo, a wandering bum, in current London slang.

"That's how we chose our name," explains Keith Relf, of The Yard Birds. The British group provided the music at July 19th's Swing-ding at City Auditorium.

Hundreds of local teenagers turned out to see the performance. Had they known that The Yardbirds had already spent two days resting at the Antlers Hotel, the singing group probably would have had little rest.

Four young men make up the group: Keith Relf, 23, Jim McCarty, 23, Chris Dreja, 21, and Jimmy Page, 22. The Yardbirds got their start playing at the Crawdaddy Club in Richmond, England, after the Rolling Stones had finished an engagement there. They were well received, and the ball started rolling.

After their rollicking show with psychodelic music and lighting effects, the exhausted musicians still had enough energy to answer questions. On the whole, they felt that Colorado Springs had a nice climate, and the "people are friendly." They registered disappointed sighs about the little sight - seeing they were able to do.

"Americans are different from the British," they agree after their sixth U.S. tour. But they can't define exactly how!

Jimmy Page is the newest addition to the group, which now numbers four instead of five. After some difficulties with former members, it was decided that they were "dispensable" in Keith's words.

Jimmy plays the guitar. The general consensus of the others is that he is a born musician. He likes to experiment with new ideas in music, art, design, or whatever. Accordingly, he designs his own shirts. After the show, he donned a bright purple-blue-patterned loose-fitting shirt with no tie and plain trousers.

His long, curly locks are another expression of his personality, as are his sleepy yet intense brown eyes. Jimmy speaks very softly, expressing his artistic views concisely.

Keith Relf does most of the vocal work on the mike. Brushing floppy, straight blond hair out of his blue eyes, he praises the new, free-loving sentiment

CHRIS CONCENTRATES — Chris Dreja, one of the guitarists with the British Yardbird, concentrates at a tricky moment during their show at the Swing-ding at City Auditorium July 19.

RHYTHM MATTERS — The beat is important, and Jimmy Page makes sure his guitar tunes right in with the new, fresh sound of The Yardbirds. The British music-makers appeared July 19 at City Auditorium.

VIEWER'S OTHER VIEW — Hundreds of teenagers flocked to the City Auditorium July 19 to see The Yardbirds, a British singing group whose latest hit was "For Your Love." This intent viewer was one of many who silently watched the 45-minute performance.

Saturday, July 29, 1967 Colorado Springs Gazette Telegraph Page 21-C

emerging from San Franicsco. He feels that Americans are generally quite conservative, and the spirit that is growing on the West Coast is a good thing.

In spite of his praise of the general "love" movement and freedom of expression, Keith dresses rather conservatively. He was wearing a plain pin-striped shirt and dark slacks.

In addition, he comments feelingly on his personal philosophy, which is understandable only to him. Nevertheless, he is a serious young man, striving to do the best he can. He is married, and will become a father in September.

Also married is Chris Dreja, who handles the rhythm guitar and the maracas. He and his "petite" wife are the parents of a little girl, Jackie. Like Keith, Chris is slightly built, with blond hair and blue eyes.

Also like Keith, his personality tends to the quiet, conservative dresser, on the whole, but has a fondness for special touches, like wearing a polka-dotted scarf instead of a tie. His quiet personality leaves the impression "still waters run deep."

Totally different from the other three is Jim McCarty, the drummer. Curly brown hair and sparkling green eyes dance with mischief as he talks about his likes and dislikes. "If I weren't one of The Yardbirds, I'd be a telegraph operator," he announces.

He likes dark girls, he maintains, as he grins at a little girl with brown hair and dark brown eyes. Jim seems to have fun all the time, and give little serious thought to anything. However, Keith implies that Jim, too, has a sober side to his personality.

After leaving here, the group went on to Denver and from there to California — Santa Rosa, Sacramento, and Santa Monica. On the whole, they feel that San Francisco has a very cosmopolitan atmosphere. Their constant traveling certainly contradicts one of the meanings of their name, which refers to those who are "confined" within a yard!

They Say Americans Are Different From British But Can't Define How . . .

MIKE CONTROL — Keith Relf, principal vocalist for The Yardbirds, handles the microphone during the group's performance July 19 at the City Auditorium.

PSYCHODELIC DRUMS — Drummer Jim McCarty, of the British group known as The Yardbirds, bangs away during the group's performance July 19 at City Auditorium."

The Church Was Right For the Film

The residents of the tiny town of LaVerne, California, 45 miles east of Los Angeles, refer to a seven - day period in June as "That Was The Week That Was."

For the first time in its seven decades of existence as a farming and citrus - growing community, it was the scene of a "location" for a motion picture production, and the townfolks had lights, cameras, movie stars and excitement brought to their doorstep.

The film was "The Graduate," directed by Mike Nichols and starring Anne Bancroft, Dustin Hoffman, Katharine Ross, Elizabeth Wilson, William Daniels, Murray Hamilton, and Brian Avery, all of whom worked in LaVerne. Each day at lunch time, youngsters from the nearby grammar and high school swarmed the troupe for autographs, during the day, the parents of many of them watched the action and shot their own film.

Nichols selected the town as a location site because a church was found there by the company's art director which exactly matched the one imagined by Buck Henry, the writer of the screenplay of "The Graduate." A modern, glass - walled house of worship, it is the scene of the marriage of Avery and Miss Ross and a resulting melee when Hoffman bodily steals the bride away from her groom.

Villa Rides In New Pic

Charles Bronson has been signed to a co - starring role in Paramount Pictures' "Villa Rides." The motion picture, which stars Yul Brynner and Robert Mitchum, is scheduled to go before the Technicolor cameras on location in Spain on August 22.

Bronson, who recently completed a role in "Guns of San Sebastian," includes among his screen credits such major motion pictures as Paramount's "This Property Is Condemned," "The Sandpiper," "The Great Escape" and "Battle of the Bulge."

"Villa Rides," which will be produced by Ted Richmond and directed by Buzz Kulik, is based on William Douglas Lansford's true story "Pancho Villa."

The view from behind: 'a group of fun-loving musicians',
Colorado Springs Gazette Telegraph (29 July 1967).

teenager's backside – 'viewer's other view' – at the 'Swing Ding', City Auditorium, Colorado Springs, on 19 July, staff writer Catherine Barnett wrote that the guitarist 'designs his own shirts. After the show, he donned a bright purple-blue patterned loosefitting shirt with no tie and plain trousers. His long curly locks are another expression of his personality, as are his sleepy yet intense brown eyes. Jimmy speaks very softly, expressing his artistic views concisely.'[89]

At the Sonoma County Fair and Expo in Santa Rosa, California, on 21 July, alongside the Sir Douglas Quintet and others, the Yardbirds played before an audience of 4,000 teenagers, who were

> sent into ecstasy[,] and an undetermined number of adults [sent] into something akin to shell-shock during Friday night's big teen bash . . . [The] Police Department received numerous complaints about the noise, as amplifiers on the instruments ran full blast. Except for several hundred fence-jumpers in the grandstand area, however, things were orderly and a groovy time was had by all.[90]

The accompanying photograph, taken from the side of the stage, showed the PA columns (the tuck 'n' roll vinyl wrap suggests these are Kustom 100W speakers), only two in number and no higher than 150 centimetres (60 in.), which would be easily overwhelmed by the amp and cabinet set-up used by Dreja and Page. The vocal PA in Sonoma, however, was still vastly superior to what they had to contend with in Santa Monica.

In one of the few despatches on the Yardbirds from Hollywood back to the *NME*, Tracy Thomas reported that 'several thousand devoted fans' in Santa Monica on 22 July were unable to hear the band due to the 'inadequacies of the sound system'. Keith Relf's voice was projected 'no further than his own hands . . . Fortunately, the instrumental amplifiers were working all right and Jimmy Page's lead guitar work was impressive. Distinguishable during the set were

—Press Democrat Photo

ENGLAND'S famed Yardbirds, a quartet which specializes in blow-your-ear-drums pop music, sent nearly 4,000 teens into ecstacy and an undetermined number of adults into something akin to shell-shock during Friday night's big teen bash at the Sonoma County Fair. In addition to the Yardbirds (guitarists Chris Dreja and Jimmy Page and vocalist Keith Relf, above), the three-hour program featured The Morning Glory, The Pullice, The Sir Douglas Quintet and The Breed, Santa Rosa Police Department received numerous complaints about the noise, as amplifiers on the instruments ran full blast. Except for several hundred fence-jumpers in the grandstand area, however, things were orderly and a groovy time was had by all.

'Specializes in blow-your-ear-drums pop music': *Press Democrat* (23 July 1967). The Yardbirds at Sonoma County Fair.

most of their single hits and Bob Dylan's "You Go Your Way and I'll Go Mine".[91] The Yardbirds were part of a line-up that included the West Coast Pop Art Experimental Band, Strawberry Alarm Clock, Captain Beefheart and Moby Grape. It was a billing that showed just how far the U.S. scene had progressed over the last twelve months. Moby Grape's three-guitar and dual-lead set-up must have given Page pause about what had been lost when Beck quit. Writing about this shambles of a concert, *Los Angeles Times* staff reporter Pete Johnson noted that Moby Grape and the 'Birds received the most fervent applause, but the latter's 'electronic pyrotechnics seemed tame either because lead guitarist Jimmy Page was hypnotized by his foot pedal, which chopped notes into wavy chunks, or because San Francisco groups have made feedback a standard item. But he is a very good guitarist.'[92]

Writing his report on the show for the *Los Angeles Free Press*, Bill Kerby began, like all others, by noting the appalling PA system – no better than 'an Alabama bus station's' – that muted the vocals of all the bands on the bill. Quick dismissals of the West Coast Pop Art Experimental Band and Strawberry Alarm Clock are followed by a qualified round of applause for Beefheart, but all eyes were on Moby Grape and the Yardbirds. Of the former, he wrote:

> Moby Grape isn't purple and it doesn't lie at the bottom of the sea. Here's what it does: it screams, it has stellar drive, it is inexhaustible, it makes wonder out of impossible, it is varied, and it could very probably turn an arrangement of Bach's B minor Mass into a thing of indescribable beauty. And the reason they do all these things is because they are great, they enjoy what they do and they must work like mules. Jerry Miller . . . must rank with Bloomfield, Clapton and Vestine [Canned Heat]. He guitared a terraced set of about ten choruses of 'Miller's Blues' displaying consummate skill and courage. The band drove his flight higher and higher, beyond reality. It was awe-inspiring.[93]

Having lost Clapton and then Beck, the Yardbirds had 'gained Jimmy Paige [*sic*] and his wah-wah pedal':

> They didn't seem to have been hurt too badly by the exchange. Their Saturday night performance was reliably

> British, refreshingly crisp, and happily insolent. To compare them to the Who would be a drastic mistake. I was unable to keep from doing so, and that's why I don't say more about them . . .
>
> Beefheart, the Grape and the Yardbirds point to a new vitality; and because we are apt not to even have a history, the perspective of time cannot function as judge in their case. All any artist can do is to find the truth in his time and serve it up to change people. And, Saturday night, they did just that.[94]

Despite all the amputations that the Yardbirds had undergone, despite all the competition from new bands, they still held the attention of a hip young audience in America; they had their respect, even if the Who could push them into the shadows.

Between 25 and 27 July (Tuesday to Thursday), the Yardbirds played the Fillmore West in San Francisco, splitting the week with the Doors, who followed on 28–30. The ballroom provided a contrast to all the state-fair and amusement-park engagements of which the tour had mostly consisted.[95] But even in these alienating spaces, well away from the main ballroom venues, or club engagements like San Antonio's Pusi-Kat (20 October), which asked audiences to 'again renter the world of psychedelia [*sic*]', or the Cheetah in Chicago (29 October), the band's dedication to their art found an appreciative audience. Bob Fiallo, who wrote for the Tampa *Tribune*, described the Yardbirds as a 'musical explosion' that 'feature an electronic, fast-moving rhythm-and-blues brand of rock. They improvise as much as a bunch of jazzmen at a jam session and base their improvisations on a foundation of musicianship and strong techniques.' Fiallo praised the band's versatility and described how their set was 'built on a wave – one which climbs up and up, and keeps the audience raving'.[96] 'Progressive nervous tension' was how Relf now described what the band were doing.[97]

One of the nights at the Fillmore was captured on tape, and although it has the audio quality of something recorded at the back of a balcony, it is remarkably listenable and gives a fair indication of how the band built their set for ballroom audiences. The show opens with 'Heart Full of Soul', which is played straight; an extended nine-minute-long 'I Wish You Would' follows, wrapped around a lengthy interlude of Donovan's 'Hey Gyp'. Garnet Mimms's 'My Baby' introduces a little soulfulness – it had been part of the set since at least April 1967. Dylan's 'Most Likely You Go Your Way, I'll Go Mine' is slipped in between that and 'Shapes of Things'. A ten-minute 'I'm a Man' ends the first set, with Page's masturbatory squealing guitar taking it to its logical conclusion after the song's intermission of Relf's wordless moaning 'n' groaning section. The second set kicks off with a relatively short five-minute 'Smokestack Lightning', Page's guitar clanging like a panel beater's hammer. McCarty and Relf then vamp their way through Sonny Boy Williamson's signature solo 'Bye Bye Bird', Page entering at the end as if he's about to take the group into 'Train Kept a-Rollin''. Instead, there's a lull before an astonishingly violent 'Happenings Ten Years Time Ago'; Page mimics Beck's solo on the original recording, but then winds up the torque in the song to breaking point as Dreja and McCarty count time. The cataclysm of their last great single is followed by two cuts from the *Little Games* album, 'Smile on Me' and a rare live outing for 'Glimpses', which sounds almost like the Velvet Underground's 'Venus in Furs' before it slips into the Pink Floyd-esque ambient section with laced and filigreed feedback. The whole a standout showpiece in the context of the Fillmore, an object example of controlled extemporization in the cathedral of improvisation as auditioned by the Grateful Dead, Jefferson Airplane and Quicksilver Messenger Service that lacks only the taped effects that Page had recorded. At the end, Relf tells the crowd that he hoped they had enjoyed being 'inside' the song in the auditorium as much as the band had up on stage. And then

WHAM! into 'Ain't Done Wrong', once forgotten but now reclaimed for the guitar bursting tour de force Beck had made it, the song elongated like the earlier 'I Wish You Would'. To balance the beginning with the end of the show, they moved on and out with 'Over Under Sideways Down' – a hit to start and to finish proceedings.

Though the standard complaint was that the Yardbirds came back from touring without any appreciable earnings, the gamble on promoting a band sometimes also came up short. Cliff Moore's White Rabbit promotions took a bet on the Yardbirds and on a bargain $2 ticket price, 50 cents lower than average, to attract the kids for a Sunday (30 July) Seattle show and a Monday (31 July) Vancouver appearance. He made a loss on the Sunday, drew only two hundred attendees for the Monday afternoon performance but pulled in 2,700 attendees for the evening slot. He walked away from the two events with '$4.40 in cash in his pockets', he said: 'Despite auto breakdowns and assorted catastrophes, the Yardbirds retained their cool throughout the weekend. "They were the most co-operative group I ever met," says Moore. They were entitled to be happy. They'd been paid $5,000 in advance,' which was about the standard fee on this tour.[98] Moore, however, couldn't have been too burnt by the experience as he booked the band back for Vancouver shows on Friday, 10 November, in the afternoon and then at 1 a.m. the following morning (later rescheduled as evening shows on Friday and Saturday at 8.30 p.m.).[99]

At tour's end, their sixth visit to the States, the Yardbirds appeared in New York at the Village Theater on Second Avenue, near Seventh Street. They got a rave review from Michael T. Kaufman in the *New York Times*:

> The quartet, a major contributor to the sonic boom shaking both sides of the Atlantic Ocean, attracted a diverse audience of youths – unkempt, barefoot, shod and kempt – with their driving and often improvisational playing.

> Tired from six weeks of one-night stands, the Yardbirds were still able to warm the theatre with their electrorock therapy. Song after song began with what amounted to a steady thumping crescendo and then, surprisingly, the music went soaring and searing. When it appeared that nothing could get louder, faster or higher, dials were twisted and the sound came out of the amplifiers, bent and refracted like columns of colored lights that flashed on the performers all through the show.
>
> At one point, the lead guitarist broke a string and had to retire to the pits for repairs. With admirable smoothness, the remaining three – bassist, drummer and singer-harmonica player – slipped into joyous up-tempo jamming. ('It blows your mind,' said a voice from the rear.) Forty-five minutes after taking the stage . . . the four performers retreated, drenched with perspiration, to the sanctuary of a tiny dressing room high above the stage.[100]

Sharing the bill with the headliners were the Youngbloods and a 'folk rock specialist named Jake Holmes, who plays an unelectric guitar, sang Southern ballads'.[101]

Reviewing two Greenwich Village houses that had emerged as 'significant talent showcases', the Bitter End Café, which had long been part of the scene, and the Village Theater, 'previously a film-house and later a Yiddish vaudery', *Variety* covered the previous Friday night's show at the latter, where a 'series of musical "explosions" staged by Don Friedman's Aurora Productions' had taken place.[102] The paper's correspondent described the Yardbirds as a 'four-man British rock group' who

> appear to be a creative force in rock music's development. Their avant-garde approach is earmarked by the fusion of jazz techniques into the electric medium. However, while

> many rocksters fall into identifiable jazz passages, the Yardbirds absorb jazz complexities into their own blues-based medium without sacrificing their identity as rock musicians.[103]

The writer hedged his bets – 'appear to be' – his opinion staid and in keeping with *Variety*'s uncertain approach to discussing the mongrel culture of rock, a low form with high aspirations. Despite such tonal turgidity, the critic's views probably appealed to the band, since it echoed their own opinions, and besides, every word he wrote *is* the gospel truth. For the record, 'The Yardbirds drew a three-quarter filled house for two shows in the 2,700-seat theatre.'[104]

The Yardbirds appearance at the Village Theater has subsequently drawn attention because it was here that the band encountered Jake Holmes, from whom they borrowed what would become a set piece of theirs and Led Zeppelin's act, 'Dazed and Confused'. Contrary to the received wisdom that Holmes performed solo and acoustically, he appeared with a three-piece electric band featuring Ted Erwin on guitar, who used 'jazz nuances and well-executed "wahs" and "wows" effected by a sound-alternating foot pedal'.[105] *Variety*'s reporter wrote that Holmes's 'material is artistic enough to be picked up by others. His approach is a conservative one, which does him justice, but the pieces are also charted to be very conducive to jazz scatting by others.'[106]

'Riots have accompanied the Yardbirds everywhere,' wrote June Harris from New York for the *NME*, echoing her January report,

> resulting in unanimous agreement between Keith Relf and Chris Dreja that America is in a big mess. During a quick visit to my office, Chris said: 'When we were in California, we attended a very peaceful love-in in Griffith Park, Los Angeles. Everything was cool – even the Hell's Angels were behaving themselves. Then a cop lets loose with his gun,

MARY QUANT

NONSTOP SAVVY

England's best-known young designer (Quant? Quite!) changed the face of fashion (she set it on its ears) and still keeps spinning out the news. Now she dips into fresh fields of color, places waistlines at low, hemlines at high. Flipsy-daisy, left, comes on strong in the calmest kind of pink—called Bermuda—with a skirt, tucked all around, that looks like perpetual motion. About $45. Backing it up: The Yardbirds, the cool sound in "Blow-Up" and on the Epic single "Little Games." Football ripples, above, in a dress pinched from a halfback: Bermuda pink with beige, tucked and pleated to touchdown! About $50. Both dresses of bonded wool jersey. Beaming approval is recording star Georgie Fame, England's Top Pop Personality in 1967. His look: a suede and lamb jacket from the Chelsea Antique Market

Psychedelic fashion props for a Mary Quant spread in *Seventeen* (September 1967).

and wow! Was there a riot. We got out of there quick!' Said Keith: 'In San Francisco we were in our dressing room at the Fillmore Auditorium when someone threw a Molotov Cocktail into the room opposite. We did a great show that night in case we got one, too!'[107]

In September, Jimmy Page carried on the conversation in an open letter published in *Melody Maker*. He ran down their July encounters with a world in upheaval:

> There's never been a tour like this! Not because of the enthusiasm of the fans or the music, or even the size of the crowds that turned up to see us. No, this is a tour we will

> always remember because of the violence. To call it explosive would be an understatement.[108]

He retold the tale of the Love-In in Griffith Park that turned nasty, adding more detail about the Molotov Cocktail incident at the Fillmore. Their three nights at the venue (25–27 July) had started well, with stars in attendance, among them Julie Christie, Jefferson Airplane and maybe Bob Dylan; then, on the second day, a race riot erupted: petrol bombs were thrown, though he doesn't say where, and the National Guard was called out. In Sacramento, a bomb scare delayed the show; in Milwaukee, more race riots had meant a nine o'clock curfew was enforced. Detroit was burning, and they were due to play there later in the tour: 'It is very worrying to know you have to go into an area during race riots – and, in most cases, these are really big riots, not minor punch-ups. We were told, for example, that Detroit has suffered a billion dollars worth of damage.'[109] The experience wasn't turned into a suite of songs, or even a side of a single; Page's story filled a few column inches and explained to British readers just where the Yardbirds had been hiding out. Elsewhere in that issue of *Melody Maker*, Page was listed alongside six other guitarists – Beck, Clapton, Green, Winwood, Townshend and Hendrix – in one of the first avowedly hagiographic pieces on 'guitar-slinging heroes with sideburns . . . The Magnificent Seven'.[110] Clapton was King, Hendrix the Pretender, Townshend the Innovator, Beck the Enigma, Green the Toughest, Winwood a space-filler to get to the Seven, and Page was 'the dark horse . . . Not so well known among the fans because since he replaced Jeff Beck in the Yardbirds the group have worked mostly in America and the group have not had an English hit for many months.'[111]

With three of the seven linked to the Yardbirds, the band's standing as an incubator of gifted guitarists took hold and, as their individual reputations grew, the smaller the band, as a collective of talent, became. Above all, Page understood this shift and capitalized on and developed his place in the pantheon. As for the Yardbirds, for the first time since they broke out from the Crawdaddy, not a single member made it into *Melody Maker*'s yearly poll, published in September.[112] The British pop audience's attention had long been directed elsewhere.

> Queen's Hall, Leeds – Friday 3rd, 8.30 p.m. to Saturday, February 4th, 6.30 a.m
> Another Mammoth All-Night Rave
> – The Cream
> Schizophrenic Psychedelic Friek Out! Schmeak Out!
> A whole show in Lighting, music, Films and Colour by
> – The Pink Floyd
> For the First Time Ever Outside London
> – Go-Go Dancers
> We're letting a live gorilla loose in the crowd at Midnight![113]

'IN CASE YOU HADN'T NOTICED, with all the noise from those freak-outs, it's 1967. And that can only mean one thing – it's not 1966 anymore, so don't get caught using 1966 words and phrases.'[114] *Melody Maker*'s Bob Dawbarn then offered his latest dictionary of hep-talk. The piece accompanied a double-page spread that put the spotlight on the Move and the Pink Floyd and asked the question 'How psychedelic is your pop?'[115] No longer can a group simply say, 'Well, mate, we can play Wilson Pickett, James Brown and all that gear.'[116] Now, according to Chris Welch and Nick Jones, 'One has to explain whether one is likely to set fire to the auditorium, or batter the audience's senses with flame, light and fiendish noises.'[117] As for the Pink Floyd, they were, it was noted, 'completely unheard of only a few weeks ago, but have already netted a residency at London's Marquee Club', while the Move 'have been building up a reputation in a maelstrom of violent "happenings"'.[118] How seriously, they asked, do the bands take their work? 'A new pattern emerges – "schizophrenic Psychedelic Pop". The Floyd are serious – while The Move . . . well.'[119]

As it referred to them, the Move's crafted play on all things psychedelic was so teasingly ambivalent that it left music journalists like Jeremy Pascall at the *NME* grasping at straws. As their debut single, 'Night of Fear', entered the charts, Pascall wrote that the Move's stage act, which included destroying two silver cars while 'two chicks' stripped and thunder clap effects exploded, was 'NOT psychedelic', while their single was. On the other hand, the band's manager, Tony Secunda, told him that the disc was 'about a guy who takes a stale dose of LSD and has a bad trip – it's a nightmare and the flip, "The Disturbance", is about madness – a guy out of his head who ends up shouting Mother and things. It's 1967 Goodtime music.'[120]

As told by Welch and Jones, the Pink Floyd were originally an R&B group that became involved in experimenting with light and sound during a workshop at Hornsey College of Art in Crouch End, Middlesex, which led to further trials. Drummer Nick Mason explained:

> When we were in our early stages, we didn't play a lot of our electronic 'inter-stellar' music and the slides were still rather amateurish. However this has developed now and our 'take off' into mainly improvised electronic scenes is much longer – and, of course, in my opinion, the slides have developed to something out of all proportion. They're just fantastic.[121]

Mason continued:

> You have to be careful when you start on this psychedelic thing . . . We don't call ourselves a psychedelic group or say that we play psychedelic pop music. It's just that people

> associate us with this and we get employed all the time at the various freak-outs and happenings in London. Let's face it, there isn't really a definition for the word 'psychedelic'. It's something that has taken place around us – not within us.[122]

For the Move, 'outrageous, trouble-making, and riotous', it wasn't about being inside or outside.[123] 'We get quite nasty to anybody who calls us psychedelic,' said singer Carl Wayne, 'the thing we'd most like to do is cause a riot.'[124] Rabble-rousing was the last thing on the Pink Floyd's agenda: 'A freak-out . . . should be relaxed, informal, and spontaneous. The best freak-out you'll ever get is at a party with about a hundred people. A freak-out shouldn't be savage mobs of geezers throwing bottles.'[125] Between the extremes, 'The Move and the Pink Floyd are two of today's groups. You may find their attitudes frightening or refreshing – fun or phoney. But by thunder – it's rhythmical' was how *Melody Maker*'s two critics summed things up.[126]

In the first week of the New Year, the *Kensington News and West London Times* filled its 'Nice and Bluesy' column with a report on the Pink Floyd, who 'over the months have perfected their own unique act. Psychedelic's the word to describe their efforts and impressive it is too.'[127] Still only semi-professional, the band were due to appear in Peter Whitehead's film *London 66–67* (aka *Tonite Let's All Make Love in London*), and they 'hope to cut their first record in the near future, it will probably be produced by Peter Asher and ex-Yardbird Paul Samwell-Smith'.[128] That potential recording collaboration linked the Yardbirds and Floyd directly, but so too did the piece's emphasis on the need for volume to produce a desired effect. Like Jeff Beck and Jimmy Page with their stacked amplifiers, the Pink Floyd promised that their audience would be confronted by '500 watts of Selmer sound and their own lighting system'.[129] When reviewing 'See Emily Play', the *Leicester Daily Mercury* made a direct link: 'The Floyd try to put too much into this release, and it comes out a little overdone . . . and is rather reminiscent of old Yardbird numbers.'[130]

Defining the scene was an ongoing project in *Melody Maker*; early in February, Nick Jones returned to the topic of 'psychedelic pop'.[131] Pete Townshend thought that you couldn't replicate a drug trip with a musical trip; he felt it all boiled down to 'is it entertaining?'[132] Was it then a joke or a serious undertaking? Jones thought that in Britain it was the former, while in the States, at least on the West Coast, it was the latter. Chet Helms, producer at the Family Dog, was in London, and Jones spoke to him about the scene with which he was involved. The Avalon Ballroom in San Francisco had a sprung 'dance floor, 360 degree projector, acoustically draped ceilings, and all the trappings of a continuum – that is, a dance that starts when you enter the ballroom and finishes when you leave the ballroom. "It's a continuous happening," says Chet.'[133] Around 1,500 people united, joining hands and dancing together all night is what defined the experience: 'The groups aren't gods anymore. Everybody participates,' said Helms.[134] 'The audience entertains the groups, the lighting men entertain the audience. Everybody just turns everybody on. The whole thing has to work together.'[135] For Jones, the U.S. scene was 'uncontrived', the opposite of what he'd found in Britain: 'England isn't ready for such social revolution yet . . . if England's social structure alters . . . our pop scene could flower in the same way [as in the United States]. It's already beginning to happen but in a very small way.'[136] He concluded with an appeal: 'Let's have less of the bandwagon-jumping by the untalented opportunists and more room for the genuinely good, hard-working, thinking young musicians of today.'[137]

For the Pink Floyd, it was less to do with an emerging youth community than with establishing an aesthetic: 'If we have to have some kind of definition, you could say we are lights and sounds. The two mediums complement each other and we definitely don't use them together as a gimmick. Our aim is simply to make the audience dig the effect,' *Record Mirror* reported. 'They don't, they say, seek to create hallucinatory effects on their audience . . . they want only to entertain. But they own up to being musical spokesmen for a mushrooming movement . . . experimentation in all the arts, including music.'[138] It was a position that the Who and the Yardbirds could share even when they were playing the Avalon Ballroom.

Keith Relf latched on to his band's experiments with light and sound when discussing psychedelia. He thought the term, as used in the United States, had validity, but in Britain it had been 'distorted': 'of course there are only certain places where you could have a light show. You can't possibly do it in the Marquee, for example, with all those columns. You've got to have a place with four bare, white walls.'[139] As for how the Yardbirds fitted in, Relf was uncertain: 'The whole scene seems to be one of artistic confusion with nobody knowing which way to turn.'[140] In Detroit, the MC5 were getting ready to make their play deep into the confusion:

> Some people call it psychedelic. The MC-5 call it the 'new music'. They should know, for they are the leading exponents of the far-out sounds in this area . . . Although the group started playing the usual rock 'n' roll, they got tired of that. 'Now,' said Wayne Kramer, 'we are taking rock 'n' roll further than it's been taken before. We're going into playing sound as a method of expression.' Robin Tyner pointed out: 'My feeling is a lot of groups are doing this kind of thing but not doing anything with it. We use sounds in definite movements and patterns.'
>
> There is a point they may reach in a song that sounds like everyone is making confusion, but it's controlled, according to Wayne. After playing together for so long, each musician knows what the other is doing. 'It's more like one big musician up on stage instead of five,' Wayne added. Although the music bewilders some listeners, many groups are picking it up. 'You find touches of it all over,' Wayne said . . .

> The MC-5 agreed that The Who and The Yardbirds are the leading exponents of the new sound. But Robin indicated: 'Each group has its own idea of what the new music is all about.'[141]

The MC5 were about to release their first record, 'One of the Guys', backed with 'I Can Only Give You Everything', which was strictly in the vein of Them and the Pretty Things – rave-up R&B. It would take the band another twelve months to get their own idea of 'going further' onto disc with 'Looking at You' and 'Borderline', but the seed had been sown.

For the *NME*'s Derek Johnson, reviewing the steady stream of psychedelic-tinged singles that passed through his column in the spring of 1967, the tag was best affixed to a sonic quality that, to his surprise, was not particularly apparent on the Pink Floyd's debut disc: 'This is the group that creates such an impact on stage with its visual effects – flashing lights, colour slides, and so on. Must say that, aurally, this doesn't strike me as very psychedelic.'[142] On the other hand, the flip side had a 'jogging jaunty beat, underlying fuzz guitar and mid-tempo pace. Solo is part sung, part whispered, with strange oscillating chanting. More like psychedelia.'[143] For Johnson, a psychedelic record was not a psychedelic record if it didn't carry with it a heavy charge of sonic oscillations.[144] With 'See Emily Play', the Pink Floyd hit Johnson's motherload: 'I felt that on Pink Floyd's last disc, the psychedelia in which they specialize didn't really come through – but golly, they've made up for it on this new one. It's crammed with weird oscillations, reverberations, electronic vibrations and fuzzy rumblings.'[145]

The Pink Floyd's first single, 'Arnold Layne', was a hit that had carried the whiff of controversy as it climbed the charts. Reviewing the single in *Melody Maker*'s 'Blind Date', Scott Walker couldn't identify the group, but he liked the disc: 'It's different and the lyrics are interesting. It's about a transvestite? I haven't tried transvestism yet.'[146] Subsequently, Nick Jones interviewed Syd Barrett about the single's 'smutty' subject; the controversy was good because if 'more people like them dislike us, more people like the underground lot are going to dig us'.[147] Jones asked the band where they felt they fitted within the pop music structure:

> 'We would like to think that we're part of the creative half in that we write our own material and don't just record other people's numbers, or copy American demo discs,' said Nick Mason. 'Our album shows part of the Pink Floyd that haven't been heard yet.' 'There's parts we haven't even heard yet,' chipped in Roger.[148]

The jibe about recording others' numbers or copying American demo discs was aimed widely, but it would also have hit the target presented by the Yardbirds with 'Little Games'.

'Games for May' was how a headlining event at the Queen Elizabeth Hall on the South Bank in London was billed. It was a prestigious engagement that promised 'Space-age relaxation for the climax of spring electronic compositions, colour and image projections, girls and the Pink Floyd'.[149] The sonic adventurism, the total show of light and sound that the Yardbirds had long promised, was now usurped; the Pink Floyd even offered girls as part of their attraction. The climax, premature or not, over all the hullabaloo around psychedelia, took place at Alexandra Palace on 29 April for the 14-Hour Technicolor Dream. Frank Zappa and the Mothers of Invention had been invited, as well as 'U.S. pop art film maker Andy "Exploding Plastic Inevitable" Warhol'.[150] The following week, *Melody Maker* added the Velvet Underground to the bill.[151] British talent scheduled to appear included Alexis Korner, Alex Harvey, Gary Farr, Graham Bond and the Pretty Things – all stalwart representatives from the bygone days of London R&B. With Champion Jack Dupree also figured to appear, it must have felt like one of those

Richmond jazz and blues festivals.[152] Pete Townshend was listed as an attraction (and was said to be recording proceedings for an album of the event to be released by Track), and the psychedelic advance guard was headed by the Pink Floyd, the Move and the Purple Gang.[153]

The Yardbirds were in France over the weekend of the Technicolor Dream, playing in Chaville, a few kilometres south-west of Paris. The outdoor concert was filmed by French television with the band, lit by bright sunshine, performing their hits in front of fin-de-siècle pin-ups. Technical hitches marred the start of the show, perhaps hindering Relf's ability to hear himself, as his singing on the seven songs is woefully out of tune. Further south, *Blow-Up* was in competition at Cannes; it went on to win the Grand Prix.[154] The Yardbirds were not involved in the film's promotion and didn't appear in any publicity material other than being featured on its soundtrack. The lack of any meaningful tie-in with the film was yet another missed opportunity to advance their cause.

Melody Maker dutifully arrived to review the country's first Human Be-In; none of the American bands or artists had turned up and, unlike the *Sunday Mirror*'s correspondent, who thought the whole thing was rather like 'the last struggle of a doomed tribe trying to save its self from extinction', Nick Jones thought it was the 'beginning of a healthy young attitude towards total freedom for the individual' as it carried 'forth some the ideals of the underground movement' to bring them 'above ground'.[155] This was not just about music, but the chance for the audience to be part of something bigger:

> Most of the artists scheduled to appear didn't make it. Hardly surprising, and fortunately the audience didn't get hostile about it. They were quite happy looning about, looking at others' clothes, eating, drinking, sleeping, dancing and just freaking about – quite at leisure to do whatever

> they damn well wanted. There was a constant supply of films, slides, joss sticks, sounds, chants, or freakers doing acrobatics on the scaffolding.
>
> Music was provided by various people ranging from the Soft Machine to Pink Floyd, an exciting new group called Tomorrow, Alex Harvey and various others . . . [But] Alexandra Palace isn't the best place for acoustics, most of the sound echoing up into the huge dome and away.[156]

According to the report in the *Sunday Mirror*, the show opened with a psychedelic striptease: model Carol Mann had her clothes cut from her by members of the audience, an appropriation of Yoko Ono's *Cut Piece* (1964). The image of Mann on a stepladder, her bra just snipped off, provided the paper with a suitably salacious photograph and added to the image of sexual anarchy where 'everyone should be free to do everything . . . to be homosexual or heterosexual, to work or not to work, to take drugs or not to take drugs.'[157]

The *Sunday Mirror* was not the only Fleet Street paper to send a reporter; a columnist for *The Observer* also attended, and posted a scurrilously racist report:

> At the door of Alexandra Palace, the Negro ticket-taker was grinning from ear to ear, saying: 'Let's having your tickets, thanking you.' A hipster stared at him, muttering: 'In the USA, Uncle Toms like you have been declared unconstitutional.'
>
> Crates of banana scrapings were stacked at the door, denied entrance. Smoking banana scrapings is the very latest thing to take a psychedelic trip on. A passing Indian pornographer, who had tried it, said: 'It's strictly a put-on. Those banana republics will stoop to anything to get rid of the stuff.'[158]

And on he rolled; deafened by the noise inside, repulsed by youthful working-class sexuality, he painted a picture of a fourteen-hour Technicolor nightmare. Out of this, the BBC procured a thirty-minute *Man Alive* programme broadcast on 17 May that featured 'the leaders and apostles of the movement – Susie Creamcheese, the Fuzzdeath Ballet, the Flies and Pink Floyd'.[159]

As much as it was a document, a film of youth in revolt against conformity, the BBC programme was also a testament to the underground's mass visibility, not only through broadcast media but via street fashion. Back during his first tour of the United States, Jimmy Page had expressed his opinion on dressing up. 'He's quite noticeable,' wrote the *Chicago Tribune* journalist:

> he has the longest hair [in the Yardbirds] and wears an old-fashioned band leader's jacket. He can't understand Americans' lack of individuality in choice of clothing, or why they worry so much about it. He wanted to wear a white silk shirt, but was scared he'd offend somebody. 'The attitudes are rather narrow-minded here, whereas in England they don't care what you wear.' He wore it for the concert anyway![160]

In Memphis, one long-haired eighteen-year-old fan, Michael Sehnert, was arrested and taken to court and charged with 'dressing as the opposite sex', the consequence of which could have meant jail time.[161] He appeared in court in the same 'tight-fitting jeans, high-heeled boots and shirt which he said he had on at the time of the arrest'.[162] All, he said, were bought at a men's clothing store, and he wore 'his hair long because he was a singer and because he just wanted to be different' (or like Keith Relf, who he somewhat resembled).[163] In court, when the Assistant City Attorney asked his mother about her son's 'feminine haircut', she replied, 'It's a feminine and masculine haircut in 1966.'[164] The judge dismissed the charge,

> noting that he did not think the hairdo was very masculine, but the prosecution had not shown the court any 'intent' on the youth's part of wanting to look feminine. He also said that he didn't know who the 'Yardbirds' were but advised the youth to 'shoot a little higher than that.'[165]

Back out on the streets, after the trial, Michael told the reporter that he had 'no intentions of cutting my hair unless it causes my mother any further grief, or unless it goes out of style – or I just get tired of it'.[166]

From 1966 into 1967, street fashion in Britain took a decidedly martial turn as the art of provocation stepped up a gear. The vogue for military apparel led by the ready availability of uniforms at I Was Lord Kitchener's Valet, as modelled by Cream in publicity pictures to promote 'Wrapping Paper' – Clapton adding to the guard's tie he'd worn in the Yardbirds – was taken to a new visibility by Hendrix's gold-embroidered Hussar tunic. Mick Jagger had also acquired a similar jacket. Hendrix was asked about his costume by the *NME*:

> Some people have told me that they think wearing a military jacket is an insult to the British army. Let me tell you I wear this old British coat out of respect. This was worn by one of those 'cats' who used to look after the donkeys which pulled the cannons way back in 1900. This coat has history – there's life to it. I don't like war but I respect a fighting man and his courage. Maybe the guy who wore this coat got killed in action. Would people rather his coat be hung up and go mouldy somewhere to be forgotten like him?[167]

Whatever the plausibility of his explanation and justification for wearing the tunic, it can't be denied he wore it with panache and style – he looked flash and fabulous. When Pete Townshend had a Union Jack flag made into a stage costume, or when he wore a row of medals and other military insignia on his shirt, his affectation was done in part to goad figures of authority – an affront to social mores. It also worked as a Pop-art assemblage, a repurposing of the everyday. Other bands took the idea of provocation but left behind Townshend's more art-orientated intentions. When Jeff Beck appeared on the cover of *Record Mirror* in July 1966, alongside Jimmy Page and the rest of his bandmates, he prominently wore an Iron Cross pinned to his lapel. Page too decorated his coats and jackets with Nazi pins and medals that he wore, on his first U.S. tour with the Yardbirds, alongside an oversized badge (perhaps made from a snuff-tin lid) commemorating the Empire – a 'souvenir of South Africa, 1900' – which had printed over a Union Jack the images of five heroes of the Boer War, including Baden-Powell. Page topped his decorative militaria and Victoriana, rather fetchingly, with a Union Army Civil War kepi.[168] Cream's dalliance with such imagery was equally jumbled (and confused).

In a February 1967 interview with the *NME*, the subject-matter meandered to the threat posed to the West by China and Communism: 'Those Red Guards are the Hitler Youth movement all over again,' said Ginger. The comment led Keith Altham to ask why Clapton was wearing an Iron Cross 'tucked discreetly inside his shirt':

> 'I don't know why there is a sudden interest in the Nazi uniforms or decorations – I wear this simply because I think the design is great,' said Eric.
>
> 'I've got an SS officer's cap,' said Ginger, 'I think it's a good thing to wear these things. It makes a few people remember there was a war – it's not a thing to forget or let happen again.'
>
> 'I think possibly the more fanatically interested have the kind of fascination for Nazi items in the same way people have a fascination for horror comics!' said Bruce.
>
> We turned to more musical subjects.[169]

Chris Farlowe had turned his interest in Nazi regalia into a business; 'his new shop sells German and Nazi war souvenirs,' wrote Bill Harry in *Record Mirror*.[170] 'I've always been collecting things concerned with the war, ever since I was a schoolboy,' said Farlowe.[171] It was all rather juvenile posturing, a playing with the forbidden – a limp joust against prohibition and a misjudged slight against the older generation who had fought the last war.

On the verge of joining the Who on a tour of Germany, John's Children were interviewed by Alan Jones for Staffordshire's local press; their manager, Simon Napier-Bell, set out their manifesto: 'John's Children are outrageously arrogant because they find other people ugly, devious and boring. They are grippingly honest because they are not sophisticated enough to be devious. They look naïve because they are young, clean and sweet.'[172] Things got easily out of hand; at one gig, the band explained, '"We were yelling Sieg Heil, the German marching cry, and the audience were shouting it back" . . . "They liked the sound of the cry . . . Nothing political. They just liked the sound" . . . Whatever they played they liked it loud,' wrote Jones.[173]

> Would they revive the war cry 'Sieg Heil' on the German tour? 'Definitely,' replied John. Offensive to the German audience? He gasped: 'Surely not. People cannot be that thick. It is a fascinating beat, that is all there is to it.' To show his innocence, John claimed he did not know what Sieg Heil meant. But then, that is part of the pop mystic. With a knowing smile, he tried to explain a new single the group were making. 'It's about a man who plays funerals in his backyard.'[174]

This was no more than another rehearsal at being outrageous, played to an audience no larger than the band's immediate peers. When John's Children's guitarist struggled to provide a convincing break, on 'But She's Mine', the B-side of their second single, 'Just What

You Want – Just What You'll Get', Napier-Bell had Jeff Beck supply the necessary sniping guitar solo. The British scene was all rather insular, self-affirming and highly solipsistic – a hall of mirrors: Jimmy, Jeff and Eric all checking out their Iron Crosses in a King's Road boutique changing room (with the Stooges' Ron Asheton sneaking a peek). Being provocative was also an act of mimicry.

Nottingham *Guardian Journal*'s columnist Richard Williams (later of *Melody Maker*) was much amused by Beck's appearance in *Blow-Up* and his 'completely manufactured frenzy' when smashing his guitar: 'Every gesture is copied from the arch-fiend of auto-destruction, Pete Townshend, and the result, for those who have seen the Who at their wildest, can only be hilarious.'[175] Williams tied his critique of Beck on film with a review of a recent appearance of his band; he was even less impressed:

> Beck seems to have dabbled in so many styles that he is now unable to co-ordinate them into one recognisable approach. He seems obsessed with the speed with which he could move his hand up and down the fingerboard. Once in a while he managed to discover a really beautiful blue chord and in one solo he couldn't resist a bow to his main influence when he quoted a few bars of Clapton's 'Steppin' Out'.
>
> Stewart is wasted. He was at his best singing gospel-blues with Long John Baldry, and since the break-up of the Hoochie Coochie Men he seems to have lost all sense of direction. He is given very little to do in his new band, and one contribution which could have been outstanding, 'Wee Wee Baby Blues', was completely ruined by over-loud intrusions. The other members of the band, drummer Aynsley Dunbar and bassist Ronnie Wood, were competent, and Wood did shine on an exciting and complex Howlin' Wolf number called 'You Gonna Wreck My Life', where his deep stabbing lines held the whole group together.

Williams's piece was headlined: 'A Group That Isn't . . .'

Debates over who was and who wasn't psychedelic, who could best provoke questions about what it was all about, continued into the summer of 1967; however, unlike those arguments that helped ferment the R&B scene, the Yardbirds were not at the centre of things, but at the periphery. *International Times* recorded that members of the Yardbirds, alongside Jimi Hendrix and Pete Townshend, had born witness to the Pink Floyd at the UFO club on 2 June and that a Soho strip club was featuring a LSD act 'consisting mainly of a chick writhing about around a giant spike while strobes and coloured lights play on the stage. The record used is "Arnold Layne".'[176] Any residual influence that the Yardbirds might have had was left to their fans to fight a rear-guard action in the letter pages of the music press. Countering the argument that the Beatles, the Pink Floyd or the Mothers of Invention were the true leaders of the psychedelic movement, Roddie the Rocker, Liverpool, wrote that it was the Who and the Yardbirds who were responsible for the 'experiments in electronics and instrumental feedback' that were at the heart of psychedelic music, and the latter's album 'was truly the most progressive yet'.[177] He suggested others who didn't share his belief were being 'brainwashed by the Pink Floyd'.[178]

Featuring singer Keith West, who with Mark Wirtz was behind the hit 'Excerpt from a Teenage Opera', guitarist Steve Howe from the Syndicats and drummer Twink from the Fairies, Tomorrow followed up their minor hit 'My White Bicycle' with 'Revolution', before setting out their psychedelic credentials in an interview with *Melody Maker*'s Nick Jones:

> It's taken us a year to sort ourselves out and work up to what we are doing now – it isn't an overnight thing. Look at Zoot Money. One minute we're watching him dropping his trousers and playing the Big Roll Band and then two weeks later he's playing the big 'psychedelic' scene. Well that

> kind of mental and musical change just doesn't happen in two weeks . . .
>
> Let's say there are five groups who all say they are playing psychedelic music. In fact they must be on five different mental levels because everybody isn't on the same level. So what happens, one of the groups starts to watch one of the others and starts digging the scene they're on. Why? Because they haven't found themselves! If you're going to be what you are then be what you are without imitating other people.[179]

The cult of originality, like the valorizing of lead guitarists, was about to go into overdrive.

In September, the *NME* announced that the Yardbirds 'may be added to the already strong bill by promoter Tito Burns of the Harold Davidson organization that was to feature the Jimi Hendrix Experience, the Move and the Turtles. Twelve dates in larger than usual venues had being scheduled, Hendrix will top the bill'. Two weeks later it was announced that Amen Corner had been added and the opening engagement would be at the Albert Hall on 14 November.[180] The final addition to the show was the Pink Floyd; there would be no further mention of the Yardbirds.[181] No explanation was given for not taking part, but the idea of playing second-fiddle to newcomer Hendrix may have been the deciding factor. Even if that wasn't the case, the plates had shifted, and the Yardbirds were no longer seen as a main attraction.

They were not alone; from their peer group, the Pretty Things had also been usurped, and Hendrix and psychedelia were the upsetters. Derek Johnson's review of the Pretties' 'Defecting Grey' encapsulated this shift:

> The Pretty Things' label switch coincides with a change of style and image. Unabashed R&B is abandoned in favour of

> 'free form' in this mixture of oom-pah waltz-time, frenzied Hendrix-like blues, and strange psychedelic noises – with a chorus of razzamatazz to round it off! Not a disc you can dance to, because of the constantly changing tempo – but certainly a disc with a difference![182]

A year earlier, the Yardbirds had been described in a Los Angeles paper as 'the sounds of tomorrow . . . Their first recording of the future was the tremendous double-sided smash, "I'm a Man" and "Still I'm Sad"', while, the reviewer wrote, The Byrds 'Eight Miles High' was a 'shift towards a Yardbirds' style of performing with an attempt at a modern sound'.[183] The pace-setters were now part of the tag team.

You get a hint of this slip into the past tense with *Hit Parader*'s review of the *Little Games* LP, which, apart from low-key German and Kiwi releases, was exclusive to the American market. There's no sense of excitement or the seeding of anticipation for prospective buyers, just the setting out of the latest product from the band: 'Jimmy Page continues the sizzling guitar tradition and the group is again experimenting with different sound effects and other fun . . . Some of the special effects make it and others seem contrived, but if you're a Yardbird fan, you should enjoy their latest and long-awaited album.'[184]

Over the years, the album has taken a reputational battering: unreleased in Britain until 1985, when vault discoveries and single A- and B-sides were added, it's been seen as a Mickie Most-orchestrated descent into pop-pap. But strip out those supplements – 'Ha! Ha! Said the Clown', 'Goodnight Sweet Josephine' and 'I Remember the Night' – and leave to the side the studio outtakes that have appeared on compact-disc sets, and the album has its own internal logic. It may not take forward the studio experiments of *Roger the Engineer*/*Over Under Sideways Down*, or compete with the attention gained by *The Who Sell Out*, *Surrealistic Pillow*, *The Doors*,

Disraeli Gears, *Axis*, *Bold As Love*, *Moby Grape*, *Velvet Underground and Nico* or *Forever Changes* (which included a Beck-esque coda on 'A House Is Not a Motel') from the same year, to say nothing of *Sgt. Pepper*, but it does contain scattered moments where it broke free from Most's worst commercial instincts and hinted at a more exciting and inventive approach.

What the album doesn't do is meet any of the ambitions that the band had set out for themselves when Page first joined – the improvisational sequences that linked with, extended, distorted and perverted even the more familiar blues and rock 'n' roll tropes in their catalogue. The lack of attention to this side of their act was perhaps why Page was disappointed in Most not being willing to go to their performances. On the other hand, it's not hard to see why the producer would turn away from their distention and extrapolation of pop forms.

Little Games is more tonally varied than *Roger*, but that only makes it more misshapen. Trite pop tunes are mixed with more satisfying pleasures like the tantric explorations of 'White Summer', Page's acoustic live showpiece, and Relf's plaintive 'Only the Black Rose', which played a similar pastoral role. The electric blasts of 'Smile on Me' and 'Drinking Muddy Water' continue the Yardbirds' grand tradition of rewriting blues staples, here Howlin' Wolf's 'Shake for Me' and Muddy Waters' 'Rollin' and Tumblin'', both superlative examples of their kind. The Lovin' Spoonful-esque 'Stealing, Stealing' is passable, but it is at best filler; as the reviewer for *Hit Parader* wrote, 'we've all heard the jug-band sounds, complete with harmonica and kazoo, many times before.'[185] 'No Excess Baggage' was written by two Brill Building songsmiths and sounds like something Most brought back home from one of his shopping excursions in New York's Tin Pan Alley. 'Tinker, Tailor, Soldier, Sailor', written by McCarty and Page, is less of a throwaway, with a driving beat and lyrics that reject off-the-shelf identities, but not much more. The album's closing track – another band original,

'Little Soldier Boy' – echoed 'Tinker' and the opening title track's theme of childhood innocence and adult guilt, but the Small Faces better delivered on the premise with 'Tin Soldier', released at the end of the year.

'Glimpses', which closes side one, is the best indicator of where the band might have taken the album had they been given the time and resources. It's the only overtly psychedelic track, the only one that spins out from the experiments of 'Happenings Ten Years Time Ago'. It refigures their trademark of Gregorian-styled chanting and harmonizing, progressing and regressing through its lock-grooved clanging chords over wah-wah guitar. Dungeon-deep bass is laid alongside the percussive snap and splash of drum and cymbal, while somewhere in the mix Relf delivers a murmured distorted spoken passage. After three minutes or so of loping distraction, the phasing enters a final orgasmic build that all but pulls the track out of its pipe-dream Limehouse exoticism. Reflected infinity and the frontiers of acquired knowledge – its 'cumular limits' – are its lysergic theme, but it ends too soon, leaving possibilities unexplored.

The provisional feel of the album, rushed and unfinished, is doubled by the dreadful faux Pop-art cover illustration, with its cartoon images of slot machines and dice and the clipped heads with hand-coloured faces of the four band members that the anonymous designer had cut-out from the photograph used on the sleeve's reverse. The art lacks entirely the vision, technique and humour of Alan Aldridge's work on the Who's *A Quick One*.

The monochrome chiaroscuro photograph of the band on the back of the jacket somewhat saves the whole aesthetic, while 'Smile on Me', 'Drinking Muddy Water', 'Tinker, Tailor, Soldier, Sailor', 'White Summer', 'Only the Black Rose' and 'Glimpses' do the same for the music. From other 1967 sessions, 'Puzzles', 'Think About It' and the slashing guitar outro from 'Ten Little Indians' might also be added alongside the more open album mono mix of 'Little Games', as both Relf and Page are on top form, even though the track misses McCarty and Dreja's involvement. It's not much of a tally, not quite an LP's worth. You can listen to these cuts for as long as you'd listen to anything from the Yardbirds' catalogue, but it's meagre pickings from a band who should have been delivering in the studio the promises made by their live shows.

Barely creating a ripple in the week's news, it was announced in *Melody Maker*, at the end of September, that the Yardbirds were in Britain but were flying back out a week later (5 October) to the USA for three and a half weeks of touring colleges. For November, a round of television and radio sessions had been arranged to promote their new single, which was being recorded before they left for America.[186] Jim McCarty was late leaving, exhaustion and drugs having finally taken their toll. He missed the first three gigs and then collapsed on stage at the Cotillion Ballroom in Wichita. His seat was filled by the drummer from the West Coast Electric Family: 'The crowd clapped along with them, danced, but most plastered themselves as close to the stage as possible. There also seemed to be a closeness between the group and the crowd. They all wanted to do their part to help the Yardbirds through.'[187]

As the tour rolled deeper into October, Page continued to receive plaudits; an evening of a double set (13 October) at the University of Tampa, Florida, was enthusiastically received. Having found Relf a remarkable harmonica talent, which was on display during a change of guitar strings when the singer went solo with 'Bye Bye Bird', Rory O'Conner still singled out Page as the 'main attraction':

> A fantastic musician, he cuts everybody with the exception of Eric Clapton. Page seemed to be off by himself on stage, playing guitar breaks that staggered the audience. Not only is he a great guitar player, but he is also a huge ham on stage, turning to face photographers behind him and in front of him whenever one appeared, which was quite often.[188]

Variety covered the band's return show to the Village Theater, 3 November, supported by Kingdom Come and Vanilla Fudge.[189] Noting a near-capacity auditorium that pulled in $16,000 out of a potential $20,000 for the 2,600-seat house, their reviewer called the band 'one of rock 'n' roll's more influential units', who 'engineered some musical innovations that have affected the attitude and approach of several other groups': 'Notable among their electronic sounds . . . were the way-out use of a "wah-wah" pedal and a violin bow on the lead guitar. Previously a quintet, the group now comprise bass, drums and a highly talented lead singer and guitarist.' The Yardbirds' staging was hampered by faulty sound equipment and a distracting, poorly executed 'psychedelic' light show by Aurora Glory Alice. Their presentation at the first show had been sloppy, a marked contrast to a commanding stint they offered in this house a few months ago.[190]

At the beginning of November, *Melody Maker* reported that the tour was being extended and the band would fly home on 12 November to promote their next single, 'Ten Little Indians', which was scheduled for release at the end of the month or in early December. Two days after returning to London, the Yardbirds had three days set aside to record a new LP for the U.S. market.[191] But hardly had those arrangements been made when it was decided to scrap plans for the single, holding off on any new release until the New Year. The band were also due to fly out to play Madison Square Garden with the Young Rascals on 23 December and then return immediately to Britain for Christmas. Another U.S. tour was planned for 22 March until 28 April.[192]

'Ten Little Indians' had been released in the States back at the beginning of October; any reticence releasing it on the British market may have been due to a lack of opportunities to promote it, but more than likely a lack of faith in it from a purely judgemental point of view. The single hadn't taken off in the United States and it sounded trite up against the latest British releases such as 'See

Emily Play', 'I Can See For Miles', 'I Can Hear the Grass Grow', 'Itchycoo Park', 'My White Bicycle', 'Whiter Shade of Pale' and 'Strange Brew', even if it held its own against Beck's 'Tallyman'. On the British market, at least, there was growing hostility against the lowly pop disc: 'Cream Declare War on Singles' ran a November *Melody Maker* headline.

'Like the arms race, the chart race is a monster nobody can stop. But a few brave spirits are shouting – "Stop the turntable – I want to get off."'[193] Among the party-killers was Scott Walker, who in 1967 preferred 'to concentrate on albums'.[194] Now, 'The Cream have announced they don't want to record any more singles. They are trying to opt out of the system where only a hit can ensure publicity, performances and money.'[195] Said Eric:

> It's not definite that we won't ever release a single again. The main reason for not wanting to do them is we are very anti the whole commercial market. The whole nature of the single-making process has caused us a lot of grief in the studios. I'm a great believer in the theory that singles will become obsolete and LPs will take their place. There will be extended LPs at 16 rpm lasting two to three hours. Singles are an anachronism.
>
> To get good music in a space of two or three minutes requires working to a formula and that part of the pop scene really leaves me cold. I hate all that rushing around trying to get a hit.[196]

If the band was to record 'something for an LP that came out short and compact', said Eric, 'we could still release it as a single.' But he thought that not only was the format 'horribly out of date', it made a lot of money for people who shouldn't be making any.[197] Asked about whether Cream would lose money by not playing the game, he responded:

> You don't make a lot of money on singles unless you have a number one. You can lose a lot of money on production and the promotion you get on singles is part of the system I would like to break down . . .
>
> The whole music scene in Britain is ruled by the chart and people are brainwashed into thinking that the number one record represents the best music available. It's horribly immature and it's got to go.[198]

The band's latest album was good, he thought, but it was recorded back in May, and they had moved on since then: 'When I hear it I feel like I'm listening to another group. It's an LP of songs and there is no extended improvisation anywhere.'[199]

In the following week's *Melody Maker*, a reader complained about Cream's new album, including 'both sides of their last single', which 'reduces the tracks to eight for most fans. And "Take It Back" sounds as if it was recorded at the nearest swimming pool.'[200] Elsewhere in that week's edition, Bob Dawbarn examined the 'swing to stereo' that favoured the long-playing album. To make his point about the superiority of stereo, he asked readers to compare the mono B-side, 'I Am the Walrus', of the Beatles' new single, 'Hello, Goodbye', with its stereo counterpart on the soon-to-be-released *Magical Mystery Tour* EP, where 'the cello figures sound great in stereo.'[201] Making the shift to stereo meant that listeners had to upgrade their system, which was costly. Classical albums were now being exclusively released in stereo by Pye and EMI, cutting the cost of producing in both formats. The pop single would remain a mono medium for the time being: 'the general feeling at the moment is that there is no real demand for stereo singles and too few single buyers have the necessary equipment to play them.'[202]

The commercial push towards stereo records, selling more equipment while cutting back on having to produce two audio formats, suited the sonic experimentation of groups like the Beatles and Cream, but it was also being led by rock groups from across the Atlantic. Nick Jones provided an overview of the 'New Wave USA', which was almost entirely devoted to recent album releases by the Doors, Moby Grape, Country Joe and the Fish, the Grateful Dead, Clear Light, Captain Beefheart and the Velvet Underground and Nico. For groups like these, singles at best promoted album sales that were no longer a mismatch of hit singles and filler.[203] Seven-inch 45 rpm discs were being surpassed as the primary, stand-alone, self-defining pop product. Confirmation of this, and the commercial standing/end point of psychedelia, was a half-page advertisement in a December issue of *Melody Maker* for the record branches of newsagents W. H. Smith, which offered the latest LPs by the Who, Traffic, Cream, Blossom Toes, Pink Floyd and Mothers of Invention, all under the banner 'Psyche Sounds '67'.[204] Jeff Beck, meanwhile, was due in the studio with Mickie Most to record his third single.[205] The Yardbirds were simply all at sea and adrift.

When the Pink Floyd's third single, 'Apples and Oranges', failed to follow its predecessors up the charts, *Melody Maker*'s Alan Walsh asked Syd Barrett for his reaction: 'Couldn't care less,' was the answer. 'For the Floyd don't really see themselves as primarily a record group. Barrett is an advocate of musical anarchy. He believes that all the group can do is make a record which pleases them. If it's not commercial too bad.'[206] Pre-dating the Desperate Bicycles by a decade, he advocated that ideally 'groups should record their own music, press their own records, distribute them and sell them.'[207]

For the Yardbirds, all this repositioning against the pop machine was, for a brief moment, encapsulated in the idea that they would become part of a ballet being organized at the Olympia in Paris on 13 and 14 December. Pans People, choreographed by Flick Collie, would perform the dances and the Yardbirds would perform all the music, which would last an hour, according to *Melody Maker*. Plans were being laid to record the shows for an LP and to stage it in Britain for television.[208] Though the event was widely plugged in the press, it never happened.[209] Some U.S. newspapers did report the event as having occurred, one in particular stitching it into a story about experiments in 'symphonic rock music' nurtured by the 'demands of its maturing audience and growing ambitions of its creators'.[210]

In his own contrary way, Pete Townshend caught something of the zeitgeist as 1967 rolled into 1968:

> Kids today are getting a fantastically raw deal as far as pop music is concerned. If you're 13 years old it's a bit much when the chart is full of 'I am a Walrus' which nobody understands. Where's the excitement of rock and roll? There's no bloody youth in music today . . . I'd like to see music right back in the early stages of Billy Fury. There's no excitement, no new ideas anymore. It's got to change and we're going to do something about it.[211]

Would that the Yardbirds had followed his lead.

9

New Heavy Beat Sound – The Underground, 1968

> Everybody under thirty years of age alive in this country today must be offered the Underground option.
>
> *INTERNATIONAL TIMES* (January 1968)

The Yardbirds were back on home turf for the New Year, and Chris Dreja made a rare appearance in *Melody Maker* alongside other pop stars discussing the 'I'm Backing Britain' campaign. The band were doing their bit by earning money in America, he said.[1] Over Christmas, *Record Mirror* reported, the band's van was looted and £2,500 worth of equipment was stolen. It was feared that the thieves might blow themselves up as the gear was set to U.S. voltage.[2] A reward had been offered, but two weeks later, the van and equipment were still missing, the reward was unclaimed and the value of the lost goods had risen by £500 to £3,000. The Yardbirds were 'working with inferior equipment' and they were 'unable to give good stage performances. They also need the original gear very urgently as they are soon to start recording a single and an album.'[3]

They played Chelmsford's Corn Exchange on 13 January before joining the hip scene at Middle Earth in Covent Garden, a smallish club that after the UFO and Happening 44 was the venue of choice for the growing London underground scene typified by the likes of Tyrannosaurus Rex, the Deviants, Soft Machine and Blossom Toes. On 26 January, Fairport Convention headlined at Middle Earth with Robert Plant's Band of Joy in support – Jeff Dexter was the house DJ and Exploding Spectrum produced the light show.

The Yardbirds were scheduled to play the night before Captain Beefheart and His Magic Band. *Melody Maker* had reported that the Americans had sold 2,000 copies of their debut album, *Safe As Milk*, on import and by word of mouth alone.[4] Tony Wilson ecstatically reviewed Beefheart's show; the Yardbirds' turn went undocumented.[5]

Early in February, the new Yardbirds single was announced, 'Goodnight Sweet Josephine', written by Tony Hazzard, who'd composed 'Ha! Ha! Said the Clown'. Hazzard had provided songs for other Mickie Most productions, including Herman's Hermits and Lulu. A 1 March release date was given alongside news of a return to the United States on 1 April for two weeks, which would be followed by a three-week tour of Australia, where their latest single was no. 5 in the charts. Other than the tour of the States, it was all hyperbole.[6] Just before the date of release arrived, it was noted that they were still to record the single and it would now reach the shops on 8 March; the U.S. tour was extended by a week beginning on 19 April in Chicago.[7] The single had originally been tracked at the end of November and in early December 1967, but that version was rejected and it was rerecorded on 13 March – the last time the band entered a British studio, though the *NME* reported that more sessions were planned.[8] *Disc* relayed the news of the single's delay and added that the band would play 'Paris Olympia on March 10, and has an album out at the end of March, tours American colleges for four weeks from April 18'.[9] The band did travel to France for a week, playing three gigs and recording the television programme *Bouton Rouge*, but the album was not released. The final tour of the States began in New York on 28 March; it had already been privately decided among the band that the Yardbirds would fold at tour's end.

The *Bouton Rouge* show featured three numbers, 'Train Kept a-Rollin'', 'Dazed and Confused' and 'Goodnight Sweet Josephine' – a fiery full-throttle start that ends in a blasé state of disinterest. Jimmy Page is dressed in his finest ruffles and frills, kick-starting proceedings with Relf pulling answering stabs on his harmonica, wearing a leather jacket and standing with feet apart on the raised podium. Dreja and McCarty are clad in satin shirts and crushed velvet trousers, looking equally resplendent. After the opening verse and chorus, Relf's harp solo is followed by Page's bursting guitar lead, but just as it builds momentum it quits – the train ride over too soon. 'Dazed' begins with a delicate guitar motif that gets pinned back by McCarty's drum stabs, the downturn into the main riff followed by a 'Glimpses'-like bowed guitar section, a psychedelic show of light and shade, before McCarty picks up the pace again and Relf and Page jump back in for the runaway false climax that brings the song back to the verse before its final petite mort. 'Sweet Josephine' ends things with the group doing a shuck 'n' jive of going through the paces promoting the non-single.

In a questionnaire for *Disc*, Jeff Beck was asked if he had any advice to give the Yardbirds. His response: 'They ought to look back and think about the old magic, in records like "For Your Love" and "Shapes of Things".'[10] He was 'pleased to be out of the Yardbirds. "When a group's doing that badly it's just punchupville."' On *Bouton Rouge*, 'Goodnight Sweet Josephine' confirmed his opinion, but 'Train Kept a-Rollin'' and 'Dazed and Confused' said otherwise.

Though it was never made commercially available in Britain, 'Goodnight Sweet Josephine', coupled with 'Think About It', was given a catalogue number (Columbia DB 8368) and it gained some reviews in the local press. The pop critic for the Runcorn *Guardian* wrote: 'This is an outstanding new single, one that must be a hit for The Yardbirds. It's certainly their best for a long time.'[11] The disc was released in April in the United States to coincide with the band's visit; *Variety*'s reviewer considered it to score 'as a cute change of pace for this British combo'. Had anything the band had previously produced been described as 'cute'?[12] The B-side put them 'back in their groove'.[13]

Bands navigating the demands of the marketplace without deminishing their own authenticity went back to the beginning of the R&B scene, not just for the Yardbirds with 'For Your Love' but for most of their peers. Early in 1964, Manfred Mann justified their servitude to the pop factory with '5-4-3-2-1' by countering that 'actually we prefer the "B" side, which had modern flute and vibes . . . We hope people will turn the record over . . . Personally, I think the group is a lot better than it sounds on records.'[14] The Yardbirds might have said the same thing four years later about any – or all – of their Mickie Most-produced singles. The problem was that in the intervening years, things had changed, and singles, as the main attraction in the pop circus, were no longer held as the currency of choice for aspiring rock bands.

'Ha! Ha! Said the Clown' featured 'Tinker, Tailor, Soldier, Sailor' on its flip, while 'Ten Little Indians' had another LP track, the infinitely superior 'Drinking Muddy Water', on its lower deck. 'Goodnight Sweet Josephine', however, was coupled with a unique band composition, 'Think About It'. Mickie Most was listed as its producer, but it's unlikely he was anywhere about when it was recorded and mixed in London back in January. In its kinship with something like Johnny Burnette Rock 'n' Roll Trio's 'Lonesome Train', the track is a return to a directness at odds with prevailing trends, reconnecting the Yardbirds with their severed rockabilly roots, punching like a search light into the underground's dim caverns.

That suggestion of travel was carried forward to when the band made their final studio recordings in New York on 3–5 April. Five tracks were auditioned; 'Avron Knows' and 'Taking a Hold On Me' were very much in the same vein as 'Think About It', the latter reusing a riff Jimmy Page had first rehearsed on 'A tout casser' at a Johnny Hallyday session the previous year, for which, alongside Micky Jones and Tommy Brown, he was credited as an arranger. But Page does more than that with the material, which his playing claimed as his alone, ripping it up and leaving Hallyday shouting from the sidelines to let him get back on board.[15] 'Taking a Hold On Me' is the better song, but it exists only with a Jim McCarty guide vocal, and like the other four tracks was not considered to be anything near a finished article. 'Avron Knows', at least, features a Relf vocal and could also have been developed into something special, given the time and inclination. 'Knowing That I'm Losing You' was eventually taken forward by Page, mutating into Led Zeppelin's 'Tangerine'. Relf's performance gives to it a haunting vulnerability, even in its half-finished state. McCarty's Morricone tribute, 'Spanish Blood', is a lot of fun, with Page pulling it into interesting corners, but the voiceover feels tentative at best. It was, like all the tracks, a 'sketch', as Page described. Only the cover of Mort Shuman and Jerry Ragovoy's 'My Baby', first recorded by Garnet Mimms, feels close to being the finished article, but that, unlike the others, had been finessed in a live setting for the best part of a year.

'My Baby' was included in the set recorded at the Anderson Theatre, New York, on 30 March, which was originally released in 1971 as *Live Yardbirds! Featuring Jimmy Page* to exploit the guitarist's success with Led Zeppelin. It was subsequently withdrawn from distribution at Page's insistence. Around 45 years later, he would craft an extraordinary remix of the original tapes that, when heard, reclaims the Yardbirds' standing as being among the very best live bands of 1967/8. 'Train Kept a-Rollin'' opens proceedings with the now-familiar slow build into the first sprint. Of the hits, there are 'Shapes of Things', 'You're a Better Man than I' and 'Over Under Sideways Down', the set climaxing with an extended 'I'm a Man'. Threaded into this well-worn raiment are the two highlights, Page's solo 'White Summer' and their arrangement of Jake Holmes's 'Dazed and Confused'. It's surprising that the latter wasn't attempted during the Columbia Studio sessions; perhaps it was put aside for when more time and resources were available for them to begin to do it halfway justice.

As a live showpiece, 'Dazed and Confused' remains a thing of wonder, the song outlining a disintegrating relationship and its emotional foment. For this drama of anguish and frustration, Page acts as a conductor – leading the band through the underworld realm of psychic distress; all shades of light and shadow displayed with the band and Relf giving fully of themselves to the service of the song. It opens with drum taps, punctuated by eerie guitar lines over which Relf hesitantly hums the melody. Then, sotto voce, he begins to express his frustration at the uncertainty of the relationship he's trapped in, but as Page's guitar becomes more insistent, punching into the riff, so Relf's singing matches his imperative; the band echoing his state of mind from perplexed passivity to the jagged raw expression of outrage. The build flounders and Relf, on his harmonica, after a pause, returns to play cat and mouse with Page's bowed guitar. The song shapes itself through a set of repeats, interpolated by a guitar solo that twists and turns, a perfect undertow to the swirling mental whirlpool of Relf's derangement. When performed by the Yardbirds, 'Dazed and Confused' is less a tour de force, the masterful statement of controlled extremes as it became with Led Zeppelin, than an intensely intimate drama, the subjective story of a lover's breakdown; a correlative to how each of the players must have felt about the imminent end of the Yardbirds.

In April, Reg Presley phoned the *NME* to talk about the U.S. tour that the Troggs were then undertaking; he was learning how to '"smarm" the Yanks', he said. He talked too about playing to 17,000 people when supporting the Who in Canada (MC5 were also on the bill): 'We'd been going down very well when half way through the act everyone started applauding and I thought that's good . . . then we discovered that the news of Lyndon Johnson's resignation had just reached the auditorium!'[16] The Who went down fine, he reported, 'but they keep getting their equipment nicked. Every time Keith Moon kicks over the drums the audience consider that he has given them a present of his kit and walk off with the drums

Yardbirds And Association Perform

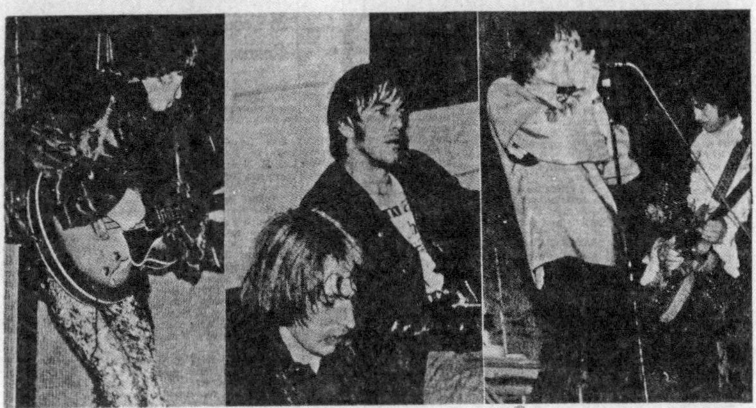

YARDBIRDS WORK UP A SWEAT — The Yardbirds, one of England's more prominent R and B groups pushed hard to produce their usual quality of music at a joint concert with the Association Saturday night at U.Mass. **Left to right** at the concert: Chris Drega, bass guitar; Keith Rielf, lead vocal, harmonica, tamborine, etc.; Jim McCarthy, drums; Keith; and Jimmy Page, lead guitar. The center picture was taken as they relaxed after the concert. (Photos by George Murphy)

4000 Jam Cage To Hear Joint Concert

By GEORGE MURPHY

Four thousand people, young and old, crowded into the Curry Hicks "Cage" Saturday night at U. Mass. ot hear a joint concert by the Yardbirds and the Association.

The Yardbirds started the performance by putting the conservative Western Mass. aduience into a trance with the clothes they wore. Some of the highlights of their garb were Rielf's purple shirt with bell sleeves; Drega's green velvet pants and emerald ruffled shirt, and Page's maroon velvet pants, flowered shawl and yards and yards of white ruffles down his chest.

The performance, which lasted about an hour, went by as quickly as if it were but 10 minutes. Jimmy Paige, lead guitarist, flew across the stage with his guitar, assumed hundreds of positions, and then took to playing his instrument with a violin bow, an art which he claims to have originated.

The original group featured bassist Chris Drega on rhthm guitar with Paul Samuel Smith on bass, and lead guitarist, Eric Clapton (now in the Cream) and eventually, Jeff Beck. Page has masterfully equaled the abilities which formerly were handled by two guitarists, one of them being credited as beong one of the top 10 in the world. year ago and is guitarist for their newest album, "Little Games," as well as doing several cuts on the groups greatest hits.

Chris Drega writhed like a snake during the entire performance but declined to move from one spot which was the left of the stage, hidden behind an amplifier. Now bassist for nearly a year, he finds he prefers it to the rhythm guitar he once played with the group. He claims he doesn't get much of a chance to play the guitar anymore because almost all his time is spent practicing.

Drummer Jim McCarthy secmed to attack his instruments rather than play them. Somehow he managed to keep himself in an upright position throughout the performance without a change in the expression on his face, though his arms never ceased to move. Ocasionally he would pull a microphone before his face and make sounds that could not be easily described.

Lead singer and harmonicist Keith Rielf nervously walked around the stage with the sweat pouring onto his newly cultivated mustache. He was constantly pulling various harmonicas out of his tight corduroy bell bottoms. He didn't hit his tambourine much but kept the audience alive by changing things around from the way they really ought to be.

In the eyes of all that attended, the concert was a complet success. The Yardbirds longed to be back in England and thought about the terrible things that happen here, like the time they were 30 minutes late for a concert in Providence, R.I. and everyone was running around screaming about how they were going to kill someone. And then of course there was the frustration of being called the Barnyards by the Association.

THE ASSOCIATION — **Left**, Larry Ramos of the Association being interviewed by T-T reporter Joan Atkociunas. Larry, the newest member of the group plays alternate lead and rhythm guitar. **Right**: On stage during the performance members of the Association **left to right** are Jim Yester on guitar; Ted Bluchel, Jr. and Russ Gigure. Other members of the group are Larry Ramos, Terry Kirkland and Brian Cole.

Association Players Are Cool, Casual

By JOAN ATKOCIUNAS

The cool, casual style of The Association wowed the audience at UMass Saturday night and had them standing on their feet begging for more.

The Association proved to be a group that was able to put themselves across, in this live performance in such a way they won the hearts of the audience by the time they had sung their second song.

The group featured a maze of various instruments. Their versatility was shown by the way they rotated the instruments and played them. Although the group in general did not favor the conservative East Coast audience, they felt that the UMass audience was among the best they had ever played for and went so far as to invite the entire 4000 attendance of the show ot come with them to Vermont for the next concert.

The group originates from Southern California, but has had some new members and changes in the past few years, though they still choose to live in their founding state.. Only one of the group was born in Southern California.

In a pre-performance interview, Larry Ramos and Brian Cole made some candid comments about their music and themselves.

Larry, the newest member of the group (he joined 18 months ago after their hit record Cherish) plays alternate lead and rhythm guitar. "We really enjoy playing for college audiences. They're always the most responsive," he said.

"No, I don't think we will change much musically so far as making any drastic changes in style. I do think we are advancing creatively, but nis is just a natural kind of evolution."

In contrast to the psychadelic garb of the Yardbirds, Larry and the other members of the group wore mod type suits Brian wore a suit of blue velour, double-breasted with bell-bottom pants. Really sharp was the Mao styled navy blue suit which Terry Kirkland wore.

Brian, a man of many opinions, dislikes having his picture taken. "I don't want to end up like Jack Lennon, having to spend thousands of dollars for a little peace of mind."

Once Brian gets started talking about California, the listener is floored with a barrage of statistics on what makes it (according to Brian) the best place in the world to live. He is also vehement about the ills of the "conservative East Coast." On stage Brian, who plays lead guitar, also makes most of the politically satirical jokes.

When asked about the group's music style, Brian yelled, "Listen, everybody ,is jumping on the psychodelic bandwagon, but we have no intention of getting in that bag. We only sing one freak-out song and that's just for a blast at the end of the show."

The over-all appearance of the group has swayed a little toward hippieness if you compare them now with their picture on their first album. Then, they all wore short hair and matching ultra conservative suits. Now the group has a few handlebar mustaches, long sideburns and, of course, a lot of showmanship.

Kirkland is now the musical genius of the group, an honor he used to share with Gary Alexander who left the group.

Other members of The Association include Russ Gigure, Jim ("Pig") Yester and Ted Bluchel.

Couture's Grove: Lord's Day operation, common victualers and pin ball machine. The weekly warrant amounted to $26,081.68.

4-H NOTE

The Southampton 4-H Jot Stitchers Knitting Club met at the home of their leader, Mrs. Oliver Press. The members are making slippers, hats, and scarfs. Refreshments were served by Helen Kaleta. Miss

Granby

MARRIAGE INTENTIONS

Marriage intentions have been filed with the town clerk by Elon W. Chartier of 232 Batchelor St., Granby, mill-wright, and Suzanne M. Beattie of 281 Morgan St., South Hadley, at home; by George K. Knight Jr.

'Yardbirds work up a sweat': *Holyoke Daily Transcript and the Holyoke Telegram* (11 April 1968).

and cymbals!'[17] He finished the call by noting that 'The Yardbirds are still out here milking what's left of the British group scene.'[18] This off-hand remark made the band appear to be a fading cabaret act, which in some senses was undoubtedly true, but their final live shows suggest that they were far from being a premature nostalgia act, revivalists before the revival.

On 6 April, 4,000 attendees crowded into the Curry Hicks 'Cage' at the University of Massachusetts to listen to the Yardbirds and the Association. Beneath a triptych of images of the band – two on stage and the centre one of McCarty and Relf sweat-soaked after the show – George Murphy for the *Holyoke Telegram* provided a rapturous report that began with a description of the band's garb, which had put the 'audience into a trance': 'Relf's purple shirt with bell sleeves; Dreja's green velvet pants and emerald ruffled shirt, and Page's maroon velvet pants, flowered shawl and yards and yards of white ruffles down his chest.'[19] The performance lasted around an hour, but

> went by as quickly as if it were but 10 minutes. Jimmy Page . . . flew across the stage with his guitar, assumed hundreds of positions, and then took to playing his instrument with a violin bow . . . Page has masterfully equalled the abilities which formerly were handled by two guitarists . . . Dreja writhed like a snake . . . McCarty seemed to attack his instruments rather than play them . . . Relf nervously walked around the stage with the sweat pouring onto his newly cultivated mustache . . . in the eyes of all that attended, the concert was a complete success.[20]

'Looking for a quick panorama of new musical sounds? Rock, jazz, pop? Don't wait for a summer festival,' wrote Philip Elwood in the *San Francisco Examiner*, reviewing the first night of three with the Yardbirds headlining at the Fillmore with support from Cecil Taylor and It's a Beautiful Day:[21]

> The Yardbirds are out of the British bag which includes Cream, the Who and in an earlier era the Rolling Stones – in other words electronic volume is part of their thing . . . Don't plan on an evening of conversation with them around. Also like the Stones of old (but in contrast to Who or Cream) the Yardbirds are sloppy and inconsistent. At times . . . Relf, arms waving and mike in hand, generates some pretty exciting stuff. More often, however, his lyrics and voice become undecipherable, and his role quite irrelevant.[22]

Elwood was even more judgemental of Page: 'not of top grade among the many fine rock guitarists these days, uses excessive volume, wah-wah foot pedal and electronic feedback. His high pitch solos are excellent; the sitar style features are most ordinary.'[23] Still, their 'abstractions in sound from traditional instruments' made Cecil Taylor's band appear 'tame', even if they were a 'far more talented and sophisticated ensemble of musicians'.[24] Summing up, he felt that 'experimental sounds, rock or jazz or whatever (from any kind of source), have developed a common audience in the last year or so.'[25] The band's penultimate Californian engagement was in Concord, where a five-band line-up, which included the Flamin' Groovies, promised a night of 'total mental experience in music and color'.[26]

The Concord gig was documented, probably by an audience member, and though Dreja's bass has fallen out of the mix, the recording is entirely listenable. The stand-out performances are a demented 'Dazed and Confused', preceded by 'You're a Better Man than I', which Page pulled apart and put back together, ramping up the excitement to an electric fever storm. This was a display of extemporization more usually reserved for 'I'm a Man' or 'Smokestack Lightning', but here Page and band burn away the pop artifice of the single and leave a scorched-earth effect that, after the return of some semblance of normalcy, is then sundered and buried with 'Dazed'.

Even if McCarty and Relf were looking forward to the end of the tour and of the band, it doesn't sound like they had given up yet. McCarty is punching hard and true, adding some inspired fills, while Relf engages with the audience in a jokey, familiar tone, his singing terse, clipped and delivered well within his range. Page though goes into overdrive, a commanding performance, his solo 'White Summer' played with a rusty razor edge. It is not pretty, but it sounds like he is far from throwing in the towel – the band will have to drag him from the stage. After a truncated 'Happenings Ten Years Time Ago', the band count military march time into a fourteen-minute 'I'm a Man', Page and Relf joyfully trading riffs, though eventually everyone gives a free pass to the guitarist, Page running through every trick in his book, working his two effects peddles, bowing and hammering his telecaster while Relf returns with his muttered psychedelic mantras about what's going on inside his mind.

Asked by *Hit Parader*'s Jim Delehant 'what sort of stuff' the Yardbirds were playing before they split, Page replied:

> The longest number we did was 'I'm a Man' because people could associate with it. We played it for ten or fifteen minutes. We even did some classical things like the '1812 Overture'. I'd play my guitar with a violin bow. It sounded like a cello. I actually started doing this two years ago. It took a while to master that but I can do it by holding the guitar the same way and I bow with a cross angle.[27]

On 31 May and 1 June, the Yardbirds played Shrine Exposition Hall in Los Angeles; only two further live engagements would follow. *Los Angeles Times* writer Pete Smith reported on the first night, and gave no intimation that it was the end of days for the band: 'Yardbirds have not had a hit in a while, but you wouldn't know it . . . [they produced] an enormous surging sound . . . Their music is loud, hard rock, violent and exciting. Within a minute of their Friday night set, nearly all the Shrine floor sitters were on their feet, transfixed by the vitality of their sound.'[28] The show was bootlegged, a lo-fi affair that was bettered by the audience recordings of the Fillmore in 1967 and the Concord that preceded it, but *The Last Rave-Up in LA* does provide the only audio of the band playing the Velvet Underground's 'I'm Waiting for the Man' interpolated within 'Smokestack Lightning' – future sounds now! Its publication date rhyming with the final show at the Shrine, *Melody Maker*'s 'Raver' column asked: 'Yardbird Jimmy Page to Settle in the States?'[29] The innuendo was that the long-rumoured death of the band was here. The book of condolence was now being prepared.

THE CRUCIAL QUESTION put in the lead letter to *Record Mirror* at the end of May 1968, printed in bold capitals, was 'Why Have the Yardbirds Deserted Britain?' Nick Lambert from Newcastle-upon-Tyne was the concerned correspondent:

> In the past year we have had one single release and two that were promised but never materialised – no albums – no TV and virtually no radio or live appearances. Yet their recent appearance on *Top Gear* was nothing short of sensational and their U.S. LP *Little Games* was simply brilliant. Britain has not forgotten the group who gave us 'For Your Love', 'Still I'm Sad', and 'Shapes of Things', so don't forget us, Yardbirds. Come back from America now, and show us where it's really at.[30]

Lambert, a true fan, had also written to *Beat Instrumental* on this topic, his letter published in their September edition.[31] The *Top Gear* session had been recorded at the beginning of March 1968 and featured 'White Summer', 'Dazed and Confused', 'Think About It' and 'Goodnight Sweet Josephine'. It was a suitably bravura valedictory blow-out, well recorded with Dreja's bass as good as it had ever sounded, like a solid, thick rubber welt wrapped around McCarty's steel sprung beats in support of Page's squealing solos and Relf's urging harp and vocal sermonizing.

Melody Maker's correspondent was right about the radio session, but his appeal for the band not to desert their British fans was already a forlorn request. On 22 June the *NME* reported that the Yardbirds were back home from the States, the 'lengthy tour estimated to have grossed 250,000 dollars'.[32] The paper also noted that starting on 14 September, college and concert dates for a six-week return to the States had been booked. But that same week, *Record Mirror* slipped out a despatch from New York with the news that 'according to Jimmy Page the Yardbirds have split up. Jim McCarty and Keith Relf are leaving the group, which means that Page is allowed to keep the name. Jimmy intends to return to London and get a new group together inside a month.'[33] The Yardbirds had played their final U.S. engagement on the back of flatbed trucks at the International Speedway Fairgrounds in Montgomery, Alabama, on 5 June.

Just how physically and mentally draining, and not even particularly remunerative, U.S. tours were in 1968 was discussed by Pete Townshend on the Who's return from yet another visit there that year. He thought it might be their last:

> not only is the work so gruelling and the travelling so tiring that there is just no time for writing songs or getting together musically with the rest of the group – financially, it's very difficult to just break even, let alone come back with pockets and bank accounts stuffed with glittering dollars. On our first tour there with Herman's Hermits we were amazed to see how scrimping the Hermits were in everyday living. We thought why the hell are they being so pennywise? We found out why – we lost 5,000 dollars on that tour.[34]

Disc's Hugh Nolan further explained that the recent tour had 'lasted six weeks and made them one of the four biggest groups in the country, grossed over 100,000 dollars – over £30,000 for the group'. But by the time they had arrived back in Britain, the four had 'earned barely £1,000 each after paying managers, agents and all the living expenses'.[35] 'It's all right onstage,' Townshend told Nolan, 'and the audiences are quite incredible. But you just keep slogging away, travelling the highways and the freeways and the byways and the airways. You can't work, you can't think – your mind's blanked out.'[36] In Britain, the scene was once more being reformulated, though this barely impacted on the Who and not at all on the Yardbirds.

Back in June, the *Derby Evening Telegraph* reported that members of the Ripley Roundtable had booked the Yardbirds for their Big Beat Barbecue on 20 July, but alas, it was noted two days before the event that the band had broken up and would be replaced by Plastic Penny.[37] A gig at Luton Technical College on 7 July is often cited as the last Yardbirds appearance; it was a booking held over from a cancelled performance that had been scheduled for 16 March, but it seems highly unlikely to have gone ahead as all other previously scheduled gigs following the return from the States had not taken place.[38] Regardless of whether the end happened in Montgomery, Alabama, or in Luton, Bedfordshire, in neither case was it or would it have been an auspicious occasion.

Ralph J. Gleason broke the news that the band had split in his *San Francisco Chronicle* column on 9 June: 'A couple of the guys will get out of the music business and stay at home in London. A couple of the others will go into other bands or studio work and Keith Relf, the lead singer, may go into film work.'[39] Thereafter, news of the break-up staggered out in the trades and music press in Britain and the United States. Fourteen days after the Alabama show, *Variety* announced that the band had disbanded: Page intended to 'restaff outfit under same handle and feature himself . . . [He] was the only

Yardbird not signed individually to Epic in addition to the combo's pact.'[40] That same week, *Go*, a weekly U.S. music paper, published an interview with Page on the break-up of the band that was carried out before he flew back from New York to London. The decision to split had been taken before the final tour: 'I had only been in the group for about 18 months, but the others were in the Yardbirds for four or five years. They had lost all their enthusiasm. Keith Relf, the singer, was fed-up for a long time and he was always threatening to leave.'[41] Disputes over the band's musical direction had split the band into two camps: Relf and McCarty had wanted to slow things down, to do something 'similar to early Simon and Garfunkel numbers', while, as Page explained, he and Dreja wanted to stick to 'a type of sound' that they were associated with, 'It's a heavy beat sound and I wanted to keep that.'[42]

On 29 June, *Melody Maker*'s New York reporter Ron Grevatt relayed the likelihood of a 'Yardbirds Split': the break-up was expected to happen on their imminent return to Britain, he wrote.[43] The news gained barely a column inch; two weeks later, the announcement that Cream were breaking up was three-quarters of the front page and an inside feature.[44] The contrast in the perceived importance of the two bands could not have been more starkly addressed. For its part, the *NME* put news of the two bands splitting into a bordered item in its 13 July issue: 'Cream Splits to Form Three Groups . . . Yardbirds Break in Two'.[45]

The Yardbirds break-up was confirmed in *Melody Maker*'s 20 July edition: 'Reason for the split: differences over musical policy. "There were no personal differences among the boys," said a spokesman. "It is just that Keith and Jim are following an entirely different musical line from Jimmy and Chris."'[46] The *NME* reported that McCarty and Relf will 'specialise in "folksy advanced pop"'.[47]

Back in early 1967, a short while after the release of the 'Little Games' single, the band had talked to Val Wilmer about how long they felt that they could continue and what they might do after things had ended, though, as Relf told her, 'It's a dodgy thing to talk about the future.'[48] But when it happened, Relf wanted to get out and work behind the scenes. Dreja intended to develop his interest in photography, while he and McCarty also had joint ownership of three grocery stores to give them a bit of security. For Page, 'the finish of the Yardbirds would only come about because "there would no longer be a market for that sort of music. Consequently I'd stop playing and go back to painting. That's all I can do apart from music."'[49] He did, however, admit to having a book of poetry underway: 'these are serious poems which I did at art school – some actually rhyme, a rare thing these days!'[50]

Page intended to supplement the heavy beat sound with a singer who could also play keyboards, specifically a mellotron. He explained: 'The whole idea is to get a new sort of collage of sound that is not the sound normally associated with a rock 'n' roll group. But, it will still have a beat backing . . . The mellotron will be there to give added interest, but the guitar will still be featured.'[51] He told *Hit Parader* he was not interested in emulating the trio set-up of Cream and the Jimi Hendrix Experience – 'definitely not. That's overplayed now.'[52]

In his 'Reports from New York' column for *Disc and Music Echo*, Richard Robinson noted that Jimmy Page was in town explaining about the new Yardbirds to the press and visiting producer Tom Wilson's recording studio.[53] Wilson had produced Dylan and the Velvet Underground; Page was not being idle, he had a vision of things to come.

THE PRIMACY OF the hit single as a measure of a band's value continued to slip, and in its place, the cultural capital of a new authenticity emerged. Talking to Pink Floyd for *Melody Maker*, Tony Wilson reported that 'fifteen months ago, the Pink Floyd, with their own avant garde electronic music and somewhat less sophisticated light show, heralded the short-lived era of love-ins, be-ins and cash-ins.'[54] With two hits, a miss and even a new single in hand, 'It Would Be So Nice', the band were turning away from chasing the charts: 'Single releases have something to do with our scene, but they are not overwhelmingly essential,' said Roger Waters: 'On LPs we can produce our best at any given time.'[55] As Wilson explained, 'The Pink Floyd are innovators and they have ideas that go beyond the normal accepted boundaries set by the economics of the pop world.'[56] The band had applied to the Arts Council for a grant to finance a project; said Waters, 'It would be a story, using other groups, written as a saga, like the Iliad, so that it doesn't just become a pop show with someone walking on and introducing groups. I don't want any of that scene.'[57] Their ambitions were shared with many others refiguring their standing in the pop world after psychedelia was felt to have exhausted itself.

Mick Farren's Deviants marketed their first self-financed and distributed album, *PTOOFF!*, as 'The sound of the underground – a new way of sound – a new way of life.' It could be bought by mail order from Underground Impresarios, 22 Betterton Street, London – 'NOW!'[58] In the same issue of *Melody Maker* in which the advert for *PTOOFF!* was run, a question was raised about what was happening:

> Pop looks doomed to destruction in these grim days of drug scandals, the breaking up of groups and the closing down of clubs. The greatest public diversion since bear baiting and cat dropping is losing favour with its supporters – and now so disgusts the Establishment, they seemed stunned into silence . . . Pop fans yawn in the face of fevered attempts to bring back the excitement of the Beatles and Stones days.[59]

Bands like the Herd and Bee Gees, 'hailed as successors', don't live up to the hype; the rock and roll revival is but a temptation to the 'jaded palate of the nation's youth' and 'our progressive bands have deserted these shores' – among those listed were Jimi Hendrix, Cream, the Who, Traffic and the Yardbirds.[60]

Seven months earlier, in his 'Pop Scene' column for *Queen* magazine, Nik Cohn had highlighted the threat to pop by the turn away from its glitz and showmanship with the emergence of the Underground scene:

> obviously pop is going to come up with some very good, progressive music in the next years. It's just that separated from all the traditional showbiz shackles, I rather doubt if I'll be interested . . . I've always been hooked on pop as a ragbag, a chaotic stew of the good and the awful, the coy and the vulgar and the heart-pumping and the downright ludicrous and, however crass it may have been, it has always toted an immense vitality. This, I think, is dying.[61]

'Underground' and 'progressive' were all but interchangeable terms by summer 1968. The letters to *Melody Maker* in this period used 'progressive' on repeat; in the 15 June issue alone, for example, there featured 'I think the Small Faces are the most progressive group in pop music today' . . . Miss J. Wilson, Luton; 'How can blues progress when so many people insist on hearing Robert Johnson and Peg Leg Peterson numbers all night long[?]' . . . Alvin Lee, Ten Years After; 'My definition, progressive pop can't exist. Progressive equals avant garde, which equals only appreciated by the discerning. Pop equals popular which equals appealing to the masses by the lowest common denominator' . . . Dave Blackhouse, Cana Variety Agency; and 'The musical tastes of English record buyers are educated towards superficial pop without interest in progressive pop – real pop made by people like Nice, Pink Floyd, Doors and Jefferson Airplane' . . . R.M.P. Neves, Portugal.[62]

At the end of July, *Melody Maker* dedicated a spread to discussing the underground scene – 'an expression much in vogue' – with

John Peel, who was fast becoming a spokesman and, through his radio show, a tastemaker on the topic (and something of a cynic):

> The Underground is like a woman who is endlessly pregnant and never has a baby. So sad. If only creative people realised they had the power to do something collectively. But it all seems to come down to people who wear the clothes, know the right words to say and do nothing . . . Isn't it true that the only audible rallying cry of the Underground has been 'legalise pot'?[63]

In the summer, Derek Boltwood started a weekly column, 'From the Underworld', in *Record Mirror*. The idea was to document and define the evolving scene of 'underground groups'. These were bands who he felt challenged pop's orthodoxy of judgements based on commercial value approved by where a single ended up in the charts:

> People who are to a large extent uncompromising – groups who don't go out of their way to make commercial records, but at the same time who are good enough to eventually sell their own sound to the public. Those who are meeting with success at the moment are just the scouts, or pioneers, of the new wave in pop – underground to a large extent now perhaps, but with enough fresh ideas and original talent to move pop in a new direction, away from the stale.[64]

From out of the psychedelic and flower-power scenes that had been hijacked by commercial interests, groups like the Pink Floyd emerged unscathed to start the recovery from pop's 'present sickness'. Others who had stopped chasing the Top 20 were Ten Years After, the Crazy World of Arthur Brown, the Nice, Fairport Convention, Jethro Tull and Tyrannosaurus Rex.

> For some reason, certain groups are labelled 'underground' – they're not given the exposure on the radio or television, or in the pop papers. Because they don't get the exposure they don't get hit records and vice-versa. A vicious circle – very vicious. It's unfortunate that this applies to some of our best groups.[65]

Subsequent columns considered the American underground with obvious contenders like Jefferson Airplane, Canned Heat and the Doors getting positive mentions alongside less likely candidates for underground status, such as Nilsson and East Coast groups Beacon Street Union and the Ultimate Spinach – 'in spite of the name, they have a great instrumental track called "Sacrifice of the Moon (In Four Parts)".'[66] At the end of August, Boltwood interviewed Marc Bolan:

> 'In my opinion,' said Marc (we were chatting in the corner of a crowded pub), 'I don't like most pubs,' he said, 'they're full of society's drop-outs. I haven't dropped out – I've dropped in. Three underground groups have made the charts – Arthur Brown, the Nice and, fortunately, ourselves' . . . [J]ust watch the king of the lizards emerge from the earth and go racing up the charts with 'One Inch Rock'. Tyrannosaurus Rex will be accepted . . . on their own terms.[67]

While bands went underground to hide and protect themselves from a rapacious, corrupting pop industry, they could still, as long as it was 'on their own terms', make forays into the charts to corrupt the machine, to unpick the pop package. But the contradictions were ever harder to supress: was the mainstream musical *Hair* a valid or exploitative underground expression? Was John Peel under- or overground? Was he part of the problem or the solution? Boltwood wrote:

> If a thing is publicised as being underground, then everybody immediately becomes suspicious – people I would consider as being 'Underground' . . . not only deny it. They refuse all knowledge of it. Last week John Peel said, 'I don't know what the Underground is. I'm not part of it.' But he did qualify it with 'Perhaps it's just an attitude, you can't pin it down.' This is where the confusion arises, for John Peel has done more for the underground groups than any other D.J. But he doesn't know what it is.[68]

If the underground was in danger of becoming pop, you can, Boltwood argued, still determine the difference between Dave Dee, Dozy, Beaky, Mick and Tich and the Nice – 'let's just remember it's just a label. Just a term of reference. I use it as a label because it refers to the sort of music I like.'[69] If the terms of reference changed, the essential debates (and contradictions) remained firmly in place for the next several years.

For its part, the *NME* fastidiously ignored the scene, leaving it to Dave Dee for some acerbic commentary on what was happening beneath their feet:

> I know there are so-called Underground groups around who wouldn't touch us with a barge-pole. Either that, or they think there's something not quite cool about the way we keep getting hits over and over again. As far as we're concerned though the Underground scene can stay there. These arty types seem to enjoy having a go at us from time to time, but some of them seem to think all they need to do to be hip is throw in an occasional 'Sock It to Me Baby'. Now that's nice enough. But who do they think they're really kidding?[70]

Like 'psychedelia', 'underground' as a descriptive term was American in origin and was used to identify music and bands that existed on the periphery of the mainstream, the two terms originally used interchangeably. An early 1967 interview with the Blues Magoos in the song-lyric magazine *Rock and Roll* was headlined 'an underground group comes out on top'.[71] The band were, the reporter explained, 'quite frankly, an "underground" group. That is, they are very "in" with a certain group of teenage avant-gardists – those who are ahead of everyone else in tastes and trends.'[72] Word of mouth was responsible for the Blues Magoos' reputation.[73] As for the band themselves,

> What we want is complete musical freedom; we'd like to present our music in just the fashion we see fit . . . Our psychedelic style just evolved out of our heads . . . Other groups are using electrical feedback on their instruments, but they do it just to create greater noise . . . Instead we do a full melodic line while creating the feedback. We use the feedback as music.[74]

Not then a manufactured product, but a music that circulates initially in a more rarefied atmosphere where reputations are built and sustained by a self-defined in-group with progressive tastes undiluted by commercial interests: 'As an "underground" group in the rock field, [Blues Magoos] are creating their own kind of musical revolution, and it's a rebellion that's quickly spreading.'[75]

In the same issue of *Rock and Roll*, there was coverage of a New York press conference, held while Beck was still in the room with the other four; the Yardbirds derided claims made by such bands as the Blues Magoos 'who haven't listened very carefully to the music that was being played three or four years ago. "They think they're into something new, but they're just repeating old, old things." The Yardbirds, at any rate, are not worried about their reputation and future popularity.'[76] This may have been true in the States, but in Britain, the Yardbirds were now discussed, if at all, as the 'old, old things'.

In November 1968, *Disc and Music Echo* caught up with Derek Boltwood and, helmed by Hugh Nolan, produced a five-page account of the underground scene. Following the introduction, there was a lexicon of underground terms and phrases – 'heavy', 'together', 'groovy', 'drop out', 'doing your thing' – an interview with Pete Brown, Cream's lyricist, and with the Action; two pages filled with John Peel's ABC of bands and solo artists (in which the Who and Pink Floyd featured, but not the Yardbirds); and Mick Farren of the Deviants' rock 'n' roll manifesto for 'revolutionary actions . . . with electric guitars and harmonicas rather than bullets and bombs'.[77] As with Peel, for Nolan, the underground was 'a state of mind rather than a time or place or a style or a sound', and it was now 'big business with 12 of the top twenty LPs in America by names which under a year ago were unheard of outside places like the Avalon and Fillmore ballrooms'.[78] Whatever future independent or collective activities the various ex-members of the Yardbirds were considering, this was the context that they now found themselves within.

AFTER THE EARLY SUMMER announcements of the band splitting, a bare sputtering of news items followed, in both Britain and the States. *Record Mirror* announced that the band had officially broken into two groups: Relf and McCarty intended to form a duo called Together, and Dreja and Page would reform the Yardbirds: 'At present the Yardbirds are working on a new LP under the direction of Jimmy Page. This does not mean that the group are to split from producer Mickie Most – Jimmy is just producing this one particular album.'[79] Relf and McCarty were working on a single, which Paul Samwell-Smith was directing. Page's Yardbirds had a ten-day tour of Scandinavia scheduled and then an extended visit to the USA in October and possibly November. It was all very underwhelming; the break-up caused barely a ripple of interest.

With Robert Plant brought on board and, speculatively, Paul Francis on drums, Chris Dreja talked to *Beat Instrumental* about the Yardbirds' new line-up. England was to be the 'target for the new onslaught. "We've definitely lost a lot of ground after spending so Long in America."'[80] But first, they were to tour Scandinavia. 'We've done a fair amount of rehearsing, with some new songs and also plenty of the old Yardbirds hits,' he said.[81] These would include 'I'm a Man' – 'it's developed just a little,' he added. 'And this looks to be the theme of the new band – continuing the Yardbirds' trademark of progressive music, but making certain that it stays appealing to the majority.'[82] By the time the magazine issue was published, Dreja had dropped out and John Paul Jones had been recruited in his place to be joined by Plant's old bandmate John Bonham on drums. By mid-August, members of the new line-up were in rehearsal.[83]

That month, *Variety* reported on the latest iteration that Page had put together, which was to be billed as 'The Yardbirds featuring Jimmy Page' when touring the United States. New recruits were 'bass player John Paul James [*sic*] and vocalist Robert Plante [*sic*]'.[84] In the 21 September issue, *Melody Maker* used its third 'Yardbirds Split' headline for a news bulletin; the latest announcement was that Dreja had now left the band and that Page had

> reformed the Yardbirds with Robert Plant (vcls), John Paul Jones (bass gtr) and John Bonham (drs). In future Jimmy plans to produce the Yardbirds discs himself and negotiations are currently going on for their release. The new Yardbirds first British date will be at London's Marquee Club on October 18. The group starts a six-week American tour on November 14.[85]

The *NME* had provided a few more details, notably that Page and manager Peter Grant had formed a company, Super-Hyp (*sic*) Recording, which will be 'responsible for the production of the

Yardbirds' discs. This means they will no longer record under the supervision of Mickie Most.'[86] Negotiations with four of the major British record companies were under way, and Warner-Reprise was thought most likely for the States. They were then on tour in Scandinavia.

The dead space between the band breaking up and the appearance of the new Yardbirds, followed by Led Zeppelin, was opportunistically filled by two unlikely candidates. Looking to create a little bit of interest in their stalled careers and maybe make a few better paying engagements, Keith Dangerfield and Dermot Hegarty both claimed to be ex-members of the Yardbirds. The latter was an Irish musician who'd released a few singles, billed as a 'former member of the English pop group, the Yardbirds, and now one of the country's top solo attractions . . . his polished act now incorporates singing to his own organ accompaniment, playing guitar and accordion as well as being one of the most personable comperes in the business.'[87] He was managed by Henry Collins, who, it was reported in the local Essex press, had met Dangerfield in the States while the singer was touring as a member of the Yardbirds. A new record was set for release – 'No Life Child' – while 'Keith may in the future appear in lunchtime shows in local factories and with other groups, give a performance in aid of Brentwood Town Football Club funds.'[88] All brazenly unscrupulous, but well below the radar, unless you read the *Brentwood Gazette and Mid-Essex Recorder* or *Wicklow People*. Both pieces were accompanied by photographs of the imposters; neither made a good match for anyone in the band, but it said something about the Yardbirds' long invisibility within British media that the two singers (or their management) thought that they could get away with their impersonations. It also said something about the band's ongoing issue with anonymity, and why Jimmy Page felt so confident about taking things forward with new members unknown to the Yardbirds' fanbase.

For the most part, Relf and McCarty had been licking their wounds back home, but they did head back towards the footlights under the name Together with a single on Columbia, to whom they were still contracted. 'Henry's Coming Home' backed with 'Love Mum and Dad' was released in mid-November, and Penny Valentine gave it a sincere review. She wrote that it was an 'intensely warm, pretty American sort of record'.[89] It reminded her of the Turtles. Ex-Shadow Tony Meehan and Paul Samwell-Smith were responsible for the production and the 'really lovely handling of strings. The whole thing is excellent and they have reason to be proud.'[90] She didn't, however, consider it to be smash-hit material, but it 'bodes well for their future' and will 'get them a lot of well-deserved attention'.[91] It did none of that, and sank without a trace; there was no promotion and no further reviews.

By the autumn, *Melody Maker* had shifted perspective a little and shone light into one corner of the underground, the blues scene. Beginning in the first week of October, the paper's long-in-the-tooth Bob Dawbarn offered a three-part survey of homegrown blues, its history and present configuration.[92] He also authored a two-part article on the contemporary pop scene that attempted to give some context and understanding to the idea of the 'progressives'.[93] Towards the end of November, Hugh Nolan reviewed the current scene for *Disc and Music Echo*: 'After all the self-conscious trends in the past ten years or so, everyone is going back to the blues: the musicians, the fans and the clubs.'[94] Chicken Shack's singer Christine Perfect said 'it's like the trad jazz boom of ten years ago . . . Everyone digs it, no one really knows why or even knows anything about it.'[95] She thought the bubble was bound to burst, but in the meantime, Nolan surveyed who was out there peddling the new wave of the blues. For originality, 'Jethro Tull are on their own,' he thought.[96] Of the more established, with John Mayall as a kind of founding father, there was Peter Green's Fleetwood Mac, Keef Hartley, Aynsley Dunbar's Retaliation, Jon Hiseman's Colosseum,

Cream ('or at any rate Clapton') and Chicken Shack. Then there was Savoy Brown Blues Band, Black Cat Bones, Doctor K's Blues Band, Duster Bennett, Love Sculpture, Tramline, Taste, Free! (*sic*) and Bakerloo Line. More names of bands followed, but in among the aforementioned was Led Zeppelin, which, as Nolan explained at the conclusion, were included 'because Jimmy IS such an outstanding guitarist': 'The blues scene, 1968, is wide open . . . the next group to score a Fleetwood Mac/Jethro Tull/Ten Years After type of success may at this moment be totally unknown, rehearing their own special brand of music in a Swansea garage, a Scarborough garret or a disused cow-barn near Leeds.'[97] Mindful of the scene's faddishness and not wanting to compete directly with either Fleetwood Mac or with the latest provincial upstarts, Page positioned himself both at the margins and in the vanguard.

When *Melody Maker* finally broke their silence around the Yardbirds' extinction with a short interview with 'good natured' Jimmy Page (the piece illustrated with a 1966 photographic portrait of him in his Civil War kepi), they had ready their own version of the question 'Whatever happened to the Yardbirds?'[98] 'One of the great mysteries of our time,' wrote Chris Welch, 'ranking with the Devil's footprints, the Marie Celeste and the Five Penny Post, is the disappearance of a group once hailed as the most progressive in Britain.'[99] Looking back, Welch recognized that the band were 'trying experimental pop long before today's Underground groups', but they were either too early 'or lacked the drive to carry their breakaway from the original blues formula through to the public.'[100] Their trips to the United States, he explained, had kept them out of the public eye in Britain. A potted history of the band was given, and now only 'new boy' Page is left to form a 'New Yardbirds . . . which threatens to be a welcome piece of fire power to the armoury of British groups.'[101] The split with the original members had been due to Relf's loss of enthusiasm, said Page, which was now made up for by the 'new chaps' in the band, who are all about nineteen years old. Whether to keep the name is still uncertain. Their debut, he noted, had been in Denmark:

> It's blues basically, but not Fleetwood Mac style. I hate that phrase progressive blues. It sounds like a hype, but it is more or less what the Yardbirds were playing at the end, but nobody knew about it because nobody saw us. We're starting work on an LP and we're going to the States in early November. I'm hoping the Marquee will be a good scene. Robert can get up and sing against anybody. He gets up and sings against Terry Reid! Those two are like brothers together.
>
> I thought I'd never get a band together. I've always shied off leadership in the past because of all that ego thing . . . I didn't want the Yardbirds to break up, but in the end it was too much of a headache. I just wanted to play guitar basically, but Keith always had this thing of being overshadowed by Jeff and that, which was nonsense. It was great when we had two lead guitars.[102]

Page, reported Welch, was all smiles and had no ill-feelings; 'he is far too excited about the future to worry about the past.'[103]

The following week, *Melody Maker* reported on the band's name change that would take place 'after two farewell performances this weekend' – at the Marquee and at the University of Liverpool.[104] The former venue advertised the gig as the band's 'debut', not its 'farewell'.[105] Led Zeppelin's coming-out gala, its 'debut', would be at the University of Surrey on Friday, 25 October. Meanwhile, manager Peter Grant was finalizing a six-week tour of the States starting around 16 November.[106] *NME* carried a similar news bulletin and added that the band had signed with agent Harold Davidson.[107]

The group would henceforth be known as Led Zeppelin. The changeover would take a short while to bed down, a headliner at

Middle Earth on 9 November, now located at the Roundhouse in Chalk Farm, was promoted as 'YARDBIRDS now known as LED ZEPPELIN', yet a show at the Bridge Place Country Club, near Canterbury, on 13 December was still being advertised as 'Yardbirds' in the *Kent Messenger* on the day of the gig itself, and earlier, on 26 October, *Disc* reported that the Yardbirds had 'backed P. J. Proby on his new single "The Day that Lorraine Came Down"'.[108] Penny Valentine reviewed the single that same week, noting that producer Steve Rowland said that it was 'right back to the good old Hollywood days when Proby sounded like Proby – basic bluesy and with hardly any other influences'.[109] The Yardbirds weren't mentioned by Valentine, though Derek Johnson did draw attention to their participation in his *NME* review of Proby's 'real wildie', which he described as 'hillbilly rock, gospel and r-and-b'.[110] Proby was still the greatest, as he told *Melody Maker*: 'I stepped out of the business for 18 months and now I heard all these guys doing the things I was doing years ago.'[111] His subsequent album, *Three Week Hero*, featured all four members of the nascent Led Zeppelin, though it was John Bonham who left the most lasting impression, with the power and verve of his drumming. Proby's oversized crown was Bonham's for the taking.

Billed as 'Formerly the Yardbirds', Led Zeppelin were booked to play the Crawdaddy Club, Richmond Athletic Ground, on 29 November, the place where Relf, Dreja, McCarty, Clapton and Samwell-Smith had first schemed and dreamed five years or so before, but, like the 'final' Yardbirds gig in Luton, this one also didn't happen; there would be no poetic return to where it all began, no neat containment or resolution before the phoenix-like Led Zeppelin rose from the ashes.

In his November 'Teen Beat' column for the *Detroit Free Press*, Richard Robinson wrote that Jimmy Page had been visiting New York for talks with Atlantic about his new band 'Lead Zeppelin [*sic*]'.[112] *Record Mirror* subsequently relayed the news that 'Atlantic

Records in America are reported to be paying $200,000 for Jimmy Paige's [*sic*] new group Led Zeppelin.'[113]

The *NME*'s New York correspondent, June Harris, also reported on Page's Manhattan ramblings and on Led Zeppelin's deal with Atlantic. She wrote that the band's soon-to-be-released LP was 'unquestionably the finest album I and several other people have ever heard as a debut effort[. It] will be released in Jan.'[114] There was some undisclosed conflict of interest here, as Harris also doubled up as an Atlantic publicist, penning the label's press releases for the album's promotion, but she was only telling it like it was.

The long-promised autumn tour of the States, first listed back in June as starting in September, then moving to October before a further shunt into November, was now definitively scheduled for a late December start. In their own way, the Yardbirds had been pathfinders on their numerous North American tours, but now the situation had changed, as Pete Townshend explained, back-tracking on the comments he'd made about the financial drag of playing in the USA. The American market was now the Who's primary concern; it was where they 'have their biggest hits, most fan fever and excitement', wrote Chris Welch.[115] 'The English scene, for us,' Townshend told him, 'doesn't compare with America. I don't think our old fans will care for that statement and new pop fans won't care at all. But the States offers us more money, fans and excitement.'[116] Implied in this change of opinion was not just the financial rewards; the very conditions of touring had been transformed. The Who were no longer playing package tours, state fairs and amusement parks, but theatres, colleges and ballrooms with booking agents, like the newly established Premier, who were dedicated to putting on rock shows, while college and FM radio provided promotional weight for rock's new hierarchy, hyping tours and record releases.

In *Disc and Music Echo*'s final edition of 1968, Richard Robinson sent notice that 'Jimmy Page and his new group, Led Zeppelin,

Orgasmic: the Yardbirds at the Boston Tea Party, 1968.

arrive in the U.S. the day after Christmas to spend Boxing Day in New York.'[117] In mid-January, he wrote:

> If you're a blues fan but still love the sound of high-powered rock, Led Zeppelin will please you. This new British group, headed by ex-Yardbird Jimmy Page, has just released their

> first album and it is a study in shotgun rock. Guitars run at screaming speeds, vocals are soft and then screaming hard, songs are impressive.[118]

With the Yardbirds' playbook providing support and direction, there was no looking back as Led Zeppelin kicked over their traces and headed rock 'n' roll's third generation into the new decade.

REFERENCES

Prologue

1 Lester Bangs, 'Psychotic Reactions and Carburetor Dung: A Tale of These Times', republished in *Psychotic Reactions and Carburetor Dung*, ed. Greil Marcus (New York, 1987), p. 5.
2 Ibid., p. 6.
3 Ibid., p. 8.
4 Lester Bangs, 'Of Pop Pies and Fun: A Program for Mass Liberation in the Form of a Stooges Review; or, Who's the Fool?' [1970], republished in *Psychotic Reactions and Carburetor Dung*, ed. Marcus, p. 40.
5 Ibid., p. 41.
6 Ibid.
7 Ibid., p. 44.
8 Ibid.

1 Modybirds and Craw-Daddies, 1963

1 Andrew Humphreys, *Raving Upon Thames: An Untold Story of Sixties London* (London, 2022), pp. 11–12.
2 Peter Hepple, 'Nightbeat: Fringe Attractions', *The Stage* (31 January 1963), p. 7.
3 Ibid.
4 Ibid.
5 Ibid.
6 Ibid.
7 Chris Roberts, 'Trend or Tripe', *Melody Maker* (5 January 1963), p. 5.
8 Ibid.
9 Ibid.
10 Ibid.
11 Ibid.
12 'Jazz Scene 1963', *Melody Maker* (5 January 1963), p. 6.
13 *Jazz News and Reviews* (9 January 1963), p. 7.
14 Ray Coleman, 'R&B Is the Threat', *Melody Maker* (2 February 1963), p. 7.
15 'Big Pete Deuchar Hits Back', *Melody Maker* (9 February 1963), p. 5.
16 Chris Roberts, 'It's All Happening Beatlewise', *Melody Maker* (9 February 1963), p. 9.
17 Ibid.
18 Ibid.
19 'Beatles Cut First LP', *Melody Maker* (16 February 1963), p. 3.
20 Norman Jopling, 'Great Unknowns: No.1 of a Great New Fortnightly Series – the Miracles', *New Record Mirror* (9 March 1963), p. 6.

21 Norman Jopling, 'A Year of R&B', *New Record Mirror* (23 March 1963), p. 7.
22 Chris Roberts, 'The Beat Boys!', *Melody Maker* (23 March 1963), pp. 8–9.
23 'Well – What Is R&B?', *Melody Maker* (30 March 1963), p. 6.
24 Ibid.
25 Ibid.
26 'Trad – It's Finished!', *Melody Maker* (6 April 1963), p. 7.
27 Laurie Henshaw, 'The Big Beat War Hots Up', *Melody Maker* (13 April 1963), p. 8.
28 Advertisement run in *New Record Mirror* (20 April 1963), p. 9.
29 Norman Jopling, 'The Soul-Beat Revival . . .', *New Record Mirror* (20 April 1963), p. 7.
30 Ibid.
31 Ibid.
32 Ibid.
33 Ibid.
34 'Jazz Clubs – London', *Melody Maker* (4 May 1963), p. 12.
35 Ibid. (11 May 1963), p. 12.
36 The article is reproduced along with more quotes from *Melody Maker* adverts for shows at the Station Hotel in Humphreys, *Raving Upon Thames*, pp. 77–8.
37 Ibid.
38 Norman Jopling, 'The Rolling Stones', *New Record Mirror* (11 May 1963), p. 2. Reprinted in Norman Jopling, *Shake It Up Baby! Notes from a Pop Music Reporter, 1961–1972* (2015), pp. 73–6.
39 Jerry Dawson and Chris Roberts, 'Liverpool v Manchester', *Melody Maker* (1 June 1963), pp. 6–7.
40 Ray Coleman, 'Blind Date', *Melody Maker* (15 June 1963), p. 6.
41 Patrick Doncaster, 'Twitching the Night Away', *Daily Mirror* (13 June 1963), p. 25.
42 Disker, 'London's Challenge to Liverpool', *Liverpool Echo and Evening Express* (8 June 1963), p. 6.
43 Ibid.
44 Norman Jopling, 'Back to Britain's Big Beat Boys', *New Record Mirror* (8 June 1963), p. 5.
45 Ibid.
46 Pete Goodman, 'Group of the Month: Rolling Stones', *Beat Monthly* (January 1964), p. 4.
47 Ibid.
48 Norman Jopling, 'I'm Still Striving for My Sound', *New Record Mirror* (22 June 1963), p. 2.
49 Ibid.
50 Ibid.
51 'Rolling Stones at the Scene', *New Record Mirror* (22 June 1963), p. 8.
52 'Blues Inc. Two Dates', *New Record Mirror* (13 July 1963), p. 6.
53 Norman Jopling, 'Are We Clairvoyant?', *New Record Mirror* (10 August 1963), p. 3.
54 Ibid.

55 Chris Roberts, 'Rolling Stones Gather Speed', *Melody Maker* (29 June 1963), pp. 8–9.
56 Ibid.
57 Ibid.
58 Jeff Bayliss, 'Provincial Round-Up', *New Record Mirror* (11 May 1963), p. 3.
59 Brian Jones, 'Everly-Diddley Tour', *New Record Mirror* (5 October 1963), p. 4.
60 Ibid.
61 Mick Jagger, 'The Everly-Bo-Richard Tour', *New Record Mirror* (12 October 1963), p. 4.
62 Ibid.
63 Bill Wyman, 'A Rolling Stone Writes', *New Record Mirror* (19 October 1963), p. 4.
64 Keith Richards, 'A Rolling Stone Writes', *New Record Mirror* (26 October 1963), p. 4.
65 Charlie Watts, 'A Rolling Stone Writes', *New Record Mirror* (2 November 1963), p. 10.
66 'Jazz Clubs – London', *Melody Maker* (19 October 1963), p. 13.
67 Jim McCarty with Dave Thompson, *Nobody Told Me! My Life with the Yardbirds, Renaissance and Other Stories* (self-published, 2018), p. 82.
68 Val Wilmer, 'Blues at Fairfield Hall', *Jazz News and Reviews* (November 1963), p. 13. The show was also covered along with the entourage's trip to Manchester in 'That Festival', *New Record Mirror* (2 November 1963), p. 2. The reporter's name isn't cited but it was most likely Guy Stevens.
69 Ibid.
70 Bob Dawbarn, 'Is Rhythm and Blues Killing Trad Jazz?', *Melody Maker* (26 October 1963), p. 8.
71 Norman Jopling, 'It's Been a Quiet Revolution', *New Record Mirror* (23 November 1963), p. 6.
72 Bob Dawbarn, 'R&B for the Masses', *Melody Maker* (22 June 1963), p. 9.
73 Jopling, 'Quiet Revolution', p. 6.
74 Jopling gave a month-by-month breakdown of how American R&B made the news in 1963 in *Record Mirror* (21 December 1963), p. 19, and (28 December 1963), p. 11.
75 G. P., 'Municipal News', *Stage and Television Today* (24 October 1963), p. 6.
76 Max Jones, 'London – It's the New Chicago!', *Melody Maker* (2 November 1963), p. 6.
77 'Jazz Clubs – London', *Melody Maker* (9 November 1963), p. 13.
78 'Jazz Clubs – London', *Melody Maker* (16 November 1963), p. 13.
79 'Jazz Clubs – London', *Melody Maker* (14 December 1963), p. 21, and (21 December 1963), p. 9.
80 'Jazz Clubs – London', *Melody Maker* (28 December 1963), p. 9.
81 Chris Roberts, 'The Heat's on Beat', *Melody Maker* (7 December 1963), p. 9.
82 Ibid.
83 Ibid.
84 Norman Jopling, 'Going Commercial? Rubbish . . .', *Record Mirror* (7 December 1963), p. 12.
85 Bob Dawbarn, 'The Year of Reckoning for Trad', *Melody Maker* (11 January 1964), p. 6.

86 Ibid.
87 'The Beat Pursuers', *Melody Maker* (11 January 1964), pp. 8–9.
88 'Mike Cotton Band Goes R&B', *Melody Maker* (29 February 1964), p. 8.
89 Ibid.
90 George Melly, *Owning-Up* (Harmondsworth, 1970), pp. 249–50.
91 Bob Dawbarn, 'Trad Survivors', *Melody Maker* (12 December 1964), p. 6.
92 Bob Dawbarn, 'Rhythm and Blues', *Melody Maker* (17 October 1964), pp. 10–11.

2 An ABC of R&B for the Purists and Bandwagon Jumpers Alike, 1964

1 Francis Wyndham, 'The Pretty Things', *Sunday Times Magazine* (12 July 1964), pp. 14–16.
2 Bob Dawbarn, 'Cyril Was *the* Man on Harmonica', *Melody Maker* (18 January 1964), p. 12.
3 Ibid.
4 Ibid.
5 'Cy Davies Dies', *Melody Maker* (18 January 1964), p. 4. His obituary: Dawbarn, 'Cyril Was *the* Man on Harmonica', p. 12.
6 Bill Carey, 'Leave the R&B Scene to the Purists', *Record Mirror* (25 January 1964), p. 6.
7 Ibid.
8 Ibid.
9 Ibid.
10 Ibid.
11 Ibid.
12 Ibid.
13 Ibid.
14 Ibid.
15 Ibid.
16 'Meet the Beat Group with a Difference', *Record Mirror* (8 February 1964), pp. 6–7.
17 Ibid. Sheffield's Dave Berry and the Cruisers were also telling a similar story to the Paramounts'. The Cruisers play, according to Berry 'an uncompromising rhythm and blues . . . it is not exactly pop music that we specialise in but it is very popular in Sheffield'. 'Sheffield the R&B City', *Record Mirror* (25 January 1964), p. 5.
18 Mick Jagger, 'The Top Spot? I Don't Care a Damn . . .', *Melody Maker* (11 July 1964), p. 3; Keith Richard, 'I'd Like to Forget About Juke Box Jury', *Melody Maker* (18 July 1964), p. 7.
19 Norman Mailer, 'The White Negro: Superficial Reflections on the Hipster', *Dissent* (Fall 1957).
20 'Kenny Talks Frankly on Jazz and R&B', *Record Mirror* (15 February 1964), p. 10.
21 Hohner advertisement, *Record Mirror* (29 February 1964), p. 12, and (7 March 1964), p. 3. The harmonica fad was covered six months later by Chris Roberts, 'Hip Harmonica!', *Melody Maker* (12 September 1964), p. 15.

22 Max Jones, 'Bilk on Beat', *Melody Maker* (11 July 1964), p. 11.
23 Ibid.
24 Bob Dawbarn, 'Barber Breaks New Ground', *Melody Maker* (12 September 1964), pp. 14–15.
25 Concert advertisement *Record Mirror* (15 February 1964), p. 12.
26 'Ottilie Patterson and Sonny Boy Williamson "Baby Please Don't Go"; (Columbia DB 7208) If you saw the old gnarled face of Sonny Boy Williamson breathing magic through his harmonica on television recently, then you'll need no urging to grab this record which has him blowing mouth organ while Miss Patterson sings. "Baby Please Don't Go", of course, is Williamson's own tune and Ottilie drives it characteristically. She's in power-pack form for the other deck too. Ivor Raymonde conducts an orchestral background for the couple, but personally I'd like to see someone repeat that bone-thudding bass fiddle accompaniment Chris Barber gave Sonny Boy on TV.' Dan Nicholl, 'Reviews', *Disc* (15 February 1964), p. 8.
27 Nigel Hunter, 'It's R&B Week', *Disc* (23 May 1964), p. 9.
28 'On the Jazz Beat!', *Jazz News and Reviews* (December 1963), p. 8.
29 Advertisement in *Record Mirror* (14 March 1964), p. 4.
30 Advertisements in *Record Mirror* (21 and 28 March 1964), p. 4.
31 Advertisements in *Record Mirror* (4 April 1964), p. 4.
32 The show was advertised in the *Liverpool Echo and Evening Express* (24 February 1964), p. 9.
33 Robert Bickford, 'Stand By for the Pretty Things', *Daily Mail* (3 April 1964), p. 10.
34 Ibid.
35 Ibid.
36 Ibid.
37 Bob Dawbarn, 'Massive Swing to R&B', *Melody Maker* (18 April 1964), pp. 8–9.
38 Ibid.
39 Ibid.
40 Ibid.
41 Hounslow's Them is featured in 'Undiscovered British Groups', *Boyfriend* (17 September 1964), p. 23.
42 Francis Hitching, 'Another Look Behind the Scenes of *Ready Steady Go!*', *Pop Weekly* (13 June 1964), n.p.
43 Ibid.
44 Ibid.
45 Ibid.
46 Guy Stevens, 'How I Write My Songs', *Record Mirror* (4 April 1964), p. 5.
47 Ibid.
48 Ian Pickstock, 'R&B with the Beatles . . .', *Jazzbeat* (February 1964), pp. 22–3.
49 Ibid.
50 Ibid.
51 Giorgio Gomelsky, 'The Rolling Stones Stake a Claim in the R&B Race', *Jazzbeat* (January 1964), pp. 22–3, and (February 1964), p. 24.
52 Ibid. (January), p. 22.

53 Ibid.
54 Ibid., p. 23.
55 Ibid.
56 Ibid.
57 Ibid. (February), p. 24.
58 Ibid.
59 Ibid.
60 Ibid.
61 Ibid.
62 Ibid.
63 Bob Dawbarn, 'Baldry Blasts R&B Greats', *Melody Maker* (30 May 1964), p. 7.
64 Mick Jagger, 'We're Not on the Wagon!', *Melody Maker* (21 March 1964), p. 3.
65 Ibid.
66 Ibid.
67 Ibid. As if countering himself that the real thing didn't sell, Jagger commented on Tommy Tucker's hit 'Hi-Heel Sneakers': 'Frankly, I didn't imagine a record like this would get in the chart over here. It's such a great, honest blues track that I can't understand why it's there in the hit parade. It's just amazing.' Ray Coleman, 'A Blues-Man Hits the Charts', *Melody Maker* (18 April 1964), p. 7.
68 Ray Coleman and Bob Dawbarn, 'Stones Stoned!', *Melody Maker* (23 May 1964), pp. 8–9.
69 Ibid.
70 Ibid.
71 Programme broadcast on 26 June 1964, Andy Neill, *Ready Steady Go! The Weekend Starts Here* (London, 2021), p. 70. *RSG*'s editor quoted from the programme for his weekly magazine column: Francis Hitching, 'The Question of R&B Crops up on *Ready Steady Go!*', *Pop Weekly* (8 August 1964), n.p.
72 Ibid.
73 Ibid.
74 Keith Richard, 'I'd Like to Forget about Juke Box Jury', *Melody Maker* (18 July 1964), p. 7.
75 'Chris Farlowe and the Thunderbirds', *Melody Maker* (2 January 1965), p. 9.
76 'The Animals', *Beat Instrumental* (October 1964), p. 6.
77 'Eleven Blues Stars for British Tour', *Melody Maker* (12 September 1964), p. 5.
78 Ibid.
79 'Top U.S. Stars Storm In', *Melody Maker* (24 October 1964), p. 1.
80 'Mailbag', *Melody Maker* (24 October 1964), p. 16.
81 Ibid.
82 Ibid.
83 Ibid.
84 Bob Dawbarn, 'Bored Mann', *Melody Maker* (31 October 1964), p. 3.
85 'R&B Quiz', *Melody Maker* (31 October 1964), p. 7.
86 Max Jones and Bob Dawbarn, 'ABC of R&B', *Melody Maker* (12 December 1964), pp. 3 and 15.
87 'You're Telling Us', *Rave* (1 September 1964), p. 47.
88 Peter Jones, 'Mickey Finn's East End Image', *Record Mirror* (18 April 1964), p. 10.

89 For the full story of the band, see Brian Neavyn, 'The Mickey Finn', *Ugly Things*, 39 (Spring/Summer 2015), pp. 41–55, and addendum: 'Mickey Finn and the Blue Men', *Ugly Things*, 40 (Fall/Winter 2015), pp. 97–9.
90 Jones, 'Mickey Finn's East End Image', p. 10.
91 Mickey Finn scored a mention when the Jamaican sound was covered by Chris Roberts in 'Blue Beat Breaks Through', *Melody Maker* (25 April 1964), n.p.
92 Charles Greville, 'It's Just Fab, Man', *Daily Mail* (2 March 1964), p. 4.
93 'Are the Stones Going Too Far?', *Beat Monthly* (March 1964), p. 6.
94 Ibid.
95 Albert Hand and David Cardwell, 'What Is Rhythm and Blues?', *Pop Weekly* (21 March 1964), p. 3.
96 Ian Dove, 'Why Elvis Failed to Start R&B Boom', *New Musical Express* (24 April 1964), p. 14.
97 Ibid.
98 Ibid.
99 Ibid.
100 Block advertisement in *New Musical Express* (27 March 1964), p. 12.
101 Peter Jones, 'R&B and Me', *Record Mirror* (28 March 1964), p. 12.
102 Pete Goodman, 'Teens Impressed Chuck Berry', *Beat Instrumental* (October 1964), p. 14.
103 David Griffiths, 'Georgie Hits Back', *Record Mirror* (11 April 1964), p. 10.
104 Ibid.
105 Quotes from the promotional leaflet were used verbatim by Peter Jones, 'The Feeling's There', *Record Mirror* (31 October 1964), p. 14. The compleat leaflet is reproduced in the booklet accompanying the CD set *Rod Stewart, 1964–1969* (NMC, 1999).
106 'Blues Beat', *Jazzbeat* (November 1964), p. 11.
107 Jerry Wexler, 'Rhythm and Blues in 1950', *Saturday Review* (24 June 1950), p. 49.
108 Ibid.
109 Ibid.
110 Ibid.
111 Ray Coleman, 'Just What Is R&B?', *Melody Maker* (9 May 1964), p. 7.
112 On this final point see also Chris Roberts, 'To Be or Not to R&B', *Melody Maker* (29 August 1964), p. 7. The question was still open to answers when posed by Bob Dawbarn's two-page investigation 'Rhythm and Blues', *Melody Maker* (17 October 1964), pp. 10–11.
113 'R&B Poll Results', *Record Mirror* (25 April 1964), p. 4.
114 Ibid.
115 Mick Jagger, 'The Top Spot? I Don't Care a Damn . . .', *Melody Maker* (11 July 1964), p. 3.
116 Ibid.
117 Ibid.
118 Ibid.
119 Bob Dawbarn, 'Where Every Harmonica Is Minted from Gold . . .', *Melody Maker* (17 October 1964), p. 10.

3 Moving Like a Crazy Caterpillar Fed on Pep Pills, 1964

1 Charles Greville, 'It's Just Fab, Man', *Daily Mail* (2 March 1964), p. 4.
2 Ibid.
3 Ibid.
4 Ibid.
5 Ibid.
6 Mike Grant, 'Starbeat', *Rave* (1 June 1964), p. 44.
7 Ibid.
8 Neil E. Slaven, 'The Mystery That Is Sonny Boy', R&B *Monthly*, 3 (April 1964), pp. 2–4.
9 Neil E. Slaven, 'The Yardbirds: Eric Clapton', R&B *Monthly*, 3 (April 1964), pp. 9–10.
10 Ibid.
11 Ibid.
12 Ibid.
13 Neil E. Slaven, 'The Yardbirds: Keith Relf', *R&B Monthly*, 4 (May 1964), pp. 5–6.
14 Neil E. Slaven, 'The Yardbirds: Chris Dreja', *R&B Monthly*, 5 (June 1964), pp. 10–11.
15 Neil E. Slaven, 'The Yardbirds: Paul Samwell-Smith and Jim McCarty', *R&B Monthly*, 6 (July 1964), pp. 10–11.
16 The contract was put up for sale on eBay UK, August 2022.
17 Advertisement in *Record Mirror* (16 May 1964), p. 14.
18 'The Beat Battle Is On', *Melody Maker* (2 May 1964), pp. 8–9.
19 Maureen Cleave, 'Disc Date: The Yardbirds: Well, They've Got a Bearded Russian Manager', *Evening Standard* (23 May 1964), p. 7.
20 Ibid.
21 Ibid.
22 'Records', *Warrington Guardian* (28 May 1964), p. 6.
23 'They're Being Mobbed', *Disc Weekly* (3 April 1965), p. 8.
24 Ibid.
25 The Pretty Things questionnaire, *Disc* (14 November 1964), p. 13.
26 Cleave, 'Disc Date', p. 7.
27 Ibid.
28 Ibid.
29 Ibid.
30 Ibid.
31 Reproduced in Norman Jopling, *Shake It Up Baby! Notes from a Pop Music Reporter, 1961–1972* (self-published, 2015), pp. 73–6.
32 Norman Jopling, 'The Blueswailers with Mod Appeal', *Record Mirror* (30 May 1964), p. 11.
33 June Southworth, 'Hi-Fab!', *Fabulous* (25 February 1964), p. 3.
34 'For Animal Lovers and (Yard) Bird Watchers', *Fabulous* (20 June 1964), p. 25.
35 June Southworth, 'London Gets the Blues in the Night', *Fabulous* (27 June 1964), p. 6.
36 Ibid.

37 Ibid.
38 Ian Dove, 'I Couldn't Afford to Sign Stones!', *New Musical Express* (3 July 1964), p. 14. It's unknown if the film still exists, but some production images from the shoot are in circulation.
39 Ibid.
40 Ibid.
41 Ibid.
42 Francis Hitching, 'Another Look Behind the Scenes of *Ready Steady Go!*', *Pop Weekly* (13 June 1964), n.p.
43 Ibid.
44 Ibid.
45 Ibid.
46 Pete Goodman, 'Yardbirds Next', *Beat Instrumental* (September 1964), n.p.
47 Ibid.
48 Ibid.
49 Ibid.
50 Il Rondo block advertisement in *Leicester Mercury* (15 July 1964), p. 3.
51 'Record Column', *Herald Express* (24 July 1964), p. 12.
52 Block advertisement, *Herald Express* (30 July 1964), p. 6.
53 Roger Bennett, 'The Pop World', *Evening Post* (28 May 1964), p. 34.
54 Bob Turner, 'Disc Date', *Runcorn Weekly News* (14 May 1964), p. 2.
55 'Record Review', *Thanet Times* (12 May 1964), p. 8.
56 'Record Review', *Wishaw Press and Advertiser* (8 May 1964), p. 4.
57 Ibid.
58 Patrick Doncaster, 'Discs', *Daily Mirror* (30 April 1964), p. 21.
59 *Record Mirror* (23 May 1964), p. 7.
60 'Singles in Brief', *Record Mirror* (2 May 1964), p. 13.
61 'Reviews in Short', *Disc* (2 May 1964), p. 10.
62 Ray Coleman, 'Pop Singles', *Melody Maker* (2 May 1964), p. 11.
63 See Andy Neill, *Ready Steady Go! The Weekend Starts Here* (London, 2021).
64 The Yardbirds television appearances are listed in Greg Russo, *Yardbirds: The Ultimate Rave-Up*, 7th edn (New York, 2022), pp. 253–5.
65 Ibid.
66 'Yardbirds Join Kramer', *New Musical Express* (10 July 1964), p. 8.
67 'Who's Your Type?', *Rave* (1 September 1964), p. 36.
68 Mike Grant, 'Starbeat', *Rave* (1 June 1964), p. 44.
69 'Our Top Tub Thumpers', *Rave* (1 October 1964), p. 62.
70 Chris Roberts, 'We're a Sort of R&B Group', *Melody Maker* (8 August 1964), p. 8.
71 Ibid.
72 Ibid.
73 Ibid.
74 Ibid.
75 'Stones – Open-Air', *Record Mirror* (18 July 1964), p. 5.
76 'Yardbird Relfe Quits Hospital', *Melody Maker* (12 September 1964), p. 4.
77 Ibid.
78 Ibid.

79 Maureen Cleave, 'Yardbird Singer Quits Hospital', *Evening Standard* (3 September 1964), p. 14.
80 Maureen Cleave, 'Yardbirds' Singer Is back', *Evening Standard* (21 September 1964), p. 11.
81 Ibid.
82 Ian Gilchrist, 'When a Yardbird Collapsed', *Rave* (1 November 1964), p. 22; Peter Jones, 'We Nearly Packed It In', *Record Mirror* (28 November 1964), n.p.
83 'Billy J., the Kinks, Etc. Had the Girls Screaming', *Grantham Journal* (16 October 1964), p. 4.
84 Ibid.
85 N.C.J., 'Exciting Birds', *Melody Maker* (31 October 1964), p. 4.
86 Ibid.
87 Ibid.
88 Patrick Doncaster, 'Discs', *Daily Mirror* (27 October 1964), p. 21.
89 Ibid.
90 Ibid.
91 Roger Bennett, 'Top Pops', *Evening Post* (7 November 1964), p. 4.
92 Ibid.
93 Ibid.
94 Ibid.
95 Ibid.
96 'New One From "Birds"', *Record Mirror* (17 October 1964), p. 9.
97 Singles reviews, *Pop Weekly* (31 October 1964), n.p.
98 Singles reviews, *Disc* (24 October 1964), p. 11.
99 'Yardbirds: Soon to Hit the Sky', *Boyfriend* (2 January 1965), p. 21.
100 'Jimmy Savile: Blind Date', *Melody Maker* (31 October 1964), p. 15.
101 Chris Welch, 'Oh No! Not a Hit Disc!', *Melody Maker* (7 November 1964), p. 3.
102 'Yardbirds', *Pop Weekly* (5 December 1964), n.p.; 'You Pick the Next Rave-Wave', *Rave* (1 June 1964), p. 62; 'They've Hit the Top', *Rave* (1 August 1964), p. 6.
103 'Yardbirds', *Pop Weekly* (5 December 1964), n.p.
104 'Yardbirds', *Pop Weekly* (12 December 1964), n.p.
105 In a comment on Howlin' Wolf's 'Smokestack Lightning' hitting the top spot in their first R&B poll, *Record Mirror*'s reporter noted that it was 'a blues standard that is performed by almost everybody on the British scene – no-one who ever saw the late Cyril Davies performing it at the Marquee sessions will be able to forget the atmosphere and excitement he generated on Chester Burnette's song' – 'All About the Poll Results', *Record Mirror* (25 April 1964), p. 5. 'Smokestack' was released in the UK as part of Pye International's R&B series and got to no. 42 in the Record Retailer chart on 27 June 1964.
106 George Melly, *Owning-Up* (Harmondsworth, 1965), p. 145.
107 Ray Coleman, 'Harmonicas? Simple, Says Mick Jagger', *Melody Maker* (13 March 1965), p. 7.
108 Letters, 'Surprise?', *Melody Maker* (5 June 1965), p. 16.
109 Ray Coleman, 'The Week's LPs', *Melody Maker* (19 December 1964), p. 20.

110 Russo, *Yardbirds: The Ultimate Rave-Up*, p. 240.
111 John Peel, 'Pop Music: Clapton', *The Listener* (27 September 1973), pp. 41–2; 'Pop Music: 1. A Short History of the Form', *The Listener* (11 June 1970), pp. 28–30.
112 Ibid.
113 'Review: *Rhythm and Blues at the Flamingo*', *Record Mirror* (7 March 1964), p. 10.
114 The album was released in the UK in February 1964, a month before the Marquee engagement.
115 Rexy Regan, 'Spins for You', *Boyfriend* (9 January 1965), p. 22.
116 Ibid.
117 Welch, 'Oh No! Not a Hit Disc!'
118 Ibid.
119 Richard Green, 'Portrait of a Year', *Record Mirror* (19 December 1964), p. 5.
120 David Griffiths, 'Tribute to the Stones', *Record Mirror* (19 December 1964), p. 4.
121 'New Faces for 1965', *Melody Maker* (26 December 1964), p. 9.
122 Mike Grant, 'Starbeat', *Rave* (1 January 1964), p. 12.
123 'New Faces for 1965'.

4 Maximum R&B: Selling (Out) the Authentic, 1965

1 Charles Greville, 'Where the Debs Play', *Daily Mail* (3 February 1965), p. 4.
2 Keith Read, 'The Beat Page', *Kentish Express* (19 March 1965), p. 17.
3 'Yardbirds Breakthrough', *Beat Instrumental* (April 1965), p. 21.
4 Ibid.
5 'Other People', *Daily Mail* (5 March 1965), p. 4.
6 'Disc Pick: Singles "For Your Love"', *Daily Mail* (5 March 1965), p. 12.
7 'Yardbird Leaving', *Disc Weekly* (6 March 1965), p. 2.
8 Ibid.
9 'New Yardbird', *New Musical Express* (26 March 1965), p. 7.
10 Chris Welch, 'Will the Yardbirds Make It with This?', *Melody Maker* (27 February 1965), p. 16.
11 Ibid.
12 Ibid.
13 Ibid.
14 'Pick of the Singles', *Melody Maker* (6 March 1965), p. 15
15 'Clapton Quits . . .', *Melody Maker* (13 March 1965), p. 5.
16 Ibid.
17 Ibid.
18 'Yardbird Leaves Group', *Record Mirror* (6 March 1965), p. 5.
19 Ibid. The Authentics were still advertised as playing the Crawdaddy clubs into mid-March.
20 'Yardbirds Breakthough', *Beat Instrumental* (April 1965).
21 Ibid.
22 'The Yardbirds Hop In . . .', *Kensington Post* (1 January 1965), p. 8.
23 *Glamorgan Gazette* (8 January 1965), p. 9.

24 Sheena Mackay, 'Yardbirds, Definitely All at Sea', *Fabulous* (5 September 1964), pp. 10–11; John McGowan, 'Yardbirds Turn Cavemen!', *Fabulous* (27 February 1965), pp. 22–3.
25 In his personal diary for 1965, the Birds guitarist, Ronnie Wood, recorded that he had heard the news, at second hand of Clapton's departure on 24 February. Ronnie Wood, *How Can It Be? A Rock and Roll Diary* (Guildford, 2015), n.p.
26 'Ex-Yardbird Joins Mayall', *Record Mirror* (17 April 1965), p. 5.
27 In a March 1970 profile of Clapton, the journalist Philip Norman broke with the received narrative when he wrote that the guitarist left the Yardbirds principally due to the attempts that 'were made to discipline their behaviour'. Philip Norman, 'The Great God Clapton', *Sunday Times Magazine* (1 March 1970), pp. 87, 89, 91.
28 Maureen Cleave, 'Success Hits the Yardbirds', *Evening Standard* (3 April 1965), p. 7.
29 Ibid.
30 Ibid.
31 Ibid.
32 Ibid.
33 Virginia Ironsides, 'In Zip the Yardbirds with a Brand New Beat', *Daily Mail* (18 March 1965), p. 14.
34 Ibid.
35 Ibid.
36 Nick Jones, 'Yardbirds – Why We Went Commercial', *Melody Maker* (17 July 1965), p. 7.
37 Ibid.
38 Ibid.
39 Ibid.
40 Ibid.
41 Derek Johnson, 'Singles', *New Musical Express* (5 March 1965), p. 4.
42 Bob Farmer, 'In the Groove', *Gloucester Citizen* (4 March 1965), p. 11.
43 Ibid.
44 Charles Fiske, 'Fiske's Discs', *Newcastle Evening Chronicle* (6 March 1965), p. 11.
45 Doris Comer, 'In the Browserie', *Faversham News* (12 March 1965), p. 3.
46 'Spotlight on Modern Youth', *Tewkesbury Register* (26 March 1965), p. 3.
47 'R&B Record Review', *Port Talbot Guardian* (2 April 1965), p. 14.
48 Ibid.
49 Jill Hansen, 'Jill's Jury', *Coventry Standard* (18 March 1965), p. 21.
50 'Cliff in "Top Pop" Riddle', *Daily Mirror* (6 April 1965), p. 1.
51 Penny Valentine, 'Singles', *Disc Weekly* (13 March 1965), p. 10.
52 Neil Jones, 'Bird Talk . . .', *Disc Weekly* (20 March 1965), p. 3.
53 'WHO – and Why', *Melody Maker* (20 March 1965), p. 7.
54 Ibid.
55 Ibid.
56 Ibid.
57 Kevin Swift, 'The Spectacular Who', *Beat Instrumental* (May 1965), p. 9.
58 Ibid.
59 Ibid.

60 Ibid.
61 Ibid.
62 Ibid.
63 Ibid.
64 Ibid.
65 Ibid.
66 Peter Jones, 'How High Will These Numbers Go?', *Record Mirror* (11 July 1964), p. 10.
67 Ibid.
68 Ibid.
69 Ibid.
70 Norrie Drummond, 'The Who – One but Four Films', *New Musical Express* (23 April 1965), p. 11.
71 Ibid.
72 '"Who" Filmed for France', *Record Mirror* (13 March 1965), p. 5.
73 'Third Time Lucky Name', *New Musical Express* (26 February 1965), p. 13.
74 'The Who', *Music Echo* (3 April 1965), p. 6.
75 Richard Green, 'The Group That Slaughters Their Amplifiers . . .', *Record Mirror* (3 April 1965), p. 9.
76 Ibid.
77 Paul Gorman, *Reasons to Be Cheerful: The Life and Work of Barney Bubbles* (London, 2010), pp. 15–16.
78 George Rooney, 'R&B Won't Last Forever Say Them', *Record Mirror* (2 February 1965), p. 5.
79 Norman Jopling, '"We Aim to Excite!" . . . Say the Art Woods', *Record Mirror* (5 June 1965), p. 5.
80 Ibid.
81 Ibid.
82 Pete Goodman, 'Keith Moon – Player of the Month', *Beat Instrumental* (July 1965), p. 6.
83 Ibid.
84 Ibid.
85 'The Who', *Beat Instrumental* (June 1965), p. 28.
86 Richard Green, 'A Disturbing Group', *Record Mirror* (6 March 1965), p. 2.
87 Nick Jones, 'Caught in the Act: Who Must Be Seen', *Melody Maker* (17 April 1965), p. 4.
88 Green, 'A Disturbing Group', p. 2.
89 Jones, 'Caught in the Act', p. 4.
90 Drummond, 'The Who – One but Four Films', p. 11.
91 'Who Make Drastic Policy Changes' *Melody Maker* (17 July 1965), p. 5.
92 Rod Harrod, 'What's Popping', *Disc Weekly* (31 July 1965), p. 13.
93 Ibid.

5 The Futuristic Sound of the Yardbirds, (1975 in) 1965

1 'Hamish I View!', *Music Echo* (27 March 1965), p. 3.
2 Alan Smith, 'Yardbirds Didn't Ape Stones', *New Musical Express* (2 April 1965), p. 8.

3 Ibid.
4 'Cathy McGowan's Diary', *Disc Weekly* (30 October 1965), p. 3.
5 Michael Aldred, 'Aldred's Eye View', *Music Echo* (20 March 1965), p. 4.
6 'Yardbirds to Record EP', *New Musical Express* (12 March 1965), p. 8.
7 'U.S. Group Joins Yardbirds Tour', *Disc Weekly* (10 April 1965), p. 2.
8 Penny Valentine 'Fans Go Kink Crazy!', *Disc Weekly* (8 May 1965), p. 4.
9 Penny Valentine, 'It's All in Fun Says Jeff', *Disc Weekly* (8 May 1965), p. 4. Mike Ledgerwood, 'Kink Mick Talks', *Disc Weekly* (29 May 1965), p. 6.
10 'New Yardbirds single . . .', *New Musical Express* (23 April 1965), pp. 8–9.
11 Ibid.
12 June Southworth, 'Black Tuesday with the Yardbirds', *Fabulous* (6 June 1965), p. 18. A full-page colour pin-up from the shoot was printed in the 17 July 1965 issue of *Fabulous*. Beyond the usual tidbits of Yardbirds news and stories, the band were covered again, this time with a photoshoot at Speaker's Corner in the summer. 'The Yardbirds Speak Up', *Fabulous* (21 August 1965), n.p. The band were given a double-page Fiona Adams pin-up in the 18 September 1965 edition and another image from the Marylebone Goods Yard was used as a single-page colour pin-up on 4 December 1965.
13 Doug Perry, 'My Kind of Girl', *Fabulous* (28 August 1965), p. 6.
14 'Personality Page', *Boyfriend* (18 December 1965), p. 2.
15 'In Step . . . Out of the Crowd', *Boyfriend* (October 9, 1965), p. 2.
16 Ibid.
17 Ibid.
18 Keith Altham, 'Yardbirds Don't Like Own Hits', *New Musical Express* (25 June 1965), p. 8.
19 Ibid.
20 Ibid.
21 'Yardbirds Breakthrough', *Beat Instrumental* (April 1965), p. 21.
22 Richard Green, 'We'll Play More Pop', *Record Mirror* (20 March 1965), p. 4.
23 Ibid. He's much more positive about the Tridents elsewhere: 'Hit It Off? Of Course We Do! New Yardbird Jeff Beck . . .', *Disc Weekly* (27 March 1965), p. 8.
24 Ibid. On their first outing to France to promote their debut EP, the Who were 'invited to play a *musique concrete* event at Le Club au Golf Drouot . . . organised by "Le Club des Rockers"'. Andy Neill and Matt Kent, *Anyway Anyhow Anywhere: The Complete Chronicle of the Who, 1958–1978* (London, 2007), p. 84.
25 Richard Green, 'The Yardbirds and Their Experiment in Sound', *Record Mirror* (17 July 1965), p. 3.
26 Ibid.
27 Mike Ledgerwood, 'Jeff Beck: The Honest Truth', *Disc Weekly* (10 July 1965), p. 3. Asked again for his opinion on the Who, he said, 'I like them very much. Both the Who and the Yardbirds share an interest in producing electronic sound.' 'They're All Raving About the Who', *Disc Weekly* (24 July 1965), p. 6.
28 'Top of the Pops', *Disc Weekly* (10 April 1965), p. 10.
29 'Pace Hots Up . . .', *Melody Maker* (3 April 1965), p. 4.
30 'Who Follow the Yardbirds', *Melody Maker* (3 April 1965), pp. 8–9.

31 Ibid.
32 Ibid.
33 Keith Altham, 'Question-Time with the Yardbirds', *New Musical Express* (9 July 1965), p. 10.
34 Ibid. Beck was still listing the Who as among his favourites in September: 'The Beat Elite: Guitarists', *Melody Maker* (18 September 1965), p. 9.
35 In one interview, Samwell-Smith cited 'What's New Pussycat?' as a stellar recording (Richard Green, 'Nothing Religious About Our Hit', *Record Mirror* (10 October 1965), pp. 8–9), and in the other, 'Trains and Boats and Planes', which he thought had the same circular structure as 'Still I'm Sad': 'It kind of goes up and around and then back to where it started.' 'Yardbirds's A+B Equals HIT!', *Disc Weekly* (9 October 1965), p. 2.
36 'The Who: Every So Often . . .', *Melody Maker* (5 June 1965), p. 7.
37 Ibid.
38 Ibid.
39 Ibid.
40 Ibid. The following month, after an irate letter from a reader dismissing the Who and their Pop-art aspirations ('Mail Bag: Pop Art? A Farce', *Melody Maker* (26 June 1965), p. 16), Nick Jones covered the topic in more detail: 'Well What Is Pop Art?', *Melody Maker* (3 July 1965), p. 11.
41 Richard Green 'The Who's Pop-Art Disc', *Record Mirror* (22 May 1965), p. 12.
42 Richard Green, 'Their Pop-Art Disc Is Like Fly Paper', *Record Mirror* (12 June 1965), p. 6.
43 Ibid.
44 Ibid.
45 Ibid.
46 Ibid.
47 Ibid.
48 Ibid.
49 Letters, 'Pop 'N', Who', *Record Mirror* (3 July 1965), p. 2.
50 'Yardbirds: Twelve-Bar Blues Are Great but Not Forever!', *Melody Maker* (26 June 1965), p. 8.
51 For a contemporary profile of Gouldman, see J. D., 'New Hitmaker Started on a Quid Guitar!', *Melody Maker* (18 September 1965), p. 21.
52 Nick Jones, 'Yardbirds – Why We Went Commercial', *Melody Maker* (17 July 1965), p. 7.
53 Derek Johnson, 'Singles', *New Musical Express* (4 June 1965), p. 4.
54 'Stars of Beat', *Melody Maker* (3 April 1965), p. 8.
55 *Melody Maker* (7 August 1965), p. 2.
56 Ibid., pp. 8–9.
57 Ibid.
58 Ibid.
59 Ibid., p. 16.
60 'Record Review by Marc Bölan', *London Life* (19 February 1966), p. 59.
61 'Mailbag', *Melody Maker* (25 September 1965), p. 20.
62 L. R. Hill, Peterborough 'Letters', *Music Echo* (18 December 1965), p. 23.
63 'The Quiet Revolution', *Melody Maker* (16 October 1965), p. 7.

64 Mike Ledgerwood, 'The Who: The Honest Truth', *Disc Weekly* (3 July 1965), p. 9. For Townshend's references to jazz guitarists, see 'The Beat Elite: Guitarists', *Melody Maker* (18 September 1965), p. 9: '"I don't use a guitar as a guitar, and if it makes sounds unlike that of a guitar, I don't care. On stage I show my lack of regard for the guitar, by hurling it about, I'm just using it to get across to the audience! . . . Now I listen to Kenny Burrel, Wes Montgomery, most of the guitarists' guitarists, although I can't use anything they do." To promote his vicious style Pete plays through two 100-watt amps, with two cabinets containing eight 12-inch speakers each.'
65 'ESP's Marquee Happening', *Melody Maker* (22 January 1966), p. 4.
66 A published report from the Beachcomber is reproduced in Joe McMichael and 'Irish' Jack Lyons, *The Who Concert File* (London, 1997), p. 38.
67 Bob Dawbarn, 'Happenings', *Melody Maker* (5 February 1966), p. 6.
68 Alana Freeman 'Five Hearts Full of Soul', *Rave* (1 November 1965), pp. 36–9.
69 Ibid.
70 *Melody Maker* (7 August 1965), p. 11.
71 Penny Valentine, 'Singles', *Disc Weekly* (7 August 1965), p. 11.
72 Mike Chamberlain, 'Singles', *Music Echo* (7 August 1965), p. 2.
73 Richard Green, 'We Don't Copy the Who', *Record Mirror* (11 September 1965), p. 2.
74 Ibid.
75 Penny Valentine, 'Quick Spins', *Disc Weekly* (23 October 1965), p. 15.
76 Ibid. (6 November 1965), p. 15.
77 'Carnaby Get in Top Gear', *Disc Weekly* (20 November 1965), p. 2.
78 Ibid.
79 Norman Jopling and Peter Jones, 'Singles Reviewed', *Record Mirror* (21 August 1965), p. 9.
80 Norman Jopling and Peter Jones, 'Singles Reviewed', *Record Mirror* (5 June 1965), p. 13.
81 Mike Ledgerwood, 'Keith Relf: The Honest Truth', *Disc Weekly* (1 May 1965), p. 4.
82 '"Oriental" Yardbirds', *Beat Instrumental* (May 1965), p. 22.
83 John Emry, 'Jeff Beck Supplies . . .', *Beat Instrumental* (June 1965), p. 38.
84 Ibid.
85 Derek Johnson, 'Singles', *New Musical Express* (30 July 1965), p. 4.
86 Penny Valentine, 'Singles', *Disc Weekly* (5 June 1965), p. 10.
87 Ibid.
88 Lois Benjamin, 'Have You Heard?', *Ladies' Home Journal* (April 1966), p. 16.
89 'Dispute Hold Up Kinks Disc', *New Musical Express* (9 July 1965), p. 7; 'Kinks Record Row Settled', *New Musical Express* (16 July 1965), p. 7.
90 Mike Chamberlain, 'Singles', *Music Echo* (31 July 1965), p. 2.
91 Pules Nurgbut, 'Mailbag', *Melody Maker* (4 June 1966), p. 24. Writing about the drone and the search for 'sonic oblivion', Harry Sword summarizes the impact on rock musicians: 'Whether or not bands fully understood the spiritual background – and most didn't – the effect was seismic. Sitar and tanpura drones were soon found in everything from brutal south London acid blues (the Pretty Things) to wide-open psychedelic folk (Incredible String

Band), American primitive rumblings (Sandy Bull and John Fahey) and bombastic hard rock (Led Zeppelin).' Harry Sword, *Monolithic Undertow: In Search of Sonic Oblivion* (London, 2021), p. 115.
92 Bob Dawbarn, 'Donovan: Now for the Comeback', *Melody Maker* (4 June 1966), p. 3.
93 Charles Greville, 'How They Got That Sound', *Daily Mail* (1 June 1966), p. 4.
94 A clip from the show is readily available on YouTube and was written about by C. B. in 'Apprehensive East Faces Swinging West', *Illustrated London News* (18 June 1966), p. 22.
95 The band discuss the recording of the EP – although not the song choice – in 'Yardbirds' Hit Written by Mockingbird!', *Disc Weekly* (10 April 1965), p. 16.
96 Joel Selvin, *Here Comes the Night: The Dark Soul of Bert Berns* (Berkeley, CA, 2014), pp. 227–31.
97 Jonathan King, 'Singles', *Disc Weekly* (21 August 1965), p. 11.
98 Keith Relf, 'Hit Talk: Yardbird's Eye View', *Disc Weekly* (6 November 1965), p. 16.
99 'Pop Eps', *Melody Maker* (28 August 1965), p. 12.
100 Penny Valentine, 'Yardbirds Try for an Indian Sound', *Disc Weekly* (19 June 1965), p. 9.
101 'Yardbirds Hat-Trick', *Disc Weekly* (7 August 1965), p. 3.
102 Brian Clark, 'Yardbirds Session', *Beat Instrumental* (October 1965), p. 32.
103 Ibid.
104 Ibid.
105 '*Rave*'s Whether Chart', *Rave* (1 November 1965), p. 45.
106 John Sandilands, 'Discs', *Daily Mail* (18 September 1965), p. 7.
107 Derek Johnson, 'Singles', *New Musical Express* (24 September 1965), p. 4.
108 Penny Valentine 'Singles', *Disc Weekly* (2 October 1965), p. 11.
109 Richard Green, 'Nothing Religious about Our Hit', *Record Mirror* (21 October 1965), pp. 8–9.
110 'Yardbirds Trip Delayed', *Melody Maker* (28 August 1965), p. 5.
111 'Names in the News', *Melody Maker* (4 September 1965), p. 15.
112 'Yardbirds Disc Delayed', *Record Mirror* (28 August 1965), p. 5.
113 Richard Green, 'We'll Cut Out Raving', *Record Mirror* (4 September 1965), p. 1.
114 Ibid.
115 Ibid.
116 Greg Russo, *Yardbirds: The Ultimate Rave-Up*, 7th edn (New York, 2022), p. 268.
117 Richard Green, 'Yardbirds Phone from a Raving Party', *Record Mirror* (18 September 1965), p. 3.
118 Louise Criscione, 'Yardbirds Wail', *KRLA the Beat* (9 October 1965), p. 3.
119 'Unwanted Visitors', *KRLA the Beat* (2 October 1965), p. 2. They had first made a featured appearance in the paper the previous month: 'Yardbirds' Faith Gave Them "Soul"', *KRLA the Beat* (4 September 1965), p. 8.
120 See, for example, Gomelsky, quoted in David French, *Heart Full of Soul: Keith Relf of the Yardbirds* (Jefferson, MO, 2020), p. 53.
121 'The Raver's U.S. Cable', *Rave* (1 November 1965), p. 48.

122 John Emry, 'Yardbirds Move On', *Beat Instrumental* (January 1966), p. 8.
123 Ibid.
124 Ibid., p. 10.
125 Derek Taylor, 'Hollywood Calling!', *Disc Weekly* (4 December 1965), p. 8.
126 'Yardbirds New Album', *Record Mirror* (30 September 1965), p. 5.
127 'The Yardbirds Have Finished . . .', *Beat Instrumental* (November 1965), p. 28.
128 'The Quiet Revolution', *Melody Maker* (16 October 1965), p. 7.
129 Ibid.
130 Ibid.
131 Ibid.
132 'Yardbirds Hope . . .', *Melody Maker* (30 October 1965), p. 4.
133 Ibid.
134 Alan Walsh, 'Sound Seekers', *Melody Maker* (6 November 1965), pp. 10–11.
135 Ibid.
136 'Who's Generation', *Disc Weekly* (20 November 1965), p. 7.
137 On release, 'My Generation' was often billed a 'protest', number, see, for example, Penny Valentine, 'Singles', *Disc Weekly* (30 October 1965), p. 11.
138 Richard Green, "The Guy Who Sings . . .', *Record Mirror* (6 November 1965), p. 16.
139 Ibid.
140 Ibid.
141 'Yardbird Reply', *Record Mirror* (13 November 1965), p. 4.
142 Roger Daltrey, 'Hit Talk', *Disc Weekly* (27 November 1965), p. 12.
143 'Clickety Click', *Rave* (1 January 1966), p. 8.
144 Richard Green "I Hate It . . . It's Rubbish . . . It's Crap', *Record Mirror* (4 December 1965), pp. 8 and 10.
145 At one point 'I'm a Man' was in contention with the Townshend composition 'Circles' to be the B-side of 'My Generation', in the event a cover of James Brown's 'Shout and Shimmy' went on the bottom deck. 'Who to Issue Record', *Melody Maker* (16 October 1965), p. 5.
146 'Out of the Bag!' *Record Mirror* (21 October 1965), p. 5. The 'other' marriage was Chris and Pat Dreja, nineteen and twenty years old, respectively. They had met at a London beat club eighteen months previously. She was an American who had come to London to work: 'I wasn't a fan,' said Pat, 'I prefer jazz to beat music and I hadn't even heard of the Yardbirds when I met Chris.' *The People* (10 October 1965), p. 11. Pat's view on the marriage was covered by June Southworth, 'A Yardbird's Nest', *Fabulous* (12 March 1966), p. 11. See also 'Yardbirds Get the Birds!', *Disc Weekly* (16 October 1965), p. 2, which covers Pat and Chris's marriage, notes Relf was going steady for more than seven months with April Liversidge. Keith and April were married at the end of February 1966, as reported in *Melody Maker* (5 February 1966), p. 2. *Disc Weekly* had earlier reported that Samwell-Smith was seeing sixteen-year-old Sue Stiles-Allen, whom he'd been dating also for seven months. 'Missing – One Yardbird!', *Disc Weekly* (28 August 1965), p. 3.
147 'Yardbirds and Mann Dates', *Record Mirror* (21 October 1965), p. 5; 'Manfred, Yardbirds Head Major Tour', *New Musical Express* (15 October 1965), p. 8.

148 'Scaffold Link-Up Manfred – Yardbirds Tour', *Music Echo* (20 November 1965), p. 9.
149 Alan Smith, 'Our Emotional Experiences in Sound!', *New Musical Express* (22 October 1965), p. 12.
150 Ibid.
151 Ibid.
152 Ibid.
153 'Mann Tour – New Script', *Record Mirror* (27 November 1965), p. 5.
154 R. N., 'Mann–Yardbirds Tour – Dynamic', *New Musical Express* (27 November 1965), p. 5.
155 'All On at Once in Zany Show', *Derby Evening Telegraph* (22 November 1965), p. 10.
156 N.E.A., 'On Tour', *Disc Weekly* (27 November 1965), p. 4.
157 S. C., 'Caught in the Act', *Melody Maker* (4 December 1965), p. 4.
158 'But Still They Screamed', *Evening Post* (4 December 1965), p. 16.
159 Ibid.
160 Caroline Silver, *The Pop Makers: British Rock 'n', Roll: The Sound, the Scene, the Action* (New York, 1966), p. 82.
161 Ibid., pp. 89–90.
162 Ibid., pp. 91 and 93.
163 Smith, 'Our Emotional Experiences in Sound!', p. 12.
164 Jane Relf, 'My Brother Keith', *Record Mirror* (30 September 1965), p. 7.
165 Dawn James, 'Five Square Yardbirds', *Rave* (1 December 1965), pp. 31–4. *Rave* magazine played on Keith's love of the pastoral: 'Keith was silent for a moment, taking in the view and the atmosphere of the river. "I feel free here, I enjoy the quietness of a river. This and music are the good things in life."' ('Yardbirds Don't Fly', *Rave* (1 July 1965), p. 35.)
166 Ibid. (July).
167 Ibid.
168 Ibid.
169 Ibid.
170 Peter Jones, 'Nico Leads Andrew's Off-Beat Company', *Record Mirror* (28 August 1965), p. 6.

6 Going Way-Out (and Then Further Still), 1966

1 Richard Green, 'Folk Fan Sam . . .', *Record Mirror* (26 February 1966), p. 6.
2 Nigel Hunter, 'No Place Like Home', *Music Echo* (5 March 1966), p. 4.
3 Pete Johnson, 'Rising Sons Sing Blue Tunes', *Los Angeles Times* (18 March 1966), p. C19.
4 Richard Green, 'Bruce Johnson', *Record Mirror* (28 May 1966), p. 3.
5 Eden, 'Having a Wild Rave-Up with Five Yardbirds', *KRLA the Beat* (29 January 1966), pp. 3–5.
6 Ibid.
7 Ibid.
8 Harrison Carroll, 'Behind the Scenes in Hollywood', *Kokomo Morning Times* (15 January 1966), p. 14.
9 Ibid.

10 'Yardbirds U.S. Rave-Up!', *Disc Weekly* (15 January 1966), p. 7.
11 Ibid.
12 Ibid.
13 Brian Clark, 'Chart Climbing Yardbirds Still Love the Blues', *Beat Instrumental* (April 1966), p. 4.
14 Derek Taylor, 'Hollywood Calling', *Disc Weekly* (22 January 1966), p. 5. On the forthcoming U.S. release of the band's 'Indian endeavour', 'Shapes of Things': 'It's great' (5 March 1966), p. 4.
15 Derek Taylor, 'Hollywood Calling', *Disc Weekly* (2 April 1966), p. 9.
16 'The Hullabaloo: The Los Angeles Club Scene', *Hit Parader* (September 1966), pp. 32–4.
17 Ibid.
18 Tracy Thomas, 'America Calling', *New Musical Express* (28 January 1966), p. 2.
19 Ibid.
20 Ibid. Giorgio Gomelsky wrote a fulsome report of the Hullabaloo shows and the party at Markley's in a letter to fan-club members (February–March 1966), which was reproduced in Richard Mackay's fanzine, *Yardbirds World* #5 (November 1983), n.p.
21 Marilyn Caldwell, 'Yardbirds Find Own Style in the Far Out', *Los Angeles Times* (26 February 1966), p. B8.
22 Ibid.
23 'Here We Are in All Our Glory', *KRLA Beat* (5 February 1966), p. 12.
24 Ibid.
25 Ibid.
26 Ibid.
27 Ibid.
28 Carol Sincak, 'The Yardbirds Throw a Bomb', *Hit Parader* (June 1966), pp. 33–4.
29 Richard Spaete, 'Mail', *Hit Parader* (August 1966), p. 52.
30 'Small Faces Get Hung Up – On Sounds', *Melody Maker* (12 February 1966), p. 9.
31 Ibid.
32 Ibid.
33 Ibid.
34 Ibid.
35 Ibid.
36 Kevin Swift, 'An Opening for the Eyes?', *Beat Instrumental* (March 1966), p. 39.
37 'Mick Jagger: Blind Date', *Melody Maker* (12 February 1966), p. 11.
38 'Dave Dee: Blind Date', *Melody Maker* (26 March 1966), p. 12.
39 'Wayne Fontana; Blind Date', *Melody Maker* (28 May 1966), p. 10.
40 'Yardbirds Split but Only for Discs', *New Musical Express* (11 March 1966), p. 2.
41 Derek Johnson, 'Singles', *New Musical Express* (25 February 1966), p. 4.
42 Norman Jopling, 'Singles', *Record Mirror* (2 February 1966), p. 10.
43 Green, 'Folk Fan Sam', p. 6.
44 Penny Valentine, 'Singles', *Disc Weekly* (19 February 1966), p. 11.
45 'Alan Price: Hit Talk', *Disc Weekly* (16 April 1966), p. 12.
46 'Yardbirds Record in a Strange Way', *KRLA the Beat* (7 May 1966), pp. 1 and 5.
47 'Singles', *Melody Maker* (19 February 1966), p. 18.

48 Nick Jones, 'Clapton – Lonely Man with Power in His Guitar', *Melody Maker* (26 March 1966), p. 11.
49 In a poetic turnaround, Williams was interviewed in *Seventeen* magazine (April 1967), p. 159: '*Crawdaddy* looks like a well-edited high-school literary magazine.'
50 Paul Williams, *Crawdaddy* (28 March 1966), p. 19.
51 Ibid.
52 'Yardbirds for San Remo', *Record Mirror* (12 January 1965), p. 5.
53 'San Remo '66', *Record Mirror* (12 February 1966), p. 10.
54 Green, 'Folk Fan Sam', p. 6.
55 Ibid.
56 Leonard Levesley, 'Discs', *The Tatler* (19 February 1966), p. 59.
57 Ibid.
58 'San Remo Should Open Up to All-comers', *Melody Maker* (5 February 1966), p. 11.
59 'Yardbirds By the Yard!', *Disc Weekly* (29 January 1966), p. 9.
60 *Record Mirror* (19 March 1966), p. 7.
61 Dreja and McCarty also raised the possibility of publishing a humorous book, but it came to nowt – 'Yardbirds Write Book!', *Disc and Music Echo* (16 July 1966), p. 6. They did, however, turn in a 'Pop Poem', in place of a review of the current charts: 'Of "Substitute" we must express/ That of the Who it's hardly the best,/ But still a good record with very good words.' ('Pop Poem', *Disc and Music Echo* (23 April 1966), p. 11.)
62 'Yardbird Goes Solo', *Melody Maker* (12 March 1966), p. 4.
63 'Yardbirds Solo Discs', *Record Mirror* (19 March 1966), p. 5.
64 'Jaggered', *Melody Maker* (12 February 1966), pp. 10–11. Manfred Mann's Paul Jones also had a big moan about playing ballrooms, it's 'a drag', he said, 'they almost make you physically sick. It's not the kids we object to, but the officious capitalists who run the ballrooms and the complete lack of essential facilities for artistes.' Mike Chamberlain, 'Ballrooms Are a Drag', *Music Echo* (10 July 1965), p. 10.
65 Mike Grant, 'Shapes of Things to Come', *Rave* (1 May 1966), p. 4.
66 Ibid., p. 5. Three of the backing tracks they laid down in these sessions would reappear in fully realized form on the album they made with Simon Napier-Bell: 'Lost Woman', 'What Do You Want' and 'He's Always There'.
67 'Yardbirds Split but Only for Discs', p. 2.
68 'The Yardbirds Blow Your Mind . . . But Why?', *Hit Parader* (September 1966), pp. 22–5.
69 'Yardbird Jeff Beck Ill', *Disc Weekly* (16 April 1966), p. 5.
70 Ibid.
71 Ibid.
72 'Yardbird Jeff Is Back', *Disc and Music Echo* (23 April 1966), p. 5. See also 'Dusty Hit Co-Writer Is Yardbirds New Manager', *New Musical Express* (15 April 1966), p. 6.
73 'Jeff Beck Collapses Taken Seriously Ill', *KRLA the Beat* (14 May 1966), p. 1.
74 'The Face', *Record Mirror* (16 April 1966), p. 12.
75 'The Face', *Record Mirror* (23 April 1966), p. 12.

76 Richard Green, 'The Yardbirds', *Record Mirror* (30 April 1966), pp. 6–7.
77 Ibid.
78 Ibid.
79 John Platt, Chris Dreja and Jim McCarty, *Yardbirds* (London, 1983), p. 84.
80 Ibid.
81 Ibid.
82 Green, 'The Yardbirds', pp. 6–7.
83 Platt, Dreja and McCarty, *Yardbirds*, p. 92.
84 'Herman: Hit Talk', *Disc and Music Echo* (2 July 1966), p. 3.
85 Green, 'Folk Fan Sam', p. 6.
86 Ibid.
87 Ibid.
88 Ibid.
89 'Keith: Back in His Own Back Yardbird!', *Disc Weekly* (9 April 1966), p. 7.
90 'Yardbirds: Must We Jump About . . .', *Disc Weekly* (26 March 1966), pp. 6–7.
91 'Yardbirds Split but Only for Discs'.
92 Ibid.
93 Alan Smith, 'Yardbirds Slam "Live Sound" Critic', *New Musical Express* (25 March 1966), p. 10.
94 Keith Altham, 'Who and 'Birds at Paris', *New Musical Express* (8 April 1966), p. 3.
95 Green, 'The Yardbirds', pp. 6–7.
96 Penny Valentine, 'Keith's Solo Bid', *Disc and Music Echo* (14 May 1966), p. 7; 'Keith: Back in His Own Back Yardbird!', *Disc Weekly* (9 April 1966), p. 7.
97 Valentine, 'Keith's Solo Bid', p. 7.
98 Penny Valentine, 'Singles', *Disc and Music Echo* (14 May 1966), p. 19.
99 Derek Johnson, 'Singles', *New Musical Express* (13 May 1966), p. 4.
100 Norman Jopling, 'Singles', *Record Mirror* (15 May 1966), p. 9.
101 Ibid.
102 'Singles', *Melody Maker* (14 May 1966), p. 12.
103 Richard Green, 'Susi Klee' and David Griffith, 'Keith Relf', *Record Mirror* (28 May 1966), p. 5.
104 Other than Relf, Klee and Doonican, Bobby Darin, Cher and Peter, Paul and Mary were reported to have recorded Lind's songs, *Record Mirror* (16 April 1966), p. 6; see also Richard Green, 'My Songs Are Photos of People', *Record Mirror* (23 March 1966), p. 5.
105 June Southworth, 'A Boy Called Keith', *Fabulous* (14 May 1966), p. 19.
106 'The Samwell-Smith Orchestra', *Beat Instrumental* (June 1966), p. 25.
107 Beck spoke obliquely about his solo plans to Mike Crofts, 'Big Band for Jeff Beck?', *Beat Instrumental* (July 1966), p. 8.
108 'Should Scott and Gary Make Solo Records?', *Disc and Music Echo* (4 June 1966), p. 11.
109 Eden, 'Keith Relf: A Man in Search', *KRLA the Beat* (23 July 1966), p. 11; see also Louise Criscione, 'Who Is This Group Called the Yardbirds', *KRLA the Beat* (16 July 1966), p. 11.
110 Louise Criscione, 'The Yardbirds from All Positions', *KRLA the Beat* (27 August 1966), p. 19.
111 Simon Napier-Bell, *You Don't Have to Say You Love Me* (London, 1998), p. 49.

112 Maureen Cleave, 'Simon Napier-Bell Always Tells the Truth . . .', *Evening Standard* (13 May 1966), p. 10.
113 Napier-Bell's father was co-owner of Basic Films (formed 1944), a successful company that made numerous government information films and industry sponsored short documentaries. In 1965, Napier-Bell Jr bought out his father's partner's shares in the business; he was not then his dad's employer. See 'Men and Matters', *Financial Times* (14 November 1966), p. 8.
114 Nik Cohn, 'Pop Scene', *Queen* (9 November 1966), p. 40.
115 'Names in the News', *Melody Maker* (14 May 1966), p. 5.
116 'EMI Inks Deal with Yardbirds', *Billboard* (28 May 1966), p. 32.
117 Ibid.
118 'Big 3, Yardbirds Make Pub. Deal', *Billboard* (25 June 1966), p. 4.
119 'Yardbirds', *Disc and Music Echo* (21 May 1966), p. 8.
120 'The Rat Race Is Tough . . .', *Disc and Music Echo* (21 May 1966), p. 14.
121 Napier-Bell, *You Don't Have to Say You Love Me*, pp. 7–8.
122 'Men and Matters', *Financial Times* (3 October 1966), p. 8.
123 Peter Jones and Norman Jopling, 'Singles', *Record Mirror* (28 May 1966), p. 9.
124 Ibid.
125 Penny Valentine, 'Singles', *Disc and Music Echo* (28 May 1966), p. 19.
126 Derek Johnson, 'Singles', *New Musical Express* (27 May 1966), p. 4.
127 'Jonathan King Column', *Disc and Music Echo* (4 June 1966), p. 12.
128 Richard Green, 'Guess What! . . . Jeff Beck', *Record Mirror* (11 June 1966), p. 6.
129 Rita F. Head, 'Mailbag', *Melody Maker* (25 June 1966), p. 16.
130 Green, 'Guess What!', p. 6.
131 'How the Yardbirds Walk the Tightrope', *Melody Maker* (11 June 1966), p. 8.
132 Ibid.
133 Ibid.
134 'Yardbirds Giant U.S. Tour', *Disc and Music Echo* (4 June 1966), p. 4.
135 'Samwell-Smith Quits Yardbirds!', *Disc and Music Echo* (25 June 1966), p. 3; 'Samwell-Smith Quits Yardbirds', *New Musical Express* (24 June 1966), p. 7.
136 'Yardbirds: Must We Jump About . . .', pp. 6–7.
137 Chris Welch, 'Birds' Brain', *Melody Maker* (19 March 1966), p. 9.
138 'How the Yardbirds Walk the Tightrope', *Melody Maker* (11 June 1966), p. 8.
139 Keith Altham, 'Yardbirds: Why I Left', *New Musical Express* (8 July 1966), p. 8. Also published as 'Why Sam Left', *Hit Parader* (November 1966), p. 10.
140 Ibid.
141 'Departing Animal and Ex-Yardbird Team Up', *New Musical Express* (26 August 1966), p. 7.
142 Brad Tolinski, *Light and Shade: Conversations with Jimmy Page* (London, 2012), p. 61.
143 'The Rat Race Is Tough . . .', *Disc and Music Echo* (21 May 1966), p. 14.
144 'Yardbird Beck Makes Solo Single', *Melody Maker* (18 June 1966), p. 5.
145 'Page Joins Yardbirds', *Melody Maker* (25 June 1966), p. 1.
146 Mike Ledgerwood, 'New Yardbird in the Nest', *Disc and Music Echo* (2 July 1966), p. 2.
147 Ibid.
148 Ibid.

149 'Jimmy, the New Yardbird, Settles In', *Melody Maker* (2 July 1966), p. 8.
150 Richard Lennox, 'We're Cheesed Off with Fans!', *Disc and Music Echo* (25 June 1966), p. 7.
151 'Jimmy, the New Yardbird, Settles In', p. 8.
152 Keith Altham, 'Yardbirds: Why I Joined', *New Musical Express* (8 July 1966), p. 8, also published as 'A New Bird in the Yard', *Hit Parader* (December 1966), p. 24.
153 Ibid.
154 Miranda Ward, 'Our Gal in London', *Hit Parader* (December 1966), p. 47.
155 Kevin Swift, 'Jimmy Will Change Yardbirds Sound!', *Beat Instrumental* (September 1966), p. 26.
156 Ibid.
157 'The Puppet Master', *Sunday Times Magazine* (20 February 1966), p. 14.
158 Ibid.
159 Ibid.
160 Allen Evans, 'Yardbirds Produce Oriental Sound on New LP', *New Musical Express* (22 July 1966), p. 12.
161 Ibid.
162 Ibid.
163 Ibid.
164 Ibid.
165 Ibid.
166 'Yardbirds: All Our Own Work', *Disc and Music Echo* (13 August 1966), p. 12.
167 'Yardbirds', *Melody Maker* (30 July 1966), p. 11.
168 Richard Green, 'Columbia 33SX 6063', *Record Mirror* (23 July 1966), p. 2.
169 Richard Green, 'I'd Say George Harrison Was Good but . . .', *Record Mirror* (13 August 1966), p. 7.
170 Richard Green, 'Mud Dominated the Windsor Jazz Festival', *Record Mirror* (6 August 1966), p. 5. For more comprehensive coverage see 'Jazz on a Summer's Weekend', *Melody Maker* (6 August 1966), p. 3.
171 Green, 'I'd Say George Harrison . . .', p. 7.
172 Nik Cohn, 'Pop Scene', *Queen* (31 August 1966), p. 24.
173 Ibid.
174 Ibid.
175 'The Yardbirds', *Record Mail* (August 1966), p. 4.
176 Ibid.
177 Michael Kac, 'Over Under Sideways Down', *Crawdaddy* (November 1966), p. 22.

7 Stock Explosions and the Perversion of Sound, 1966

1 Eric Clapton, 'Expert Advice', *Melody Maker* (22 January 1966), p. 12.
2 Christine Osbourne, 'We Don't Want a Big Hit', *Music Echo* (5 March 1966), p. 7.
3 'Beck and Super Pop', *Melody Maker* (5 March 1966), pp. 8–9.
4 Ibid.
5 Chris Welch, 'Group's Group', *Melody Maker* (5 March 1966), p. 9.
6 'The Raver', *Melody Maker* (16 April 1966), p. 2; 'Mailbag', *Melody Maker* (19 March 1966), p. 20, and (16 April 1966), p. 16.

7 Nick Jones, 'Clapton – Lonely Man with Power in His Guitar', *Melody Maker* (26 March 1966), p. 11.
8 Ibid.
9 Ibid.
10 Ibid.
11 Ibid.
12 Ibid.
13 Richard Vernon, 'Reviews', *R&B Monthly*, 24 (January/February 1966), p. 21.
14 A rumour that Clapton was splitting from the Bluesbreakers was mentioned in *Melody Maker*'s 'The Raver' column, but it appears he was just taking a leave of absence (21 August 1965), p. 2.
15 Mark Powell, booklet notes accompanying *Blues Breakers John Mayall with Eric Clapton*, Deluxe Edition (Universal, 2006).
16 George Ellis, 'Record Reviews', *Jazzbeat* (October 1966), p. 27.
17 'LP Reviews', *Beat Instrumental* (September 1966), p. 21.
18 'New Records', *Melody Maker* (6 August 1966), p. 12.
19 'Eric, Ginger and Jack Team Up', *Melody Maker* (11 June 1966), p. 4.
20 'Bruce-Clapton-Baker Group Debut', *Melody Maker* (25 June 1966), p. 2. News of the naming of the band was carried by the other music papers a week later: 'The Cream', *Record Mirror* (2 July 1966), p. 4.
21 Dawn James, 'Stirring – the Cream', *Rave* (1 October 1966), p. 13.
22 Chris Welch, 'Sweet 'n Sour Rock 'n Roll', *Melody Maker* (30 July 1966), p. 7.
23 Ibid.
24 Ibid.
25 Ibid.
26 Richard Green, 'Mud Dominated the Windsor Jazz Festival', *Record Mirror* (6 August 1966), p. 5.
27 'Jazz on a Summer's Weekend', *Melody Maker* (6 August 1966), p. 3.
28 Green, 'Mud Dominated the Windsor Jazz Festival', p. 5.
29 'Jazz on a Summer's Weekend', p. 3.
30 R. S., 'The Cream: Caught in the Act', *Melody Maker* (6 August 1966), p. 16.
31 'Expert Advice', *Melody Maker* (13 August 1966), p. 12.
32 Ibid.
33 'Fresh Cream Whips Up Hit!', *Disc and Music Echo* (29 October 1966), p. 8.
34 Kevin Swift, 'Eric Clapton', *Beat Instrumental* (August 1966), p. 15.
35 Ibid.
36 Ibid.
37 Mike Crofts, 'Big Changes For Mayall', *Beat Instrumental* (October 1966), p. 11.
38 Richard Green, 'I'd Say George Harrison Was Good but . . .', *Record Mirror* (18 August 1966), p. 7.
39 Keith Altham, 'Cream Are the Very End!', *New Musical Express* (28 October 1966), p. 10.
40 James, 'Stirring – the Cream', p. 13.
41 Ibid.
42 Ibid.
43 Ibid.
44 Ibid.

45 Ibid.
46 Ibid.
47 Richard Green, 'If You're Puzzled Why', *Record Mirror* (5 November 1966), p. 4.
48 Ibid.
49 Norman Jopling, 'Singles', *Record Mirror* (8 October 1966), p. 9.
50 'Singles', *Melody Maker* (1 October 1966), p. 11.
51 'The Cream Want a Bit of Butter on Their Bread', *Disc and Music Echo* (5 November 1966), p. 20.
52 Ibid.
53 Kevin Swift, 'Jack Bruce Explains Cream Policy', *Beat Instrumental* (November 1966), p. 14.
54 'Paragon Launched', *Music Echo* (19 March 1966), p. 8.
55 Hugh Nolan, 'Can You Tell Cream from Butterfield?' *Disc and Music Echo* (19 November 1966), p. 11.
56 'Fresh Cream Whips Up Hit!', *Disc and Music Echo* (29 October 1966), p. 8.
57 For further comparisons between the two bands, see also Keith Altham, 'Cream Are the Very End!', *New Musical Express* (28 October 1966), p. 10.
58 'Mailbag', *Melody Maker* (8 October 1966), p. 20.
59 Ibid.
60 Ibid.
61 Ibid.
62 Ibid.
63 Nick Jones, 'Clapton Revs into a New Gear', *Melody Maker* (15 October 1966), p. 7.
64 See the two full-page advertisements in *Star Tribune* (31 July 1966), p. 26, and (1 August 1966), p. 25.
65 'Mary Quant: Nonstop Savvy', *Seventeen* (September 1967), pp. 120–21.
66 'Music Just Happens F=for Yardbird Quintet', *Minneapolis Star* (8 August 1966), p. 6B.
67 Ibid.
68 Marg Storhoff, 'Are They Attractive? Naturally!', *Minneapolis Tribune* (12 August 1966), p. 13.
69 'Yardbirds', *Disc and Music Echo* (13 August 1966), p. 5.
70 'Yardbirds to Appear Friday at the Col', *Quad City Times Democrat* (2 August 1966), p. 23.
71 Pamela Bassett, 'Young Fans Dig English Yardbirds', *Chicago Tribune* (12 August 1966), p. 45; see also John Platt, Chris Dreja and Jim McCarty, *Yardbirds* (London, 1983), p. 88.
72 'Let There Be Screams', *Great Falls Tribune* (15 August 1966), p. 8.
73 Carol Crane, 'Screams of Teenage Girls . . .', *Arizona Daily Star* (22 August 1966), p. 2A.
74 Ibid.
75 Ibid.
76 'Open Letter to Five Yardbirds', *KRLA the Beat* (22 October 1966), p. 8.
77 Ibid.
78 'Mail', *Hit Parader* (October 1966), p. 56.
79 'Second Keith Relf Solo Disc', *Disc and Music Echo* (30 July 1966), p. 5.

80 'The Yardbirds appear to be having a fantastic time on their American tour . . .', *Fab 208* (3 September 1966), p. 3; 'Yardbird Op.', *Fab 208* (17 September 1966), p. 20.
81 'Yardbird Jeff Beck Ill', *Disc and Music Echo* (6 August 1966), p. 4; 'Jeff Ill', *Melody Maker* (6 August 1966), p. 4.
82 'Keith Relf Denies Yardbird Split-Up', *KRLA the Beat* (19 November 1966), p. 2, and more on those rumours in the same edition, Louise Criscione, 'On the Beat', p. 3. See also 'Yardbirds Carry on Minus Beck', *New Musical Express* (9 September 1966), p. 7, and 'Yardbird Out of Hospital', *New Musical Express* (16 September 1966), p. 9.
83 'Beck Ill', *Melody Maker* (10 September 1966), p. 4.
84 'Yardbirds Quartet Tours America', *Disc and Music Echo* (12 September 1966), p. 10.
85 Ibid.
86 Lillian Roxon, 'Psychedelics: That's the New Fad', *Sydney Morning Herald* (17 July 1966), pp. 45 and 83.
87 Ibid.
88 Ibid.
89 Ibid.
90 Ibid.
91 Norman Jopling, 'Freak Out!', *Record Mirror* (22 October 1966), p. 5.
92 Ibid.
93 Ibid.
94 Walter Blum, 'The Big Beat Generation', *San Francisco Examiner* (27 March 1967), pp. 22, 25, 27 and 29.
95 Paul Drummond, *Eye Mind: The Saga of Roky Erickson and the 13th Floor Elevators, the Pioneers of Psychedelic Sound* (Los Angeles, CA, 2007), pp. 87 and 92.
96 Ibid., p. 100.
97 She doesn't say where, but a good guess would be Green's Pavilion at Lakeview Park in Manitou Beach, Michigan, where support was provided by Detroit's favourite sons, the Rationals. See 'At Manitou Beach', *Detroit Free Press* (5 August 1966).
98 Loraine Alterman, 'Yardbirds Are Alive; They Click; They Have Fun', *Detroit Free Press* (26 August 1966), p. 5C.
99 Ibid.
100 Norrie Drummond, 'Big Night for the Stones', *New Musical Express* (30 September 1966), p. 13.
101 Mike Ledgerwood, 'Stones Stampede', *Disc and Music Echo* (1 October 1966), pp. 10–11 and 17.
102 Alan Walsh, 'Pandemonium!', *Melody Maker* (1 October 1966), pp. 8–9.
103 The Millionaire, 'Pop . . . Pop . . . Ouch!', *International Times*, 1 (14 October 1966), p. 11.
104 Walsh, 'Pandemonium!'
105 Ibid.
106 Mike Ledgerwood, 'Yardbirds Deny "Splitting" Rumours', *Disc and Music Echo* (15 October 1966), p. 13.

107 Ibid.
108 Rick Dane, 'Yardbirds Shake the Scene Again', *The Tatler* (29 October 1966), p. 39.
109 Norman Jopling, 'Singles', *Record Mirror* (22 October 1966), p. 9.
110 Derek Johnson, 'Singles', *New Musical Express* (21 October 1966), p. 8.
111 'Jonathan King Column', *Disc and Music Echo* (22 October 1966), p. 12.
112 Penny Valentine, 'Singles', *Disc and Music Echo* (22 October 1966), p. 15.
113 'Recording Notes', *Beat Instrumental* (November 1966), p. 29.
114 Pete Goodman, 'Beach Boys Used Theremin for Success', *Beat Instrumental* (December 1966), pp. 13–14.
115 'Different Sounds', *Record Mail* (November 1966), p. 3.
116 Ibid.
117 'John Castle Writes . . .', *Record Mail* (December 1966), p. 4.
118 Hunter Davies, 'Psychedelic', *Sunday Times* (30 October 1966), p. 13.
119 Ibid.
120 'Scene', *Disc and Music Echo* (19 November 1966), p. 2.
121 Ibid.
122 Chris Welch and Bob Dawbarn, 'Psychedelia', *Melody Maker* (22 October 1966), pp. 10–12.
123 Ibid.
124 'Count Five', *Hit Parader* (February 1967), p. 31.
125 'Rock 'n', Roll "Rough"', *Hammond Times* (24 June 1966), p. 1B.
126 Carol Dunlop, 'Quintet to Change Name, Sound', *Wichita Beacon* (4 January 1967), p. 3C.
127 Charles Jackson, 'Draggin' Takes Back Seat to Yardbirds', *Wichita Beacon* (19 August 1966), p. 2B.
128 As an example of this conflation of the Yardbirds with psychedelia: '[The McCoys] concluded their first set with their first big hit, "Hang on Sloopy", and their second with a wild, lengthy number featuring psychedelic guitar a la the Yardbirds. It was, however, their own composition, they said.' (Carol Dunlop, 'Young Ideas '67', *Wichita Beacon* (12 July 1967), p. 17.)
129 Ibid.
130 Ibid.
131 'Singles', *Melody Maker* (22 October 1966), p. 15.
132 Ibid.
133 Ibid.
134 Bob Dawbarn and Barry Fantoni, 'Exclusive! Psychedelic from the Inside', *Melody Maker* (12 November 1966), p. 12.
135 June Southworth, 'Psychedelia Sixty Seven', *Fab 208* (31 December 1966), p. 5.
136 Ibid.
137 Ibid.
138 Derek Johnson, 'More Single Reviews', *New Musical Express* (24 December 1966), p. 10.
139 Ibid.
140 More than echoing the points raised here, the Misunderstood were interviewed in *Beat Instrumental* (January 1967), p. 39.

141 Ren Grevatt, 'British Pop Is Finished', *Melody Maker* (5 November 1966), p. 4.
142 'Platter Chatter', *Hit Parader* (September 19966), p. 51.
143 Derek Johnson, 'Singles', *New Musical Express* (21 October 1966), p. 8.
144 Eden, 'Yardbirds: Kids Want More Quality', *KRLA the Beat* (3 December 1966), p. 13.
145 Ibid.
146 Ibid.
147 Ibid.
148 Eden, 'Jeff Beck: Alone in the Yardbirds', *KRLA the Beat* (17 December 1966), p. 7.
149 'Yardbirds Coming Stateside Once More', *KRLA the Beat* (5 November 1966), p. 5; 'Keith Relf to Quit Yardbirds?', *Melody Maker* (22 October 1966), p. 1.
150 Ed Denson, 'The Folk Scene', *Berkeley Barb* (28 October 1966), p. 6.
151 Ibid.
152 Ibid.
153 Ibid.
154 Ibid.
155 Ibid.
156 Drummond, *Eye Mind*, p. 186.
157 Shirley Davis, 'Teens Scream Approval of "Rock"', *Quad City Times-Democrat* (9 November 1966), p. 21.
158 Ibid.
159 'The Move are constantly experimenting with new sounds and lead guitarist Roy Wood can even play his guitar with a violin bow.' 'On the Move From Birmingham', *Melody Maker* (30 April 1966), p. 8.
160 'Food Fair News', *Detroit Free Press* (13 November 1966).
161 Loraine Alterman, 'Where the Action Is', *Detroit Free Press* (21 October 1966).
162 Ibid.
163 'Artist's Mod Wedding All Set, Except . . .', *Detroit Free Press* (31 October 1966), n.p.
164 'The Nation's . . .', *Detroit Free Press* (4 November 1966), n.p.
165 Lois Sutherland, 'Their Wedding Is Proof It's a Mod, Mod World', *Detroit Free Press* (13 November 1966), pp. 1A–2A.
166 Ibid. for a report on 'Up-Tight with Andy Warhol and the Velvet Underground' show see Frank Uhle, *Cinema Ann Arbor: How Campus Rebels Forged A Singular Film Culture* (Ann Arbor, MI, 2023), pp. 62–6.
167 June Harris, 'America Calling', *New Musical Express* (26 November 1966), p. 14.
168 Ibid.
169 Ibid. Napier-Bell hyped John's Children in *KRLA the Beat*, calling them a 'musical plea to the new wave generation', and the 'children of English aristocrats', giving each member of the band double-barrelled names while noting that on stage they wore 'white high-necked sweaters and mystical medallions'. 'Beat Showcase', *KRLA the Beat* (17 December 1966), p. 7.
170 Van Sauter, 'A Mod Pair Joined in Holy Matrimony', *Detroit Free Press* (21 November 1966), pp. 3A and 8A.
171 Ibid.
172 Ibid.
173 Ibid.

174 Gary Grimshaw, 'I'm Just Mod about Weddings', *Fifth Estate* (1–15 December 1966), p. 5.
175 Ibid.
176 Reproduced in *Vox Teen Beat: The Complete Collection, 1965–67* (London, 2023), p. 82.
177 Dylan Jones, *Loaded: The Life (and Afterlife) of the Velvet Underground* (London, 2023), pp. 89–90. Page told Jones he'd seen the Velvets in July 1966 but that date is clearly wrong: he wasn't in the States with the Yardbirds at that point and Lou Reed and co. did not play the Scene club that month. But he was in and around New York during the Velvets 12 day residency in January 1967.
178 Ibid. Page remembers talking to Reed after one of the shows, asking what his points of reference were; Reed told him 'Eight Miles High'. In the Lou Reed archives is a copy of the 2011 Sundazed issue of a previously unreleased recording of that song with a card from Page: 'Thought you might enjoy a little more Coltrane!!', 'Inside Lou Reed's Revelatory New Public Archive', www.rollingstone.com, accessed 2 May 2024. The Scene club, with the Velvets playing, was documented by Richard Goldstein in his 'Pop Eye', column for *Village Voice* (19 January 1967) and reproduced in his *Goldstein's Greatest Hits* (New York, 1970), pp. 221–8. See also Virginia Lee Warren, 'A Different Kind of Senior Prom', *New York Times* (8 June 1966), p. 77.
179 Jonathan King, 'Singles', *Disc Weekly* (21 August 1965); and 'Blind Date', *Melody Maker* (28 August 1965).
180 Patrick Doncaster, 'Discs', *Daily Mirror* (19 August 1965), p. 19.
181 Peter Jones, 'Nico Leads Andrew's Off Beat Company', *Record Mirror* (28 August 1966), p. 6.
182 Ibid.
183 Keith Altham, 'Oldham: Talented, Insulting, Outrageous', *New Musical Express* (5 August 1966), p. 3.
184 Platt, *Yardbirds*, p. 78. Images from the gig were published in *Hit Parader* (March and April 1966).
185 Ibid., pp. 85, 130–33; French, *Heart Full of Soul*, p. 89.
186 'U.S. Pop Art Man . . .', *Melody Maker* (29 April 1967), p. 2.
187 Nick Jones, 'Move', *Melody Maker* (29 October 1966), p. 6.
188 'Listings', *Melody Maker* (17 December 1966), p. 29.
189 'Clubs' listing, *Melody Maker* (29 October 1966), p. 20.
190 Nick Jones, 'Psychedelicamania at Roundhouse', *Melody Maker* (7 January 1967), p. 2.
191 Ibid.
192 Derek Johnson, 'Singles', *New Musical Express* (21 October 1966), p. 8.
193 Norman Jopling and Peter Jones, 'Singles', *Record Mirror* (3 December 1966), p. 9.
194 Derek Johnson, 'Singles', *New Musical Express* (3 December 1966), p. 6.
195 Penny Valentine, 'Singles', *Disc and Music Echo* (26 November 1966), p. 19.
196 Penny Valentine, 'Singles', *Disc and Music Echo* (3 December 1966), p. 15.
197 Greg Russo, *Yardbirds: The Ultimate Rave-Up*, 7th edn (New York, 2022), p. 72. Louise Alterman reported that the band had written three numbers for the film. ('Where the Action Is', *Detroit Free Press* (21 October 1966), p. 44.)

198 Mike Jenking, 'Let's Rock! . . . £10 for an LP', *Record Mirror* (9 April 1966), p. 6. Review of reissued R&R Trio LP, 'Best track, as selected by a recent poll, is "The Train Kept A-Rollin'" which should . . . be issued as a single'. *Record Mirror* (15 October 1966), p. 8.
199 'Eye View', *Music Echo* (3 July 1965), p. 4.
200 Brian Harvey, 'Singles', *Music Echo* (29 May 1965), p. 2.
201 Don Paulsen, 'Yardbird Jeff Beck', *Hit Parader* (April 1967), pp. 48–9.
202 Antonioni's attendance was reported in *Melody Maker* (11 December 1965), p. 5.
203 Mike Gershman, 'The "Smashing" Who', *Press Democrat* (1 April 1968), p. 20.
204 Victor Bockris and Gerard Malanga, *Up-Tight: The Velvet Underground Story* (London, 1983), p. 676.
205 '2500 Ball at IT-Launch', *International Times*, 2 (31 October 1966), p. 14.
206 The Nashville recording is listed as taking place on 16 November 1966 with McCarty on drums, in Russo, *Yardbirds: The Ultimate Rave-Up*, p. 73. McKay makes a cameo appearance in Platt et al., *Yardbirds*, p. 113, and in photographs in the Caravan's bus and elsewhere, pp. 148–9. BBC Radio One DJ Tony Blackburn also covered 'I Can't Make Your Way' on *Tony Blackburn Sings* (1968), which has a passable imitation of Beck's solo, some hearty handclaps and backing vocalists intoning 'he can't make it' into the outro. Blackburn's singing is as flat as a Dutchman's cap.
207 The campaign ran in *Fab 208* (22 October and 26 November 1966) and in *Rave* (December 1966). The Hollies were also used to promote Miss Disc cosmetics.
208 'Yardbirds Reach 1984', *Tulsa World* (19 August 1966), p. 17.
209 Ibid.
210 Vicki Boles, 'Coliseum Show: It Was Like Some Imaginary World', *Twin City Sentinel* (2 December 1966), p. 8.
211 Ibid.
212 Ibid.
213 Ibid.
214 'Yardbirds Due Later', *Lima News* (9 October 1966), p. 5C.
215 Ibid.
216 Chris Guagenti, 'So What's All That Interesting?', *Lima News* (11 December 1966), pp. 1C–2C.
217 Ibid.
218 Ibid.
219 Ibid.
220 Ibid.
221 Ibid.
222 Wanel Norman and Vicki Birchfield, 'Caravan of Stars 1 Termed "Success" . . .', *Alexandria Daily Town Talk* (5 November 1966), p. 10.
223 Catherine Barnett, 'Bum, Is a Hobo, Is a Group of Fun-Loving Musicians . . .', *Colorado Springs Gazette Telegraph* (29 July 1967), pp. 20C–21C.
224 Ibid.
225 Ibid.
226 Ibid.
227 Tracy Thomas, 'America Calling', *New Musical Express* (3 December 1966), p. 6.
228 'Yardbirds Split Is Definite', *New Musical Express* (17 December 1966), p. 8.

229 Ibid.
230 Ibid.
231 'Page to Quit Yardbirds', *Disc and Music Echo* (10 December 1966), p. 7. Two weeks later, the paper confirmed Beck had left: 'Jeff Beck Splits', *Disc and Music Echo* (24 December 1966), p. 6.
232 'Jeff Beck Column', *Beat Instrumental* (January 1967), p. 9.
233 Ibid.
234 See Platt et al., *Yardbirds*, including photographs, pp. 100–103.
235 Ibid.
236 Ibid.
237 *Beat Instrumental* Gold Star Award (January 1967), pp. 20–21.
238 'Yardbird Joins Most', *New Musical Express* (31 December 1966), p. 7.
239 Paulsen, 'Yardbird Jeff Beck', pp. 48–9.
240 Ibid.
241 Ibid.

8 Electrorock Therapy and the 14-Hour Technicolor Dream Machine, 1967

1 'Hit Talk: Roy Wood', *Disc and Music Echo* (21 January 1967), p. 3.
2 Ibid.
3 Ibid.
4 Ibid.
5 Ibid.
6 Ibid.
7 June Harris, 'America Calling', *New Musical Express* (14 January 1967), p. 14.
8 Ibid.
9 'The Jeff Beck Column', *Beat Instrumental* (February 1967), p. 9.
10 Ibid.
11 Ibid.
12 Ibid.
13 'The Jeff Beck Column', *Beat Instrumental* (March 1967), p. 9.
14 Jack Bentley, 'Pop Groups, Sex-Mad Girls . . .', *Sunday Mirror* (12 March 1967), p. 29.
15 Ibid.
16 Don Short, 'Pop Star Sued . . .', *Daily Mirror* (15 November 1967), p. 20.
17 Derek Boltwood, 'Jeff Beck', *Record Mirror* (26 August 1967), p. 5.
18 'Jeff Beck's First Vocal Disc Set', *Disc and Music Echo* (25 February 1967), p. 7.
19 Penny Valentine 'Singles', *Disc and Music Echo* (4 March 1967), p. 15.
20 Peter Jones, 'Singles', *Record Mirror* (25 March 1967), p. 9.
21 'Beck Is Back with a Bang', *Disc and Music Echo* (22 April 1967), p. 5.
22 Valerie Wilmer, 'Jeff's Future Beckons', *Hit Parader* (July 1967), p. 23.
23 Mike Ledgerwood, 'Disappointing, but Orbison Scores', *Disc and Music Echo* (11 March 1967), p. 16.
24 Chris Welch, 'Beck Leaves Tour', *Melody Maker* (11 March 1967), p. 1.
25 'Jeff Beck Quits Faces-Orbison Tour', *Disc and Music Echo* (11 March 1967), p. 4.
26 Ibid.
27 Ibid.

28 Ibid.
29 Chris Welch, 'Beck Leaves Tour', *Melody Maker* (11 March 1967), p. 1.
30 Keith Altham, 'Guitarist Beck Has Hit as Singer', *New Musical Express* (15 April 1967), p. 14.
31 Chris Welch, 'Jeff Beck: When the "Big Break" Leads to Disaster', *Melody Maker* (25 March 1967), pp. 10–11.
32 Chris Welch, 'But, for Jeff . . .', *Melody Maker* (25 March 1967), pp. 10–11.
33 Ibid. Wood too was temporarily out of the band, Dave Ambrose his replacement on bass; see Altham, 'Guitarist Beck . . .' pp. 10–11.
34 'Jeff Beck Change', *Disc and Music Echo* (15 April 1967), p. 4.
35 Peter Jones, 'Jeff Won't . . .', *Record Mirror* (24 April 1967), p. 6.
36 Ibid.
37 Alan Jones, 'Debut Turned Out a Fiasco', *Lincolnshire Echo* (16 May 1967), p. 7.
38 Ibid.
39 Jones, 'Jeff Won't . . .', p. 6.
40 Peter Jones, 'Singles', *Record Mirror* (25 March 1967), p. 9; Derek Johnson, 'Singles', *New Musical Express* (25 March 1967), p. 6.
41 Virginia Ironside, 'Pops', *Daily Mail* (18 March 1967), p. 12.
42 Welch, 'But, for Jeff . . .', pp. 10–11.
43 Keith Altham, 'Hendrix Is Out of This World', *New Musical Express* (15 April 1967), p. 4.
44 Eden, 'Jeff Beck: Alone in the Yardbirds', *KRLA the Beat* (17 December 1966), p. 7.
45 Ibid.
46 The subsequent takes of the participants involved in the session are ably recorded alongside Simon Napier-Bell's visceral dislike of Jimmy Page in Chris Salewicz, *Jimmy Page: The Definitive Biography* (London, 2020), pp. 89–93. See also Simon Napier-Bell, *Sour Mouth, Sweet Bottom: Lessons From a Dissolute Life* (London, 2022), pp. 106–11.
47 Derek Boltwood, 'Jeff Beck', *Record Mirror* (26 August 1967), p. 5.
48 Jim Delehant, 'Yardbird Jimmy Page Says . . .', *Hip Parader* (March 1967), pp. 20–21.
49 'Yardbirds Down Under', *Record Mirror* (7 January 1967), p. 4.
50 Ibid.
51 Bob Dawbarn, 'We've Gone Stale . . .', *Melody Maker* (21 January 1967), p. 15. It wasn't clear if not being allowed to record was a temporary union injunction or simply a product of there being no time in their schedule.
52 'Yardbirds TV Film', *Disc and Music Echo* (21 January 1967), p. 5, and 'The Yardbirds', *Record Mirror* (21 January 1967), p. 4.
53 'Yardbirds May Do Horror Song', *Disc and Music Echo* (28 January 1967), p. 6; 'Yardbirds Sing', *Melody Maker* (28 January 1967), p. 4.
54 'Scene', *Disc and Music Echo* (4 February 1967), p. 2.
55 'Swinger with a Camera', *Disc and Music Echo* (11 March 1967), p. 16.
56 *Melody Maker* reported that the 'single will be chosen from four titles record for Mickie Most on Sunday' (4 March 1967), p. 6.
57 'EP Reviews', *Record Mirror* (11 February 1967), p. 8.
58 'The Raver's Weekly Tonic', *Melody Maker* (21 January 1967), p. 2.
59 Bob Dawbarn, 'We've Gone Stale . . .', *Melody Maker* (21 January 1967), p. 15.

60 Ibid.
61 Ibid.
62 Ibid.
63 Ibid.
64 Pamela Bassett, 'Young Fans Dig English Yardbirds', *Chicago Tribune* (12 August 1966), p. 45.
65 Ibid.
66 Penny Valentine, 'Singles', *Disc and Music Echo* (15 April 1967), p. 15.
67 Derek Johnson, 'Singles', *New Musical Express* (15 April 1967), p. 6.
68 Ramsden Greig, 'Discs', *Evening Standard* (15 April 1967), p. 7.
69 Peter Jones, 'Singles', *Record Mirror* (15 April 1967), p. 9.
70 'Blind Date: Cat Stevens', *Melody Maker* (15 April 1967), p. 10.
71 Ibid.
72 'Bill Harry's Pop Talk', *Record Mirror* (20 May 1967), p. 4.
73 'Reviews', *Runcorn Weekly News* (20 April 1967), p. 5; 'Singles Review Column', *Buckinghamshire Examiner* (21 April 1967), p. 7.
74 'Tailpieces', *New Musical Express* (20 May 1967), p. 16.
75 Derek Taylor, 'Our Man in America', *Disc and Music Echo* (20 May 1967), p. 14.
76 Valerie Wilmer, 'The Yardbirds Without Jeff Beck', *Hit Parader* (September 1967), pp. 15–16.
77 Alan Smith, 'Hit-Maker Mickie . . .', *New Musical Express* (3 June 1967), p. 2.
78 Bill Harry, 'The Secret of Mickie Most's Huge Success', *Record Mirror* (13 May 1967), p. 2.
79 Jim Delehant, 'Jimmy Page's New Yardbirds', *Hit Parader* (December 1968), pp. 52–3.
80 Ibid.
81 Derek Boltwood, 'Jeff Beck', *Record Mirror* (26 August 1967), p. 5.
82 Ibid.
83 Douglas Marlborough, 'The Faceless Men Behind the Top Pops', *Daily Mail* (14 August 1967), p. 9.
84 'My Lost Date . . .', *Daily Mail* (19 May 1967), p. 3.
85 Keith Altham, 'Jeff Beck Not Nearly So Wicked . . .', *New Musical Express* (27 May 1967), p. 13.
86 'Yardbirds Go East', *New Musical Express* (8 July 1967), p. 8; '"Ha Ha" Yardbirds', *Disc and Music Echo* (7 July 1967), p. 7.
87 Wilmer, 'The Yardbirds Without Jeff Beck', pp. 15–16.
88 'Jimmy Page Gives Yardbirds New Idea', *Beat Instrumental* (April 1967), p. 25.
89 Catherine Barnett, 'Bum, Is a Hobo, Is a Group of Fun-Loving Musicians . . .', *Colorado Springs Gazette Telegraph* (29 July 1967), pp. 20C–21C.
90 'England's Famed Yardbirds', *Santa Rosa Press Democrat* (23 July 1967), p. 12A. More photographs of the bands, audience and after-show enthusiasm followed the following week in the paper's 'Teens Today' page (30 July 1967), p. 37.
91 Tracy Thomas, 'American Calling', *New Musical Express* (5 August 1967), p. 10.
92 Pete Johnson, 'Santa Monica Concert Features the Yardbirds', *Los Angeles Times* (25 July 1967), p. D7.
93 Bill Kerby, 'Silent-Rock at SM Civic', *Los Angeles Free Press* (28 July 1967), p. 28.
94 Ibid.

95 'Dance Concerts', *San Francisco Examiner* (23 July 1967), p. 23.
96 Bob Fiallo, 'Teen Topics: The Yardbirds', *Tampa Tribune* (20 July 1967), p. 16-E.
97 Ibid.
98 Jack Wasserman column, *Vancouver Sun* (2 August 1967), p. 29. On fees, see the discussion of booking the Yardbirds to replace the Animals at a state fair. 'Fair Board to Meet Sat. On "Animals" Replacement', *Bucyrus Telegraph-Forum* (27 April 1967), p. 1.
99 Advertisement in *Vancouver Sun* (20 October 1967), p. 35. Terry David Mulligan, 'The Yardbirds . . . at the PNE', *The Province* (9 November 1968), p. 9.
100 Michael T. Kaufman, 'Yardbirds Complete 6th Mission to Expand Young Minds in U.S.', *New York Times* (28 August 1967), p. 36.
101 Ibid.
102 Bent, 'Two Greenwich Village Sites Score as Top Summer Talent Showcases', *Variety* (6 September 1967), p. 50.
103 Ibid.
104 Ibid.
105 Bent, 'Jake Holmes: Bitter End Café', *Variety* (30 August 1967), p. 60.
106 Ibid.
107 June Harris, 'New York', *New Musical Express* (26 August 1967), p. 9.
108 Jimmy Page, 'And Yardbirds Get the Full Treatment in U.S.', *Melody Maker* (9 September 1967), p. 10.
109 Ibid.
110 Chris Welch, 'Magnificent Seven', *Melody Maker* (9 September 1967), p. 8.
111 Ibid.
112 *Melody Maker* (23 September 1967).
113 Advertising copy for All-Night Rave, 4 February 1967, *Melody Maker* (28 January 1967), p.5.
114 Bob Dawbarn, 'Like, Baby Let's Turn On . . .', *Melody Maker* (14 January 1967), pp. 8–9.
115 Nick Jones and Chris Welch, 'Who's Psychedelic Now?', *Melody Maker* (14 January 1967), pp. 8–9.
116 Ibid.
117 Ibid.
118 Ibid.
119 Ibid.
120 Jeremy Pascall, 'Smashing Move', *New Musical Express* (7 January 1967), p. 10.
121 Ibid.
122 Ibid.
123 Ibid.
124 Ibid.
125 Ibid.
126 Ibid.
127 P. S., 'Red Letter Days for the Pink Floyd', *Kensington News and West London Times* (6 January 1967), p. 6.
128 Ibid.
129 Ibid.
130 Sheila Gray, 'Records Reviewed', *Leicester Daily Mercury* (15 June 1967), p. 14.

131 Nick Jones, 'Psychedelic Pop', *Melody Maker* (11 February 1967), p. 11.
132 'Pop Think In: Pete Townshend', *Melody Maker* (14 January 1967), p. 7.
133 Ibid.
134 Ibid.
135 Ibid.
136 Ibid.
137 Ibid.
138 'Quote from the Pink Floyd', *Record Mirror* (3 March 1967), p. 7.
139 Bob Dawbarn, 'We've Gone Stale . . .', *Melody Maker* (21 January 1967), p. 15.
140 Ibid.
141 Loraine Alterman 'The MC-5: More Like One Big Musician', *Detroit Free Press* (17 February 1967), p. 3B.
142 Derek Johnson, 'Singles', *New Musical Express* (18 March 1967), p. 10.
143 Ibid.
144 See his reviews of the Electric Prunes' singles, such as 'Get Me to the World on Time: 'Raving Psychedelia . . . A fantastic rhythm combines with all the way-out sounds and oscillations you could imagine.' Derek Johnson, 'Singles', *New Musical Express* (22 April 1967), p. 6.
145 Derek Johnson, 'Singles', *New Musical Express* (17 June 1967), p. 4.
146 'Blind Date: Scott Walker', *Melody Maker* (18 March 1967), p. 10.
147 Nick Jones, 'Freaking Out with Pink Floyd', *Melody Maker* (1 April 1967), p. 8.
148 Ibid.
149 Block advertisement in *Melody Maker* (6 May 1967), p. 16.
150 'Huge U.S. Freak-Out Is Heading Our Way', *Melody Maker* (15 April 1967), p. 2.
151 'Dream Wave', *Melody Maker* (22 April 1967), p. 4. On being interviewed on a trip to London, Warhol was asked about his involvement with the band. He said: '"I found the Velvet Underground a year and a half ago. They've been playing colleges and are getting more people. Isn't the record somewhere around?", Paul, one of his actors, found the record with its sleeve of one big yellow banana. The banana – Warhol's current hang up – peels to show pink underneath.' The Velvets with Nico were expected in London in July, it was reported (Prue Vosper, 'Warhol!', *International Times*, 14 (2 June 1967), p. 10).
152 Ibid.
153 'Townshend "in Technicolor"', *Disc and Music Echo* (29 April 1967), p. 6.
154 'Yardbirds Back to U.S., Paris', *New Musical Express* (22 April 1967), p. 10; 'Yardbirds Back', *Melody Maker* (22 April 1967), p. 5.
155 Nick Jones, 'Technicolour Dream Stirs Underground', *Melody Maker* (6 May 1967), p. 15.
156 Ibid.
157 Ronald Maxwell, 'SNIP, SNIP! The Great Freak-In', *Sunday Mirror* (30 April 1967), p. 19.
158 John Crosby, 'It Happens All the Time', *The Observer* (7 May 1967), p. 38.
159 'Television Today', *Evening Standard* (17 May 1967), p. 4.
160 Pamela Bassett, 'Young Fans Dig English Yardbirds', *Chicago Tribune* (12 August 1966), p. 45.
161 Whitley Perry, 'Youth Is Freed, Tresses and All', *Commercial Appeal* (15 June 1966), n.p.

162 Ibid.
163 Ibid.
164 Ibid.
165 Ibid.
166 Ibid.
167 John King, 'Scene's Wildest Raver!', *New Musical Express* (28 January 1967), p. 2.
168 For an unsourced anecdote about Page and Beck being spat on in Scotland for wearing Iron Crosses, see Salewicz, *Jimmy Page*, p. 96.
169 Keith Altham, 'Cream Cut Loose', *New Musical Express* (4 February 1967), p. 11.
170 Bill Harry, 'I'm a Very Emotional Person', *Record Mirror* (16 December 1967), p. 2.
171 Ibid.
172 Alan Jones, 'In the Groove', *Evening Sentinel* (8 April 1967), p. 4.
173 Ibid.
174 Ibid.
175 Richard Williams, 'A Group That Isn't . . .', *Guardian Journal* (13 May 1967), p. 5.
176 'Record Crowd at U.F.O.', *International Times*, 15 (16 June 1967), p. 10.
177 Roddie the Rocker, 'Original Freakout', *Record Mirror* (16 September 1967), p. 2.
178 Ibid.
179 Nick Jones, 'Tomorrow Are Saying It Today', *Melody Maker* (9 September 1967), p. 14.
180 'Hendrix–Move–Turtles Tour', *New Musical Express* (16 September 1967), p. 9; 'More Hendrix', *New Musical Express* (30 September 1967), p. 8.
181 'Floyd Join Hendrix', *New Musical Express* (14 October 1967), p. 10.
182 Derek Johnson. 'Singles', *New Musical Express* (11 November 1967), p. 4.
183 John Bethea, 'Disc-ussion', *Press-Telegram* (24 March 1966), p. 18.
184 'Platter Chatter', *Hit Parader* (December 1967), p. 58.
185 Ibid.
186 'Yardbirds Back', *Melody Maker* (30 September 1967), p. 3.
187 Cathy Henkel, 'Yardbirds Carry On Without Drummer', *Wichita Beacon* (25 October 1967), p. 23.
188 Rory O'Connor, 'Teen Topics: The Yardbirds' Concert', *Tampa Tribune* (19 October 1967), p. 8E.
189 The gig had been noted in Nancy Lewis's despatches, 'New York News', *Disc and Music Echo* (4 November 1967), p. 14.
190 'Yardbirds Near-Capacity . . .', *Variety* (8 November 1967), p. 50.
191 'Yardbirds' Disc', *Melody Maker* (4 November 1967), p. 2.
192 'Yardbirds for U.S.', *Melody Maker* (18 November 1967), p. 3.
193 'Cream Declare War on Singles', *Melody Maker* (18 November 1967), p. 12.
194 Ibid.
195 Ibid.
196 Ibid.
197 Ibid.
198 Ibid.
199 Ibid. Jack Bruce more or less reiterated the points made by Clapton: 'It's not releasing singles that we object to – it is the process of setting out to make a single and then having it sold like a manufactured product. The whole thing

becomes such a strain.' (Nick Logan, 'What Stirs Inside Cream', *New Musical Express* (27 January 1968), p. 13.) Rejecting the commercial merry-go-round of plugging a new single would be why Led Zeppelin also disparaged the format, especially in Britain.

200 Steve Thomas, 'Mailbag', *Melody Maker* (25 November 1967), p. 24.
201 Bob Dawbarn, 'Making the Public Stereo Minded', *Melody Maker* (25 November 1967), p. 16.
202 Ibid.
203 Nick Jones, 'New Wave USA', *Melody Maker* (25 November 1967), p. 10.
204 *Melody Maker* (2 December 1967), p. 17.
205 'Jeff Off to U.S.', *Melody Maker* (2 December 1967), p. 3.
206 Alan Walsh, 'Hits? The Floyd Couldn't Care Less', *Melody Maker* (9 December 1967), p. 9.
207 Ibid.
208 'Yardbirds Ballet', *Melody Maker* (9 December 1967), p. 3.
209 For example, 'Yardbirds Ballet', *Thanet Times* (12 December 1967), p. 2.
210 John Crabtree, 'Serious Business . . .', *Kenosha News* (19 January 1968), p. 16.
211 'Who's Pete . . .', *Disc and Music Echo* (6 January 1968), p. 10.

9 New Heavy Beat Sound – The Underground, 1968

1 Chris Welch, 'Right Then Who's Backing Britain?', *Melody Maker* (20 January 1968), p. 10.
2 'Yardbirds', *Record Mirror* (6 January 1967), p. 4.
3 'Yardbirds', *Record Mirror* (20 January 1967), p. 4.
4 'Beefheart Due', *Melody Maker* (20 January 1968), p. 3.
5 Tony Wilson, 'Caught in the Act' and 'Captain Beefheart's Miserable Mystery Tour', *Melody Maker* (27 January 1968), pp. 4 and 7.
6 'Yardbirds', *Record Mirror* (10 February 1968), p. 3; 'Yardbirds Single', *Disc and Music Echo* (10 February 1968), p. 7.
7 'News', *Record Mirror* (2 March 1968), p. 4.
8 'Yardbirds Away Again', *New Musical Express* (23 March 1968), p. 12.
9 'Birds to Paris', *Disc and Music Echo* (2 March 1968), p. 6.
10 Steve Webb, 'Me: Jeff Beck', *Disc and Music Echo* (23 March 1968), p. 10.
11 'Teenage Topics', Runcorn *Guardian* (29 February 1968), p. 5; also reviewed in Wishaw, *Press and Advertiser* (1 March 1968), p. 11.
12 'Top Singles of the Week', *Variety* (10 April 1968), p. 56.
13 Ibid.
14 Bob Dawbarn, 'The Singular Mr Mann', *Melody Maker* (25 January 1964), p. 12.
15 Page also contributed to Hallyday's 'Psychedelic', for which, paradoxically, he appears to have retreated to using as fuzzbox circa 1964/5.
16 'Trogg Reg Phones from U.S.', *New Musical Express* (13 April 1968), p. 5.
17 Ibid.
18 Ibid.
19 George Murphy, 'Yardbirds and Association Perform', *Holyoke Telegram* (11 April 1968), p. 18.
20 Ibid.

21 Philip Elwood, 'A Wide Range of New Sounds', *San Francisco Examiner* (24 May 1968), p. 27.
22 Ibid.
23 Ibid.
24 Ibid.
25 Ibid.
26 'Yardbirds', *Concord Transcript* (29 May 1968), p. 5.
27 Jim Delehant, 'Jimmy Page's New Yardbirds', *Hit Parader* (December 1968), pp. 52–3.
28 Pete Johnson, 'Yardbirds Featured at Shrine Exposition', *Los Angeles Times* (4 June 1968), p. F14.
29 'The Raver', *Melody Maker* (1 June 1968), p. 6.
30 Nick Lambert, 'Your Page', *Record Mirror* (25 May 1968), p. 2.
31 Nick Lambert, 'Your Letters', *Beat Instrumental* (September 1968), p. 41.
32 'Yardbirds to U.S. Again', *New Musical Express* (22 June 1968), p. 9.
33 'From New York the Hawk Report', *Record Mirror* (22 June 1968), p. 2.
34 Hugh Nolan, 'Who: U.S. Tours Are a Drag!', *Disc and Music Echo* (4 May 1968), p. 20.
35 Ibid.
36 Ibid.
37 '41 Club Win Foulkes Trophy', *Derby Evening Telegraph* (5 June 1968), n.p., and 'Big Beat Event', *Derby Evening Telegraph* (18 July 1968), n.p.
38 Hedging their bets, but only a little, Dave Lewis and Mike Tremaglio list the Luton gig as 'unconfirmed' but note it is 'highly unlikely' to have taken place (*Evenings with Led Zeppelin: The Complete Chronicle* (London, 2021), p. 21). On the other hand, Russo has reproduced a flyer for the gig as 'evidence that the show took place!' (p. 117).
39 Ralph J. Gleason, 'Lively Arts', *San Francisco Chronicle* (9 June 1968), p. 157.
40 'Yardbirds Disband . . .', *Variety* (19 June 1968), p. 56; 'Yardbirds to Make Changes', *Billboard* (29 June 1968), p. 12.
41 'Yardbirds Split – but the Name Goes On', *Go* (21 June 1968), n.p.
42 Ibid.
43 'Yardbirds Split?', *Melody Maker* (29 June 1968), p. 3.
44 'Cream Split Up', *Melody Maker* (13 July 1968), p. 1.
45 'Yardbirds Break in Two', *New Musical Express* (13 July 1968), pp. 8–9.
46 'Yardbirds Split', *Melody Maker* (20 July 1968), p. 3.
47 'Yardbirds Break in Two', pp. 8–9.
48 Valerie Wilmer, 'The Yardbirds Without Jeff Beck', *Hit Parader* (September 1967), pp. 15–16.
49 Ibid.
50 Ibid.
51 Ibid.
52 Jim Delehant, 'Jimmy Page's New Yardbirds', *Hit Parader* (December 1968), pp. 52–3.
53 Richard Robinson, 'Reports From New York', *Disc and Music Echo* (22 June 1968), p. 9.

54 Tony Wilson, 'Pink Floyd on a New Art Form', *Melody Maker* (18 May 1968), p. 7.
55 Ibid.
56 Ibid.
57 Ibid.
58 Advertisement in *Melody Maker* (1 June 1968), p. 2.
59 'Pop Scene '68 Freaking Out!', *Melody Maker* (1 June 1968), pp. 12–13.
60 Ibid.
61 Nik Cohn, 'Pop Scene', *Queen* (26 November 1967), pp. 36 and 41.
62 'Mailbag', *Melody Maker* (15 June 1968), p. 20.
63 'Underground', *Melody Maker* (27 July 1968), pp. 12–13.
64 Derek Boltwood, 'From the Underworld', *Record Mirror* (10 August 1968), p. 10.
65 Ibid.
66 Derek Boltwood, 'From the Underworld', *Record Mirror* (24 August 1968), p. 7.
67 Derek Boltwood, 'A Combination, and a Daring Duo', *Record Mirror* (31 August 1968), p. 3.
68 Boltwood, 'From the Underworld', p. 3.
69 Ibid.
70 Alan Smith, 'Dave Dee Has a Go at the Underground', *New Musical Express* (12 October 1968), p. 18.
71 'An Underground Group Comes Out on Top', *Rock and Roll* (May 1967), pp. 12–13.
72 Ibid.
73 Ibid.
74 Ibid.
75 Ibid.
76 'Press Conference with the Yardbirds', *Rock and Roll* (May 1967), pp. 18–19.
77 Hugh Nolan, 'Underground: Revolution – With Guitars Not Bullets', *Disc and Music Echo* (2 November 1968), p. 20.
78 Hugh Nolan, 'Underground: Let's Kill All Barriers in Music', *Disc and Music Echo* (2 November 1968), p. 16.
79 'Yardbirds', *Record Mirror* (20 July 1968), p. 4.
80 Rick Sanders, 'Yardbirds Home to Roost', *Beat Instrumental* (September 1968), p. 8.
81 Ibid.
82 Ibid.
83 The new line-up was listed in 'Yardbird Shuffle', *Beat Instrumental* (October 1968), p. 29. This period and the shifting shape of the band is comprehensively covered in Dave Lewis and Mike Tremaglio, *Evenings with Led Zeppelin: The Complete Chronicle* (London, 2021), pp. 26–9.
84 'Disbanded Yardbirds Regroup Under Page', *Variety* (15 August 1968), p. 53.
85 'Yardbirds Split', *Melody Maker* (21 September 1968), p. 4.
86 'Yardbirds Reshaped', *New Musical Express* (14 September 1968), p. 9.
87 'A Quick Follow Up . . .', *Wicklow People* (17 August 1968), n.p.
88 'Pop Star Picks Brentwood', *Brentwood Gazette and Mid-Essex Recorder* (21 June 1968), p. 5.

89 Penny Valentine, 'Singles', *Disc and Music Echo* (16 November 1968), p. 23.
90 Ibid.
91 Ibid.
92 Bob Dawbarn, 'The Blues British Style – Part 1', *Melody Maker* (5 October 1968), pp. 14–15; Part 2 (12 October 1968), pp. 20–21; Part 3 (19 October 1968), pp. 13 and 23.
93 Bob Dawbarn, 'Pop Today and Tomorrow – Part 1', *Melody Maker* (12 October 1968), pp. 16–17; Part 2 (19 October 1968), pp. 14–15; Part 3 (26 October 1968), p. 13.
94 Hugh Nolan, 'These Are the Big New Names to Watch', *Disc and Music Echo* (23 November 1968), p. 18.
95 Ibid.
96 Ibid.
97 Ibid.
98 Chris Welch, 'Only Jimmy Left to Form the New Yardbirds', *Melody Maker* (12 October 1968), p. 24.
99 Ibid.
100 Ibid.
101 Ibid.
102 Ibid.
103 Ibid.
104 'Yardbirds Change', *Melody Maker* (19 October 1968), p. 3.
105 Marquee Club advertisement in *Melody Maker* (19 October 1968), p. 25.
106 'Led Zeppelin Debut', *Melody Maker* (26 October 1968), p. 4.
107 'Yardbirds Goodbye', *New Musical Express* (12 October 1968), p. 8.
108 'Yardbirds *Backed . . .*', *Disc and Music Echo* (26 October 1968), p. 2.
109 Penny Valentine, 'Singles', *Disc and Music Echo* (26 October 1968), p. 23.
110 Derek Johnson, 'Singles', *New Musical Express* (26 October 1968), p. 14.
111 'Says P. J. Proby', *Melody Maker* (12 October 1968), p. 6.
112 Richard Robinson, 'The Teen Beat', *Detroit Free Press* (22 November 1968), p. 31.
113 'The Face', *Record Mirror* (7 December 1968), p. 12.
114 June Harris, 'In New York', *New Musical Express* (23 November 1968), p. 16.
115 Chris Welch, 'Bus Ride Back to Pop 30 for Who', *Melody Maker* (21 September 1968), p. 11.
116 Ibid.
117 Richard Robinson, 'New York Reporter', *Disc and Music Echo* (28 December 1968), p. 14.
118 Richard Robinson, 'The Teen Beat', *Detroit Free Press* (17 January 1969), p. 6D.

SELECT BIBLIOGRAPHY

Bangs, Lester, *Psychotic Reactions and Carburetor Dung*, ed. Greil Marcus (New York, 1987)

Bockris, Victor, and Gerard Malanga, *Up-Tight: The Velvet Underground Story* (London, 1983)

Chapman, Rob, *Syd Barrett: A Very Irregular Head* (London, 2010)

—, *Psychedelia and Other Colours* (London, 2017)

Clayson, Alan, *The Yardbirds* (London, 2002)

Drummond, Paul, *Eye Mind: The Saga of Roky Erickson and the 13th Floor Elevators, the Pioneers of Psychedelic Sound* (Los Angeles, CA, 2007)

Frame, Pete, *The Restless Generation: How Rock Music Changed the Face of 1950s Britain* (London, 2007)

French, David, *Heart Full of Soul: Keith Relf of the Yardbirds* (Jefferson, MO, 2020)

Garcia, Alfredo, *The Inevitable World of the Velvet Underground* (Madrid, 2011)

Humphreys, Andrew, *Raving Upon Thames: An Untold Story of Sixties London* (London, 2022)

Jopling, Norman, *Shake It Up Baby! Notes from a Pop Music Reporter, 1961–1972* (self-published, 2015)

Lewis, Dave, and Mike Tremaglio, *Evenings with Led Zeppelin: The Complete Chronicle* (London, 2021), pp. 26–9

McCarty, Jim, with Dave Thompson, *Nobody Told Me! My Life with the Yardbirds, Renaissance and Other Stories* (self-published, 2018)

Mansfield, John and Colin, *As You Were: The True Adventures of the Ricky-Tick Club* (self-published, 2019)

Melly, George, *Owning-Up* (Harmondsworth, 1970)

Napier-Bell, Simon, *You Don't Have to Say You Love Me* (London, 1998)

—, *Sour Mouth, Sweet Bottom: Lessons from a Dissolute Life* (London, 2022)

Neill, Andy, *Ready Steady Go! The Weekend Starts Here* (London, 2021)

—, and Matt Kent, *Anyway Anyhow Anywhere: The Complete Chronicle of the Who, 1958–1978* (London, 2007)

Nevill, Brian, *Boom Baby: The Escape from 60s Suburban Culture* (London, 2013)

Platt, John, Chris Dreja and Jim McCarty, *Yardbirds* (London, 1983)

Russo, Greg, *Yardbirds: The Ultimate Rave-Up*, 7th edn (New York, 2022)

Salewicz, Chris, *Jimmy Page: The Definitive Biography* (London, 2020)

Savage, Jon, *1966: The Year the Decade Exploded* (London, 2015)

Sellers, Robert, *Marquee: The Story of the World's Greatest Music Venue* (London, 2022)

Silver, Caroline, *The Pop Makers: British Rock 'n' Roll: The Sound, the Scene, the Action* (New York, 1966)

Stevlor, Stephen, *Dave Godin: A Northern Soul* (self-published, 2020)
Sword, Harry, *Monolithic Undertow: In Search of Sonic Oblivion* (London, 2021)
Watts, Peter, *Denmark Street: London's Street of Sound* (London, 2023)

ACKNOWLEDGEMENTS

This book took shape across a number of email exchanges with the Seth Man about Led Zeppelin. I doubt I'd have found my way back to their catalogue, which I'd left behind during the heady days of punk, without his guidance. Along the way, Mike Stax (*Ugly Things*) has also been a guiding light, and I've had help from Peter Wilkinson, Allan Crockford (Galileo 7), Andrew Humphreys (Paradise Road), Frank Krutnik, Phil King, Brian Nevill (*Boom Baby*), Andrea Wordsworth (for permission to quote from her Eel Pie Island diary) and Eugene Reingold. My thanks to each and every one of them. A special note should also be made of Greg Russo's lists of gigs, television appearances and studio sessions in *The Yardbirds: The Ultimate Rave-Up*; it is an invaluable resource. Finally, my thanks to my editor at Reaktion, David Hayden. For more, see www.peterstanfield.com.

PHOTO ACKNOWLEDGEMENTS

The author and publishers wish to express their thanks to the sources listed below for illustrative material and/or permission to reproduce it:

Collection of the author: pp. 72, 83, 146, 155, 176, 190, 217, 218, 245, 301; Heritage Auctions, HA.com: pp. 30, 374; David McEnery/Shutterstock: p. 68.

INDEX

Page numbers in *italics* refer to illustrations